SOCIAL WELFARE POLICY AND SOCIAL PROGRAMS

A Values Perspective

SECOND EDITION

Elizabeth A. Segal

Arizona State University

BROOKS/COLE
CENGAGE Learning

Australia • Brazil • Japan • Korea • Mexico • Singapore • Spain • United Kingdom • United States

BROOKS/COLE
CENGAGE Learning™

Social Welfare Policy and Social Programs:
A Values Perspective, Second Edition

Elizabeth A. Segal

Aquisitions Editor: Seth Dobrin

Editorial Assistant: Rachel McDonald

Technology Project Manager:
Andrew Keay

Marketing Manager: Trent Whatcott

Marketing Assistant: Darlene Macanan

Marketing Communications
Manager: Tami Strang

Editorial Production: Matt Ballantyne

Art Director: Caryl Gorska

Print Buyer: Linda Hsu

Permissions Editor (image): Don Schlotman

Permissions Editor (text): Margaret
Chamberlain-Gaston

Production Service: Pre-Press PMG

For product information and technology assistance, contact us at
Cengage Learning Customer & Sales Support, 1-800-354-9706

For permission to use material from this text or product,
submit all requests online at **cengage.com/permissions**
Further permissions questions can be emailed to
permissionrequest@cengage.com

Library of Congress Control Number: 2009924508

ISBN-13: 978-0-495-60419-8

ISBN-10: 0-495-60419-4

Cengage Learning
10 Davis Drive
Belmont, CA 94002-3098
USA

Cengage Learning is a leading provider of customized learning solutions with office locations around the globe, including Singapore, the United Kingdom, Australia, Mexico, Brazil, and Japan. Locate your local office at: **international.cengage.com/region**

Cengage Learning products are represented in Canada by Nelson Education, Ltd.

For your course and learning solutions, visit **academic.cengage.com**

Purchase any of our products at your local college store or at our preferred online store **www.ichapters.com**

Printed in the United States of America
2 3 4 5 6 7 13 12 11 10

BRIEF CONTENTS

CONTENTS

CHAPTER 7   SOCIAL INSURANCE   151

CHAPTER 8   POVERTY AND ECONOMIC INEQUALITY   172

PREFACE

Every day of our lives we are confronted by social welfare issues. In a typical day in America the news reports that the President and Congress cannot agree on how to balance the national budget...the number of people with Alzheimer's disease is growing...states are voting whether or not to provide health care for immigrants...jobs are lost in the United States because another factory moved overseas...these are all social welfare concerns. Every time you receive a paycheck, dollars are withheld to pay taxes and you become an active participant in our social welfare system. When you drive your car on public roads or visit a public library, you are benefiting from government services. Social welfare policy touches every facet of our professional and personal lives.

This book is a comprehensive introductory social welfare policy text for both undergraduate and graduate students who are new to social work and human services. The book is designed to help students understand what drives social welfare policy, how it affects people's lives, and to gain insight into key issues of social concern. Unique to this social welfare policy text is a discussion of the values and beliefs that drive our social welfare system. These conflicting values and beliefs are presented throughout the book and help to explain the divergent approaches used to address social concerns. By emphasizing the conflicting values and beliefs that people hold, it is possible to better understand the motivations behind our social welfare policies. This book guides the reader through areas of social policy concern, including poverty, health care, child welfare, and aging, with a foundation of ideologies, theories, values, and beliefs to help explain our social welfare system. Added to this edition is more material on conducting policy analyses and guidance for influencing the policy arena.

Newcomers to the study of social welfare policy will find this book extremely helpful. The American system of social welfare is so broad and complex that it would be impossible to include in-depth coverage of every policy issue. Instead, this book serves as a comprehensive overview to the social welfare policy arena. The text is designed to help the reader to feel comfortable with social welfare policy concepts and to serve as a guide for conducting social welfare policy analyses. This text examines the major social welfare policies and programs in the United States from colonial times into the 2009 legislative year. Reading through the entire book will help students to become "policy literate"—able to understand, analyze, and influence public policies.

This book reflects my experiences teaching undergraduate and graduate social work students for over 20 years. The organization of the book follows the best way I have found for teaching the material. However, I encourage users of this book to arrange the order of the chapters that best suits your needs. I have organized the chapters to build on each other, but I have also tried to format them to stand alone should an instructor prefer a different order. I owe a great deal to my students for helping me shape this text. I hope I have responded well to their questions, comments, and suggestions. I have also been blessed with wonderful colleagues and friends who over the years have indulged in my thinking out loud to craft so many of the ideas reflected in this book. Of course the content is solely my doing, and I take total responsibility for the accuracy and presentation of all the material.

I would also like to thank the reviewers for making valuable suggestions and comments. I appreciate the time and effort they took to carefully review the manuscript.

Publishing a book involves many people behind the scenes, some directly and some indirectly. I am grateful to the staff at Cengage for all their efforts to turn a pile of manuscript pages into a beautiful, bound book. I especially thank my parents, who taught me the power of social welfare policy to promote social justice. I am eternally grateful to them for giving me the gift of education and the support and role modeling to follow a lifetime of learning.

Liz Segal

SOCIAL WELFARE POLICY AND UNDERLYING VALUES

How often do you drive on an interstate highway? Did you attend a public school? Did you file an income tax form with the Internal Revenue Service this year? All these actions involve you in social welfare policies and programs in the United States. Have you ever held a job and received a paycheck and found that part of your earnings was deducted for something called FICA? If so, you are part of the largest social welfare program in America, commonly known as **Social Security**. Almost every job in this country is part of the Social Security system. The **Federal Insurance Contribution Act (FICA)** requires an employer to withhold a percentage of an employee's salary for the **Social Security Trust Fund**. How much do you know about FICA? Do you know the exact percentage that is withheld from your paycheck? Do you know what you will receive in return for this contribution? Should you know? And if so, why? Social Security is just one of the many social welfare policies and programs that are part of Americans' daily lives. Take the test in Box 1.1 and see what you know about U.S. social welfare policies.

WHAT IS SOCIAL WELFARE?

In the term *social welfare*, "social" speaks to the collective nature of U.S. society. Citizens are all part of many systems, and those systems combine to form the larger society. For example, a person is part of his or her family, neighborhood, school or workplace, and social class. Each person is also defined by different identities, such as ethnicity, race, gender, religion, physical and mental abilities, sexual orientation,

BOX 1.1	MORE ABOUT SOCIAL WELFARE POLICIES

Test Your Knowledge

1. What percentage of your paycheck is taken to pay for Social Security?
2. What percentage of children under 18 years of age are living in poverty?
3. How many members of Congress are there?
   a. How many are in the House of Representatives?
   b. How many are in the Senate?
4. What is the name of the federal medical assistance program for the poor?
5. What is the name of the federal medical insurance program for the elderly?
6. What is the federal/state cash assistance program that has been designed to aid poor children?
7. What major social welfare legislation did Congress pass in 1935?
8. Which social welfare program is the most costly for the federal government?
9. What is the current amount of the minimum wage?
10. How many judges sit on the United States Supreme Court?
11. If you need to take time off to care for a sick child, how much time are you entitled to by law?
12. Is this paid leave or unpaid leave?

Answers
1. 2009—7.65 percent   2. 2007—18 percent   3. 535   a. 435   b. 100   4. Medicaid   5. Medicare
6. Temporary Assistance for Needy Families (TANF)   7. The Social Security Act   8. Social insurance or Social Security
9. 2009—$7.25   10. 9   11. 12 weeks under the Family and Medical Leave Act of 1993   12. It is unpaid leave.

and age. "Welfare" speaks to well-being, the state of healthy balance for people. Therefore, **social welfare** means the well-being of society.

The maintenance of the well-being of society is the domain of **social welfare policy**. Social welfare policy is the collective response to social problems. Policy implies assuming a position, but that position does not necessarily require action. It can be an all-out effort to eradicate a social problem or a choice to ignore a social problem. For example, from 1983 to 1990 the federal government did not have any public policy related to AIDS. Although the illness had been documented as a growing national concern since 1983, no federal legislation was enacted until 1990. In part, this inaction represented a federal decision to let local communities and social service agencies deal with AIDS. It also reflected a decision not to treat AIDS as a national concern. The choice *not* to intervene on the federal level also represented a policy. Thus, social welfare policy is a position to act, or not to act, on a social issue or problem on behalf of society. And these efforts, or lack of efforts, can be found in federal, state, tribal and local government agencies; nonprofit and for-profit organizations; religious institutions; and community groups.

Social welfare programs are the products of social welfare policies. As mentioned previously, an example of a social welfare program that touches all of us is social insurance, or what we commonly refer to as Social Security. This program began as a response to the economic and social conditions of the Great Depression, which was a time of economic insecurity for millions of people. Something had to be done to correct the imbalance in the economy and provide some level of economic support for people. The solution was passage of the **1935 Social Security Act**.

As is so often the case, the public was aware of the problem long before policies and programs addressed it. Decades went by before social insurance was established. In 1935, the force of government legislation created a social economic safety net. The result was the foundation of today's Social Security and public assistance programs. Although this example is simplified, it demonstrates the process by which social concerns lead to social welfare programs.

WHY STUDY SOCIAL WELFARE?

To understand the social welfare system is to gain power—the power to question, advocate for change, and make good decisions about people's lives. If you know the strengths and weaknesses of social programs, you can better plan for your future. As a professional in the field of human services, you can be a better leader and better source of information for clients.

Social work, by its nature and professional ethics, is concerned with the well-being of all members of society. According to the National Association of Social Workers Code of Ethics, "Social workers should promote the general welfare of society." Section 6.04(a) states that "Social workers should be aware of the impact of the political arena on practice and should advocate for changes in policy and legislation to improve social conditions in order to meet basic human needs and promote social justice" (National Association of Social Workers, 2008). Study of social welfare policy, programs, and practice is therefore imperative for preparing to become a social worker.

PREMISES FOR STUDYING SOCIAL WELFARE

This book is based on several general guidelines. First, each person is a part of the social welfare system. At different times in your life your role will vary, but simply by being a member of society you are automatically part of the system.

Second, this book is posited on the idea that all Americans are both providers and recipients of social welfare. Every time you earn a paycheck, taxes are withheld so that the government can pay to provide services. Each year you are required by law to file income tax returns and to report and pay federal and state taxes. Every purchase made that requires the payment of a sales tax provides dollars that pay for public services. Many of those services, such as interstate highways and public parks, are used by everyone. Some services, such as literacy training or home-delivered meals, are used only by those who need them. When the government uses tax dollars to provide social welfare services, it is taking on a **provider** role. Every time you drive on a public road, take a book out of the public library, rely on fire or police protection, or go to school, you are receiving public social welfare services and are taking on a **recipient** role. For example, most universities and colleges, public or private, receive some government assistance. Whether it is in the form of state tax dollars, federal money for financial aid, or a tax-exempt status as a nonprofit institution, social welfare provides benefits to schools, which are recipients.

Third, there are a number of different approaches to providing social welfare services. Social programs vary according to the approach used. Examination of the principles that underlie social services helps us to understand the social welfare system.

Fourth, public and private efforts contribute to social welfare. Citizens are involved in making social welfare policy. Participating in an election contributes to the making of social welfare policy because the officials elected develop and enact public laws. Not voting is also a way of participating in policy making because a nonvoter is letting those who *do* vote make the choice. Private efforts are also part of the overall social welfare system. The United Way or a shelter for physically abused women is an example of a private service that promotes societal well-being. Private efforts usually are intertwined with public services, adding to the breadth of the social welfare system.

The fifth and final premise of this book concerns the influence of values and beliefs on the U.S. social welfare system. Social welfare efforts are based on social values and beliefs that shift over time. A **value** is the worth, desirability, or usefulness placed on something, whereas a **belief** is an opinion or conviction (Oxford American Dictionary, 1999). Values and beliefs join together when people feel that something is worth an investment or commitment of money, time, or public awareness. Because people's values and beliefs are individual forms of expression, getting a consensus for a national commitment is difficult. Just as values have changed over time, so too have the policies and programs that have been shaped by those values. For example, some people once considered slavery to be an acceptable social order that should be enforced by public policies and laws. Others did not think that slavery was acceptable and waged a civil war to end it and change the policies and laws enforcing it. Even after slavery was abolished, conflicting values and beliefs fueled dissent over racial issues. This book explores the conflicting values and beliefs that shape social welfare policies and programs. Understanding the underlying values and beliefs that have shaped the social conscience of America illuminates the current state of the social welfare system.

The newcomer to social work and social services will find this book of great assistance in understanding the social welfare system. The book begins with a history of social welfare policies in America and provides a theoretical foundation for the U.S. social welfare system. The importance of social justice and civil rights is discussed. The tools needed to analyze policy are covered, followed by key areas of social concern. The book concludes with a discussion of the impact of social welfare policy. This book serves as a guide to understanding the overall structure of the U.S. social welfare system and as a resource to help you effect change in the system.

A word of caution is necessary here in regard to terminology. The word *system* suggests an organized, standardized, cohesive set of policies and programs. This is far from the reality of social services in the United States. The network of social services includes a variety of programs based on different policies, developed over decades, often without cohesiveness or connection. Keep this caveat in mind as you study this system.

Each Person Is a Part of the Social Welfare System

People are members of different social, political, cultural, and economic groups. Within each of these groups, a person has a different role and responsibility. Therefore, each person must navigate a complex social network. Ideally, navigation would occur smoothly, but in reality, this is not the case. Values and priorities within each domain vary and conflict. For example, on the individual level, a person's role as a parent may conflict with his or her role as an employee. Can a person care for children and be active in the workplace at the same time? Sometimes the conflicts are on a larger scale. Can a person earn enough to live on at the same time that his or her employer earns enough to make a profit? What happens when the employer needs to pay less in wages? The employer may move to a new geographic location in which wages are lower, and jobs may be eliminated in the original location. Conflicts are inevitable in the social system, and interventions are needed to lessen or minimize their impact. The goal is to create a sense of well-being in society. Because systems often conflict and many of these systems are extensive, there is a need for intervention on a broad scale. Social welfare policies and programs are created to fulfill this need.

Our **social welfare system** consists of the organized efforts and structures used to provide for societal well-being. In its simplest form, the system can be conceptualized as having four interrelated parts: (1) social issues, (2) policy goals, (3) legislation and regulation, and (4) social welfare programs. The social welfare system starts with identified social issues. Once an issue has been recognized as a social concern, policy goals must be articulated. When these goals have been defined, a public position can be created through legislation or regulation. Finally, legislation is translated into action through the implementation of a social welfare program (Figure 1.1). Typically, these steps flow in linear fashion. That is, first an issue is identified as a social concern before there would be a public response.

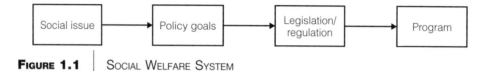

FIGURE 1.1 | SOCIAL WELFARE SYSTEM

During the early years of President George W. Bush's first administration, the public was concerned about the high cost of medications for senior citizens. Many elderly people on fixed incomes could not afford to pay for their medical prescriptions. This issue was identified as a problem in need of social intervention. Politicians responded in 2003 by developing legislation to amend the Medicare program and expand coverage to include prescription drugs. The legislation created a new program for seniors. This example demonstrates the flow of the social welfare system.

The following questions are important when studying the social welfare system. The term in parentheses is often used to describe the gist of the question.

What is the issue of concern? (Problem identification)

What would we like to change or achieve? (Goals)

How have we mandated a response to this issue? (Legislation or regulation)

What programs and services have resulted from this mandate? (Service delivery system)

To understand the American social welfare system, these questions must be asked and the answers analyzed. Chapter 6 presents an in-depth way to analyze the system. The extent to which the changes in Medicare have alleviated the problem of high costs for medication for seniors requires social policy analysis.

PROVISION OF SOCIAL WELFARE SERVICES

All Americans are providers *and* recipients of social welfare services. The roles change from situation to situation. The foundation of a social welfare system is people contributing to care for others and for themselves. The system exists for two primary reasons: (1) to create a "safety net" for all people, and (2) to provide services that individuals cannot provide for themselves, such as fire protection and interstate highways. Obviously, individuals cannot easily pave their own roads or protect themselves from emergencies such as fires. The larger society needs a system to economically and efficiently provide for social needs. Analysis of social welfare policy allows people to assess whether the system has achieved this goal. At times, problems arise that demonstrate that the system is not effective. Through social welfare policy analysis we can determine what works, what does not, why a program is not working, and how we might change the system. This ability to analyze social welfare policy is an integral part of the social work profession.

APPROACHES TO THE PROVISION OF SOCIAL WELFARE

Several key concepts form the foundation of social welfare services. These concepts include residual, institutional, universal, and selective approaches to the development of social welfare policies and programs.

Residual Versus Institutional Approaches   Historically, changing economic and social conditions moved the country from reliance on private social welfare programs to acceptance of public social welfare programs. This shift was characterized by two competing conceptions of social welfare policy: **residual** and **institutional** approaches (Wilensky & Lebeaux, 1965). The first concept, **residual social welfare policy,** calls for organized public intervention only when the normal resources of family and marketplace break down. Social welfare services are called into play *after* a problem is identified and cannot be addressed through a person's own means. Social services become available in an emergency. The focus is on individual behaviors and responsibility. The second concept, **institutional social welfare policy,** calls for the existence of social welfare programs as part of the social structure and as part of the normal function of society. Social welfare programs are seen as a preventive effort built into the social system. Institutional policy is based on the premise that providing services is a legitimate function of society. The complexities and difficulties of modern life are ever present. Therefore, it is normal for individuals at times to require the assistance of social institutions. Institutional social welfare policy focuses on prevention and collective responsibility.

Examination of a social concern helps to illuminate the differences between a residual and an institutional approach to social welfare policy and programs. For example, politicians, the public, and social service providers often view teenage pregnancy as a social problem. Becoming a mother at an early age may limit a young woman's opportunities for education and employment. Opportunities may also be limited for the children born to young mothers because the parents and children may experience emotional, economic, and social stress. A residual approach to the social issue of teenage pregnancy would focus on providing services *after* the teenager becomes pregnant. Residual programs might include specialized prenatal care for teenage mothers, school programs held on weekends and nights, and parenting skills classes. An institutional approach would be to help teenagers *before* pregnancy occurred. Institutional programs might include establishing school family planning courses that stress delaying parenthood and providing access to birth control resources.

The difference between the residual and institutional approaches is a good example of the struggle in developing social welfare policy and programs. To what extent should individuals be responsible, and to what extent should society be responsible? For the most part, social welfare policy in this country has followed the residual approach. Most social programs were created to respond to an identified need after it occurred. The result of this approach is a categorization system used to identify who should receive services and who should not.

Universal Versus Selective Provision of Services   The principle of **universality** calls for social services that provide benefits to *all* members of society, regardless of their income or means. **Selectivity** means that services are restricted to those who can demonstrate need through established eligibility criteria. A major difference between universal and selective programs is the extent of the stigma attached to receiving services. Universal services are available to all, whereas selective services are available only to recipients who are identified as incapable of providing for themselves.

The advantage of universal coverage is that everyone receives the benefit, which prevents many social problems. A major disadvantage of such an approach is its cost. Selective coverage ensures that only those most in need will be covered. Such targeted coverage is less expensive, but it stigmatizes the recipient and can be too narrow. Those who do not fit the prescribed criteria exactly will not receive anything.

Blending Social Welfare Policy Approaches   How do the concepts of residual and institutional approaches fit with universal and selective approaches? Figure 1.2 demonstrates how some common programs fit these conceptions of social welfare policy. Most social services are residual and selective, are developed in response to breakdown, and are available only to those who demonstrate a need. Examples of selective residual services include public cash assistance and most other aid given to those who are poor. Very few residual services are universal. One program that is universal is administered by the Federal Emergency Management Agency (FEMA). The services are available in a crisis such as an earthquake, regardless of whether a person has financial means. Of course, the effectiveness of those services depends on the quality of the agency, as Hurricane Katrina demonstrated in New Orleans. In spite of poor response, the design of FEMA is to universally respond to an emergency, which is a residual approach.

The clearest examples of universal institutional services are public education and fire and police protection, which are available to all regardless of income. Some institutional services are selective. Many may argue that the program commonly referred to as Social Security is a universal institutional program. The program is actually a selective institutional program: Only those who have worked in covered employment are eligible to receive benefits, and benefits are determined according to the person's history of contributions. It feels universal because today almost 97 percent of all workers are covered. The structure of the Social Security program is discussed in greater detail in Chapter 7.

	Residual	Institutional
Universal	Federal Emergency Management Agency	Public Education Fire and Police Protection
Selective	Temporary Assistance for Needy Families (public cash assistance program for poor families)	Social Security

FIGURE 1.2 | SOCIAL WELFARE POLICY BLEND

Some social welfare programs can be defined as institutional and universal, yet the actual implementation of many of these programs suggests otherwise. For example, public education is available to all, although the resources and quality of education vary by region and community. Jonathan Kozol, in *Savage Inequalities: Children in America's Schools* (1991), argued that there has been a long history of inequality in the educational system. School spending on children in the suburban communities outside of New York City, for example, is more than twice as high as spending for children in city schools. Across the nation, there is great variability. For example, teaching salaries average highs of $59,825 in California and $59,304 in Connecticut to lows of $34,709 in South Dakota, and $38,284 in West Virginia (National Education Association, 2007). Disparity in resources for public education demonstrates that although all children in this country are entitled to public education, they do not necessarily receive the same education.

Finally, there is a flow between residual and institutional approaches in the development of social welfare policies. Let us return to the example of public education. We have been discussing it as a universal institutional social welfare program, but it has not always fit into this category. Public education began as a residual response to the problem of juvenile crime and idleness. If young people were required to attend school, they would be off the streets and would become better socialized for work and participation in society. Public education was not originally conceived of or developed as an institutional program, but rather, it evolved into one. Many institutional social welfare policies and programs evolved out of residual policy responses.

HOW ARE PEOPLE INVOLVED? PUBLIC AND PRIVATE EFFORTS

Participation in the social welfare system may be as simple as driving on a publicly funded highway, attending a public school, visiting a county hospital or library, mailing a letter, or working for the city, state, or federal government. It includes paying taxes on items we buy and wages we earn, taxes that help fund the social welfare system.

Corporations also receive public support. Private sports teams, for instance, which are owned by companies or groups of investors, often receive large tax breaks and even public dollars so they can build stadiums. Many private companies depend on federal government projects to keep their businesses solvent. States provide tax deferrals, tax abatements, and low-interest loans to corporations. The federal government developed tax-free enterprise zones for businesses and created rules that allow tax breaks (e.g., companies can subtract the costs of their equipment before the equipment actually wears out) (Abramovitz, 2001). When deep financial stress hit in 2007 and 2008, the federal government intervened with public support programs that used billions of dollars of public funds to keep private institutions afloat.

Even when people think they are not involved in the public realm of social welfare, they often are. Thousands of private companies earn contracts to produce goods or render services funded by the public. For example, a military contract to build airplanes for the air force goes to a private company. The funds to pay for the airplanes come from federal taxes collected by the government. Those funds create the means for corporations to employ people and pay wages that in turn support families and keep the economy running. And the government, in turn, is able to tap the expertise of specialists such as airplane manufacturers without having to create a separate government agency.

WHY DO WE HAVE A SOCIAL WELFARE SYSTEM?

The United States is considered the primary working example of capitalism and a market-place economy. The economy operates through an exchange of goods and services—for a day's work one receives a salary that in turn allows one to purchase what one needs or wants. However, this system does not always cover all members of society. For those who cannot work because of health or physical limitations, for those who cannot find work, or for those who are excluded because of their race, sex, age, physical ability, or sexual orientation, there is no market exchange of salary. As a result, the market system does not provide sufficient resources for some people.

To provide for those outside the market system and keep the system in check, the U.S. government plays a crucial role in maintaining the social well-being of the country. For example, the federal government provides services to help people find work through programs such as job training. The government also provides for those who cannot work due to physical disability through programs legislated under the Social Security Act. These are examples of federal government intervention in the marketplace economy. State and local governments operate in much the same way. For example, schools are run by local people elected to serve on school boards. Their decisions direct and control the public education each child receives.

Although the underlying principle of the social welfare system is government involvement, not all people agree with this position. Since the earliest history of this nation, people have argued for and against government involvement in the social arena. Those arguments and the types of government roles and systems developed over the history of this nation are reflected in society's values and beliefs. Thus, to fully understand the social welfare policies and programs in this country, it is imperative to analyze the underlying social values and beliefs that have guided the development of the social welfare system.

VALUES AND BELIEFS AS THE CORNERSTONE OF SOCIAL WELFARE IN AMERICA

Social welfare efforts throughout American history have reflected the dominant values and beliefs of society. Remember, a value is the worth, desirability, or usefulness placed on something and a belief is an opinion or conviction. Those values and beliefs shift, and as a consequence, so too have public policies. For example, at one time in this country, the "desirability" of slavery was upheld as legitimate public policy, only to later become an issue so divisive that the nation faced civil war. One of the outcomes of the Civil War was that slavery was abolished and became illegal. Shifts in public values create shifts in public policy. Understanding the underlying values and beliefs that shape the social conscience of America helps us understand how the social welfare system of today came to be. Two currents underlie the values that have shaped social welfare policies, religious beliefs, and social beliefs.

The evolution of these values and beliefs has not been smooth, and today's policy reflects many conflicting values and beliefs. This conflict makes the creation and implementation of social welfare policies and programs difficult in the United States.

RELIGIOUS VALUES

Religion has held a strong position in maintaining the well-being of U.S. society. A large proportion of Americans identify with established religions (see Box 1.2). The development of social welfare services can be traced back to values reflected in the dominant religions of the early history of this nation. Those dominant religions were primarily Protestant. The goals of religious charitable efforts were to uphold moral character, maintain humbleness, and help those less fortunate. Famous Biblical quotations such as "It is harder for the rich man to enter heaven than for a camel to fit through the eye of a needle" (from the Book of Matthew in the New Testament) and "Love thy neighbor as thyself" (from the Book of Leviticus in the Old Testament) reflect a strong symbolism of charity and concern for the needy:

> Christian tradition mandates a *sympathetic* attitude and practice towards the poor, disadvantaged, or diseased. There is nothing in the Bible resembling advocacy of material redistribution of resources, much less social or political revolution. The poor, the ill, the imprisoned, and the weak are to be treated with kindness and love, but the Bible deals with this as a matter of personal sentiment and moral obligation. (Wagner, 1999, p. 76)

For the most part, religious values in America have been translated into individual reform, not social change. The emphasis was on individual behaviors of both those giving and those receiving. These emphases are apparent in social welfare efforts of many religious organizations today.

The roles of religion and social welfare are further complicated by the mandates of the Constitution. The United States was founded on the principle that religion and government should not be related. Thomas Jefferson was a firm advocate of the "separation of church and state," and this sentiment is codified in the Constitution under the first part of Amendment I of the Bill of Rights: "Congress shall make no law respecting an establishment of religion, or prohibiting the free exercise thereof." Although religious sentiments influenced charity and social welfare

---

BOX 1.2   **CONSIDER THIS . . .**

- Approximately 163 million Americans (63 percent) identify themselves as affiliated with a religious denomination.
- Members of American Protestant churches total 94 million persons across 220 particular denominations.

- Over 60 million people identify themselves as Roman Catholics, making Catholicism the single largest denomination.
- There are more than 300,000 local congregations in the United States.

Eck (2002)

in this country, the law was clear that the government should not be involved in the establishment of religion, and at the same time, the government should not interfere with the free practice of religion. These two values are also an influential part of the social welfare system. Thus, although there is a religious imperative to help, by law it must be done without blending the roles of government and religious organizations.

The constellation of social services today challenges this separation. There are social welfare agencies such as Catholic Charities, Lutheran Social Services, and Jewish Family and Children Services, to name only a few. These organizations clearly are identified with religious organizations yet receive public funds and are therefore part of the social welfare system. The issue of separation of church and state that these efforts raise is not new and continues to challenge providers of social services. Box 1.3 presents a point of view that critiques the reality of separation of church and state for one particular organization, but the point could be argued for all groups that are affiliated with religions.

The impact of religion in the political arena may follow economic and social trends. The proportion of Americans who identify as having strong religious beliefs declined from the mid-1990s to 2007 (Pew Research Center for the People and the Press, 2007). Dionne (2008) suggests that a look at history since the 1920s reveals shifts between public attention on religion and morals to economics and secular values. He argues that when economic concerns grow, less attention is paid to cultural issues, and he suggests that 2008 may have ushered in a shift and the years to come will be a period when economic prosperity becomes more important than religion and culture.

PERSONAL VALUES

Related to religious values are personal values. Each of us has his or her beliefs, shaped by our life experiences and backgrounds. It is difficult to separate what is important to us personally from what might be important socially. In fact, personal

---

BOX 1.3	CONTROVERSIAL PERSPECTIVES . . .

Should public dollars be used by religious organizations to provide social services?

"Although Catholic Charities has a strong reliance on public funding, it may not be operating from a strict separation-of-church-and-state philosophy. It is clear that Catholic Charities has been influenced by the teachings of the Catholic Church. . . .

In a time when the United States has great levels of cultural, religious, sexual, and racial diversity, is it appropriate and ethical for social services organizations such as Catholic Charities to receive public funding and yet maintain their religious identity? Although the public funds that local Catholic Charities agencies receive are given with the condition that clients are not discriminated against or denied services on the basis of race, cultural background, and sexual preference, the reality of how able and willing Catholic Charities agencies are to offer clients a full range and choice of services can be questioned given its religious identification."

Degeneffe (2003), p. 382

beliefs can drive us to be involved publicly. Although we all carry our own values and beliefs, it is important when analyzing social issues and providing social services that we strive to be aware of which values and beliefs are our own, which are dominant in society, and the intersection of the two.

SOCIAL VALUES

As the United States was founded on the principle of separation of religion and state, strong values emerged based on membership in society. Two strong social values that shaped social welfare policy are social responsibility and citizenship. Americans have long held the values of hard work and self-sufficiency. However, at the same time, social responsibility has been valued. Recent opinion polls reflect this conflicting sentiment (Pew Research Center for the People and the Press, 2007). Americans value individual enterprise. Almost two thirds (62 percent) polled disagreed with the idea that "success in life is pretty much determined by forces outside our control" and 68 percent disagreed with the statement "hard work offers little guarantee of success." Although Americans strongly feel that individual effort is rewarded, public opinion also expresses the need for government intervention. More than two thirds (69 percent) say it is the responsibility of the government to take care of people who cannot care for themselves. Also, 69 percent believe that the government should guarantee every citizen enough to eat and a place to sleep. Although these numbers suggest that the majority of people favor government social welfare services, a more accurate picture is seen when one examines the views of those who identify with one of the two major political parties. Box 1.4 demonstrates the disparity.

The role of government in aiding its citizens is closely related to the expectation that citizens will be involved in society. American history is replete with active civic involvement.

> An extensive and participatory civil society took shape from the start of U.S. nationhood, even as life for the vast majority of Americans proceeded on farms or in small towns. In the era between the Revolution and the Civil War, voluntary groups multiplied and formed links across localities, spurred on by government activities and popular political contention in the new republic and by competitive religious evangelism in a nation without an established church. (Skocpol, 1999, p. 37)

BOX 1.4 | **CONSIDER THIS . . .**

Seventy-nine percent of Democrats compared to 58 percent of Republicans say it is the government's responsibility to "take care of people who can't take care of themselves."

Eighty-three percent of Democrats compared to 47 percent of Republicans say the government should "guarantee every citizen enough to eat and a place to sleep."

Pew Research Center for the People & the Press (2007)

BOX 1.5 | **CONSIDER THIS . . .**

"Democracy, civil rights, and representative government—to name a few of the key institutions that foster human dignity and wealth—were brought about by people involved in spontaneous collective action, fighting not for their selfish ends but for a vision for all of humanity. Our freedom is based on the emotional commitments of generations past."

Gintis (2001), pp. xvii–xviii

A democracy by definition demands participation of its citizens. A democratic government is founded on the principle that the entire population is involved in the election of representatives, and hence each person is part of the government system (see Box 1.5). As Theda Skocpol (1999) discovered in her research on the history of civic engagement, the nature of American government from the beginning encouraged participation, from political action in competing groups to mobilization for revolution, the Civil War, and both world wars.

Social justice is another value that is integral to the social work profession: "Social workers promote social justice and social change" (Preamble, NASW Code of Ethics, 2008). Social justice describes the level of fairness that exists in society. *The Social Work Dictionary* (Barker, 2003) defines it as:

> An ideal condition in which all members of society have the same basic rights, protection, opportunities, obligations, and social benefits. Implicit in this concept is the notion that historical inequities should be acknowledged and remedied through specific measures. (pp. 404–405)

Thus, religious and social values place importance on the principles of charity, caring for others, government involvement, and civic responsibility. With such positive principles guiding the nation, why is the development of social welfare policy so fraught with dissension? Why is it so difficult for people to agree on the best way to help each other? The struggle for agreement on social welfare policy rests with attitudes, the beliefs that underlie the principles of caring for others and responsibility.

CONFLICTING VALUES AND BELIEFS IN SOCIAL WELFARE POLICY

Americans support the values of helping those in need, contributing to charity, being socially caring, and participating as a citizen. Nevertheless, people view those values differently. Box 1.6 outlines three general areas where social values conflict. Do we think responsibility for people's well-being is personal and private, or should it fall under collective and public concern? Should we respond to social needs as they occur, or should we take a long-term approach? Values are not fixed, so people may opt for personal responsibility as the foremost solution for some issues and collective attention for other issues. Values may change over time for the nation as a whole or for some individuals. For example, suppose you believe

| BOX 1.6 | CONSIDER THIS . . . |

General Values—What Is Most Important?

Who do we view as responsible for people's well-being?

Personal or Collective?

Where do we place responsibility for people's well-being?

Private or Public?

When should social welfare interventions occur?

Immediate or Long-Term?

strongly in personal and private responsibility. Paying Social Security taxes would be disturbing to your sense of what is important, your values. Years later, when you face retirement, you may rethink your value of private responsibility and welcome the collective aspects of Social Security benefits. Fluidity is the reality (Box 1.6). Values can shift over time and in terms of the issue.

Behind these general values are powerful competing beliefs that lead to disagreement. The author proposes that the struggles in society to achieve the aforementioned values grow out of conflicting beliefs. The following 12 conflicting beliefs can be found in responses to social problems and throughout the U.S. social welfare system (see Figure 1.3). Each chapter of the book concludes with a discussion of relevant conflicting values and beliefs.

UNDESERVING VERSUS DESERVING

Most Americans support the idea of helping people in need, as long as the people are worthy of help. They must be seen as trying hard, willing to work if given the chance, and grateful for any and all opportunities. The belief that there are deserving and undeserving people dates back to the colonial period (1700s) and is still significant today in discussions of need. Early colonial laws considered widows, orphans, elderly people, and people with a physical disability as worthy of assistance. The characteristic they shared was that they were in need through circumstances beyond their control. That view persists today. In political speeches given in the House of Representatives hours before the approval of the 1996 welfare reform legislation, the overriding concern of lawmakers was self-sufficiency and serving the truly needy (Segal & Kilty, 2003). If a person is perceived as being able to work but still poor, then the belief is that the person is not worthy of assistance.

Distinguishing between who is deserving and who is undeserving may seem like a clear and logical process. Any reasonable person should be able to decide who should receive social welfare and who should not. However, the difference between who is worthy and who is not is based on an individual's view of the circumstances that led to the need. What is missing from this perspective is the consideration of cause. For example, is poverty the result of personal failure or of societal structures that create

Undeserving—should be able to be responsible for self	*Deserving*—worthy of help
Personal Failure—conditions of need brought on by individual's failure	*System Failure*—conditions of need brought on by economic, political, and social conditions
Individual Responsibility—people should take care of themselves; no outside support	*Social Responsibility*—people are all responsible for each other; society should care for all
Individual Change—adaptation by the person	*Social Change*—structural changes of society
Self-sufficiency—ability to care for oneself	*Social Support*—receiving care and help from others
Handout—charity	*Entitlement*—earned right or access
Aid to Those We Know—inclined to help when there is a personal relationship	*Aid to Strangers*—willing to help people unknown to us
Religious and Faith-Based Practice—social services based in religious organizations and infused with religious values and beliefs	*Separation of Church and State*—nonsectarian; no religious connection to social services
Crisis response—mobilize only for a critical event	*Prevention*—provide services before there is a problem; services are ongoing and comprehensive
Sympathy—sorrow for a person's misfortune	*Empathy*—identification with another person's life situation
Suspicion—wariness of person's motives	*Trust*—positive regard for person's motives
Emotions—feelings	*Rationality*—factual and dispassionate analysis

FIGURE 1.3 | CONFLICTING BELIEFS

barriers to resources? Should we focus on the individual or on society? The next pair of conflicting beliefs relate more specifically to this dilemma.

PERSONAL FAILURE VERSUS SYSTEM FAILURE

Many people question a person who looks healthy but is receiving government assistance: Why isn't the person working? It is difficult not to immediately compare your own ability to hold a job and earn enough to support yourself and your family with another person's inability to do so and therefore receive assistance without working. Many people feel it is unfair and believe the person to be undeserving. However, what is often lacking in understanding need in America is consideration of the impact of economic, social, and political systems on access and opportunity. Racism limits people's opportunities. Women are treated differently than men.

Companies find it cost-effective to close plants and move, leaving hundreds of workers without jobs. Many do not have the skills to quickly find another job. Higher education and training are not available for all, so some young people do not learn the skills that would help them get jobs. We must question whether these are instances of personal failure or whether something is wrong with society's social interactions, economic policies, or educational systems. This raises the next question: Who is responsible for people's well-being—each individual or society?

INDIVIDUAL RESPONSIBILITY VERSUS SOCIAL RESPONSIBILITY

As has already been discussed, Americans are torn in their beliefs about who should be responsible for people's well-being. The belief that the individual is responsible for his or her state in the world is strong, but so is the belief that the government should step in and aid people when they are in need. This split in the public consciousness plagues the development of social welfare policy. Although by definition social welfare involves the general public, the form of that involvement is the subject of debate. If a person believes strongly in individual responsibility, then that person will see personal needs such as poverty, mental illness, and family breakdown as issues that should be addressed by individual effort. For the person who believes strongly in social responsibility, many of these problems are social issues that should be addressed by public intervention. One's beliefs in terms of responsibility will shape the direction of social policy.

Who comes first, the individual or the community? This is the question underlying the individual versus social responsibility debate. Many cultures believe that people are part of a collective, a larger group, and individuals are not the focus. Other cultures emphasize individuality and the worth of each person over and above the collective society. American tradition is firmly rooted in individualism, and yet democracy calls for collective participation. The disparity between these two beliefs gives rise to disagreements about approaches to social welfare.

INDIVIDUAL CHANGE VERSUS SOCIAL CHANGE

If a person is a strong advocate of individual responsibility, then it is likely that when social welfare policies and programs are called into play, he or she will emphasize the individual. If the problem, for example, is unemployment, then the emphasis will be on trying to get the unemployed person a job. If a person holds strong beliefs about social responsibility, then he or she will focus on social change. The emphasis will be on promoting the development of new jobs and general economic well-being for the community.

SELF-SUFFICIENCY VERSUS SOCIAL SUPPORT

Similar to the individual responsibility versus social responsibility debate is the debate over where support should ultimately rest. Should we promote self-sufficiency (i.e., individual support), or should we accept ongoing need addressed by social support? Self-sufficiency stresses individualism and personal achievement, whereas social support stresses collectivity. For some, the belief in social support is so strong that it may not matter why a person has a social need. They feel that the responsibility to others supercedes all and that we must take care of all people regardless of the cause of their need.

ENTITLEMENT VERSUS "HANDOUT"

Attitudes toward assistance are also fraught with conflict. Some believe that assistance and social support are rights and—that people are entitled to a basic standard of living. Often an entitlement is viewed as something that a person has earned and therefore has a right to claim. The opposite belief is that assistance is given out by those with the power and means to provide for people without power and in need and is hence a "handout." There is no stigma attached to service as entitlement because the recipient is owed the service. There *is* stigma attached to service as a handout because the recipient has not earned the service.

AID TO THOSE WE KNOW VERSUS AID TO STRANGERS

One pervasive characteristic of our society is the tendency to be more comfortable and more inclined to help people we know, or feel we know, rather than help strangers. Class differences in American society insulate people with wealth or even comfortable means from contact with people who are poor. What little contact they have is typically not on a personal level. It usually takes place through the media or through hierarchical relationships. Those with means are served in restaurants or have their lawns mowed by those who can barely make ends meet. Racial divisions are powerful in society. People of different races often do not get to know each other. Thus, when one racial group is called on to support social services, they are often asked to help people from another racial group. They may be reluctant to do so. This reluctance has proved to be a challenge in American society.

RELIGIOUS AND FAITH-BASED PRACTICE VERSUS SEPARATION OF CHURCH AND STATE

As discussed earlier under religious values, the mixing of religion and social welfare is highly contested. Although the constitutional prohibition is strong, there is much debate about the appropriate role of religious organizations in the care and support of people. Recently, there has been more emphasis from politicians on the provision of social welfare services by faith-based institutions. This question will continue to influence the development of social welfare policy.

CRISIS RESPONSE VERSUS PREVENTION

The outpouring of relief and donations after the attack on the World Trade Center and Pentagon on 9/11 was overwhelming. So much blood was donated that there was a surplus, and some had to be destroyed. On an average day at most blood banks, there is a shortage of blood and never a surplus. It is typical for people to mobilize for a tangible crisis. The need for prevention, on the other hand, is usually invisible and not compelling and is therefore much more difficult to enact.

Sympathy Versus Empathy

Usually sympathy and empathy are considered the same emotion: caring for others. But these responses are distinctly different when applied to social well-being. Both responses involve the ability and willingness to share feelings with another. However, **sympathy** involves compassion, which is sorrow for someone's misfortune and a desire to alleviate his or her suffering. **Empathy** requires identifying oneself with another, thereby entering into the other's experience. Empathy does not presuppose misfortune as does sympathy. Although an empathic person will undoubtedly feel another's pain if the conditions of the person's life are miserable, his or her perspective is larger. An empathic person takes into consideration the external conditions that may contribute to the person's misfortune. Sympathy, with its concurrent compassion, typically creates a hierarchy in which those who are more fortunate help those who are more unfortunate. Empathy suggests that any of us could find ourselves in the same situation as the other, given life events, and does not lead to a hierarchy of giver and receiver.

Trust Versus Suspicion

Giving a person money for necessities involves trust. If that person should instead use the money to buy drugs, the giver feels exploited and suspicious of how the receiver is living his or her life. Recipients are free to make bad choices, but when they misuse resources provided by others, the givers feel as though there has been a breach of trust.

Rationality Versus Emotions

Facts and dispassionate analysis are keys to rational thinking. Should all social issues be approached using only a rational perspective? Do emotions play a role? Shouldn't human beings have emotions when they are considering issues as painful as poverty, violence, and poor health? Public policy makers struggle with developing rational, sensible policies and policies that appeal to the emotions. When creating laws that govern treatment of the American flag, for example, legislators often cite the flag's symbolic meaning rather than refer to it as merely a beautiful piece of cloth. This example demonstrates that beliefs and the emotional meaning of a symbol are more powerful than the construction of an object, which is a rational act.

Values and Beliefs Guide Policy Making

Values and beliefs tend to flow together. Although people may take differing positions on concerns, beliefs tend to follow a general value framework. Beliefs reflect values. Figure 1.4 outlines the beliefs that support specific values.

How does knowing that we are a nation with conflicting values and beliefs help in understanding the social welfare system? Rather than becoming polarized by the traditional divisions among policy makers and citizens—Republican versus Democrat, liberal versus conservative, right wing versus left wing—we should strive to understand the belief systems that guide our views. We may feel torn between two conflicting values, sometimes believing strongly in one and sometimes in the other.

PERSONAL	vs	COLLECTIVE
Personal failure		System failure
Individual responsibility		Social responsibility
Individual change		Social change
Self-sufficiency		Social support
Aid to those we know		Aid to strangers
Religious		Separation of church and state
Sympathy		Empathy

PRIVATE	vs	PUBLIC
Undeserving		Deserving
Personal failure		System failure
Individual responsibility		Social responsibility
Individual change		Social change
Self-sufficiency		Social support
Aid to those we know		Aid to strangers
Religious		Separation of church and state
Sympathy		Empathy
Emotions		Rationality

IMMEDIATE	vs	LONG TERM
Undeserving		Deserving
Personal failure		System failure
Handout		Entitlement
Crisis response		Prevention
Sympathy		Empathy
Suspicion		Trust
Emotions		Rationality

FIGURE 1.4 | BELIEFS SUPPORTING GENERAL VALUES

For example, we want government involvement in some things and privacy in others. Usually when political groups differ, they are arguing about beliefs. The preceding list covers most of the disagreements in the public policy arena. Figure 1.5 outlines some of the typical beliefs that support and oppose government involvement. If a person holds beliefs that are in the first column, he or she is more likely to expect individuals to be responsible for the conditions of life. Rather than argue for more government programs, we need to address these important ideas and explore the meaning of these beliefs. When we clarify values and beliefs and understand people's positions, we can better develop social policies. And even if we cannot agree with all beliefs, exploring them helps us to more accurately discuss the true conflicts in social discourse.

Unlikely to Support Government Social Programs	More Likely to Support Government Social Programs
Undeserving—should be able to be responsible for self	*Deserving*—worthy of help
Personal Failure—conditions of need brought on by individual's failure	*System Failure*—conditions of need brought on by economic, political, and social conditions
Individual responsibility—people should take care of themselves; no outside support	*Social Responsibility*—people are all responsible for each other; society should care for all
Helping Those We Know—inclined to help when there is a personal relationship	*Helping Strangers*—willing to help people unknown to us
Crisis—mobilize only for a critical event	*Prevention*—provide services before there is a problem; ongoing and comprehensive
Individual Change—adaptation by the person	*Social Change*—structural changes of society

FIGURE 1.5 | CONFLICTING BELIEFS THAT SUPPORT OR OPPOSE GOVERNMENT INTERVENTION

Throughout the rest of this book, the relevant values and beliefs will be discussed to better understand the social welfare system in America.

CHANGING DEMOGRAPHICS AND THE NEED FOR SOCIAL WELFARE POLICIES AND PROGRAMS

The population of the United States includes more than 300 million people. This makes this country larger than most nations; only China and India have a larger population. The United States is almost ten times more populous than Canada, five times more populous than the United Kingdom and France, three times more populous than Mexico, twice as populous as Russia, and 30 times more populous than Sweden. We are a diverse nation, and that diversity is changing. Census data (U.S. Census Bureau, 2007) reveal that we are aging. In 1980 the median age was 30 years, it grew to more than 36 years of age in 2006, and it is projected to increase to 39 years of age by 2050 when 26 percent of the population is expected to be over 60 years old compared to 16 percent in 2000. Racial composition is also changing. In 2000, 19 percent of the population was categorized as people of color and by 2015 that is expected to increase to 37 percent. The presidential and vice presidential candidates of 2008 reflected those changes. The election of the first person of color as president in over 230 years of United States government reflects those changes. In terms of social welfare policy, it portends an exciting time of change. Public policy reflects the needs and concerns of social and economic groups. For example, with the aging of the population, programs and services that address the needs of people as they age will most likely become more pronounced in policy debates. Already changes in racial composition are taking precedence as in the discussions surrounding immigration. Following social welfare requires keen awareness of social trends. Shifts in population typically influence public policy discussions, often serving as the catalyst for social change.

FINAL THOUGHTS

Changing social and economic conditions coupled with the ways people's beliefs and values influence their interpretations of these events influence the development of social welfare policies and programs. Part of the belief system in the United States is that people have freedom of choice and that is what distinguishes Americans from so many citizens of other nations. Americans treasure their freedom and consider the United States to be the most open and free country in the world. That belief is so deep that they rarely question it. Yet, is it true that all Americans are free to choose how they lead their lives? Within the framework of lawful behavior, do we have choice?

To have free choice in the public domain, it means that:

All options are open and available.

Each person is aware of those options.

Each person fully understands all the options, as well as the qualifications needed to participate in the options.

Each person understands the consequences, impact, and possible outcomes of all choices.

Sufficient resources are available for all to take advantage of all choices.

Sufficient support is available to sustain a person in his or her choice.

People have the abilities, skills, self-confidence, realistic assessment, and motivation needed to take advantage of all choices.

Although some people may never have all of the pieces of the framework when they make choices, some people will have more pieces than others. The more pieces you have, the better suited you are to take advantage of free choice. In fact, these aspects of free choice are the basis of social justice. The reality in America is that for poor, oppressed, and disenfranchised people, choice is often not a reality. The result is social injustice. Social welfare policies and programs are one of the ways that society tries to provide more choices for more people and give them the skills necessary to take advantage of those choices.

You may be asking whether social welfare policies and programs make a difference. Are they worth the social and economic investment? The answer is that social welfare programs do help and make a difference. This book is based on that premise. For example, more than 20 years ago, Lisbeth Schorr (1988) put together a volume describing numerous social programs for children that had proved to be highly successful. She concluded that "we know how to organize health programs, family agencies, child care, and schools to strengthen families and to prevent casualties at the transition from childhood to adulthood. We know how to intervene to reduce the rotten outcomes of adolescence and to help break the cycle that reaches into succeeding generations" (p. 294). Years later, Jonathan Crane (2000) used rigorous research techniques to identify successful social welfare programs. He concluded that "a number of programs have had a substantial, positive impact on the lives of the people they have served and have benefited society as a whole" (p. 1). He writes further that "although there have been many disappointments in the past 35 years, we have learned a tremendous amount. If we let this knowledge go to waste, then the money spent on programs over the years will have gone for naught. If instead, we capitalize on the handful of successes that we have worked so hard to develop, then all the money, the failures, and the disappointments will have been worthwhile after all" (p. 40).

Understanding what works and what does not work creates better social policy and programs. This book provides the foundation and guidelines you need to understand the U.S. social welfare system, the public policies and programs that contribute to it, and the underlying values and beliefs that shape social welfare policies.

Key Terms

social welfare	recipient	social welfare system	universality
social welfare policy	value	residual social welfare policy	selectivity
social welfare programs	belief	institutional social welfare policy	social justice
provider			

Questions for Discussion

1. How would you describe what our social welfare system is to a friend who is not taking this class?
2. What is the difference between a provider and a recipient in the U.S. social welfare system?
3. Explain the difference between a value and a belief. Give an example of each.
4. Why do you think it is important to study social welfare policy?
5. Find data on population growth in the United States between 1980 and today. How has the composition of our population changed and how do you think that might influence social welfare policy?

Excercises

1. Based on your initial understanding of social welfare policy, what policies and programs do you think benefit you? Why? Write these down and put them away until the end of the course. At that time, look at what you wrote and consider how your thinking and understanding may have changed over the course. Are there different social welfare policies and programs that you can identify as beneficial to you?
2. Look at your list of policies and programs. Can you identify which are institutional and which are residual? Can you determine which are universal and which are selective?
3. Consider the values and beliefs identified in this chapter. Where do your own values and beliefs fit? Again, write down where you think you fit in terms of the values and beliefs listed in this chapter. At the end of the course, review what you wrote and consider how your views may or may not have changed. Why?
4. Read through a newspaper or a news magazine such as *Time* or *Newsweek*. How

many articles are related to social welfare issues? How are the issues presented? Does the discussion seem relevant to social work practice? How do these issues affect you, your family, and your friends?

5. Visit the web site of a local or national elected politician. Can you identify values and beliefs held by this elected official? How do you think those values and beliefs might influence his or her policy-making?

References

Abramovitz, M. (2001). Everyone is still on welfare: The role of redistribution in social policy. *Social Work* 46(4):297–308.

Barker, R. L. (2003). *The social work dictionary*, 5th ed. Washington, DC: National Association of Social Workers.

Crane, J. (ed.). (2000). *Social programs that work*. New York: Russell Sage Foundation.

Degeneffe, C. E. (2003). What is Catholic about Catholic Charities? *Social Work* 48(3):374–383.

Dionne, E. J. (2008). Culture wars: The era of Americans voting on the basis of 'moral values' is over. *Washington Post National Weekly Edition* 25(22):25.

Eck, D. L. (2002). *A new religious America*. San Francisco: HarperCollins.

Gintis, H. (2001). Foreword: Beyond selfishness in modeling human behavior. In R. M. Nesse (ed.), *Evolution and the capacity for commitment*. New York: Russell Sage Foundation.

Kozol, J. (1991). *Savage inequalities: Children in America's schools*. New York: Crown.

National Education Association. (2007). *Rankings and estimates*. Washington, DC: NEA Research.

National Association of Social Workers. (2008). *NASW code of ethics*. Washington, DC: Author.

Oxford American Dictionary of Current English. (1999). New York: Oxford University Press.

Pew Research Center for the People and the Press. (2007). *Trends in political values and core attitudes: 1987–2007*. Washington, DC: Author.

Schorr, L. B. (1988). *Within our reach: Breaking the cycle of disadvantage*. New York: Anchor Press Doubleday.

Segal, E. A., & Kilty, K. M. (2003). Political promises for welfare reform. *Journal of Poverty* 7(1/2):51–68.

Skocpol, T. (1999). How Americans became civic. In T. Skocpol & M. P. Fiorina (eds.), *Civic engagement in American democracy*. Washington, DC: Brookings Institution.

U.S. Census Bureau. (2007). *Statistical abstract of the United States: 2008*. 127th ed. Washington, DC: U.S. Government Printing Office.

Wagner, D. (1999). *What's love got to do with it? A critical look at American charity*. New York: New Press.

Wilensky, H. I., & Lebeaux, C. N. (1965). *Industrial society and social welfare*. New York: Free Press.

HISTORICAL FOUNDATIONS OF SOCIAL WELFARE IN AMERICA

Today's social welfare policies have been shaped by historical events and molded by changing social values and beliefs. Exploring the history of social welfare policy in the United States can help us better understand today's social welfare system.

The political system of a democratic government rests on the principle that people or their elected representatives make policy decisions. The majority usually decides elections and makes decisions. In the United States, that majority mirrors those who control the most resources. Social welfare policy evolves in ways that reflect the majority culture and its values. That majority has usually been concerned with maintaining the status quo rather than risking social upheaval. Examples of efforts to maintain the status quo can be seen in the treatment of women and nondominant groups. Social welfare policy in this country has tended to reinforce traditional family ethics, which kept women at home (Abramovitz, 1996) and restricted nondominant people and immigrants from full economic participation (Patterson, 2000).

In spite of the overriding goal of protecting the status quo and maintaining control for the majority, change has occurred from colonial times to the present. Some social welfare policy changes were dramatic and far-reaching. Others were slow and gradual. Because the social welfare system reflects economic fluctuations, political changes, and shifting values and beliefs, it is important to examine the system within the context of history.

COLONIAL PERIOD (1690–1800)

Social welfare—the concern with societal well-being—dates back to the time of the earliest European settlers. The colonial period was a time of great uncertainty. To the Europeans who first landed in this country, North America did not seem to possess established social, political, or economic systems. The settlers lacked awareness of native cultures that had been in existence for centuries. The New World of the European settlers was actually a place of thriving, populated communities.

| BOX 2.1 | MORE ABOUT THE FIRST NATIONS OF NORTH AMERICA |

At the time of the earliest European contact with North America, there were no "American Indians." The aboriginal inhabitants of North America encountered by European travelers spoke a myriad of languages; possessed a wide variety of cultures; displayed a broad diversity of social, economic, and political organization; and had no conception of themselves as a single "race," group, or people. The common label "Indians" in fact told more about the visitors than about the natives. First, the label revealed an unfounded geographic optimism about the discovery of a route to the East Indies; if this was India, these must surely be Indians. More important, this strategy of simplistic collective desig-

nation reflected a racially compartmentalized worldview that would come to guide the colonial policies of Europeans for nearly five centuries on as many continents. These policies divided human populations into two camps: those who were civilized and those who needed to be civilized; those manifestly destined to rule and those in need of rule. Finally, the uniformity implied by the common label "Indian" reflected the singleness of purpose in European, and later American, social, economic, political, and military dealings with the various indigenous communities they confronted: an unrelenting demand for native land and resources (Nagel, 1997, p. 3).

Many indigenous people lived in North America (see Box 2.1). The population is estimated to have been as high as 18 million before 1492. In the 130 years after that date, 95 percent of the indigenous people died from diseases brought by Europeans and from conflicts that occurred as white settlement expanded (Mann, 2002).

The settlers who came to America during the late 1600s and early 1700s either ignored cultures and mores that were not their own or found ways to destroy those cultures. Consequently, the earliest settlers relied on laws from their countries of origin in creating their first social welfare system. The earliest form of legislated so-cial welfare policy came with the importation of the **Elizabethan Poor Laws** (Tratt-ner, 1999). Passed in 1601 in England, the Elizabethan Poor Laws embodied the first public legislation outlining a public response to social welfare needs. As the feudal system changed in England, the problem of what to do about people in dire need surfaced as a public concern. With people leaving the countryside, where they were under the rule and care of feudal lords, towns became populated by people without sufficient resources to survive. Feudal lords, in power through birth, mar-riage, and at the behest of the monarchy, were responsible for a geographic area and all the people who lived there. Towns tended to be separate, and became a place where people from the countryside came to try and improve their economic well-being. Arriving poor, they put a strain on the local towns. The Elizabethan laws were passed primarily out of necessity, to designate a system of care for the poor and indigent—not because of a commitment to social well-being. Landowners and church leaders were not able to care for all those in economic need.

A number of key components characterized the Elizabethan Poor Laws (Axinn & Stern, 2008). Landowners and lawmakers of the time categorized need by distinguish-ing between those deserving of aid, the "worthy poor," and those not deserving, the "unworthy poor." The **worthy poor** included widows, orphans, the elderly, and peo-ple with disabilities. These groups were viewed as worthy because their circumstances of need were perceived to be beyond their control. The **unworthy poor** were able-bodied single adults and unmarried women with out-of-wedlock children. These groups were unworthy because either they could work and were not doing so or they did not follow the expected social norms. These distinctions are important be-cause they permeate the U.S. social welfare system to this day and are reflected in the belief of "deserving versus undeserving," as described in Chapter 1.

In addition to categorizing people in need, the Elizabethan Poor Laws institu-tionalized structures that remain a part of the social welfare system. The Elizabe-than Poor Laws stipulated that the economic support of those in need must first come from within the family. Only when the family could not afford to care for a person did local authorities take public responsibility for his or her care. Another stipulation was that the person in need had to be a legal resident of the community. In this way, the generosity of the local government would be provided for commu-nity residents rather than outsiders. Funding for public assistance came from money collected from local residents who could afford to pay. The tendency to support people we know rather than strangers continues to be strong to this day.

The Elizabethan Poor Laws established a single relief system coordinated by civil authorities. The system was intended to provide support for those who de-served assistance. It was not seen as a way to eradicate poverty. The colonists be-lieved strongly in the work ethic. Those who could work must work. They also believed that jobs were available for anyone willing to work and that hard work would lead to moral uprightness and individual well-being. In other words, they valued self-sufficiency more than social support.

These earliest social welfare laws set the stage for all social welfare policy to come. In summary, the major principles of the Elizabethan Poor Laws included (1) a distinction between the worthy and unworthy poor, (2) the idea that the family is responsible first and foremost for the care of its members and that only after the family cannot provide support will local authorities intervene, (3) the stipulation that only residents of a community were eligible to receive assistance, and (4) the provision that assistance would be given only when dire necessity required it and would be terminated when the recipient achieved the ultimate goal of employment or marriage to someone who was employed. Poverty was seen as an individual shortcoming, not a structural or societal failure. One key outcome of the colonial period was the belief that social welfare was a partnership between private care and public aid.

The American South was similar to the North in its adherence to the Elizabethan Poor Laws, but it differed in regard to its economic structure. The agricultural economy of the South relied on large numbers of laborers. African slaves provided an inexpensive source of labor. From the 1600s through the late 1700s, almost 600,000 Europeans came to America and 300,000 Africans were brought here as slaves (Daniels, 1990). Almost all of the Africans lived in southern states. The colonists from Europe, most of whom were British, controlled the economic and social order of colonial America. By 1661, the South had institutionalized slavery. The care of slaves was the responsibility of their owners. The Elizabethan Poor Laws were not applicable to slaves, who had no legal claim to social welfare support from local governments. As in the North, these policies set the foundation for the public response to social welfare needs for years to come.

During the colonial period, America was perceived as a land of abundant resources with plenty of room for growth. The native people, like the African slaves, were regarded by the colonists as nonpersons with no rights to the land or resources (Nagel, 1997). The colonists considered American Indians to be a nuisance blocking the growth of the colonial empire (Nabokov, 1991). The differences in culture between the colonists and the native peoples were significant. Misunderstanding and mistrust between the two groups lasted for centuries. For the American Indian tribes, the white colonists, in the words of a member of the Santee, were:

> . . . a heartless nation. They have made some of their people servants . . . We have never believed in keeping slaves, but it seems that these Washichu [white people] do . . . The greatest object of their lives seems to be to acquire possessions—to be rich. They desire to possess the whole world. For thirty years they were trying to entice us to sell them our land. Finally the outbreak [of illness] gave them all, and we have been driven away from our beautiful country. (Nabokov, 1991, p. 22)

Such differences in beliefs and the success of the settlers in pushing the native peoples westward caused the colonies to grow and prosper. Because of economic growth and a rich base of natural resources, the belief that poverty was inevitable or structural never became part of the national consciousness. In fact, because of the abundant resources and expansion, poverty was viewed as a personal misfortune, not a public responsibility.

IMPACT OF THE COLONIAL PERIOD

The policies and practices of colonial America serve as the foundation for the U.S. social welfare system and beliefs. The strong values of work, individualism, and aggressive expansion blended to create an ongoing American way of life. This way of life promotes economic gain and individual achievement. Americans value the entrepreneurial and adventurous spirit of early explorers and settlers. Also, the acclaimed superiority of Anglo-European colonists over indigenous cultures and African slaves set the stage for racial conflicts that continue today.

CONFLICTING BELIEFS OF THE COLONIAL PERIOD

The colonial period gave rise to a number of the conflicting beliefs that influence U.S. social welfare policies of today. Most significant is the emphasis on distinguishing between those who are deserving of aid and those who are not, the worthy and unworthy poor. The emphasis on the individual reflected the colonial values of individual responsibility, self-sufficiency as the preferred way of living, and the work ethic. Also codified in the Elizabethan Poor Laws was the tendency to help those we know rather than strangers. These beliefs permeate the social policies and programs that constitute the current social welfare system.

PRE–CIVIL WAR PERIOD (1800–1860)

After the American Revolution in 1776 and the formation of the United States, economic, political, and social forces changed the face of the nation. The economic structure of the country changed from primarily agrarian to primarily industrial. More and more immigrants from European countries settled in America. With growing immigration and industrialization, workers in search of employment gravitated toward cities, and the America of the 1800s became more urbanized.

The social welfare system in the United States changed with the increase in industrialization, immigration, urbanization, and western expansion. Although the fundamental precepts of the Elizabethan Poor Laws were still accepted, local authorities were facing greater social problems and need. Conditions such as mental illness and disabilities and the plight of orphaned children seemed impossible to solve through distribution of aid to individuals. One solution was the building of **residential institutions** to care for such people (Leiby, 1978). Institutions were believed to be the way of eliminating social problems through rehabilitation of poor people and others deemed as having social problems and in turn setting examples of proper ways to live (Rothman, 1971). The institutions, also known as **indoor relief,** included hospitals, almshouses for the poor, and orphanages for children (Axinn & Stern, 2008).

Colonial and pre–Civil War America reflected a strong religious background, which greatly influenced how early Americans viewed social problems (Jansson, 2009). The dominant ideology was a religious moralistic perspective that regarded individual behavior as the root of most problems. This perspective reinforced the emphasis on correcting behavior through rehabilitation and life in institutions. Although the goal of institutional living was to rehabilitate people, the reality differed. Institutions often became places where people who were destitute or suffering from mental illness were warehoused, and no efforts at rehabilitation were undertaken. The conditions were often substandard, and inmates were treated poorly.

IMPACT OF THE PRE–CIVIL WAR PERIOD

The use of institutions in caring for people became an established social service approach during this period. Care from sources other than families and friends was accepted as a legitimate way to treat social problems. In addition, although the separation of church and state was outlined in the Constitution, religious organizations played a role in caring for people.

CONFLICTING BELIEFS OF THE PRE–CIVIL WAR PERIOD

The concept of rugged individualism permeated the society of the 1800s. America was still seen as a nation rich in resources, and opportunities for hard work were perceived to be plentiful. Therefore, anyone not working or poor was regarded with suspicion. Poverty was viewed as an individual condition and, hence, a personal failure, not a societal failure. This belief reinforced the value of economic self-sufficiency.

However, the concept of available work for every person who wanted it was, and continues to be, a distortion of historical reality (Katz, 1986). As has been true during many periods of history, viable employment for unskilled or semiskilled workers was not universally available. Although there have always been rich and poor people in American society, the industrialization of the 1800s created broader differences and a greater disparity in resources between those at the top and those at the bottom.

CIVIL WAR AND POSTWAR PERIOD (1861–1874)

The Civil War awakened the new nation to social unrest, regional nationalism, and economic disparity. The difference between the North and the South was not simply a matter of abolition versus institutionalization of slavery. The industrialized North had an economic base that differed from the more agrarian economy of the South. The Civil War and its aftermath created a tremendous need for relief efforts. As a result of poor sanitary conditions, public health emerged as a social welfare concern, as did the need for national government intervention.

For the first time in the nation's history, the federal government made a brief foray into providing social welfare benefits. Before the Civil War, all social welfare programs fell under the control of private charity groups and local governments. With the magnitude of the Civil War and the North's successful efforts to abolish slavery came the postwar need to provide for those displaced by the war. In 1865, the new federal government established the **Freedman's Bureau,** which provided temporary relief for newly freed slaves, managed abandoned and confiscated property, helped to reunite families, provided medical supplies and food rations, and established institutions such as hospitals, schools, and orphanages (Trattner, 1999).

The Freedman's Bureau was placed in the War Department, an action that ensured that the bureau would remain temporary. It was disbanded in 1872 (Jansson, 2009). The development of the bureau raised the question of what role the federal government should take in the creation of social welfare policy and the provision of services. The bureau was seen only as a postwar effort and not as a way of altering the social or economic structure that had given rise to the Civil War. It provided the minimum services needed immediately after the war.

Although slavery officially ended with the Civil War, racial differences remained deeply embedded in American society. African Americans were technically free people but were still subject to the will of the majority. Even many northern abolitionists who had fought for the end of slavery perceived African Americans as morally inferior to whites (Jansson, 2009). Forcing people to leave their native land and culture and then depriving them of any chance to develop their own resources and a new culture set the stage for long-standing racial imbalances. How could newly freed African Americans begin to achieve the social, political, and economic success that the founders of this country had secured for themselves almost 200 years before? Early settlers had access to land and resources, and by the 1800s controlled the political and social economy. Even with the end of the Civil War, African Americans were not included in those systems. Freed slaves had no belongings, no land, and no education, and therefore had no chance to integrate into the mainstream society. What institutional slavery accomplished before the Civil War, social values and structural systems maintained after the war.

Women fared a bit better after the Civil War. The war had drawn women out of their homes and into the social structure to a greater degree. Women found a place for themselves in social welfare services and public health careers. Following the war, the country experienced enhanced economic wealth and an improved standard of living. Women from families who were economically well off found opportunities to do social welfare service work outside the home.

During the years following the Civil War, Anglo-Americans decimated the resources and culture of American Indians. Thousands of miles of railways opened the way for westward expansion, and white settlers took the land as they moved across the country. In 1887, the **Dawes Act** destroyed Native American culture by dividing native lands among individuals. Needing resources, many Native Americans sold their land for little money or were cheated out of it. Ninety million acres were transferred to whites, and 90,000 American Indians were left homeless. Also in 1887, the government provided funds for missionary groups to create boarding schools. American Indian children were forced to attend these schools and consequently lost contact with their families, communities, and culture (Day, 2006).

IMPACT OF THE CIVIL WAR AND POSTWAR PERIOD

The greatest contribution of this time to social welfare was the involvement of the federal government in the delivery of social services. The idea of the highest level of government stepping in to address social problems was new to the nation.

Although it was a short-lived effort, it left an indelible mark on the social welfare system. Also, the impact of the Civil War was to be felt for generations to come. The rift between the North and the South, and the ill feelings it left, continue to affect social beliefs today. The aftereffects of slavery lingered for over 100 years, and the economic, social, and political separations between whites and African Americans are still evident today.

CONFLICTING BELIEFS OF THE CIVIL WAR AND POSTWAR PERIOD

Disproportionate economic growth, renewal of immigration, increased industrialization, urbanization, and western expansion characterized the period from the 1870s through the beginning of the 1900s. The industrial development fostered by the war laid the foundation for postwar expansion and growth in individual wealth (Axinn & Stern, 2008). It also set the foundation for intensified economic disparity, poverty, regional differences, and racial strife. The high level of unemployment at the end of the 1800s challenged the American belief in individualism and the availability of work for anyone who wanted it (Bremner, 1956). People began to accept the possibility that there might be structural reasons beyond the control of the individual that contributed to poverty. Societal structure and system failure, instead of personal failure, were seen as possible contributors to poverty.

Severe bouts of economic depression, particularly during the late 1800s, gave rise to a tremendous need for social welfare intervention and recognition of the large-scale needs of many population groups. Social responsibility began to emerge. Out of this period came the seeds of government-supported social services and federal social welfare policy.

PROGRESSIVE ERA (1875–1925)

The late 1800s and early 1900s witnessed two opposite but related trends: economic growth and increased poverty. Urban areas grew tremendously, and industry expanded. Immigrants were hired to fill dangerous and low-paying jobs, and wealth became concentrated in the hands of the few who were at the top. Poverty was prevalent among industrial workers, immigrants, and rural southern African Americans (Wenocur & Reisch, 1989). The wide schism between the "haves" and "have-nots" produced great social need. Change was rapid, and the social problems that surfaced were far beyond the capabilities of the existing private charities.

The growing disparity between rich and poor fueled political and social dissatisfaction that in turn gave rise to a new political movement. This period, the **progressive era**, witnessed a shift in social welfare policy and programs from family and private responsibility to community and government responsibility. Unlike during the expansionary years after the Civil War, economic conditions at the turn of the century worsened, and the nation began to regard problems such as poverty as social concerns rather than individual problems (Trattner, 1999). This new concern included closer examination of the structural forces that led to personal misfortune.

Among the numerous social problems during this period were terrible labor conditions, particularly for women and children; poor health, especially among those living in crowded urban tenement areas; lack of understanding of mental health needs, which led to mistreatment of those deemed to be "insane"; poor treatment of children and lack of educational opportunities; and overall poverty among a significant portion of the population.

Social welfare programs and the provision of services during the progressive era were embodied in two distinct movements: the **Charity Organization Societies (COS)** and the **settlement movement**. The role of these movements in the foundation of the profession of social work is discussed in Chapter 4. Briefly, COS and settlements dominated the social service system of the progressive era.

CHARITY ORGANIZATION SOCIETIES

Modeled after groups in London, the first Charity Organization was established in 1877 in Buffalo, New York. COS workers tried to eliminate poverty by discovering its causes among individuals and then removing those causes from society (Erickson, 1987). Objective techniques stressing scientific methods were considered the best way to solve the problem of poverty. Through coordinated relief giving and modeling of appropriate behavior by "friendly visitors," families would receive relief without duplication of services and would be shown how to live a respectable life. Those most involved in COS believed that poverty was rooted in the personal character of the poor person (Germain & Hartman, 1980).

SETTLEMENT MOVEMENT

The settlement movement was influential at the turn of the century. The work of the settlements was based on a completely different perspective than that of the COS regarding the causes of poverty and social need. The settlement movement officially began in this country in 1887 with the establishment of the Neighborhood Guild in New York City. It was based on a similar model in England, the famous Toynbee Hall (Reid, 1981). The philosophy behind the settlement movement was that social workers should live among the people to best serve communities. Established as neighborhood centers where all were welcome, settlements served both as housing for settlement workers and meeting places for local people. The settlement movement philosophy combined the achievement of individual growth with satisfying social relations and social responsibility. Unlike the narrow individual focus of the COS, the settlements emphasized community and society. The settlements held a holistic perspective of the person in society and regarded a person's inner well-being as inseparable from external forces. The settlement philosophy held that people could become full citizens through participation in social systems, including the family, neighborhood, ethnic groups, and place of employment.

IMPACT OF THE PROGRESSIVE ERA

The progressive era witnessed tremendous political change. For the first time in America, industrial workers began to organize and demand better working conditions and wages. Although management was still in control of production, unions were organized for numerous trades and provided newfound strength for workers. Women found a place in the changing economic and political environment, becoming employed in social welfare services and seeking increased political involvement. The **suffrage movement** gained public attention and culminated in 1920 with passage of the constitutional amendment awarding women the right to vote. Women fought for and achieved access to higher education and professions (Boulding, 1992).

African Americans did not fare as well as other groups during the progressive years. White workers, women, and children gained rights, but most of the freed slaves of the South remained in poverty and were excluded from political and social realms. Many became tenant farmers, economically enslaved to their former owners. Some moved to the North to find jobs in urban centers. Although life in the North was better than life in the South, northern African Americans were barred from union membership and did not benefit from the progress of white workers (Jansson, 2009). The newly created social welfare services were not available to African Americans, so they created a separate network of services to meet their needs. Although the National Urban League in 1910 and the National Association for the Advancement of Colored People (NAACP) in 1912 were established (Axinn & Stern, 2008), racial divisions and hierarchies remained firmly rooted in America.

In spite of political change and progress, the underlying economic and social structure of the United States remained intact. The severe economic depressions of the turn of the century gave way to a resurgence of social stability. World War I brought a sense of common purpose to the nation, put people to work, and halted immigration, giving the country time to absorb the people of diverse cultures that had flocked to America in the late 1800s and early 1900s. By the 1920s the nation was relatively prosperous and the social changes of the progressive era had slowed. "Old American values" resurfaced, and a return to majority conservatism dominated (Daniels, 1990, p. 281).

CONFLICTING BELIEFS OF THE PROGRESSIVE ERA

Social welfare policy still remained in the hands of private charities and localities. The involvement of religious and faith-based groups in the delivery of social services called into question the separation of church and state. The federal government was not yet a provider of services, although stronger seeds of federal involvement in social welfare had been sown during the progressive era. The federal government had passed legislation regulating work, protecting women and children, placing restrictions on factory owners, and protecting American workers. A shift in values from individual responsibility to social responsibility created a foundation for believing in social support in addition to self-sufficiency. Although emphasis was still placed on each person's abilities, there was growing awareness that the larger society had some role in the care of those who were less fortunate.

THE GREAT DEPRESSION AND THE NEW DEAL (1925–1940)

Economic instability and depression were remote concerns during the 1920s. The "Roaring Twenties" were years of economic prosperity and extravagant living. Certainly there were poor people, but their problems were geographically and socially confined. Those in political power and those who controlled industry remained oblivious to the needs of the poor. Much of the population was living beyond their means, buying on credit and saving little or nothing. Market speculation and fraudulent stock deals were common. Shrewd but shady business dealings that resulted in profit were viewed as acceptable. There was a general feeling that anyone who worked hard and had some business savvy could "make it" economically.

The stock market crash of October 1929 brought an abrupt end to the nation's strong faith in the market system and the prosperity of the 1920s. The warning signs of extended credit, little savings, and market speculation had gone unheeded. The nation's social structure and charitable organizations were totally unprepared to meet the incredible social needs and demands of Americans during the Great Depression of the 1930s. The economic changes were staggering: in 1929 almost 1.6 million people were unemployed; in 1931, 8 million were unemployed; and by 1933 almost 13 million were out of work—more than 25 percent of the civilian labor force (U.S. Bureau of the Census, 1975). In addition, the gross national product fell from $103 billion in 1929 to $56 billion in 1933 (U.S. Bureau of the Census, 1975). Millions of families were impoverished because of the widespread unemployment of the main breadwinner.

The shock of the Great Depression paved the way for the election of Franklin Delano Roosevelt to the presidency. The nation was in the depths of severe economic destitution and ready for a new leader with new ideas.

> One of the factors that made Roosevelt a great leader was that his beliefs so neatly coincided with popular values in the thirties...What was good, decent, fair, and just—what was "right"—was also what a majority of people wanted and, hence, what was expedient. (McElvaine, 1993, p. 325)

Roosevelt had a genuine concern for others, a noblesse oblige combined with his understanding of struggle based on his own experience with polio. He believed that the Depression was the result of factors that could be changed through federal action. His policies, referred to as the **New Deal**, were designed to reverse the economic misfortunes of the nation.

The **Social Security Act of 1935** was the most significant federal legislation to develop out of the Great Depression and Roosevelt's New Deal efforts. It represented a major change in the country's approach to social welfare policies and programs. Although a number of smaller federal efforts were undertaken during the early 1930s, the groundwork for passage of the Social Security Act was set from three efforts: the **Federal Emergency Relief Act (FERA)**, the **Civilian Conservation Corps (CCC)**, and the **Works Progress Administration (WPA)** (Axinn & Stern, 2008; Trattner, 1999).

FERA was the first federal economic relief agency to be established since the Freedman's Bureau after the Civil War. The magnitude of poverty was so great that many agreed that the federal government needed to be the direct provider of relief to local public agencies through which individuals would receive aid. The relief was intended to be temporary, available only until people became employed.

By 1933, the creation and provision of jobs were the dominant goals of the social welfare policies under the New Deal. The CCC and the WPA were created to develop employment for those on relief. The WPA provided 8 million government jobs ranging from heavy construction work to playing in orchestras (Axinn & Stern, 2008). WPA projects included the building of post offices, schools, and government buildings. The CCC provided employment for thousands of young men, who worked on conservation projects, including reforestation and flood control (Trattner, 1999).

The Roosevelt administration planned to use FERA to provide direct relief and the WPA and CCC to provide temporary employment through the worst of the Depression. Once basic relief had been achieved, permanent solutions were needed. Two key advisors to the president at this time were both social workers: Harry Hopkins and Frances Perkins. Harry Hopkins, born in Iowa, started his social work career as a Settlement House worker in New York City. He went on to work as an advocate for the poor and served in the New York State Bureau of Family Rehabilitation and Relief. Hopkins served as the director of FERA and acted as a personal advisor to Roosevelt. Frances Perkins, the first woman appointed to a presidential cabinet position, served as the secretary of labor throughout the Roosevelt administration. Frances Perkins had begun her career as a public investigator of labor conditions and was deeply committed to improving the lives of workers. Her work as a member of FDR's cabinet demonstrated her commitment to enhancing labor conditions and promoting federal social welfare services. Perkins chaired the Committee on Economic Security, which developed the Social Security program still in place today (McSteen, 1985; Severn, 1976).

The Great Depression disproved the concept that poverty was always the result of personal laziness and unworthiness. During the Depression millions of hardworking, responsible, and previously economically stable workers found themselves without work. The circumstances of their poverty were out of their control. The economic upheaval of the Depression altered public opinion toward social welfare policy and programs. The overall failure of economic institutions lessened the resistance of the voting public to adopting a national social welfare policy (Dobelstein, 1980).

The failure of the economic system brought the federal government into the direct provision of social welfare services. The enactment of the Social Security Act established the two main social welfare programs of today: social insurance and public assistance (Berkowitz & McQuaid, 1988). The social security programs reflected Roosevelt's New Deal efforts of providing relief in times of economic downturn while stressing employment as the key to economic well-being.

The **Social Security Act**, passed in August of 1935, represented a compromise between radical and conservative ideologies. Conservatives were concerned that federal social welfare policy would destroy individual responsibility and self-determination. Radical proposals called for large payments and federal responsibility for the economic well-being of all Americans. In response to these competing political pressures, the act included provisions for economic security for the aged, unemployment insurance, and assistance for dependent children, as well as funds for states to provide services to promote vocational rehabilitation, infant and maternal health, public health, and aid to children and people with disabilities. The overall aim was to reinforce the work ethic by rewarding employment while at the same time providing a federal safety net of economic relief for those most in need.

The Social Security Act created two main social welfare programs: (1) **social insurance**, including Old-Age Insurance and Unemployment Insurance, and (2) **public assistance**, including Old-Age Assistance, Aid to Dependent Children, and Aid to the Blind. Over the years the act has been amended numerous times to include other provisions. The details of economic assistance and the Social Security Act are explained more fully in Chapters 7 and 8 as part of the discussions on social insurance, poverty, and economic inequality.

The Social Security Act put into place two programs with very different approaches to providing economic assistance. Social insurance is a collectively funded program for workers and their dependents that provides economic resources at the conclusion of employment due to retirement, disability, or death. It is *social* because anyone who works is covered, provided he or she has paid into it while they worked, and it is *insurance* because the payments guarantee coverage for the rest of the recipient's life. Public assistance, on the other hand, does not require any involvement prior to economic need. It is a government-funded effort to assist people whose income falls below a certain level and are considered to be in poverty. It is *public* because it is funded through general revenue collected by the government, and it is *assistance* because it is meant to be temporary and aid people in distress, not provide support for life.

The social insurance provisions of the Social Security Act were appealing for a number of reasons. Initial acceptance was aided by the bias in the system: early entrants were favored with a high benefit-to-cost ratio, that is, in the early years of the program, people would receive benefits after paying into the program for only a short time. The program had an incremental structure: Costs were low at first and then increased gradually. This structure made it more acceptable to the taxpaying public. Also, the program's design ensured that there was no stigma attached to receiving benefits; workers had "paid" for the benefits with payroll taxes. A person earned credits by working and did not have to prove financial need.

The public assistance provisions did not receive as much public support. Because of the tremendous poverty of the Great Depression, people needed immediate economic aid. The overall plan was that public assistance was to be temporary. Once the immediate economic crisis passed and all were employed (or related to someone employed), there would no longer be a need for public assistance. The severity of the Great Depression and the political savvy of Roosevelt and his supporters lessened public opposition to both programs and reluctance to accept their benefits. In the end, the Social Security Act reflected many compromises and contained many ambiguities so that different interest groups could support it (Derthick, 1979).

The establishment of the Social Security Act in 1935 marked the beginning of a new era in social welfare policy in the United States. The act ushered in a period of significant change in the ideological stance of the federal government: It marked the beginning of the modern welfare state. Since 1935, almost all significant social welfare policy has been enacted as part of the Social Security Act or an outgrowth of it. Its programs account for most of the coverage, recipients, benefits, and expenses for social welfare from 1935 to the present. In addition, the creation of social insurance and public assistance through the Social Security Act gave rise to several major shifts: there has been tremendous growth in the federal bureaucracy and in the number of people working on social welfare issues, and the federal government has been established as the institution that takes on projects disowned or ignored by the private sector (Berkowitz & McQuaid, 1988).

IMPACT OF THE GREAT DEPRESSION AND NEW DEAL ERA

During the 1930s, significant social welfare policy shifts occurred. Human rights were given more priority than property rights; the movement toward equality in access to employment and education was initiated; legislation was passed to promote better health and economic security; and the federal government began to intervene in the nation's economy. All of these changes helped to push forward the development of professional social work (Fisher, 1980).

CONFLICTING BELIEFS DURING THE GREAT DEPRESSION AND NEW DEAL ERA

Existing social services and relief organizations could not deal with the millions in need. The private charitable groups of the 1920s had been concerned with individuals and small-scale need, and they lacked the skills and resources to deal with the tremendous social and economic upheaval of the Great Depression. Public opinion changed because of the magnitude of the Depression. People who were hardworking and had trusted the market system were suddenly without work. They lost savings and had no prospects for self-support. The situation could not be explained by the American belief in individualism and the inevitability that hard work and honesty would always be rewarded. The market system had failed, and poverty had become a societal concern. The combined failures of the economic system, private charitable agencies, and state and local governments to address economic need placed social welfare on the agenda of the federal government: "As a result of the Depression, many people came to realize that the fortunes of individual Americans were interdependent, and many adopted the belief that it was the duty of the federal government to prevent new depressions" (Gronbjerg, Street, & Suttles, 1978, p. 46).

The belief in social responsibility and social change was significant during this time period. Also for the first time, people became aware of how difficult it was to respond to a crisis situation. They began to feel that prevention could be an important part of the social welfare system. The Social Security Act demonstrated that legislators had a positive belief in both immediate responses to crisis and preventive actions to ward off future crises.

President Roosevelt was the first national leader to demonstrate empathy over sympathy in social well-being. Although leaders before him, such as Lincoln, demonstrated great concern for the plight of people who were oppressed and destitute, Roosevelt promoted programs based on the premise that unfortunate circumstances could happen to anyone and that the response should be empathic, not just sympathetic. Economic downturn could hit people who had always worked hard, and, therefore, social programs needed to be developed to guard against the vicissitudes of the marketplace. Social Security was the proposed solution.

Prior to the 1930s, the federal government had played a secondary role to private organizations and states and localities in social welfare policy. The federal government had begun to intercede through regulation but had for the most part left the market system alone. Therefore, those who did not benefit from the market—poor workers, women and children, racial minorities, and immigrants—had received no federal support. The economic upheaval of the Great Depression changed the federal role, and social responsibility gained national support. Although in the years to come those opposed to government involvement in personal life would challenge this support, the federal government was firmly entrenched in the provision of social welfare services by the end of the 1930s.

WORLD WAR II AND THE POSTWAR ERA (1940–1960)

Challenged by international events, President Roosevelt was forced to focus on World War II and abandon his primary concern with the social reforms of the New Deal. World War II did what all the employment programs of the New Deal could not: It put most Americans back to work. The war effort employed millions through enlistment in the armed services and employment in war-related industries and technologies. The war brought about social changes because the country was closed to immigration and military personnel were exposed to foreign cultures. It brought full employment and finally ended the economic downturn of the Great Depression.

In addition to bringing the economy out of the Depression, World War II permanently expanded the social role of the federal government. "New Deal spending in the years 1937 through 1941 averaged $9.2 billion a year. By the years 1947 to 1950, however, federal expenditures averaged $37.8 billion. A four-fold increase in government spending had occurred almost unnoticed" (Berkowitz & McQuaid, 1988, p. 147).

Expansion of the military also changed the social environment. With so many men in the armed services, women were brought into the workforce and introduced to nontraditional jobs. The famous "Rosie the Riveter" exalted the efforts of women in jobs that men had formerly held. As the war went on, social mores gave way to military necessity. African Americans were brought into the military and slowly began to be integrated into the larger military system. The liberation of women and the integration of African Americans were short lived, however. After the war, the nation shifted into a period of private interest, a focus on the family, and a conservatism not witnessed since the 1920s.

Immediately following the war, the federal government passed the **Servicemen's Readjustment Act of 1944**, commonly known as the **GI bill**. It reflected the sentiment that the nation owed much to its veterans and therefore funded provisions for education and training, home and business loans, and employment services designed to help the returning soldiers adapt to civilian life (Axinn & Stern, 2008). Although today the GI bill is viewed as a major piece of legislation, its original sponsors planned it to be nothing more than a modest support for readjustment (Lemann, 1993). However, millions of people took full advantage of the educational provisions. The act contributed to a lasting positive view of the federal response to returning veterans.

Although the federal government was permanently drawn into the provision of social welfare services during the 1930s and 1940s, the efforts of the 1950s centered on incremental changes and services that reinforced the private domain. Federal subsidies for housing, mortgages, and transportation made it possible for postwar families to leave cities and live in newly developed suburban areas (Ehrenreich, 1985).

The one major social welfare policy development of the decade was the addition of disability insurance to the Social Security Act. This addition exemplifies the development of social welfare policy during the 1950s. Change was incremental in nature. It took years to convince policy makers to extend social insurance to cover workers who became disabled and their families.

IMPACT OF WORLD WAR II AND THE POSTWAR ERA

The addition of disability coverage to Social Security reflected the mood of the times: It demonstrated how difficult it was to expand the coverage of the existing Social Security Act. The conservative mood made developing any new social welfare policies extremely difficult. The 1950s witnessed a postwar prosperity that emphasized private well-being. Although women had left the family to work outside the home during the war, they returned during the 1950s to cultivate the family and private interests. Reform in social welfare policy and social values would not come for another decade.

CONFLICTING BELIEFS OF THE WORLD WAR II ERA AND THE POSTWAR ERA

Whereas the New Deal era promoted social responsibility, the post–World War II period was an era in which individual responsibility was promoted. The crises of the Great Depression and the war had passed, and the focus was once again on the individual. Rational, incremental change was the preferred response to social well-being. Economic growth and suburban development reinforced a concentration on personal life, and social responsibility faded in importance.

SOCIAL REFORM (1960–1970s)

The private focus and relative economic stability of the 1950s was broken by the revelations of the 1960s. The economy had generally prospered. However, research uncovered large segments of the population who had not benefited from the post–World War II prosperity and were living in poverty. Michael Harrington's book *The Other America: Poverty in the United States* (1962), which described the economic misfortunes of so many Americans, is credited with initiating the **War on Poverty**. A massive migration of African Americans from the South to the North had created densely populated urban areas untouched by the economic prosperity of the 1950s (Jansson, 2009).

The 1960s, like the early 1900s and the 1930s, was a period of social welfare policy development. In response to the "rediscovery" of poverty and the demographic shifts, two major social welfare policy initiatives were passed by 1964: the Civil Rights Act and the War on Poverty. The **Civil Rights Act of 1964** codified protection of racial minorities by requiring desegregation of public facilities and prohibiting discriminatory hiring practices (Jansson, 2009). President Lyndon Johnson launched the War on Poverty as an effort to start his own New Deal (Trattner, 1999). The **Economic Opportunity Act** outlined the administration's antipoverty attempts. Among the provisions were the Job Corps program, which helped youths to prepare for employment; VISTA (Volunteers in Service to America), which stressed community service in impoverished neighborhoods; and **Community Action Programs,** which provided federal funds for community programs working toward the elimination of poverty (Axinn & Stern, 2008). Also in 1964, the **Food Stamp Program** was enacted to address the growing need to alleviate hunger in America.

Additional legislation was enacted in 1965. The **Older Americans Act** developed a nationwide network to coordinate services for the elderly. The coverage of the Social Security Act was expanded by the addition of two major social welfare programs, **Medicare** and **Medicaid,** to address health care for the elderly, the poor, and people with disabilities. Early efforts during the 1920s and 1930s to include health coverage in the Social Security Act had failed. Supporters of health care insurance and assistance had spent 30 years lobbying for health coverage. As participants in the War on Poverty, they were successful in gaining passage of Medicare, which is part of the social insurance program of the Social Security Act, and Medicaid, which provides health coverage as part of public assistance. The addition of Medicare broadened the safety net of Social Security for the elderly and workers who became disabled. The constellation of health services for the poor was expanded through Medicaid.

The War on Poverty also affected other areas of social welfare. As a result of the Economic Opportunity Act, **Head Start** was established in 1965. The goal of Head Start was to prevent poverty by providing services for poor preschool children and their families. The services included medical care, nutrition, school preparation, and parental education (Gustavsson & Segal, 1994). Civil rights legislation also expanded. Chapter 5 provides greater detail about advances in desegregation and policies enacted to ensure protection based on race and gender.

IMPACT OF THE SOCIAL REFORM PERIOD

In a relatively short time, the face of social welfare policy was again dramatically altered. Building on the programs of the New Deal era, social reformers in the 1960s promoted expansion of both social insurance and public assistance at the federal level. Public health insurance was enacted to complete the coverage of the Social Security Act. The War on Poverty brought the issue of social need back to the forefront of the nation's consciousness. The **Civil Rights movement** gained momentum through public legislation as well as growth in public awareness. The increased awareness extended to other social groups, as the women's rights, American Indian rights, farm workers' rights, and gay rights movements all coalesced during the 1960s.

CONFLICTING BELIEFS OF THE SOCIAL REFORM PERIOD

Public consciousness was at a high level during the 1960s. In reaction to the conservatism of the 1950s, the focus shifted from the individual back to social responsibility and social change. Emotions ran high. Leaders attempted to craft public policies that would address social system failures. Poverty was again regarded as a social ill more than as an individual shortcoming. Social support was one of the key sentiments fueling the momentum to create a more just and fair society. The Civil Rights marches and demonstrations represented, in addition to social change and responsibility, a concern for people who were strangers, a sentiment that was not seen during the post–World War II years.

RETRENCHMENT: SOCIAL WELFARE PULL-BACK STARTING IN THE 1970s AND THROUGH THE 1990s

For social welfare activists, the 1960s was a time of optimism, when it seemed that all social problems could and would be addressed. Policies and programs were created and supported by the government and the voters alike. No matter how liberal and reformist the new legislative efforts might have been, however, conservative ideologies were still evident. By the later 1960s, efforts were begun to curtail the social largess of the decade. Public assistance, developed as part of the New Deal, had shifted from aid for the elderly, those with disabilities, and widows and their children to aid for a new population, the dependent children of unmarried, abandoned, or divorced women (Berkowitz & McQuaid, 1988).

By the late 1960s, the growth in the caseloads of single mothers and families of color in the Aid to Families with Dependent Children (AFDC) program (expanded in 1962 from the original Aid to Dependent Children program of the Social Security Act) prompted more punitive measures. The program was perceived as having changed from one of income support for the worthy poor—widows and orphans—to one of subsidizing women whose lifestyle differed from the norm and who were not concerned with the nation's family ethic (Abramovitz, 1996). The economy began to stagnate. The War on Poverty of the 1960s, although regarded as worthy, did not eradicate poverty. The costs of the Vietnam War led to inflation. People began to view government skeptically. Thus, during the 1970s, the efforts of the previous decade underwent a reversal.

Despite the shifting ideology of the 1970s and President Richard Nixon's conservative policies, a number of incremental policy initiatives developed. In 1973 the federal government passed the Comprehensive Employment and Training Act (CETA), designed to help the unemployed, and a year later Title XX was added to the Social Security Act to provide funds directly to the states for social welfare services for the poor. Both initiatives reflected the more conservative elements of the times, with reliance on local authority and the private market for implementation rather than the federal government (Trattner, 1999).

The activism of the 1960s did not disappear during the 1970s. The women's movement gained momentum in gaining equal rights and protection from discrimination. Groups such as the National Organization for Women (NOW), organized in 1966, established themselves as national representatives for women's issues. In

1973, the landmark legal case of *Roe v. Wade* legalized abortion and in the process gave women of all economic and social backgrounds access to the medical procedure. Gay rights advocates mark the 1969 Stonewall riot as the beginning of the gay rights movement. The riot was a violent, 5-day confrontation between the police and the gay patrons of the Stonewall bar in New York City. The confrontation politicized many gay people and resulted in intensified organizing for equal rights and protection from discrimination (Marcus, 1992).

The renewed conservatism of the 1970s settled in during the 1980s, however. Represented by the presidency of Ronald Reagan, the entire decade was a time of preoccupation with private interests. The Reagan administration focused on three fundamental goals: shifting responsibility and power from the federal government to states and localities, relying on the private sector to provide for social welfare needs, and reducing federal programs and spending for social welfare initiatives (Rochefort, 1986). The concept of **devolution** of social services marked public policy. Devolution sought the return of control of social services from the federal level to the state or local levels. This shift, supporters of devolution argued, would save costs for the federal government and let those closest to the problems, localities, develop appropriate programs. While this concept had merit, it ignored the reason the federal government became the provider of many social services in the first place—left to their own, localities either did not have sufficient resources or the will to provide services.

Social welfare policy legislation enacted during the 1980s was meager and often punitive, taking resources away from social welfare services under the guise of "less government." This punitive response was particularly felt by poor women who relied on government cash benefits to support their families. After cuts in AFDC were made law in 1983 under President Reagan, the Family Support Act of 1988 was passed to amend the AFDC program. Described as "welfare reform," the act was punitive and restrictive, giving poor women less support and protection from economic hardship (Segal, 1989).

When social welfare policy was enacted during the 1980s, it often came long after a social problem had gained national attention. For example, in 1987, years after researchers and mayors of urban cities had recognized the problem, the federal government finally passed legislation to provide support for people who were homeless. The Stewart B. McKinney Homeless Assistance Act was passed in July 1987, but was never fully funded. From 1987 to 1991, Congress authorized $3.3 billion, yet only $2.4 billion was actually appropriated to be spent on services for people who were homeless (U.S. General Accounting Office, 1992).

Just as slow in coming was the federal response to AIDS, a disease that had gained public attention as early as 1983 (Shilts, 1987). The federal government did not respond with AIDS-related legislation until 1990, when the Ryan White Comprehensive AIDS Resources Emergency (CARE) Act was passed. It was designed to provide services for people with AIDS. As with other legislation of the time, full funding was not forthcoming. In 1991 and 1992, the act received less than one-fourth the authorized amount of almost $900 million (Select Committee on Children, Youth, and Families, 1992).

At the same time that social welfare services were being rescinded and underlying social problems were being ignored, the federal government invested untold billions in supporting corporate America. The $7.5 billion bailout of Continental

BOX 2.2 | CONSIDER THIS ...

Technology has entered people's lives at a rapid pace. "In 1980, IBM projected that the total U.S. market for personal computers for the next 5 years would be 241,000 machines. The actual number was almost exactly 100 times that" (Garreau, 2001, p. 7).

Bank in 1984 (Congressional Quarterly, 1985) and the more than $100 billion spent between 1989 and 1993 for resolving the savings and loan scandal (Congressional Quarterly, 1993) are the most publicized instances. Other subsidies of agriculture, energy, and technology groups were significant.

The decade of the 1990s can best be summarized as one of economic fluctuations. The early years were bleak because the nation was mired in a recession. Then the economy expanded at an unexpected rate. From July 1990 through March 1991, the nation was in deep recession. During the next 18 months, the nation was technically not in a recession, but the atmosphere was recession-like (Rushefsky, 2002). Then, the nation rebounded and experienced an unprecedented period of economic growth, which lasted until 2000. In addition to, and perhaps as a contributor to, the economic expansion, technology found its way into thousands of homes. It changed the way people communicate and gain access to information and changed worker productivity (see Box 2.2).

The 1990s was also a period of political divisiveness. Republicans and Democrats were deeply divided. Congress was controlled by the Democrats under the Republican President George H. W. Bush. In 1994, the Republicans took control under the Democratic President Bill Clinton. The divided federal legislative and executive branches contributed to contentious public policy confrontations.

In spite of division in government and retraction in social welfare spending and programs, gains in civil rights were made during the 1990s. In 1990, the **Americans with Disabilities Act** was passed, mandating protections from discrimination for people with disabilities. In 1991, after civil rights gains had been chipped away for years, the Civil Rights Restoration Act expanded many of the protections of earlier legislation. In the spring of 1993, gay advocates organized the largest civil rights demonstration in American history with the March on Washington. Nearly a million people demonstrated for equal rights and an end to discrimination based on a person's sexual orientation.

The election of Democrat Bill Clinton to the White House in 1992 ended 12 years of Republican control. Under President Clinton, several major pieces of legislation were passed after they had languished for years in Republican administrations. After twice being vetoed by President George H. W. Bush in 1988 and 1990, the **Family and Medical Leave Act (FMLA)** was passed and signed into law in January of 1993. Although it was minimal in its coverage and far less than what activists had hoped to achieve, the FMLA marked the first time in history that the federal government had mandated employers to guarantee unpaid leave for workers after the birth or adoption of a child, or during the illness of a dependent or family member. Other social welfare legislation passed under President Clinton included the

Brady Bill, which enacted controls on the purchase and ownership of handguns, and the Anti-Crime Bill, which outlawed automatic assault weapons. These two bills had been introduced to Congress during the Reagan and Bush administrations and had met with defeat each time.

Democratic control of Congress was short lived. After the 1994 election, Republicans took control of both the House and the Senate for the first time in more than 40 years. The Republican platform called for retraction of social welfare services and a shift away from federal support. The Republican "Contract with America" pledged to decrease federal control of social welfare services with a move to turn over the responsibility to state and local governments. These positions built on those espoused during the 1980s under the Reagan presidency. The Republican agenda of limiting social welfare programs and removing the federal government from the social welfare system was reflected in the **Personal Responsibility and Work Opportunity Reconciliation Act (PRWORA)**, signed into law by President Clinton in August of 1996. This piece of social welfare policy represented a radical shift in public assistance. Since 1935, the Aid to Families with Dependent Children (AFDC) program had guaranteed cash assistance to any family with a very low income. The new legislation canceled a guarantee that had been in place for more than 60 years. The AFDC program was phased out and replaced by the **Temporary Assistance for Needy Families (TANF)** program.

The new legislation removed unified federal guidelines for the program (Center on Budget and Policy Priorities, 1996). Today, as a result of PRWORA, public assistance programs vary by state. If a state runs out of money in a given year, it can stop providing economic aid. Poor families have to wait until the next year for assistance. In addition, there is a time limit on cash assistance. No family can receive more than 5 years of assistance over its lifetime. The new law is very complicated and contains numerous sections. A full discussion of TANF and the full impact of this policy change are found in Chapter 8.

IMPACT OF THE RETRENCHMENT YEARS

What characterized the 1980s was less government support for poor and disenfranchised people and more government support for corporate America. This seeming contradiction reflected the priority of support for private interests rather than social welfare programs. Less government was viewed as better government. This view led to cutbacks in social welfare spending at the federal level, which in turn caused rescinding of services at the state and local levels. Disparities between those with high incomes and those with low incomes grew, leaving a larger gap between the rich and the poor. From 1980 to 1990, household incomes rose by more than 20 percent for the highest fifth, more than $20,000 in real dollars, compared with an increase of seven percent, or $650, for those in the bottom fifth (DeNavas-Walt, Proctor, & Lee, 2005).

The historical lesson of the 1990s is that even in modern times, economics has a major impact on social welfare. Although the fluctuations of the Great Depression were more volatile and extreme, the economic changes of the 1990s were also profound. Social welfare policies were mixed, perhaps reflecting the shifts in the economy. Although civil rights gained some ground, public assistance was cut back extensively and was viewed harshly by policy makers and the public.

Political rancor soured people on government, and this had a negative effect on social programs. Public support declined, and punitive and restrictive measures were enacted. Dissatisfaction with the federal government promoted moving social welfare services to state and local levels, furthering the decentralization begun during the Reagan years. The impact of this shift has been strongly felt by social work practitioners, who provide much of the staff for social welfare programs.

CONFLICTING BELIEFS OF THE RETRENCHMENT YEARS

Distinction between deserving and undeserving people resurfaced by the 1980s. The social responsibility ethos of the 1960s receded, and individual and private interests had become the hallmark by the end of the 1980s. Whatever regard people had had for prevention in social services prior to this period disappeared. The focus was on personal failure as the reason for social problems rather than systemic failures. The view of social welfare as a "hand-out" rather than an entitlement dominated the public policy landscape. The desire to shift responsibility for social welfare from the federal government to localities was also pronounced during the years of retrenchment.

The 1990s witnessed the full return of differentiating between deserving and undeserving people. Poor women on public assistance were viewed as undeserving, and subsequent legislation codified that belief. This perspective fueled beliefs in personal failure as the reason for poverty and destitution. The full force of the belief in the primacy of individual responsibility and self-sufficiency was evident in PRWORA. For the most part, social responsibility and social change were marginal sentiments during the 1990s. These narrow perspectives on and conflicting beliefs about social welfare policy set the stage for struggles to come over the next ten years.

THE NEW CENTURY

The first decade of the 21st century opened with some of the same conditions of the previous decade. The contentious 2000 election, which gave a plurality of popular votes to Democrat Al Gore but gave the electoral vote and, hence, the presidency to George W. Bush, marked the beginning of the century. The bitter division of electoral politics that influenced the 1990s became more entrenched during the new decade. With the return of the presidency to the Republican party, the ideas of limited government and individual responsibility were reinforced. Less government was thought to be better, and lowering taxes was the rallying point for the Bush presidency.

However, the tragic events of September 11, 2001, with the terrorist attack on the World Trade Center buildings and the Pentagon, rocked the nation. Although the lasting effect of that event remains to be seen, it is likely to have been a pivotal point in U.S. history (Garreau, 2001). The events of 9/11 did demonstrate the impact of crisis and the readiness of Americans and the government to respond. Although President Bush was a strong advocate of less government intervention, he instituted federal relief efforts on a major scale following the events of 9/11. These efforts included restitution to families of those who died in the attacks, major monetary grants for emergency efforts, and economic support and loans for corporate airlines and airports. Directly as an outcome of 9/11, the cabinet level Department of Homeland

Security was created through the National Strategy for Homeland Security and the Homeland Security Act of 2002. The Department of Homeland Security (DHS) was developed to provide one unifying agency responsible for the national network of organizations and institutions involved in efforts to secure the nation, and does so with 180,000 federal employees. Within DHS is the Transportation Security Administration (TSA). TSA is responsible for security of the nation's transportation systems and oversees the security for the highways, railroads, buses, mass transit systems, ports, and 450 airports in the United States. TSA employs approximately 50,000 people from Alaska to Puerto Rico. Very quickly, in response to the crisis of 9/11, the arm of the federal government grew instead of diminishing.

The early part of the decade also included major public policy changes, specifically Medicare reform. In December 2003, President Bush signed into law a Medicare prescription drug benefit. The goal is to help seniors pay for the high cost of prescription drugs, but the program is such a complicated combination of options and partial coverage that analysts fear it "will make it harder, not easier, for the nation's senior citizens to navigate health care in this country" (Dallek, 2003, p. 22). The program combines public and private services and is optional. The many options in the program resulted from the need to find consensus among diverse policy makers in order to pass it, but these options make for a very complicated program (see Box 2.3). It began in 2006 and within the first two years had grown to cover over 27 million people (Centers for Medicare and Medicaid Services, 2008). A detailed description of the new benefit is given in Chapter 11.

The war in Iraq, which officially began in March 2003, went from a planned short-term "shock and awe" blitz to a long-term costly war that has stretched on for years. At the five-year anniversary in 2008, more than 4,000 American military personnel had died and tens of thousands had been wounded. By the close of 2007, the financial cost to the federal government for the global war on terror had been $700 billion. Future costs will depend on the numbers of troops deployed. Over the next ten years, troop levels of 30,000 to 75,000 are estimated to cost an additional $1.2 trillion to $1.7 trillion (Congressional Budget Office, 2008). The financial costs and human casualties of the war abroad have greatly affected the resources available and needs for social services at home. This shift will have repercussions on the United States for years to come.

Furthermore, the 2005 failure of the federal government and local authorities to respond adequately to the disaster brought on by Hurricane Katrina in New Orleans raised questions about the adequacy of social welfare policies and programs. The abilities of local authorities and the Federal Emergency Management Agency (FEMA) to respond to the crisis and aftermath were sorely inadequate. Even several years post Katrina, rebuilding efforts and the return of residents were inadequate. Hurricane Katrina also revealed how long-standing social and economic divisions are worsened by natural disaster. The poor of New Orleans, primarily African American, lived in areas hardest hit and suffered significantly, with minimal resources to rebuild their lives (White, Philpot, Wylie, and McGowen, 2007).

Immigration gained significant attention by 2007. Initial focus on immigration was prompted by efforts to ensure unauthorized people do not enter or illegally remain in the United States as did some of the 9/11 terrorists. However, by 2008, the focus on immigration centered on unauthorized workers who were primarily from

| BOX 2.3 | CONTROVERSIAL PERSPECTIVES . . . |

Will the Medicare Reform of 2003 Help Seniors?

The Medicare reform policy of 2003 was passed with the intent of helping low-income seniors to pay for prescription drugs. Should the federal government pay this expense? When the legislation was passed, the estimated cost of the program was $400 billion over ten years. By February 2005, the estimate had grown considerably to at least $720 billion over the next ten years (VandeHei, 2005). In 2008 the Congressional Budget Office revised the estimate for federal spending and figured that with the offset of premiums the government cost would be about $625 billion for the first ten years, but costs by 2017 would be almost three times higher than in 2007. Can we afford this cost as a nation? Some people argue that prescription medications should be covered under the health care policies of Medicare. Others argue that pharmaceutical companies are making large sums of money through the sale of prescription medications and that the government should intercede in the market and broker group prices for medica-

tions as is done for other health care services. And still others argue that the public was misled. One of the pressing questions that arose when the higher costs of the Medicare reform program were announced with the presidential budget for fiscal year 2006 was this: How could the original estimate be so wrong? That is, how could the ten-year cost in 2003 balloon from $400 billion to $600–700 billion? Part of the answer is that the program was not slated to become fully operational until 2006. The costs from 2003 until 2006 would merely be planning costs. Therefore, the first few years of the ten-year plan would be much less costly than the ten-year costs, when the program would be fully operative. The larger question is this: Was the cost of $400 billion used because it was lower and therefore more palatable to the public and policy makers, even though it was not reflective of the cost once the program was fully up and running? Did advocates of the policy have a responsibility to disclose the full operating costs rather than base their estimates on the lesser startup costs?

Latin American countries. Opponents of open immigration argue that these undocumented people compromise security, while advocates argue that people come for economic opportunities and serve in needed areas of employment. The issue of immigration is dealt with more thoroughly in Chapter 13. Like previous events, the immigration debate raised questions about race and economics in America, issues that are very relevant to social welfare policy.

The last major concern of the first decade of the new century was the economy. The housing market, fueled by easy-to-get mortgages, fell and banks with heavy exposure to the housing market suffered severe financial losses. Federal interventions through the Federal Reserve Board and mortgage support efforts developed by the President and administered through the Federal Housing Administration were initiated in 2007 to stem the negative financial impact. By 2008, the federal government had become deeply involved in the domain of private businesses and banks. With passage of the Housing and Recovery Act of 2008, the Treasury Department took over the government-sponsored but privately run mortgage agencies known as

Fannie Mae and Freddie Mac. This effort is discussed in more detail in Chapter 9. From a historical standpoint, this federal move, coupled with government bailouts of other financial firms, shifted the federal government from the role of outside regulator to inside operator within the for-profit financial business sector. The full impact and cost of this shift will unfold over the next decade. These initiatives will increase federal spending, and with the tax decreases initiated in the first years of the Bush administration, further increase the national deficit. The state of the economy has significant implications for social welfare and is addressed more fully in Chapter 9.

It is too early to tell what impact the first decade of the new century will have on our social welfare system or what conflicting beliefs will dominate. We have witnessed the nation's capacity to respond to a major crisis such as 9/11. However, that crisis has caused increased mistrust of strangers and people different from the majority culture. Significant efforts at social welfare reform have been attempted, such as the Medicare changes. For the first time in history an African American and a woman were viable candidates to be nominated by a major party for president, and a woman nominated for vice president. The election of Barack Obama, the first African American to hold the highest political office in the United States, is a remarkable social and political shift in America. President Obama's cabinet reflects the broad diversity of the American people, and as such suggests that a broader scope of policy interventions will follow. A window into poverty was opened with the aftermath of Hurricane Katrina. The federal government expanded in response to national security. The economy faltered demanding federal interventions. The economic interventions begun by the federal government in 2008 under President Bush continued under the new Presidency of Barack Obama with the American Recovery and Reinvestment Act of 2009. This public law earmarked $787 billion to invest in jobs, infrastructure, energy efficiency, science unemployment assistance, and funds to aid state and local governments. These events suggest that the population of the United States expects government to intercede. However, the impact of these events and what role in maintaining social well-being the government will continue to play remain to be seen.

FINAL THOUGHTS

No matter what kind of social welfare policy decisions are made in the future, it is certain that changes will build on the achievements and failures of the past. To be prepared to participate in the dialogue for social welfare policy change, it is imperative to understand its history. We really can, and should, learn from history. In this chapter, an overview of the history of social welfare policy in America has been provided that can serve as a foundation for understanding the U.S. social welfare system.

Key Terms

Elizabethan Poor Laws	unworthy poor	Freedman's Bureau	progressive era
worthy poor	indoor relief	Dawes Act	

Charity Organization Societies

settlement movement

New Deal

Social Security Act of 1935

social insurance

public assistance

Servicemen's Readjustment Act of 1944

GI bill

War on Poverty

Civil Rights Act of 1964

Economic Opportunity Act

Food Stamp Program

Older Americans Act

Medicare

Medicaid

Head Start

devolution

Americans with Disabilities Act

Family and Medical Leave Act

Personal Responsibility and Work Opportunity Reconciliation Act

Temporary Assistance for Needy Families (TANF)

Questions for Discussion

1. What can people learn from studying the history of social welfare policy in America?
2. Identify a period of history in which individualism seemed strong. What were the social welfare responses of the time that reflected the strong beliefs in individualism?
3. Identify a period of history in which social responsibility seemed strong. What were the social welfare responses of the time that reflected the strong beliefs in social responsibility?
4. When did the federal government seem to become entrenched in the provision of social welfare services? Do you think this has been a positive or negative trend? Why or why not?
5. Give a recent example of new intervention or expanded intervention by the federal government. Do you think this expansion is good for the nation? Why?

Excercises

1. Ask someone older than you if he or she will reminisce about what they remember about social conditions throughout their life. Were they alive during the Great Depression? Do they remember World War II? Were they involved in social movements of the 1960s? Do they remember the struggle over civil rights? Try to link their personal experiences with the historical events outlined in this chapter.
2. Read a historical novel to help bring to life some of the periods highlighted in the chapter. As a class project, several groups can be formed, each focusing on a different time period. The task is to find a novel written about the time period and analyze the experience of the characters in relation to historical events. For example, a group might read *The Grapes of Wrath* for the Great Depression or *Forrest Gump* for the 1960s. Are the books realistic portrayals? Why or why not?
3. For each of the historical periods, list the most significant social welfare policy change of the time. Are those changes still evident in our social welfare system today? Why or why not?
4. Browse through current news magazines or online news sites. Is there a current event that you think is becoming or might become in the near future a major social welfare issue? Bring it to class and share it with your fellow students. Do they agree or disagree? Why?

References

Abramovitz, M. (1996). *Regulating the lives of women*, Revised edition. Boston: South End Press.

Axinn, J., & Stern, M. J. (2008). *Social welfare: A history of the American response to need*, 7th ed. Boston: Allyn and Bacon.

Berkowitz, E., & McQuaid, K. (1988). *Creating the welfare state*, 2nd ed. New York: Praeger.

Boulding, E. (1992). *The underside of history*. Vol. 2. Newbury Park, CA: Sage.

Bremner, R. H. (1956). *The discovery of poverty in the United States*. New York: New York University Press.

Center on Budget and Policy Priorities. (1996). *The new welfare law*. Washington, DC: Author.

Centers for Medicare and Medicaid Services. (2008). *Monthly contract summary report*. Washington, DC: Department of Health and Human Services.

Children's Defense Fund. (1996). *Legislative Update (8-2-96)*. Washington, DC: Author.

Congressional Budget Office. (2008). *The budget and economic outlook: Fiscal years 2008 to 2018*. Washington, DC: Congress of the United States.

Congressional Quarterly. (1993). Hill votes more funds for thrift bailout. *1993 CQ Almanac*, p. 150. Washington, DC: Author.

Congressional Quarterly. (1985). *Congress and the nation 1981–1984*. Vol. VI. Washington, DC: Author.

Dallek, G. (2003). A prescription for confusion. *Washington Post National Weekly Edition* 21(8):22.

Daniels, R. (1990). *Coming to America: A history of immigration and ethnicity in American life*. Princeton, NJ: Harper Perennial.

Day, P. J. (2006). *A new history of social welfare*, 5th ed. Boston: Allyn and Bacon.

Derthick, M. (1979). *Policymaking for Social Security*. Washington, DC: Brookings Institution.

DeNavas-Walt, C., Proctor, B. D. & Lee, C. H. (2005). Income, poverty and health insurance coverage in the United States: 2004. *Current Population Reports*, P60–229. Washington, DC: US Census Bureau.

Dobelstein, A. W. (1980). *Politics, economics, and public welfare*. Englewood Cliffs, NJ: Prentice Hall.

Ehrenreich, J. H. (1985). *The altruistic imagination: A history of social work and social policy in the United States*. Ithaca, NY: Cornell University Press.

Erickson, A. G. (1987). Family services. *Encyclopedia of social work*. Vol. 1, pp. 589–593. Silver Spring, MD: National Association of Social Workers, Inc.

Fisher, J. (1980). *The response of social work to the Depression*. Boston: G. K. Hall.

Garreau, J. (2001). Hinge moments in history. *Washington Post National Weekly Edition* 18(52):6–7.

Germain, C. B., & Hartman, A. (1980). People and ideas in the history of social work practice. *Social Casework* 61(6):323–331.

Gronbjerg, K., Street, D., & Suttles, G. D. (1978). *Poverty and social change*. Chicago: University of Chicago Press.

Gustavsson, N. S., & Segal, E. A. (1994). *Critical issues in child welfare*. Thousand Oaks, CA: Sage.

Harrington, M. (1962). *The other America: Poverty in the United States*. Baltimore: Penguin.

Jansson, B. S. (2009). *The reluctant welfare state*, 6th ed. Belmont, CA: Brooks/Cole.

Katz, M. B. (1986). *In the shadow of the poorhouse*. New York: Basic Books.

Leiby, J. (1978). *A history of social welfare and social work in the United States*. New York: Columbia University Press.

Lemann, N. (1993). GI bill nostalgia. *Washington Post National Weekly Edition*. (September 6–12).

Mann, C. C. (2002). 1491. *The Atlantic Monthly* 289(3):41–53.

Marcus, E. (1992). *Making history: The struggle for gay and lesbian equal rights*. New York: HarperCollins.

McElvaine, R. S. (1993). *The Great Depression: America 1929–1941*. New York: Times Books.

McSteen, M. A. (1985). Fifty years of social security. *Social Security Bulletin* 48(8):37–44.

Nabokov, P. (ed.). (1991). *Native American testimony*. New York: Penguin.

Nagel, J. (1997). *American Indian ethnic renewal: Red power and the resurgence of identity and culture*. New York: Oxford University Press.

Patterson, J. T. (2000). *America's struggle against poverty in the twentieth century*. Cambridge, MA: Harvard University Press.

Reid, K. E. (1981). *From character building to social treatment*. Westport, CT: Greenwood.

Rochefort, D. A. (1986). *American social welfare policy: Dynamics of formulation and change*. Boulder, CO: Westview.

Rothman, D. J. (1971). *The discovery of the asylum: Social order and disorder in the new republic*. Boston: Little, Brown.

Rushefsky, M. E. (2002). *Public policy in the United States*, 3rd ed. Armonk, NY: M. E. Sharpe.

Segal, E. A. (1989). Welfare reform: Help for poor women and children? *Affilia* 4(3)42–50.

Select Committee on Children, Youth, and Families. (1992). *A decade of denial: Teens and AIDS in America*. House of Representatives Report 102-1074. Washington, DC: U.S. Government Printing Office.

Severn, B. (1976). *Frances Perkins: A member of the cabinet*. New York: Hawthorn.

Shilts, R. (1987). *And the band played on*. New York: St. Martin's.

Trattner, W. I. (1999). *From poor law to welfare state*, 6th ed. New York: Free Press.

United States Bureau of the Census. (1975). *Historical statistics of the United States*. Washington, DC: U.S. Government Printing Office.

United States General Accounting Office. (1992). *Homelessness: McKinney Act programs and funding through fiscal year 1991. GAO/RCED-93-39*. Washington, DC: U.S. Government Printing Office.

VandeHei, J. (2005). So much for "limited government." *Washington Post National Weekly Edition* 22(17):11.

Wenocur, S., & Reisch, M. (1989). *From charity to enterprise: The development of American social work in a market economy*. Urbana, IL: University of Illinois Press.

White, I. K, Philpot, T. S., Wylie, K., & McGowen, E. (2007). Feeling the pain of my people: Hurricane Katrina, racial inequality, and the psyche of Black America. *Journal of Black Studies* 37:523–533.

CONCEPTUAL FOUNDATIONS OF SOCIAL WELFARE POLICY

CHAPTER 3

David Bacon/Image Works

Social welfare policy usually represents the culmination of many social, political, and economic events. A policy is shaped by the values and beliefs of its supporters and influenced by social and economic conditions, timing of policy development, or a combination of these and other factors. Many theories attempt to explain why policy evolves the way it does. To understand social welfare policy, students should become familiar with some of the leading ideologies, theories, and paradigms. These three terms are often used interchangeably. However, for our purposes they are defined as follows: **Ideologies** are ideas or bodies of thought that offer guidance; **theories** are systems of ideas that explain a phenomenon; and **paradigms** are patterns or models that provide a conceptual framework. As Figure 3.1 illustrates, the three concepts are interrelated. Ideologies are the building blocks for theories. Paradigms are built on both ideologies and theories.

This chapter presents ideologies, theories, and paradigms that attempt to explain why and how social welfare policy develops. The social conditions and values that influence policy are also discussed. The synthesis of these factors is the foundation for the analysis of the social welfare policies and programs discussed in this book. The array of ideologies, theories, and paradigms is great. Consider that these concepts are tools to help you analyze social welfare policies. Most public policies reflect several of these concepts. The same social issue can be interpreted by one set of ideas, only to shift to another over time. A clear example is the policy of slavery in this country. Slavery was a policy based on ideologies, theories, and paradigms that have changed over time. The changes in perspectives ultimately led to the abolition of slavery. Knowledge of ideologies, theories, and paradigms helps us to analyze policy and subsequently understand how and why policies and programs have evolved. One point worth noting is that the same issue over time can be analyzed from different perspectives. Ideologies, theories, and paradigms are dynamic, and change in response to new information, research, and societal events.

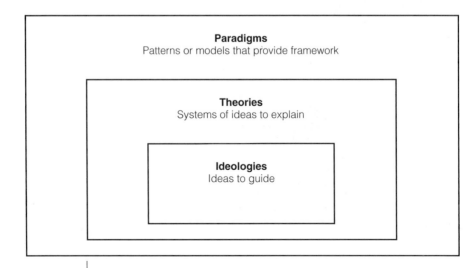

Paradigms
Patterns or models that provide framework

Theories
Systems of ideas to explain

Ideologies
Ideas to guide

FIGURE 3.1 | PARADIGMS, THEORIES, AND IDEOLOGIES

IDEOLOGIES OF THE SOCIAL WELFARE SYSTEM

Many concepts in social welfare policy are based on ideologies, which are ideas that influence our thinking. Many ideologies influence the design of the American social welfare system. Understanding ideologies helps to clarify some of the inconsistencies in policies and explain why the system looks the way it does today.

CAUSE AND FUNCTION

In the early years of the social work profession, the role of human services was the focus of much debate. In 1929, the president of the first professional organization, the National Conference on Social Work, addressed the issue. Porter Lee (1929) differentiated between two aspects of social work: cause and function. **Cause** is the issue on which people take a moral position to improve society. **Function** is the day-to-day effort to provide services. Lee believed that workers should support the cause while carrying out the function of their daily duties.

The conflict between cause and function is always present. To what extent should people take action and fight for a cause, and to what extent should they tend to the daily needs of the recipients of social services? Lee's exhortation that one should embrace the cause at the same time that one is carrying out daily duties is a very tall order. Some theorists argue that supporting both cause and function is impossible and that one must choose between the two. The War on Poverty of the 1960s demonstrated elements of this conflict. Some advocates felt that the public assistance system was punitive. To labor in service of the system, or in Lee's terms to provide function, was to continue to impose a system that was not helpful. Instead, it was important to fight for the cause—better treatment of those who are poor and receive public assistance—and to change the selective residual program to a more universal institutional program. These fighters believed that the cause prevented workers from functioning well.

The struggle between cause and function is often seen in social welfare history, and social service providers face it today. For example, when a client lives in a dangerous neighborhood, should the social worker help the client move or should the worker fight to change the neighborhood? Often, it is easier to change the individual's situation than to change an entire community.

BLAMING THE VICTIM

Individual responsibility is a key belief shaping the U.S. social welfare system. Holding each person responsible for his or her own circumstances is a significant part of American ideology (as discussed in Chapter 1). One variation of the ideology of individual responsibility is **blaming the victim**.

The concept of blaming the victim was introduced by William Ryan (1971) to explain why poverty and other concerns are viewed as personal rather than social problems. Ryan argues that it is easier and more comfortable to blame the individual who is poor than to blame all of society. Social welfare in America has been much influenced by this ideology. Citizens often prefer "to treat what we call social problems, such as poverty, disease, and mental illness, in terms of the individual deviance of the special, unusual groups of persons who had those problems" (Ryan, 1971, p. 16). If defects can be identified in the community and the environment, responsibility for them can be placed on all members of society. Ryan argues that because of self-interest and class interest, most people prefer to see social problems as a result of individual defect rather than the result of a social system that is unfair and exclusionary. If the individual is to blame, then the rest of society is not responsible for making changes or offering help.

For example, if urban poverty is the fault of those who live in poor areas of a city, then it is the poor residents' responsibility to correct their behaviors and improve their surroundings. On the other hand, if urban poverty is the result of the economic system, then social change is needed to provide work for unemployed people.

Those who benefit from society the way it is are reluctant to criticize a system that has been good to them. At the same time, there may be genuine concern for those who are disadvantaged. The best way to reconcile concern for the poor with respect for the status quo is to blame the victim and create social welfare services that focus on changing the individual.

An extension of this theory is second-order victim blaming (Dressel, Carter, & Balachandran, 1995). This theory explains the reasons why social welfare programs fail. For example, a social problem such as poverty gives rise to programs such as Temporary Assistance for Needy Families (TANF). If the programs fail, critics claim that recipients are at fault rather than the programs. An illustration will clarify this point further. If a client fails to show up for a scheduled appointment, the client is viewed as "noncompliant." The possibility that the social service office is not accessible to the client because public transportation is not available is ignored. This level of victim blaming is important to social workers and their clients. If a client is not benefiting from a social service, workers should examine the service's design, funding, and implementation before considering the individual's motivation. Are the program components sound? Are services accessible? If not, how can the program be changed? Too often, program failures are blamed on individual recipients instead of poorly designed and implemented programs. This is second-order victim blaming.

THE CULTURE OF POVERTY AND THE UNDERCLASS

Social services are often developed to assist those whose needs are greater than their resources or the resources of their family. Therefore, ideologies related to poverty and how we view the poor are important to understand. The ideology of a **culture of poverty** goes hand in hand with the concept of blaming the victim. This ideology asserts that some people are born poor and socialized to remain poor. Poverty is a cultural destiny passed on from one generation to another. Poverty is viewed as a set of attitudes and behaviors; the only way to help the poor is to teach them to take on a new culture, the dominant culture. This idea was prevalent in discussions of poverty in the 1960s, but it began much earlier. For example, at the beginning of the 20th century, Charity Organization Society "friendly visitors" entered the homes of poor people to model ideal behaviors for them.

In the years following the 1960s, a new version of the culture of poverty surfaced. Several social scientists, particularly William Julius Wilson (1987), have described the permanent underclass and the culture of the ghetto. Wilson cites both the individual and society as having responsibility for social conditions, specifically poverty. He argues that because of economic isolation and distress, urban ghettos produce a unique culture that is antithetical to the behaviors, beliefs, and values of the majority culture. As Wilson sees it, the solution to poverty and related problems is for both institutions and individuals to change. Social welfare programs and the economic system must become more sensitive to the needs of the individual, and each person must take responsibility for his or her personal behavior.

CONSERVATIVE AND LIBERAL POLITICAL PERSPECTIVES

The degree of commitment to conservative and liberal beliefs about social welfare policy differs. Conservatives generally oppose government intervention as a waste of taxpayers' money. Social programs are viewed as providing benefits to those who do not need them or as creating a dependency that encourages people to stop caring for themselves. (This perspective is found in many of the previously discussed ideologies.)

Liberals generally support active intervention by the federal government. Social welfare policies are regarded as being so important that they should be legislated by the government. Implicit in this view is the idea that the welfare of society cannot be left to freely operate without some controls. Liberals view the government as being a referee to ensure fairness and a provider to correct imbalances and inequities.

Conservative and liberal views are often considered to be contradictory and exclusionary, that is, a person can hold one belief or the other but not both. The politics of the 1990s and 2000s has demonstrated how polarizing this dichotomy can be. Radio talk shows identifying themselves as conservative have flourished, giving rise to competing liberal-oriented shows. The media conflict reinforces the public debate and dichotomy. It is possible, and some people identify this way, to hold both perspectives. For example, you might hear someone describe him or herself as fiscally conservative and socially liberal. What he or she mean is that he or she do not support major government intervention in the economic realm but favor government roles in social services and in promoting civil rights. If the social welfare of all citizens is a high priority for policy makers, then the debate about which perspective is better needs to be changed to the perspective of what will be most beneficial for the most people.

BIOLOGICAL DETERMINISM

Many of the ideologies already discussed are related to the concept of **biological determinism**. Biological heredity is seen as determining how people behave. This view holds that one's heredity predetermines, or at least strongly influences, the level of social and economic position a person achieves. Biological determinism is not new. It has surfaced at numerous times throughout western history. It gained early legitimacy through science. Darwin's concept of "survival of the fittest" was applied to human beings to explain poverty, racial differences, and gender differences (Harvey & Reed, 1992; Shipman, 1994). Supporters of social Darwinism argue that those at the top economically and socially got there because of innate inherited abilities. This approach ignores environment, social surroundings, access to opportunities such as educational and employment opportunities, and resources and privileges available to a person born to the right parents, classes, races, or social stratification.

Biological determinism flourished during the 1920s, resurfaced during the 1970s, and again gained popularity during the 1990s. The book *The Bell Curve* (Hernstein & Murray, 1994) claims that intelligence is inherited and therefore predetermined. This ideology, like all forms of biological determinism, is antithetical to the social work belief that people are affected by the environment and, therefore, have the ability to change. Social welfare policies are often responses to inequalities in the social and economic environment. Policies are public attempts to make changes in the social environment so that people may grow and change. Adherence to biological determinism blocks the development of social welfare policy.

SOCIAL WELFARE SERVICES AS A RIGHT

The last ideology to be discussed here is the perspective that social welfare services are a right. Most of the values and beliefs behind the U.S. social welfare system reflect an emphasis on the individual. If one focuses on the individual and his or her abilities or means, then one can ignore the larger social and economic structure. For example, people who view the failure of the War on Poverty to eradicate poverty as a result of badly planned programs or the unwillingness of poor people to change ignore the reality of the economic system.

Theorists such as Richard M. Titmuss (1968) have argued that the private market system is plagued by problems of inequality, social injustice, and exclusion. Poorly educated, ill-clothed, homeless, disenfranchised individuals cannot participate fully in the market system because they are so far outside of it. Their opportunities are limited because of where they were born and where they live, as well as their skin color, gender, physical ability, sexual orientation, and other factors. Individuals cannot control or change the discrimination and exclusion put on them by others. Therefore, the system and society as a whole must be held responsible for the social well-being of these individuals.

This ideology holds that social welfare programs should not be viewed as an afterthought provided selectively but as a social right provided through a universal system. Health care is a good illustration of this ideology. Relying on the marketplace to provide health coverage has meant that large groups of people have no health insurance coverage. Social welfare rights advocates believe that health care coverage is a right to which all people are entitled, regardless of their own resources. The only way to make health care a right is through universal coverage provided by the federal government. Social welfare services as a right is a function of public purpose over private interest.

THEORIES OF THE EVOLUTION OF THE SOCIAL WELFARE SYSTEM

Social welfare policies and programs in this country evolved over time. How did the current social welfare system come to be? What factors precipitated the development of social welfare policies, and how were the policies influenced? Several theories have been developed to explain why the social welfare system evolved as it did. Six of these theories are discussed here. This section closes with a view of how appropriate these theories are for the new information and globalization era of the 21st century. Again, keep in mind that no one theory explains all social policy. Different perspectives fit for different issues and different times in our history.

INDUSTRIALIZATION AND THE SOCIAL WELFARE SYSTEM

The structure of the modern social welfare system was created when the Social Security Act was passed in 1935. This legislation created a permanent role for the federal government as guardian of the social well-being of the entire nation (see Chapter 2). Passage of the act marked the culmination of many events and social conditions.

According to the industrialization theory outlined by Wilensky and Lebeaux (1965), today's social welfare state traces its beginnings to the advent of the industrial era. From the 1850s to the 1920s, tremendous industrial expansion and urbanization occurred in the United States. The result was both a greater need for social welfare services and the means to cover that need: industrial growth and urban crowding gave rise to social conditions that demanded attention, and greater productivity gave rise to greater economic resources to address human needs.

Industrialization led to new methods of manufacturing and new types of jobs. It also led to modernization and attempts to produce more at less cost. The workers' standard of living improved with increased production and incomes, but the magnates' desire to maximize profits also caused poor working conditions to proliferate. The changes in the workplace led to worker dependence on the owners of businesses. This dependence gave rise to concerns about unemployment, job-related disability, health care, and the care of dependent children and widows when a worker was disabled or died.

Social conditions were also changing during the industrial era. With improvement in health care and modernization of living conditions, life expectancy increased and retirement became a real possibility. Family incomes rose, and people became more mobile. Consequently, the extended family that had lived in the same area in previous generations disappeared and with it the safety net it had provided.

The changes in economics, communities, and family relations altered the provision of social welfare services. Although the individual was still primarily responsible for his or her well-being, workers also expected industry and government to ensure that certain basic needs were met. Those needs included safety in the workplace, a guaranteed minimum wage, regulated work hours and conditions, social insurance for retirement, disability compensation, and survivors' benefits in the event of death. Industrialization had led to general acceptance of the federal, state, and local governments having key roles in maintaining the social well-being of all citizens. Although the government had provided temporary services during the early years of the United States, by the 1950s the government had become a permanent provider of social welfare services.

CYCLES OF HISTORY

Most social welfare programs and services in this country are residual in response and selective in coverage (see Chapter 1). The residual and selective design of social welfare policy largely reflects the ideologies, values, and beliefs of U.S. society. This country was founded on individualism and self-sufficiency. Government intervention is contrary to this philosophy, yet Americans also believe in helping those in need. The tensions between these conflicting beliefs, individual responsibility and social responsibility, have played a key role in the development of social welfare policy.

Schlesinger (1986) views American history as a cycle between individual responsibility and social responsibility. He describes a "continuing shift in national involvement between public purpose and private interest" (p. 27). During the cycles, each period runs its course and brings about a change. When public purpose is the dominant influence, sweeping changes are made in a short period of time. Sustained public action, however, requires energy and intense political commitment. People tire of this level of activity and need to regroup. Therefore, periods of public purpose are followed by times of private interest, when people become immersed in their personal lives. During periods of private interest, changes brought about by public action are absorbed and people focus on privatization and personal acquisition. Eventually, however, private interest leads to dissatisfaction because acquisition is not possible for everyone and segments of society are in need. People begin to feel that the system is not fair, and they press for public change and social responsibility. In this way, the course of history shifts from private interest to public purpose.

The cycles shift with generations. Schlesinger posits 30-year cycles. During the late 19th and early 20th centuries, the cycles shifted several times. For example, around the turn of the century the progressive movement called for public action. The materialistic, acquisitive period of the 1920s followed. The next shift occurred with the Great Depression and the accompanying outcry for public action. Public action in the 1930s consisted of the New Deal and government provision of social welfare services to individuals. In the 1950s, there was a return to private interest characterized by conservatism and material growth. A shift occurred again in the 1960s, which was a period of public action. Interest and energy ebbed, and by the 1980s the nation had once again settled into a period of private interest. According to the historical cycles theory of social welfare policy development, the 1990s might have ushered in a new period of public action and social change, but the theory did not hold up in this instance. Although policies that had languished during the 1980s, such as the Family and Medical Leave Act and civil rights legislation, were passed during the 1990s, the 1990s was overall a weak period of social responsibility. It remains to be seen how the cycle will shift in the early decades of the 21st century. Regardless of whether the time frames fit (30-year cycles) the concept of moving back and forth from periods of private focus to public action, it seems to help explain the shifts we have seen in social welfare policy over the past 100 years.

SOCIAL CONTROL

Some theorists view the development of social welfare policy as a tool of **social control**. Those in positions of power use the institutions of the social welfare system to control and direct the behavior of the needy. Piven and Cloward (1971), in *Regulating the Poor*, cited public assistance as a tool used by those in political power to quell social unrest and reinforce the employment system. By creating a residual social welfare program and keeping benefits low, the powers that be ensure that most people will not be inclined to rely on public assistance and will instead be willing to work, even at low-paying jobs. In time, when benefits are too low to meet people's basic needs, social unrest develops, and programs are expanded. In this way, shifts are made in benefit amounts and eligibility but the basic system remains intact.

Like the historical cycles theory, the social unrest theory views social welfare policy as alternating between periods of minimal benefits and periods of broader services. The movement on this continuum reflects ongoing efforts by those in political power to keep social unrest at a minimum by first providing generous benefits and then encouraging people to work by cutting back on benefits and tightening eligibility requirements. This fluctuation has often occurred. Piven and Cloward point to the 1930s and the 1960s as times when coverage and benefits for public assistance expanded. These periods are evidence of attempts to regulate the poor through social control. Both the 1930s and 1960s began with social movements and ended with expansions in the social welfare system. After the expansions, social unrest dissipated. The poor were successfully regulated through changes in social welfare benefits.

ELITE POWER THEORY

The **elite power theory** is built on the idea that a handful of people control the policies that govern all of society. It is related to social control theory. Domhoff (1990) describes the elite control of public policy as the domination of the nation by a small capitalist class. This dominant elite class is well connected to those who make public policy.

> There usually are very narrow limits to what can be accomplished by poor people, minorities, trade unionists, and liberals through elections and the legislative process. The costs of running for office are enormous for average people in terms of time and money, and the impediments to change built into the legislative process make it very hard to sustain a pressure-group coalition or legislative social movement that does not have a great amount of money and patience. (Domhoff, 1990, p. 260)

Domhoff agrees with the social control theory on the fact that power gets redistributed when average people organize to disrupt the system. Although the conditions and reasons that motivate people to disrupt the system vary and cannot be predicted, the process does occur and is often supported by those in power. That support is, however, both a response to disruption *and* an attempt by the elite class to hold onto its position of power. The concept of a ruling elite is controversial. Box 3.1 discusses this in more detail.

| BOX 3.1 | CONTROVERSIAL PERSPECTIVES . . . |

Is the country run by an elite group?

The idea that a small, powerful group of people are making pivotal decisions and are in control of policy flies in the face of our belief in our democratic system. We believe that all people have a say in their government. According to our Declaration of Independence, our government derives its power from the consent of the governed. We have a Constitution that outlines the right of the people to govern themselves. So how can we have an elite group with power and control of America? Dye (2002) argues that power in America rests with a handful of people by virtue of the positions they hold:

> A few thousand individuals out of 281 million Americans decide about war and peace, wages and prices, consumption and investment, employment and production, law and justice, taxes and benefits, education and learning, health and welfare . . . In all societies—primitive and advanced, totalitarian and democratic, capitalist and socialist—only a few people exercise great power. This is true whether or not such power is exercised in the name of "the people." (p. 1)

Dye (p. 10) identifies a total of 7,314 elite people, that is, less than three-thousandths of 1 percent of the nation's population, who:

> control over one half of the nation's industrial assets;
>
> control over one half of all U.S. banking assets;
>
> control over three quarters of all insurance assets;
>
> direct Wall Street's largest investment firms;
>
> control all the television networks;
>
> control all the major media conglomerates;
>
> control almost half of all the assets of private foundations;
>
> control two thirds of all private university endowments;
>
> direct the nation's largest and best-known New York and Washington law firms;
>
> occupy key federal government positions in the executive, legislative, and judicial branches.

ECONOMICS AS A DETERMINANT OF SOCIAL WELFARE POLICY

All of the theories discussed so far have a number of common characteristics. Each theory suggests that social welfare policy is a consequence of historical events. Several identify a cyclical pattern, and all have an economic component. Industrialization changed the economy of this country, giving rise to the modern social welfare system. Social values and beliefs changed as the acquisition of resources shifted: when private interests were not being met through sufficient growth in income, people looked to the government for remedies. Benefits expanded in response to social unrest. Often that social unrest was sparked by economic upheaval, as during the Great Depression.

Analysis of history and policy evolution suggests that economics is a driving force behind the policies and politics of social well-being (Segal, 1987). Chapter 2 traced the historical ebb and flow between periods of economic growth and economic hardship. A pattern seems to emerge of policies changing in response to economic shifts. Times of growth are marked by emphasis on individual responsibility and times of economic contraction by increased demands for the government to take responsibility for people's well-being.

As we have seen, the value placed on individual responsibility dates back to the earliest times in America. Rugged individualism meant that each person was responsible for his or her own welfare. This responsibility extended to the individual's family and sometimes to the well-being of the immediate community. Throughout American history, however, there have been national upheavals, such as industrialization, urbanization, depression, and war, which have altered the marketplace. During national upheavals, individuals could not adequately provide for their own well-being. At these times, government was called to step in and take over the responsibilities of individuals and families. Thus, in spite of the idealized image of the rugged individual, the reality of life is that government has always stepped in to aid individuals (Dolgoff, Feldstein, & Skolnik, 1993). From the earliest history of this country to the present, government has helped to support medical care, economic credit, industrial development, and general social well-being.

The theory of economics as a determinant of social welfare policy focused on the public perception of government intervention. When the economy is strong, opportunity for economic gain appears limitless. If there are jobs and growth and yet a person is not working, that person is viewed as lazy. Government assistance is seen as evidence that an individual is weak and not taking responsibility. When the economy is bad, however, the market system is blamed rather than the individual. People turn to the government for assistance, and seeking help is not seen as a weakness. The Great Depression is the most significant illustration of this phenomenon. The rate of unemployment during the Great Depression exceeded 25 percent. With so many previously employed people out of work, public attention focused on the failures of the economic structure and people were open to government intervention. As discussed previously, the dire economic conditions resulted in the enactment of the Social Security Act and the birth of the modern social welfare system. The recession of 2007–2009, which officially began in December of 2007, and the accompanying economic meltdowns of the housing and financial markets demonstrate the theory as well. The federal government has embarked on an economic intervention not seen since the days of the Great Depression. Once all the interventions are tallied, the economic stimulus provided by the federal government may total in the trillions of dollars.

Public debate on national health insurance coverage is another example of how economic pressure can influence social welfare policy. For decades, advocates have been calling for a national health care program but policy makers have paid little attention. Following the election of Bill Clinton, as the nation was coming out of an economic recession, there was a flurry of activity on health care reform. The federal government considered developing a comprehensive health care system. Federal attention diminished with the election of George W. Bush and a commitment to private sector management. However, state governments still struggled with the issue. Why? According to the economic determinants theory, health care is an area in which the marketplace has failed, because individual needs are not being met. Many people today are employed and working full time but do not have adequate health care coverage for themselves or their families. Or, they have lost their jobs due broader economic conditions. They are participating in the economy but are not receiving what they need to pay for health care. When such an imbalance occurs, people look to government to correct the inequity. With the economic downturn of the late 2000s and the presidential campaign of 2008, the issue of national health care returned. The election of Barack Obama as president, who has pledged support for a broader national approach to health care, suggests that the electorate is once again asking for that policy. Thus we see that one driving force behind the push for government intervention in addition to economic conditions is a sense that those who participate fully in the marketplace are not reaping the rewards of their efforts. Other economic variables have pushed the health insurance debate. Support for government-funded health insurance has grown not only in response to public concern about the economic imbalance between working and not receiving health care coverage but in response to the economic bottom line for businesses—profitability. Corporations and businesses are finding the cost of health insurance for employees is growing and affecting their economic profitability. If the federal government steps in to provide health insurance, businesses will be able to remove themselves from the role and cost of being the source of health insurance. Thus, individual, social, and even corporate economics can be a driving force behind social welfare policy.

CRITICAL THEORY

Critical theory combines elements of social control, elite power, and economics in explaining the evolution of social welfare policy. **Critical theory** examines social life with the goal of evaluating U.S. social order and the ways in which power and domination affect people's lives. Critical knowledge helps us discern ways that oppression and domination can be changed (Bentz & Shapiro, 1998; Fay, 1987). Although analysis of social interactions is important, critical theory includes prescriptions for change that liberate oppressed people from people in power. We must examine the U.S. social world from many perspectives to find power imbalances, including those involving class, race, and gender (Agger, 1991; Thayer-Bacon, 2000).

An illustration of this theory is found in a critical theorist's view of public assistance. Although Temporary Assistance for Needy Families is a social welfare program that addresses poverty, its recipients are primarily low-income single women and children who are disproportionately people of color. The public policy-makers who crafted TANF are mostly white male legislators with high levels of education and income. Therefore, a deconstruction of TANF from a critical theory perspective means not only looking at the economics of poverty but also at the ways in which gender, race, class, and family composition fit in and at who is making the decisions on how the program is constructed (Segal & Kilty, 2003). How well did those who made the decisions about TANF understand the conditions of those who live under the program? A comparison of lawmakers and for whom the law was made reveal vast differences in class, race, and gender.

Critical theory includes a call for action. Paulo Freire's work (1990) emphasizes this important piece of critical theory—the element of consciousness raising and praxis or social action. Critical theory includes the process of self-reflection and ultimately should result in social change. Once people understand the imbalance of power, they can begin the process of social change to liberate those who are oppressed. It is action oriented, because it calls for social change to even out power imbalances. Critical theory is a controversial way to analyze the U.S. social welfare system because it challenges the status quo.

POSTINDUSTRIALIZATION AND GLOBALIZATION

The theories already discussed have emphasized the influence of the industrial era and political elites. The United States underwent a major shift in the late 20th century. The production era of industrialization that lasted from the 1950s through the 1970s ended. And the nation entered a new economic period of services. This new period, begun in the 1980s, is often referred to as the **postindustrial era**. Postindustrial production centers on service delivery, examples of which include health care, technology, financial and legal information, and personal care. The other significant influence since the 1980s has been **globalization**, the increasing connectedness of the world's economy. Theories about postindustrial changes and globalization shaping social welfare policy since the 1980s posit that these changes are different than those of the industrial period following World War II and continuing through the 1970s.

Myles and Quadagno (2002) discuss the influences of postindustrialism, globalization, and two other social forces, gender and aging of the workforce. They find that neither postindustrialism nor globalization have changed the structure of the U.S. social welfare system. Although economic downturns have resulted in retractions, the structure of the system as it evolved out of the industrial era is still intact. Two other issues have been the main influences: the movement of women into the labor force and the aging of the U.S. population. The demographic shift of women in the workplace has affected social welfare policies more than any other single factor in recent years. During the postwar years, social welfare proponents were concerned with creating a safety net to be used in the event that the typical male breadwinner lost his job because of illness, unemployment, or old age. With the increase in the number of women working, the social welfare system has been pushed to accommodate women and family needs. "The pattern of the welfare state reform since the 1980s has not just been a story of retrenchment but also one of significant restructuring. At the same time that traditional benefits have been scaled down, new entitlements are being created" (Myles and Quadagno, 2002, p. 49). So although traditional social services related to the needs of the male breadwinner have been cut back, new women- and family-centered policies, such as family leave and child care credits, have been increased. Therefore, Myles and Quadagno argue the social welfare system has not radically changed since the industrial era; rather, it has been restructured and the focus has shifted to accommodate the changing demographic and social needs of the nation.

PARADIGMS OF THE SOCIAL WELFARE SYSTEM

Paradigms are patterns or models that form a picture to help us understand social phenomena. By analyzing social welfare policy with these models, we can understand why policies evolved the way they did. With those insights, we can find ways to make social welfare policies and programs more effective and appropriate. Once again, social issues can fit multiple paradigms, although typically there is a dominant model based on the issue and historical context that helps to explain how specific social policies come to be.

SOCIAL CONSTRUCTION

People create a shared reality. We attribute various characteristics to groups. For example, we may believe stereotypes that "all men are strong" or "all women are nurturers." These views are reinforced through values and beliefs, and then passed on to others through stories, language, and interpretations. These images are seen as reality, although they are social constructions. **Social construction** occurs when those who are dominant in a society define a group's characteristics and determine the group's value. The dominant perceptions are accepted by society as the norm.

The social construction of racial groups has changed enormously, with a tremendous impact on American society. Racial differences have historically been promoted as facts of nature. However, many have realized that "the racial categories with which we have become so familiar are the result of our imposing arbitrary cultural boundaries in order to partition gradual biological variation" (Marks, 1994, p. 34). In fact, the mapping of the human genetic code reveals that there is very little differentiation between people all over the world—we are about 99.9 percent genetically identical—and that "race itself has no genetic basis. No genes, either by themselves or in concert with others, were able to predict which race each person had claimed to be" (Weiss, 2001, p. 7). Race has been socially constructed to label some people as inferior and others as superior. The labels are not based on biological reality.

Social construction means that people give meaning and importance to characteristics and that those differences are not based on physical realities. That meaning is reinforced through public policy (Schneider & Ingram, 2005). Slavery, and then later the abolition of slavery, are major historical examples of public policy reinforcing social construction, in this case the view that one race was superior to another. Public policy formalizes this view, and then the impact over time from the policies "proves" the veracity of the social construction. For example, segregation in the United States ensured that people of color, particularly African Americans, were educated separately from whites. Even when freed slavers were finally allowed to attend school, they attended separate schools that were poorly funded and inferior to the schools attended by whites. This led to continued low levels of education for many African Americans, and this outcome served as proof supporting the original social construction of inferiority due to race.

As a paradigm, social construction provides a lens through which to analyze social welfare policy. If social programs are designed to support the family model of two heterosexual parents, with the male working full-time outside the home and the female staying home to care for children, and if families no longer look like that, then social construction allows one to examine the structure of today's families and, in turn, what social supports those families need. If women are working full-time, then child care policies need to be considered. Rather than insisting on the genetic "fact" that men work and women stay at home, social constructionists push us to see whether this is a physiological reality or a socially constructed norm.

Social construction can also lead to social change. If indeed all policies are framed by values and beliefs reinforced by dominant groups, then we have the power to change the way issues are viewed and hence change policy. Social construction not only explains why things are the way they are but can also provide a method to create social change. For example, the nation experiencing an African American and a woman running for president challenges the historically dominant view that U.S. Presidents are always white men, as had been the case for hundreds of years. The outcome of the 2008 election proved that there can be different social constructions of the qualifications for the highest political office. There is no doubt that 100 years ago society held strongly to the view that it was a factual impossibility that an African-American person or a woman could hold such a political leadership position. Now that possibility exists with the election of an African American man, even though the physical attributes have not changed over the past 100 years. Social perspectives and dominant ideologies have changed, and that is social construction.

CRITICAL ANALYSIS

Critical analysis, which is based on critical theory, is a way of viewing the world that combines deconstruction, self-reflection, and praxis or social action (Fay, 1987). It includes norms or values. It is not value neutral (Bentz & Shapiro, 1998). One technique used for critical analysis is **deconstruction** (Agger, 1991), which is discussed in more detail in Box 3.2. What a person's language or writings appears to mean on the surface may not be what is truly meant. People use analysis to take apart what is said or written to identify who is speaking and why, what the

---

| **BOX 3.2** | **MORE ABOUT DECONSTRUCTION** |

Jacques Derrida is one of the most famous critical theorists who used the technique of deconstruction. Here he differentiates between the process of deconstruction, examining law, and the impulse or feeling of justice, which is a drive and not something to be deconstructed:

There is a history of legal systems, of rights, of laws, of positive laws, and this history is a history of the transformation of laws. That is why they are there. You can improve law, you can replace one law by another one. There are constitutions and institutions. This is a history, and a history, as such, can be deconstructed. Each time you replace one legal system by another one, one law by another one, or you improve the

law, that is a kind of deconstruction, a critique and deconstruction. So, the law as such can be deconstructed and has to be deconstructed. That is the condition of historicity, revolution, morals, ethics, and progress. But justice is not the law. Justice is what gives us the impulse, the drive, or the movement to improve the law, that is, to deconstruct the law. Without a call for justice we would not have any interest in deconstructing the law. That is why I said that the condition of possibility of deconstruction is a call for justice. Justice is not reducible to the law, to a given system of legal structures. That means that justice is always unequal to itself. (Caputo, J. D., 1997, pp. 16–17)

words mean to different people, and how the historical and current contexts influence the words. Why is critical analysis being promoted at this time, and by whom? Critical analysis draws further on critical theory, examines power relations, and calls for change if there are imbalances in power. If one group dominates another who is oppressed, then action must be planned to address this imbalance.

Critical analysis can be very controversial because it calls for action to change the control and distribution of power in policy-making. Based on social construction, critical analysis identifies the dominant culture and its values. Critical analysis goes beyond the assessment of dominant culture and outlines ways that it can be changed. Critical analysis looks closely at the impact of power and dominant control of society, assesses how those in control use their power to reinforce the status quo, and looks for ways to change the distribution of power. Civil rights movements often reflect critical analysis. Disenfranchised groups identify how they are oppressed and make demands to change social structures to include or protect them. For example, the women's movement was based on critical analysis of how men had dominated social, political, and economic domains in society and women had been relegated to secondary status. Awareness of this difference led to a social movement demanding changes that allowed women access to the same levels of power that men had. Over the decades since the beginning of the women's movement, social change has evolved—women's wages have grown, the numbers of women in male-dominated professions has increased, and women are actively involved in politics and elected office. Policy analysis of gender differences in society, accompanied by social action to change that imbalance combined to demonstrate the application of the critical analysis paradigm.

DISTRIBUTIVE JUSTICE

Distributive justice describes the social obligation of the state to all its citizens to provide agreed-upon social benefits that are not only fair to the recipients but that contribute to the betterment of U.S. society (Rawls, 1971). Rawls argued that the public adherence to justice is fundamental to a well-ordered society. In terms of social welfare policy, distributive justice involves attention to both the individual and society, providing a framework that combines the two:

> Justice is a matter of allocating social resources fairly, and injustices can be rectified either by helping an individual to work within the current system to obtain the needed resources or by getting society to change the system of allocation. The justice account has no problem integrating indirect and direct services, policy and treatment, as justice-related interventions. (Wakefield, 1988, p. 208)

A distributive justice paradigm calls for us to identify what social benefits should be provided to all citizens and then create ways to ensure a fair allocation of those benefits. So, if education is believed to be a social benefit (i.e., that the receipt of it helps both the individual and all of society), then we must strive to find ways to ensure that all citizens have access to quality education. Although there is attention to both the individual and society, this distributive justice approach to social welfare policy emphasizes social responsibility.

STRENGTHS-BASED MODEL

The strengths-based focus is an intervention model posited to guide social service providers to emphasize the positive attributes of a person over the person's deficits or needs.

> A strength's perspective assumes that when people's positive capacities are supported, they are more likely to act on their strengths. Thus, a belief in people's inherent capacity for growth and well-being requires an intense attention to people's own resources: their talents, experiences, and aspirations. Through this active attention, the probability for positive growth is significantly enhanced. (Saleeby, 1992, p. 25)

In social welfare policy, this means building policies and programs on peoples' existing strengths. For example, if parents want to stay at home with their children, and there is a social benefit from adults being at home and available to their children, regardless of whether they are single parents or married, then social supports should be found to allow parents to stay home. This solution builds on the strengths of adult caregiving for children without emphasizing how a family should be structured—that is single or married parents. The strengths perspective can be seen as a corollary to the social construction model. Again, using family structure as an example, a strengths focus for policy is to look at how to support all parenting regardless of marriage status of the parent. Individuals bring skills and abilities to parenting, so how can social policy reinforce those abilities for the individuals? What social structures need to be in place to support those individuals and bring out their strengths as parents? By doing so, the focus is on parenting and not on the composition of families. And in this process, we can socially reconstruct what is good parenting and move away from the social construction that good parenting is only achievable with two parents.

SOCIAL EMPATHY

Empathy is the ability to understand the situation and experiences of another person. **Social empathy** (Segal, 2006) calls for us to use insight gained about people's lives to develop public policies that are sensitive to people's needs based on the realities of their living situations. A social empathy paradigm provides a framework with which to analyze social concerns and develop policies that reflect the lived experiences of people.

If people want to address social problems in the United States and change the conditions that perpetuate economic and social disparity and exclusion, then they must address the conflict in attitudes and experiences. People who have never been poor or never experienced discrimination that has prevented them from educational and employment opportunities, for example, may have trouble understanding values like prevention and social support. If a person's frame of reference is that everything in life depends on individual efforts, then the person will not see any value in social responsibility.

Although there are other ways to address social well-being, we need to help people who have no personal experience or insight into what it means to grow up poor or disadvantaged or discriminated against in America to see what that looks and feels like. I suggest that we begin to explore ways to develop **social empathy**—increasing the capacity of people to understand and experience the conditions of others who are not like them.

Teaching individuals empathy is difficult, yet it is considered an important part of social relationships and development. It is key to the ability to adapt and change (Watson, 2002). Empathy is critical to becoming an emotionally intelligent person (Goleman, 1994). When people develop empathy, they are more likely to understand other people's needs and develop ways to build a better society.

The likelihood of someone who is wealthy knowing or understanding the day-to-day life of someone who is poor is small today. Yet we know that people learn best from firsthand experience. How can educators close the experience gap between those at the top and those at the bottom? They must begin to find ways to teach policy makers, voters, and people who have never experienced need and inequality what it is like. They need to find ways to develop social empathy, the ability to feel and understand what others are experiencing in American society, and what it would be like to live the lives of others.

SOCIAL WORK PROFESSIONAL PARADIGM

Social work has professional principles and ethics. Each social worker, in receiving a degree, agrees to abide by the profession's values. These values include fostering self-determination on the part of clients and promoting the general welfare of society (see Box 3.3). They also demonstrate that workers are obligated to advocate for social welfare policies and programs that promote social justice, respect diversity, and improve social conditions.

BOX 3.3 | MORE ABOUT SOCIAL WORK VALUES

Section 6. The Social Workers' Ethical Responsibilities to the Broader Society

6.01 Social Welfare
Social workers should promote the general welfare of society, from local to global levels, and the development of people, their communities, and their environments. Social workers should advocate for living conditions conducive to the fulfillment of basic human needs and should promote social, economic, political, and cultural values and institutions that are compatible with the realization of social justice.

6.02 Public Participation
Social workers should facilitate informed participation by the public in shaping social policies and institutions.

6.03 Public Emergencies
Social workers should provide appropriate professional services in public emergencies to the greatest extent possible.

6.04 Social and Political Action
(a) Social workers should engage in social and political action that seeks to ensure that all people have equal access to the resources, employment, services, and opportunities they require to meet their basic human needs and to develop fully. Social workers should be aware of the impact of the political arena on practice and should advocate for changes in policy and legislation to improve social conditions in order to meet basic human needs and promote social justice.

| BOX 3.3 | **MORE ABOUT SOCIAL WORK VALUES** *continued* |

(b) Social workers should act to expand choice and opportunity for all people, with special regard for vulnerable, disadvantaged, oppressed, and exploited people and groups.

(c) Social workers should promote conditions that encourage respect for cultural and social diversity within the United States and globally. Social workers should promote policies and practices that demonstrate respect for difference, support the expansion of cultural knowledge and resources, advocate for programs and institutions that demonstrate cultural competence, and promote policies

that safeguard the rights of and confirm equity and social justice for all people.

(d) Social workers should act to prevent and eliminate domination of, exploitation of, and discrimination against any person, group, or class on the basis of race, ethnicity, national origin, color, sex, sexual orientation, gender identity or expression, age, marital status, political belief, religion, or mental or physical disability.

Revised by the 2008 NASW Delegate Assembly
NASW (2008)

The ideologies, theories, and paradigms presented here are not mutually exclusive—they are interrelated. Some build on others, as suggested in Figure 3.1. They are tools for analyzing social welfare policies and programs and the social conditions and social needs that are part of society. It is likely that particular paradigms may appeal more than others. Some policy analysts prefer to use one paradigm consistently. They might refer to it as the "lens" through which they perceive social conditions. The author prefers to see the paradigms as an arsenal of tools that can be used to decipher why the U.S. social welfare system is the way it is.

CONFLICTING VALUES AND BELIEFS AND THE THEORETICAL FOUNDATION OF SOCIAL WELFARE POLICY

So how do conflicting beliefs enter into the discussion of ideologies, theories, and paradigms? Beliefs sway thinking and hence play a significant role in people's interests in a particular ideology, theory, or paradigm. For example, if a person feels strongly that social responsibility is important, the person might be drawn to the paradigms of critical analysis and social empathy because both emphasize social change. If a person is more focused on individual change, then distributive justice or strengths-based paradigms may be a better fit. Understanding one's *own* beliefs is an important first step in analyzing social welfare policies. Once people are aware of their own biases and preferences, they can better understand how and why they perceive their social surroundings the way they do.

FINAL THOUGHTS ON THE CONCEPTUAL FOUNDATION OF SOCIAL WELFARE POLICY

This chapter has presented the broad concepts of the foundations of social welfare policy. Understanding these ideas helps us to analyze social welfare policy in

America. At different times in history, these perspectives dominated social thought. At first reading they may seem complicated and varied; however, it is important to become familiar with them. They are key to understanding our social welfare system. These principles help to explain why and how the social welfare policies of today came to be. Without understanding their evolution, it is impossible to intelligently evaluate them and make meaningful changes. Parts of all of these concepts can be found in the patchwork of the social welfare system. Throughout the rest of this book, I will refer to these ideas in explaining social welfare policies, programs, and practices.

Key Terms

ideologies	blaming the victim	elite power	social construction
theories	culture of poverty	critical theory	distributive justice
paradigms	biological determinism	postindustrial era	social empathy
cause and function	social control	globalization	

Questions for Discussion

1. What is the difference between an ideology, a theory, and a paradigm?
2. Consider the roles of men and women in our society. How have these roles been socially constructed? Have those constructions changed over time? Describe.
3. How have economics played a part in the development of social welfare policy?
4. What is critical theory? How can you use it to apply critical analysis to the study of social welfare policy?
5. What is social empathy? Do you think that our social programs are built using social empathy? Why?

Excercises

1. Choose one theory of the U.S. social welfare system. List the strengths and weaknesses of this theory. Does it help to explain the evolution of social welfare policy in this country? Why or why not?
2. Choose a social issue or problem. Choose a partner. Each partner should take one side of an opposing position based on the ideologies presented in the chapter. After five minutes of debate, switch sides. Which perspective was easier to articulate? Why? How did your own feelings or values affect your arguments?
3. Obtain a copy of the mission statement of a social service organization in your community. Does it reflect the social worker's ethical responsibility to society as described in the NASW Code of Ethics in Box 3.3?
4. Choose a social characteristic—a race, gender, class, or sexual orientation. List all the attributes you can think of that are associated with that characteristic. Now review the list. Are these attributes biologically predetermined or socially constructed? Share your list with a classmate and discuss.

References

Agger, B. (1991). *A critical theory of public life: Knowledge, discourse, and politics in an age of decline*. New York: Falmer.

Bentz, V. M., & Shapiro, J. J. (1998). *Mindful inquiry in social research*. Thousand Oaks, CA: Sage.

Caputo, J. D. (ed.). (1997). *Deconstruction in a nutshell: A conversation with Jacques Derrida*. New York: Fordham University Press.

Dolgoff, R., Feldstein, D., & Skolnik, L. (1993). *Understanding social welfare*, 3rd ed. New York: Longman.

Domhoff, C. W. (1990). *The power elite and the state: How policy is made in America*. New York: Aldine De Gruyter.

Dressel, P. L., Carter, V., & Balachandran, A. (1995). Second-order victim-blaming. *Journal of Sociology & Social Welfare* 21(2), 107–123.

Dye, T. R. (2002). *Who's running America?* 7th ed. Upper Saddle River, NJ: Prentice Hall.

Fay, B. (1987). *Critical social science*. Ithaca, NY: Cornell University Press.

Freire, P. (1990). *Pedagogy of the oppressed*. New York: Continuum.

Goleman, D. (1994). *Emotional intelligence*. New York: Bantam.

Harvey, D. L., & Reed, M. (1992). Paradigms of poverty: A critical assessment of contemporary perspective. *International Journal of Politics, Culture, and Society* 6: 269–297.

Hernstein, R. J., & Murray, C. (1994). *The bell curve: Intelligence and class structure in American life*. New York: Free Press.

Lee, P. (1929). Social work as cause and function. *Proceedings of the National Conference of Social Work*. Chicago: University of Chicago Press.

Marks, J. (1994). Blacks, whites, other. *Natural History* December, pp. 32–35.

Myles, J., & Quadagno, J. (2002). Political theories of the welfare state. *Social Service Review* 76(1):34–57.

National Association of Social Workers. (2008). *Code of Ethics*. Washington, DC: Author.

Piven, F. F., & Cloward, R. A. (1971). *Regulating the poor: The functions of public welfare*. New York: Random House.

Rawls, J. (1971). *A theory of justice*. Cambridge, MA: Harvard University Press.

Ryan, W. (1971). *Blaming the victim*. New York: Pantheon.

Saleeby, D. (1992). *The strengths perspective in social work*. New York: Longman.

Schlesinger, A. M., Jr. (1986). *The cycles of American history*. Boston: Houghton Mifflin.

Schneider, A. L. & Ingram, H. M. (2005). Public policy and the social construction of deservedness. In Schneider, A. L. & Ingram, H. M. (eds.), *Deserving and entitled Social constructions and public policy* (pp. 1–28). Albany, NY: State University of New York Press.

Segal, E. A. (2006). Welfare as we *should* know it: Social empathy and welfare reform. In Kilty, K. M & Segal, E. A., Eds. *The promise of welfare reform: Rhetoric or reality?*, pp. 265–274. Binghamton, NY: Haworth Press.

Segal, E. A. (1987). *Social welfare policy in response to economic change: Fifty years of social security*. Doctoral dissertation, University of Illinois at Chicago.

Segal, E. A., & Kilty, K. M. (2003). Political promises for welfare reform. *Journal of Poverty* 7(1/2):51–67.

Shipman, P. (1994). *The evolution of racism*. New York: Simon & Schuster.

Thayer-Bacon, B. J. (2000). *Transforming critical thinking*. New York: Columbia University Press.

Titmuss, R. M. (1968). *Commitment to welfare*. New York: Pantheon.

Wakefield, J. C. (1988). Psychotherapy, distributive justice, and social work. *Social Service Review* 62:187–210.

Watson, J. C. (2002). Re-visioning empathy. In D. J. Cain & J. Seeman (eds.). *Humanistic psychotherapies: Handbook of research and practice*, pp. 445–471. Washington, DC: American Psychological Association.

Weiss, R. (2001). Breaking the human code. *Washington Post National Weekly Edition* 18(17):6–7.

Wilensky, H. I., & Lebeaux, C. N. (1965). *Industrial society and social welfare*. New York: Free Press.

Wilson, W. J. (1987). *The truly disadvantaged: The inner city, the underclass, and public policy*. Chicago: University of Chicago Press.

THE DELIVERY OF SOCIAL WELFARE SERVICES

Social workers are involved directly and indirectly in the provision of social welfare services and need to understand how the delivery system operates. Like the social welfare system as a whole, the delivery of services is complicated and involves different levels of government and numerous types of agencies. The structure of various services varies. This chapter describes the structures for social welfare services delivery, or what we might call the "nuts and bolts" of the social welfare system.

THE PROFESSIONALIZATION OF SOCIAL WELFARE SERVICES

The structure of today's social welfare system is relatively new. As described in Chapter 2, the nationalization of services did not evolve until the 1930s. Before that time, services were delivered in a piecemeal fashion and often by reluctant providers. When the large and multilayered system of social welfare of today developed, social service providers became professionalized. This professionalization in turn contributed to the multifaceted nature of social service delivery.

HISTORY OF SOCIAL WORK

The year 1898 is considered the year in which social work was founded. In 1898, the New York Charity Organization Society held its first professional social service training program. By the 1960s, this program had become the Columbia School of Social Work (Frumkin & Lloyd, 1995). As discussed in Chapter 2, the workers in the major movements of the 1890s, the settlement movement and Charity Organization Societies, had major disagreements on how to work with people and communities.

> The settlers defined problems environmentally and engaged in social melioration. The charity workers, for the most part, defined problems as personal deficiencies and emphasized the need for moral uplift to achieve social betterment.... The conflict continued and left the new profession with a legacy of struggle between those who seek to change people and those who seek to change environment. (Germain & Hartman, 1980, p. 329)

The earliest debates within the social work profession grew out of the disagreement between the **Settlement Movement** and the **Charity Organization Societies** as to whether to focus on personal deficiencies or environmental problems. This struggle underlies the more than 110-year history of the social work profession.

Outside criticism of the developing profession was heard early. In 1915, Dr. Abraham Flexner, who represented the General Education Board and was a leading authority on graduate professional education, addressed the question "Is Social Work a Profession?" in a paper he delivered to the National Conference on Social Welfare. His conclusion was that social work was not a profession because it lacked a unique methodology. "Lacking its own 'technique which is communicable by an educational process,' social work was no profession" (Trattner, 1994, p. 258). Flexner's criticism propelled leaders in the profession to define the role of social workers and determine what made social work unique.

Porter R. Lee, president of the National Conference of Social Work, in his 1929 presidential address, was supportive of his profession but outlined the struggle in a slightly different way. Lee viewed the struggle as a pull between the "cause and function" dichotomy inherent in professional social work. Lee felt that the social worker of his day was "meeting more exacting demands for performance, assuming a more specific type of responsibility, meeting with fair success more intricate and elusive problems" (Lee, 1929, p. 12). Because of these critiques and ongoing debate, the professional social worker was impelled to take on a more functional role by focusing on organization, techniques, efficiency, standards, and accountability.

The challenge as Lee saw it was to find a way to balance cause, which was the belief in ideology, and function, which was the administration of that belief. In the end, Lee believed that although those with a cause may sway the beliefs of people, it should be the professional social worker's role "to administer a routine functional responsibility in the spirit of the servant in a cause" (p. 20).

Bertha Capen Reynolds, who in recent years has been embraced as the inspiration for a progressive social work movement, embodies the personal cost of the struggle for social work's professional identity. Although trained in the psychoanalytic tradition, she questioned the effectiveness of this practice. Her criticism of mainstream social work practice of the 1930s led to her removal from the Smith College School of Social Work in 1938 (Freedberg, 1986). Reynolds' beliefs demonstrated the "fundamental conflict in the definition of social work: the professional individualized approach to human beings in trouble comes up against the intractable fact of a social service that ultimately is dependent upon the resources of the larger community" (Freedberg, 1986, p. 105). Reynolds's push for social action kept her at odds with the then mainstream professional shift toward individual casework.

> In 1951, the National Council on Social Work Education supported a project to answer the question of what social work was and was not. The task was difficult: Any attempt to define the scope and functions of social work must grapple with many formidable obstacles, the most insurmountable of which is the absence of criteria that can be used to identify a professional social worker. (as cited in Brieland, 1977, p. 342)

The task force summarized the current state of the profession as indefinable and not yet professional:

> There is not yet enough of an analysis of social work practice to identify the major functions of positions that should be classified as professional. (as cited in Brieland, 1977, p. 342)

Over the past 25 years, the debate about purpose has continued. Frumkin and O'Connor (1985) viewed the profession as "adrift" and "failing to maintain a core identity" by the 1980s. They argued that the profession had abandoned working with both client and environment, and in place of that dual focus, social work leaders had "called for the establishment of a psychologically oriented view of social work practice stressing intrapsychic and interpersonal dynamics and intervention strategies aimed principally at influencing changes in individual behavior, family or group dynamics" (p. 14).

Specht and Courtney (1994) argued that social work was not simply struggling to find its identity, but that the profession had "abandoned its mission." They argued that the historical mission of social work to deal with social problems had been upended by a move to embrace psychotherapy.

> The concern of psychotherapy is with helping people to deal with feelings, perceptions, and emotions that prevent them from performing their normal life tasks because of impairment or insufficient development of emotional and cognitive functions that are intimately related to the self. Social Workers help people make use of and develop community and social resources to build connections with others and reduce alienation and isolation; psychotherapists help people to alter, reconstruct, and improve the self. (p. 26)

Specht and Courtney (1994) held that "the popular psychotherapies have diverted social work from its original mission and vision of the perfectibility of society" (p. 27). They argued that there is no place for psychotherapy in social work: "It is not possible to integrate the practice of individual psychotherapy with the practice of communally based systems of social care" (p. 170), and they concluded that psychotherapy "is an unsuitable mode of intervention for social work" (p. 172).

Ehrenreich (1985) summarizes this historical struggle to identify the uniqueness and importance of the social work profession. He argues that the tension between individual and societal change is based in values and assumptions.

> On the one hand, there are those theories that emphasize the problems of the individual and see casework as the solution. On the other hand, there are the theories that emphasize the problems of society and see social reform as the solution. These theories are more readily understood as the ideologies and battle cries of particular groups within and outside the profession, struggling for power in the profession, than as exclusively true, well-validated (or even capable of being validated) theories of human behavior (p. 227).

The struggle between emphasizing services to the individual and focusing on social change is not the divisive issue it once was. The latest standards for social work education open with the sentence that "The purpose of the social work profession is to promote human and community well-being" (CSWE, 2008, p. 1) giving equal weight to individual and social concerns. These Educational Policy Standards stress intervention across all levels—individuals, families, groups, and communities. Although as a profession we equally commit to all these levels of practice, the ability to serve both individual needs and social reform is a constant challenge. As you read through this chapter on service delivery, keep in mind the historical conflict of focusing on the individual or committing to social change.

PROFESSIONAL CONTRIBUTIONS OF THE CHARITY ORGANIZATION SOCIETIES AND SETTLEMENT MOVEMENT

Social work owes a great deal to two distinct but overlapping movements: the Charity Organization Societies and the Settlement Movement. Together they formed the foundation of the profession of social work that exists today. They also represent two different perspectives and traditions for serving those in need, the micro and macro approaches.

Charity Organization Societies   Three main principles guided the Charity Organization Societies: (1) urban poverty was rooted in moral and character deficiencies of the individual; (2) once poor people had been helped to recognize and correct their flawed characters, poverty could be abolished; and (3) the goal of ending poverty could only be reached if the Charitable Societies cooperated and organized so as to stop providing overlapping resources (Boyer, 1989).

Perhaps the most famous COS worker was **Mary Richmond**. She began work in Baltimore in 1891 as an administrator and a friendly visitor. Over the years, she advocated for the training of social work professionals. She wrote *Social Diagnosis*, which presented theory and practice in how to identify clients' problems. Her work served as the foundation for establishing professional social work (Erickson, 1987).

Although the Charity Organization Societies were widespread, their focus on individual change in spite of terrible economic and social conditions was not sufficient to eradicate the poverty of the early 1900s. Recurring economic depressions and mass destitution were beyond the reach of the COS movement (Katz, 1986). Moreover, the theory on which COS was based was paternalistic and blamed the individual for his or her condition (Ehrenreich, 1985). COS did nothing to change the environmental conditions that contributed to impoverishment, unequal opportunities, illness, and lack of social support.

Although the COS movement failed to eradicate poverty or significantly improve the lives of those in need, it made lasting contributions to the social welfare system and the development of the social work profession (see Box 4.1). The Societies embodied the concept that social services should be provided by formal organizations whose workers were trained to provide support and relief funds. Organizations should focus on the unique concerns of individuals and not assume that all situations were alike. Scientific methods should be used to assess needs. This belief paved the way for research on and investigation of individual and

BOX 4.1	MORE ABOUT CONTRIBUTIONS TO THE PROFESSIONALIZATION OF SOCIAL WORK	
	Charity Organization Societies	**Settlement Movement**
Focus:	Specialized focus on individuals and families	Focus on individuals as part of their communities
Practice Emphasis:	Casework	Group work and community organizing
Macro Emphasis:	Coordination and organization of social services	Social reform and political action
Research Focus:	Scientific methods used to determine need emphasizing research on the individual	Research on the community and social needs assessment
Contribution to the Field:	Training of professional social service providers	Understanding strengths of cultural diversity

family needs. The Societies were the forerunners of today's family service agencies (Erickson, 1987).

Settlement Movement Discussion of the Settlement Movement would not be complete without mention of **Jane Addams.** For more than 30 years, Jane Addams was a powerful force behind the Settlement Movement (Germain & Hartman, 1980). In 1889, she and Ellen Gates Starr founded Hull House in Chicago, the most famous of the settlements. Hull House was located on the west side of Chicago, where poor immigrant groups lived in crowded, unhealthy, unsafe conditions. The goals and activities of Hull House set the tone for settlements across the nation.

Most settlement houses were founded in poor neighborhoods occupied mostly by recent immigrants. The early goals of the settlement movement were to help socialize people to their new homeland and alleviate the tremendous economic and social disparity between the newcomers and the established wealthier classes. Settlement leaders emphasized the need to direct reform efforts toward the environment. Activities within the settlement movement included social clubs, which provided vocational training and educational opportunities, recreation programs, playgrounds and gymnasiums, and classes in drama, music, and art. Although socialization was a key element, the goals of helping immigrants adapt to their new home and of shrinking the gap between the wealthy and the poor were always significant in settlement work. The settlements, more than any other institutions in America, emphasized work with immigrants and minorities through intelligent and sympathetic approaches (Kogut, 1972).

After establishment of Hull House, the settlement movement grew rapidly. In 1891, there were six settlements; by 1897, 74 settlements; and by 1900, more than 100 settlements. The movement peaked in 1910 with 400 settlements (Davis, 1984). The settlements provided places for local people to meet and discuss the politics of the day. The settlement houses became clearinghouses for urban reform and played a vital role in the progressive, or social justice, movement of the 1900s (Trattner, 1999).

The settlement movement is credited with contributing to the establishment of a number of social reforms. These included regulation of child labor, compulsory school attendance laws, maximum hours and minimum wages for female workers, workers' compensation, mothers' pensions, new standards for public sanitation and health, special courts for juvenile offenders, visiting nurses, and visiting teachers (Chambers, 1974).

Jane Addams herself was very involved in efforts for environmental reform and became a political figure. She was a powerful public speaker and prolific writer who used both venues to reach the American people. For 20 years she enjoyed public admiration, but she fell out of favor with the public when she expressed opposition to World War I. She was an outspoken leader of the peace movement and one of the founders of the Women's International League for Peace and Freedom (Addams, 1922; 1937). Years after the war, her efforts on behalf of world peace were recognized. She received the Nobel Peace Prize in 1931. Although she was at odds with social workers who focused on individual change rather than social reform, she was universally admired.

Settlement workers believed they could solve social problems by living in poor neighborhoods. They were reformers who helped people who lacked power to organize locally and nationally. Settlements were a strong force during the progressive era and contributed to the development of social welfare policies and organizations, including the National Child Labor Committee, National Women's Trade Union League, National Association for the Advancement of Colored People, and American Civil Liberties Union (Davis, 1984). When the American public shifted its focus during World War I, however, the settlements declined in importance. The prosperity of the postwar period masked the concerns of the poor, and the pressing social needs that had given rise to the settlement movement seemed to dissipate. Nevertheless, the settlement movement made significant contributions to ways of providing social welfare services.

The settlement movement is a model for social work involvement in social welfare policy and political action (see Box 4.1). Group work, community organization, and social action emerged from the settlements. Settlements such as Hull House were very involved in gathering data on their surrounding communities and used their findings to document the need for social change. The settlement movement embodied the values of the progressive era: helping economically and socially disadvantaged people integrate into society, while simultaneously working for structural changes designed to improve labor conditions and alleviate poverty.

PUBLIC AND PRIVATE PROVIDERS OF SOCIAL WELFARE SERVICES

The work of the Charity Organization Societies and the settlements, although dedicated to public service, was conducted through organizations that were **private social service agencies**, that is, they were separate from the government. As discussed in Chapter 2, the severity of the Great Depression brought the federal government into the provision of social welfare services. Since that time, all levels of government—federal, state, and local—have become deeply embedded as providers, funders, and facilitators of human services.

GOVERNMENT ROLES

Today it is impossible to fully separate private social services from government services. The government regulates, sponsors, and financially contributes to social welfare services. The relationship between private organizations and the government is complicated. Interactions take place more often behind the scenes than at the point where services are directly provided. For example, although the federal government, in partnership with state governments, funds the Medicaid program (medical assistance to low-income people), medical services are actually provided by a variety of public and private groups. It is important to understand the relationship between the private sector and the government because it is crucial to the operation of the social welfare system in the United States.

Public involvement in social services is widespread because there are so many levels of government, as demonstrated by the statistics in Box 4.2. Thousands of government bodies, including states, cities, counties, and sovereign tribal organizations, are involved in the social service system of this nation.

| BOX 4.2 | MORE ABOUT THE LEVELS OF GOVERNMENT IN THE UNITED STATES |

U.S. federal government	1
State governments	50
Local governments	87,525
County	3,034
Municipal	19,429
Township/town	16,504
School district	13,506
Special district	35,052
Tribal governments	1 for each registered tribe (over 300)

Source: U.S. Bureau of the Census, 2007

Federal Government   The federal government is the largest player in the social welfare arena. The federal government spends more than a trillion dollars each year on direct and indirect assistance. For example, in 2006 the federal government transferred $546 billion for Social Security payments; $407 billion for Medicare payments; $256 billion for health care under Medicaid; and billions more for education, social services, and community development (Social Security Administration, 2008). Much of these funds were channeled through state and local governments. In 2004, states and localities received $426 billion from the federal government to cover public welfare, education, transportation, health, housing, and community development (U.S. Census Bureau, 2007). In addition, the federal government sponsors services related to national defense, agriculture, scientific and space research, transportation, and the administration of justice. In fact, the federal government is involved in almost every aspect of citizens' lives. Therefore, when one speaks about social well-being in this country and the delivery of social welfare services, one cannot ignore the role of the federal government, which is pervasive and of the utmost significance.

In addition to funding services, the federal government mandates and regulates the policies that govern the social service arena. Federal overview of the social welfare system is conducted through laws, regulations, and court actions. These actions are described in detail in subsequent chapters. This chapter explores the structures of service delivery and the relationships between the government and the providers of services.

State Governments   State governments typically operate in a similar fashion to that of the federal government. Each state is headed by a governor, just as the president heads the nation. Legislators are elected to fill each statehouse, which is similar to Congress. Departments run the day-to-day operations of each state. States, like the federal government, raise revenues through taxes and fees and, in turn, use those funds to provide services. State governments often receive federal funds for the provision of social services. This fact is particularly important in understanding the operations of the social welfare system.

For example, the federal government may pass a policy regarding care for abused children. The law outlines how federal funds will be distributed to state governments, which will either offer the service or make a contract with a private agency that will offer the service. Thus, a local agency might provide parent training for families in which abusive behaviors have occurred. This training service is provided by the local agency through a contract with the state, which in turn pays for the service with federal dollars. The service offered fulfills the federal government goal outlined by the policy regarding care for abused children. This is the typical process of service delivery in the United States. It is a mixed system in which federal, state, and local governments work with private organizations in making policies, raising funds, and delivering services.

Local Governments   Local governments vary greatly, and include cities, townships, counties, and districts. There are about 90,000 such government bodies in the United States today. The number and diversity of these governing entities make it impossible to summarize their characteristics and operations. Local governing bodies may include city or town councils, school boards, sanitation commissions, and fire districts, just to name a few. All of these bodies are public and therefore subject to public policies and regulations, and all have close relationships with elected officials. As government organizations, they are open to public inspection, scrutiny, and accountability.

Tribal Governments   There are over 300 officially recognized tribes in the contiguous United States (Nagel, 1997) and possibly another 200 in Alaska and Hawaii. Some tribes are still not officially recognized. All recognized tribes in the lower 48 states are officially sovereign. In recent years, the courts have extended recognition of sovereignty to Alaskan Natives. Tribal sovereignty for Hawaiian Nationals, however, is still being debated. Each officially recognized tribe is a distinct sovereign entity. As a sovereign nation, each tribe is responsible for management of its local policies and governing actions. The history of sovereignty reflects the history of federal treatment of native nations in the United States. Sovereignty today means that tribal governments operate autonomously from state governments and are responsive to federal law and eligible for federal services. Tribes have a long history of forced assimilation (see Chapter 5) and denial of autonomy. Sovereignty stresses autonomy for Native American tribes and as such is an important value to native peoples. Sovereignty means that tribal governments are responsible for the management of federal resources for social services in the same way that state governments are.

Should the Federal Government Provide Social Services?

Today there is much controversy over the role of public agencies in the provision of social welfare services. The dislike of government involvement in social welfare has ebbed and flowed over the years, and gained strong support during the 1980s and 1990s. Sentiments such as "Less government is better" and "Get government off our backs" have been voiced by policy analysts, radio personalities, taxpayers, and even politicians. The pros and cons of public social welfare are raised in Box 4.3.

| BOX 4.3 | MORE ABOUT THE VALUE OF PUBLIC SERVICE |

Public service means equal treatment by law. All who are eligible, no matter how severe or complex the need, will be served. No one can be turned away by a public service agency if they fit the criteria for service. One opposing argument is that public services can create dependency. If the government takes care of needs, what responsibility does the individual have?

Should the government be in the business of people's personal lives? In what ways do we want government intervention, and in what ways do we dislike government intervention? A supporting argument is that if we value social justice, then we must help all people, and do so fairly. Public service is part of a socially just society.

Social workers have differing opinions on the subject. Their work is centered on social well-being and hence the role of public agencies in providing for human need. The Code of Ethics (NASW, 2008) prescribes public participation in a number of ways, including promotion of the general welfare of society, facilitation of informed participation by the public in shaping social policy and institutions, and service in public emergencies (Sections 6.01, 6.02, and 6.03). Social workers are mandated to advocate for changes in policy and legislation to improve social conditions (Section 6.04). Although these actions can be carried out in private settings, the contribution to public well-being is paramount. Therefore, the shift away from a positive view of public involvement and the denigration of public service is contrary to some of the essential tenets of the social work profession that emphasize public service.

Besides the social work value in public service, there is another fact that compels people to support government funding and provision of services. Much of the work done by public social service providers would not be done by private organizations. There are numerous social services that promote well-being but cannot be done well with an economic profit. Providing emergency medical treatment to people without insurance or the means to pay would bankrupt a private medical facility. Providing schools for children with mental and physical disabilities would not be possible if each family had to pay for all the services and facilities needed. How could each of us afford to ensure that streets and highways are paved and maintained properly? How much profit can be made by private companies for such services? Historically the role of government has been to promote social well-being, even when services are costly and not profitable. In fact, the most pressing reasons for government services has been precisely in those areas that the private sector cannot operate profitably or prices are driven high by the need to be profitable. The debate over health insurance rests on this dilemma—is it better in terms of cost, coverage, and quality of services to provide health insurance through the federal government or through the current system of private health insurance companies? Of course this question is complicated, like so many areas of social welfare policy. The federal government already provides health insurance for some groups, such as the elderly through Medicare and low-income people through Medicaid. So the real question is, should the federal government *extend* its provision of health insurance to all citizens?

| BOX 4.4 | CONSIDER THIS... |

Did you know that 22 million people were employed directly by federal, state, and local governments with a payroll of $72 billion in 2005? This represents 15 percent of all employed people in the United States. That means that about one out of six people receives a paycheck directly from a government organization. Countless other employees indirectly receive their income through government contracts for services. Therefore, when we call for the reduction of government services and say that "less government is better," we are also calling for cutting jobs and employment for many American workers. This creates a public dilemma that is often sidestepped in discussions of public services.

Source: U.S. Census Bureau, 2007

Another reality is that public social agencies are staffed by people from the community. About one of six people works directly for the federal, state, or local government (see Box 4.4). Countless other people are paid from funds that are supplemented by government monies. For example, the public transportation system is run by a public agency but uses equipment that is purchased from private companies. Contracts for purchase are funded by public money but allow private companies to employ millions of workers. Therefore, removing government from the social service system would affect every facet of citizens' lives.

PRIVATE AGENCIES

The social welfare system in this country is a mixture of the public and private sectors. Private groups dominated the early days of social work; large-scale public government involvement took over in the 20th century; and over the past 25 years the private sector has again moved to the forefront. The move to privatization has not really been a departure from public involvement but rather a public **contracting out** of services, that is, services are funded by public money but delivered by private organizations. For example, community mental health services are funded by the federal and state governments and provided both by for-profit behavioral health care companies and nonprofit organizations.

It is important to distinguish between these social welfare providers. The three entities, public agencies, private for-profit agencies, and private nonprofit agencies, have significantly different goals and missions. Austin (2002) describes the three as follows: Nonprofit organizations have deeply held values, and the services offered are a reflection of those values. Governmental or public organizations are subject to political majorities and political power. Usually the mission is related to the delivery of public goods or services. For-profit organizations are designed to produce economic benefits, typically for the shareholders or owners of the company.

Another way to distinguish the three types of social service providers is by their legal titles. **Public** refers to government; **voluntary** refers to private nonprofit; and **commercial** refers to private for-profit (Burch, 1999). Public agencies include departments, service entities, boards, and businesses such as Amtrak railway service.

Voluntary providers, although private, do not have the legal authorization to make a profit on the services they offer. Commercial providers are legally designed to be financially profitable as they provide services.

Nonprofit Organizations   Nonprofit organizations are defined as voluntary charity groups that fall under Internal Revenue Code section 501(c)(3). This distinction means that the organization uses all of its income for the delivery of cultural, educational, social, or health services and is accountable to the public through external audits of its finances. As a 501(c)(3) agency, it cannot participate in partisan politics (i.e., advocate for a candidate or lobby for specific issues). There is a provision for nonprofit voluntary organizations to engage in political advocacy through the creation of a separate entity subject to Internal Revenue Code 501(c)(4). Although both types of agencies are nonprofit, the biggest tax distinction is that donations to a 501(c)(3) organization are tax deductible whereas donations to a 501(c)(4) organization are not. This separation of function between service delivery and political action is monitored by the Internal Revenue Service, a public federal agency.

Tax laws are one of the major ways that government monitors the actions of social service delivery agencies. Functions and roles are also mandated by tax laws. For example, donations to public institutions are not tax deductible. For this reason, public universities develop private foundations whose roles and obligations fall under the laws regulating 501(c)(3) organizations. Social work practitioners should be aware of these regulations because so many agencies are administered under them.

For-Profit Organizations   Commercial agencies that provide social services operate on private business principles. The goal is to provide services in economical ways but also create a funding profit. This private format is favored by those who believe that efficiency and effectiveness are enhanced when profit principles are applied. Those opposing it feel that human needs cannot be treated effectively or humanely through the private market goal of making a profit. See Box 4.5 for some frequently asked questions about the value of for-profit and nonprofit organizations.

FORMS OF SOCIAL WELFARE ASSISTANCE

Understanding the values that have influenced social welfare policy and the theories of how the social welfare system evolved is necessary preparation for analyzing current policies and influencing the creation of new policies. In the next section of this chapter, terms used to describe types of social welfare services are defined. The social welfare system offers a combination of forms of assistance, and they account for most of the social services provided. Which form of assistance is used is based on the values held by the persons responsible for shaping social welfare policy.

PUBLIC ASSISTANCE AND SOCIAL INSURANCE

The Social Security Act of 1935 codified two parts of our social welfare system: **public assistance** and **social insurance**. Originally, planners thought that these two

| BOX 4.5 | CONTROVERSIAL PERSPECTIVES... |

What are the pros and cons of for-profit and nonprofit social services?

Why supporters of private for-profit services favor this approach:

For-profit agencies can earn profits, which can translate into higher salaries for workers and more money for innovations and new technology.

Financial stability depends on clients choosing to use an agency, so the competition for users promotes higher-level services.

Use of business principles and techniques can enhance profitability.

Why critics of private for-profit services dislike this approach:

The best way to care for human need is not always profitable.

The drive to make a profit leads to serving only those who can afford to pay and have less severe problems.

Professional judgment about what is best for the client gets ignored if it is expensive and instead ensuring a profit after all services are delivered becomes primary.

Why supporters of private nonprofit services favor this approach:

The motives for providing service are based on a mission that is related to caring and concern.

Nonprofit services can be cost-effective because they are not subject to all the limitations of public regulations.

When no profit is drawn out, there are more funds to use for services and rates can be lower for clients.

Caseloads and staffing can be regulated by the agency.

Nonprofit services embrace volunteers and therefore can promote the spirit of volunteerism.

Why critics of private nonprofit services dislike this approach:

The agencies must raise funds, and such sources of revenue are unpredictable.

Fundraising can be time-consuming and uses money that does not go to service provision.

Agencies can be inefficient and so specialized that management and services are not effective.

approaches to support would complement each other and that in time, social insurance would erase the need for public assistance.

Social insurance benefits are cash benefits in the form of a transfer of money from the government to the individual. Eligibility for benefits differs, however. For social insurance, individuals pay into a program over time in exchange for future coverage. Social Security is the most prominent example of social insurance (see Chapter 7). Simply stated, most employees pay a prescribed amount into the system based on their earnings and that amount is matched or supplemented by their employers. They become eligible for benefits when they retire or become disabled. Those who are dependent on a covered person, typically the wage earner's spouse or children, become eligible to receive benefits if the worker dies. They are regarded as survivors and are entitled to certain benefits based on the employment history of the worker. The recipients receive a monthly cash payment based on the contributions made while the wage earner was working. This system allows the individual complete freedom to choose how the money is spent. Unlike in the cash assistance program, a person's need does not affect how much he or she receives. Benefits are based on the contributions made, regardless of a person's financial situation at the time benefits are paid.

The overriding concept behind social insurance is that because a person has paid in, he or she is entitled to receive benefits. In addition, there is a shared responsibility for the program. The social insurance system is not a personal savings account where benefits total exactly what a person paid in over the years. Rather, a standardized formula is used that calculates a person's benefits based on years worked and earnings history, with a set bottom and ceiling below or above which no one can receive benefits. An individual may receive more in benefits than he or she paid in or less than he or she paid in. The program is designed to insure society as a whole, not simply individuals.

CASH ASSISTANCE PROGRAMS

The most common form of public assistance is government payment of money from general taxes to those in need. Recipients of **cash assistance** receive a check for an amount that is determined according to a particular program's rules and the recipient's characteristics. The recipient is free to spend the money as he or she sees fit, although the money is intended to pay for basic necessities such as housing, food, and clothing. Often cash assistance raises the most resistance from the public because the recipient is in complete control of how the money is ultimately spent. Because of that resistance, cash assistance benefits are typically paid at a lower level than social insurance benefits. For example, in 2006 the average monthly Social Security benefit for a retired worker was $1,044 compared to $423 for a poor elderly person under the cash assistance program of Supplemental Security Income and $166 for a person in the public assistance program Temporary Assistance for Needy Families (Social Security Administration, 2008).

IN-KIND BENEFIT PROGRAMS

In-kind benefits are a more limited form of public assistance. **In-kind benefits** are services or commodities provided to eligible recipients. Medical care and public housing are examples of in-kind benefits. Rather than receiving cash, people receive the service directly. For example, instead of receiving money for rent, a person lives in an apartment that is paid for by the government. In place of choosing any doctor and paying for services, a person qualifies to receive medical treatment at a health clinic. Individuals receiving these benefits are not allowed to have any role in the exchange of resources and often have only limited choices in the provision of the service.

VOUCHERS

Vouchers are a cross between in-kind benefits and cash assistance. Vouchers are earmarked for a specific service or commodity, but the recipient is free to use them as he or she sees fit. Recent debate has centered on proposals for educational vouchers. Parents receiving a voucher valid for a child's school tuition could choose which school the child would attend. The Food Stamp Program operates in the same way. Although food stamps are most often considered in-kind benefits, they more closely resemble vouchers. Food stamps can be used only for food, but the recipient can choose the store at which to use them. Food stamp credit cards are programmed for a certain cash amount. They cannot be exchanged for money, however; they can only be used for food items.

ENTITLEMENT

The term **entitlement** is often misused in discussions about social welfare services. The most common use is in complaints about those who seem arrogant about receiving aid ("He feels *entitled* to have anything he wants!"). This kind of "entitlement" has nothing to do with an entitlement program. According to budget regulations, **entitlement programs** are mandated by law to give aid to all who are eligible to receive the aid regardless of the total cost in any given year or fiscal period. For example, Social Security is an entitlement program. No matter how many people are eligible for Social Security in a fiscal year, the federal government must pay each person what he or she are due by law. Even if the government needs to borrow money from other places to pay for benefits, the public is entitled to receive them. Contrary to public opinion, welfare, or public assistance, is no longer an entitlement program. The funding for it is capped, and when the federal allocation runs out for a given year, states and localities do not receive any additional funding to cover the programs. Of course the government itself sets these rules. Social Security has been an entitlement program since its inception in 1935, whereas public assistance was changed from its original design in 1935 as an entitlement program to a capped, limited program as part of the welfare reform legislation of 1996. The implications of this funding system are explored in detail in Chapters 7 and 8.

SOCIAL INVESTMENT

Social investment is the spending of public money to help people and communities grow and develop, so that individuals will enjoy better social well-being. For example, the Head Start program could be considered a social investment. Low-income children are provided with educational and social services at a young age to offset the possible disadvantages of growing up poor. The theory is that providing these services to very young children will "pay off" as a social investment when the children attend school and are better prepared educationally and socially. Higher education student loans are another form of social investment. Helping students pay for college who could not otherwise do so is a way for the government to help more adults acquire the education and skills that are valuable for the economic development of the nation. Some people argue that dollars spent for social facilities such as public libraries and parks and interstate highways are also forms of social investment. These social welfare expenditures promote social and economic growth and therefore are considered an investment in future social productivity.

ECONOMIC DEVELOPMENT

Economic development is a form of social investment specifically designed to enhance community and individual economic growth. Policy forms of this approach include the creation of enterprise zones. The government provides tax incentives for private industries to develop certain urban areas (enterprise zones), which in turn creates employment opportunities for local residents. Increased employment in low-income areas will pay off as the area's economy becomes stronger. Economically sound neighborhoods tend to have lower crime rates and higher outcomes for future generations. Preferential tax treatments such as reduced or waived property taxes for private building ventures is another example of economic development through social welfare policy and spending. The goal is that by making private building ventures more attractive, companies will develop areas of cities and communities that might otherwise not be developed because the cost or the anticipated profit is too low to attract private development. The thinking follows that with these private developments, new jobs and additional revenue will flow. Publicly funded sports stadiums fall under this rationale for government subsidized development.

CONFLICTING VALUES AND BELIEFS

The types of assistance described are the most widely used ways of delivering social welfare services. Each type varies by degree of individual versus social choice and regulation, and who makes decisions for whom. The question of whether the government should provide social support or whether private organizations should provide it continues to be debated. Which side one takes reflects the degree of one's belief in the value of individual responsibility versus social responsibility and also the extent to which one values personal self-sufficiency versus social support. As social work professionals, we have a mission that outlines public support and therefore the provision of social welfare services directly or in partnership with our government.

Analyzing underlying values and beliefs to our social service delivery system returns us to the issue raised in the beginning of the chapter, whether to focus on serving individuals or changing social structures. Sometimes, as recipients of public dollars, social service organizations are caught between the two. What if your social service agency, which is funded through public dollars, finds mental health services to treat depression for poor individuals is never ending because so many of their life conditions due to living in a poor community are intractable? Do you use the public money for individual intervention to help the person deal with the depression, or to change the entire neighborhood to develop more jobs, better housing, and safer living conditions? This is the micro/macro practice debate complicated by the funding mandates. Sometimes social service practitioners are hesitant to demand social reform because it feels like "biting the hand that feeds you," that is, fighting against the very structure that funds your job. This can create a very powerful tension for social service providers and their agencies.

FINAL THOUGHTS ON THE DELIVERY OF SOCIAL WELFARE SERVICES

The system for delivery of social services is complicated. Most services rely on some form of collaboration between the public and private domains. The relationship can vary by community, agency, and even specific service. This mix often makes it difficult to track the flow of funds and regulations. The strong connection between public and private sectors is evident, underscoring the necessity that all social service funders, policy makers, and providers work together to ensure a strong and effective social welfare system.

Key Terms

Charity Organization Societies (COS)

Mary Richmond

Settlement Movement

Jane Addams

private social service agencies

contracting out

public

voluntary

commercial

nonprofit organizations

for-profit organizations public assistance

social insurance

cash assistance

in-kind benefits

vouchers

entitlement

social investment

economic development

Questions for Discussion

1. What are the key differences between the Charity Organization Societies and the Settlement Movement?
2. How are the differences in the COS and Settlement Movement apparent in social work practice today?
3. What are the strengths of public social services? What are the weaknesses?
4. What are the strengths of private social services? What are the weaknesses?
5. How might you reconcile the tension between working to help individuals and working to change social systems?

Excercises

1. Visit a social service agency. Find out if it is a for-profit or nonprofit organization. How does it get its funding? Does it receive private funds or public funds, or both?
2. Make a list of services or benefits provided by a local social service agency. Can you identify whether the services are in-kind services, cash assistance, vouchers, or social insurance? Explain the differences.
3. Get a copy of the book *Unfaithful Angels: How Social Work Has Abandoned Its Mission* by Specht and Courtney. Review the key points of the authors. Do you

agree? Do you think that social work has left its foundation and is not true to its original mission?
4. Identify a social service provided in your community. Trace its delivery back through all the stages of service to its origin. Are the state and local levels involved? Does the authority or funding, or both, go back to the federal government?
5. Visit a low-income neighborhood. What social services are provided? Do the services stress individual intervention or community change?

References

Addams, J. (1937). *Twenty years at Hull House.* New York: Macmillan.

Addams, J. (1922). *Peace and bread in time of war.* New York: Macmillan.

Austin, D. M. (2002). *Human services management: Organizational leadership in social work practice.* New York: Columbia University Press.

Boyer, P. (1989). Building character among the urban poor: The Charity Organization Movement. In I. C. Colby (ed.), *Social welfare policy: Perspectives, patterns, insights,* pp. 113–134. Chicago: Dorsey.

Brieland, D. (1977). Historical overview. *Social Work* 22:341–346.

Burch, H. A. (1999). *Social welfare policy analysis and choices.* New York: Haworth Press.

Chambers, C. A. (1974). An historical perspective on political action vs. individualized treatment. In P. Weinberger (ed.), *Perspectives on social welfare.* New York: Macmillan.

Council on Social Work Education. (2008). *Educational policy and accreditation standards.* Washington, DC: Author.

Davis, A. F. (1984). *Spearheads for reform.* New Brunswick, NJ: Rutgers University Press.

Ehrenreich, J. H. (1985). *The altruistic imagination: A history of social work and social policy in the United States.* Ithaca, NY: Cornell University Press.

Erickson, A. G. (1987). Family services. In *Encyclopedia of Social Work*, 18th ed. Vol. 1, pp. 589–593. Silver Spring, MD: National Association of Social Workers.

Freedberg, S. (1986). Religion, profession, and politics: Bertha Capen Reynolds' challenge to social work. *Smith College Studies in Social Work* 56:95–110.

Frumkin, M., & Lloyd, G. A. (1995). Social work education. In *Encyclopedia of Social Work*, 19th ed. *Vol. 3*, pp. 2338–2247. Washington, DC: National Association of Social Workers.

Frumkin, M., & O'Connor, G. (1985). Where has the profession gone? Social work's search for identity. *Urban and Social Change Review* 18(1):13–18.

Germain, C. B., & Hartman, A. (1980). People and ideas in the history of social work practice. *Social Casework* 61:323–331.

Katz, M. B. (1986). *In the shadow of the poorhouse.* New York: Basic Books.

Kogut, A. (1972). The settlements and ethnicity: 1890–1914. *Social Work* 17(3):22–31.

Lee, P. R. (1929). *Social work: Cause and function presidential address.* Washington, DC: National Conference on Social Welfare.

Nagel, J. (1997). *American Indian ethnic renewal.* New York: Oxford University Press.

National Association of Social Workers. (2008). *NASW Code of Ethics.* Washington, DC: Author.

Social Security Administration. (2008). *Annual statistical supplement to the Social Security Bulletin,* 2007. Washington, DC: Author.

Specht, H., & Courtney, M. E. (1994). *Unfaithful angels: How social work has abandoned its mission.* New York: Free Press.

Trattner, W. I. (1999). *From poor law to welfare state: A history of social welfare in America,* 6th ed. New York: Free Press.

Trattner, W. I. (1994). *From poor law to welfare state: A history of social welfare in America,* 5th ed. New York: Free Press.

U.S. Census Bureau. (2007). *Statistical abstract of the United States: 2008,* 127th ed. Washington, DC: U.S. Government Printing Office.

5 | SOCIAL JUSTICE AND CIVIL RIGHTS

David Young-Wolff/PhotoEdit

The issue of rights—what people deserve and what they are entitled to—versus the issue of social welfare services—what the government or other groups in power are willing to provide—dates back to the earliest years of the United States. Questions regarding the government's role in ensuring and protecting rights (i.e., What is a right and what is not a right? and What rights exist for whom?) dominate social welfare policy debates today. Affirmative action, abortion rights, gay rights, and immigration policies are all examples of social issues that involve questions of civil rights and social welfare services. **Civil rights** are rights to which people are entitled because they are members of society. Rights are often ensured and protected through laws, resources, and services. Social welfare services, on the other hand, are provided only when deemed necessary by a majority of voters. Civil rights are protected and guaranteed by the law, whereas social welfare services are created and dispensed in accord with the decisions of policy makers. Therefore, social welfare services are more easily changed and rescinded.

Social justice is an important component of civil rights. As defined in Chapter 1, social justice reflects fairness to all in society. All people have the same basic rights, protections, opportunities, and social benefits, as well as the same social obligations. When those rights are not upheld or there are barriers to achieving fairness, government has been called upon to ensure the establishment of social justice. But government is a reflection of the majority's will, so there has been, and continues to be, a struggle to achieve social justice in our society.

BARRIERS TO SOCIAL JUSTICE AND CIVIL RIGHTS

Three barriers may prevent the achievement of social justice: prejudice, discrimination, and oppression. **Prejudice** is a belief or attitude of dislike for a group based on myths and misconceptions. Although it is difficult to have a belief but not act on it, it is possible for people to be prejudiced in their thinking but not act in a socially unjust manner. When prejudice is acted upon, discrimination results. **Discrimination** is the action of treating people differently based on their identity, because of prejudice. When discrimination becomes widespread and systematic, it becomes **oppression**. Therefore, thinking a racial group is inferior is prejudice; denying a member of that racial group a job because you think the person is inferior is discrimination; discriminatory actions by a number of people constitute oppression. Prejudice, discrimination, and oppression occur in numerous forms, and each can build on the other two. They affect people of racial, cultural, sexual identity, ability, class, gender, and age groups. Box 5.1 outlines the most pervasive forms of social injustice that plague our society.

Although the legal and political rights of citizens have been a public concern throughout American history, civil rights protections have been, and continue to be, slow in coming for some members of society. For example, early citizenship rights such as the eligibility to vote were restricted to white men, generally those who owned property. Women were not protected by government laws to the same extent as men for most of American history. For hundreds of years, African Americans and American Indians were not allowed the same rights as whites solely because of racial prejudice. In spite of the limited nature of early civil rights in this

BOX 5.1 | MORE ABOUT PREJUDICE, DISCRIMINATION, AND OPPRESSION

Racism: Belief or doctrine that inherent differences among various human races determine cultural or individual achievement, usually involving the idea that one's own race is superior; policy or system of government based on such a doctrine

Ethnocentrism: Belief in the inherent superiority of one's own ethnic group or culture

Sexism: Discrimination or prejudice based on a person's gender, especially discrimination against women

Homophobia: Unreasonable fear of or antipathy toward homosexuals and homosexuality

Classism: Biased or discriminatory attitude based on distinctions made between social or economic classes

Xenophobia: Unreasonable fear or hatred of foreigners or strangers

Ageism: Belief in the superiority of youth over age

Source: Based on *Webster's College Dictionary,* 1991

country, later periods of social upheaval, political organizing, and public outcry brought about major civil rights changes. The efforts continue today.

Discussions of people's civil rights raise the issues of inequality and social injustice. When one group has rights and protections that others do not, it creates a sense of relative inequality. When only men had the right to vote, for example, there was an inequality for women. When only whites could sit in the front of public buses, African Americans were being treated in an unequal way. For people or groups who perceive that their rights or access to services and resources are blocked, there is an imbalance. That imbalance is inequality and social injustice.

Human rights are also important. The term sometimes is used synonymously with civil rights, but it often is considered to have a broader scope because it conveys political and humanitarian concerns. The strongest statement outlining the need for human rights is the **Universal Declaration of Human Rights,** passed without a dissenting vote by the United Nations General Assembly in 1948. The declaration calls for all nations to recognize "the inherent dignity" and "the equal and inalienable rights of all members of the human family" and for all nations to "promote social progress and better standards of life." Therefore, human rights include civil rights and social justice, with the goal of making all nations places where social, political, and economic progress and improved standards of life are promoted. The international context of human rights is discussed more fully in Chapter 13.

This book posits that certain rights, such as citizenship, freedom of expression, and protection from discrimination, are or should be available to *all* people, regardless of age, income, gender, race, ability, ethnicity, sexual orientation, or gender expression. For these rights to be guaranteed, they must be supported by the power of public law and government. When laws are created and enforced to uphold civil rights, people are protected in every facet of their lives from discrimination. This chapter traces the history of civil rights in America, discusses those rights, and highlights the social welfare policy implications of civil rights.

THE CONSTITUTION: CORNERSTONE OF CIVIL RIGHTS

The foundation in law for protection of people's rights rests with the Constitution (The Constitution of the United States, 1986). Following the Revolutionary War, the newly established leaders of the nation turned their attention to developing a system of government that was more democratic than the British monarchy. The Constitution, as originally passed and later amended, serves as the basis for civil rights and protections in America. It provides the framework for our system of government, our electoral process, rights related to personal expression and behavior, and protection of the nation's and the citizens' well-being.

The United States Constitution, consisting of seven articles, was agreed to in 1789. Article I outlines the legislative branch, and Articles II and III establish the executive and judicial branches, respectively. The separation of powers was deemed necessary to provide a system of "checks and balances" with the design of "popular control of government" (Oleszek, 2007, p. 3). The structure of our government and details about the three branches can be found in Chapter 14.

Furthermore, the Constitution settled the question of whether the government should be representative of the national citizenry or a federation representing states (Jacobson, 1987). A national government would be based on representation according to population, whereas a federal system would be based on representation of the states. For large states with great numbers of people, representation according to population was advantageous. For small states, equal representation for each state was much more appealing. Together, the House of Representatives and the Senate make up the Congress of the United States. The system that prevailed was a compromise between these two positions.

The form of government established was based on a bicameral, or two-chamber, system. The House of Representatives was made up of members elected by the people according to the population of each state, and the Senate was made up of two members from each state, regardless of the state's size. Senators were originally chosen by state legislatures, but in 1913 the Constitution was amended to allow for direct election of senators by citizens. This system remains in effect today.

Although the question of representation was settled through development of the democratic process, participation in the process of selection was limited. The right to vote was initially addressed by the Constitution in a general way, with the specifics left to states. Over time, the Constitution was amended to more clearly delineate the parameters of the right to vote. Voting as a specific right took decades to resolve and is discussed in further detail in the next section.

The **Bill of Rights** identifies the central tenets of civil rights in America (see Box 5.2). It consists of the first ten amendments to the Constitution, which were ratified in 1791, two years after the first Constitutional Convention and the original passage of the Constitution. The First Amendment protects freedom of religion, speech, and the press; the right of people to assemble peaceably; and the right of people to petition government:

> Congress shall make no law respecting an establishment of religion, or prohibiting the free exercise thereof; or abridging the freedom of speech, or of the press; or the right of the people peaceably to assemble, and to petition the Government for a redress of grievances.

BOX 5.2	**MORE ABOUT THE BILL OF RIGHTS, RATIFIED ON DECEMBER 15, 1791**

Amendment I: Congress shall make no law respecting an establishment of religion, or prohibiting the free exercise thereof; or abridging the freedom of speech, or of the press; or the right of the people peaceably to assemble, and to petition the Government for a redress of grievances.

Amendment II: A well regulated Militia, being necessary to the security of a free State, the right of the people to keep and bear Arms, shall not be infringed.

Amendment III: No Soldier shall, in time of peace be quartered in any house, without the Consent of the Owner, nor in time of war, but in a manner to be prescribed by law.

Amendment IV: The right of the people to be secure in their persons, houses, papers, and effects, against unreasonable searches and seizures, shall not be violated, and no Warrants shall issue, but upon probable cause, supported by Oath or affirmation, and particularly describing the place to be searched, and the persons or things to be seized.

Amendment V: No person shall be held to answer for a capital, or otherwise infamous crime, unless on a presentment or indictment of a Grand Jury, except in cases arising in the land or naval forces, or in the Militia, when in actual service in time of War or public danger; nor shall any person be subject for the same offence to be twice put in jeopardy of life or limb; nor shall he be compelled in any criminal case to be a witness against himself, nor be deprived of life, liberty, or property without due process of law; nor shall private property be taken for public use, without just compensation.

Amendment VI: In all criminal prosecutions, the accused shall enjoy the right to a speedy and public trial, by an impartial jury of the State and district wherein the crime shall have been committed, which district shall have been previously ascertained by law, and to be informed of the nature and cause of the accusation; to be confronted with the witnesses against him; to have compulsory process for obtaining witnesses in his favor, and to have the assistance of counsel for his defense.

Amendment VII: In suits at common law, where the value in controversy shall exceed twenty dollars, the right of trial by jury shall be preserved, and no fact tried by a jury, shall be otherwise reexamined in any court of the United States, than according to the rules of common law.

Amendment VIII: Excessive bail shall not be required, nor excessive fines imposed, nor cruel and unusual punishments inflicted.

Amendment IX: The enumeration in the Constitution, of certain rights, shall not be construed to deny or disparage others retained by the people.

Amendment X: The powers not delegated to the United States by the Constitution, nor prohibited by it to the states, are reserved to the States respectively, or to the people.

These protections create a foundation of civil rights in this country. Other amendments were added as the struggle for civil rights expanded the meaning of these liberties. Today the Constitution and all its amendments serve as the basis for legal decisions in this country.

THE HISTORY OF VOTING RIGHTS IN THE UNITED STATES

The right to vote was not clearly spelled out by the Constitution. Decisions about the specifics of who was eligible to vote were left to the states. Consequently, after ratification of the Constitution and prior to the Civil War, voting was predominantly a right of white men who owned property. This meant that many other

Americans were denied the right to vote. Because voting entitles one to a voice in government and political decisions, and voting was restricted to white men, most public policies ignored or did not protect the rights of all people. Women, slaves, and those who did not own land were not envisioned as full citizens. For almost 100 years, these omissions in civil rights were ignored by those in power. Not until after the Civil War did the government have to make concessions to protect the rights of more citizens.

VOTING RIGHTS FOR AFRICAN-AMERICAN MEN

The Civil War began the movement to expand the rights of African Americans. Until the Civil War, black slaves brought from Africa lacked any civil rights or personal protections. In fact, they were considered the property of their owners. One of the political outcomes of the Civil War was that the federal government intervened and passed the Fourteenth Amendment in 1868 and the Fifteenth Amendment in 1870.

The original intent of the Fourteenth Amendment was to establish the full rights of citizenship and equality for all, including African Americans:

> All persons born or naturalized in the United States, and subject to the jurisdiction thereof, are citizens of the United States and of the State wherein they reside. No state shall make or enforce any law which shall abridge the privileges or immunities of citizens of the United States; nor shall any state deprive any person of life, liberty, or property, without due process of law; nor deny to any person within its jurisdiction the equal protection of the laws.

The words "persons" and "citizens" in the Constitution referred to men. Consequently, the rights of citizenship were extended to all men but not to women. Two years later, in 1870, the issue of voting rights was clearly spelled out in the Fifteenth Amendment, which gave the right to vote to any male, regardless of race or color:

> The right of citizens of the United States to vote shall not be denied or abridged by the United States or by any State on account of race, color, or previous condition of servitude.

Although the intent of the Fourteenth Amendment was to give freedom and civil rights to former slaves, interpretation in the courts limited its impact. The Supreme Court's *Plessy v. Ferguson* decision in 1896 mandated that equal protection did not preclude segregation. The decision justified separate but equal public facilities. However, the government's will to enforce the decision was minimal, and the historical result was that segregation and "separate and unequal" actions dominated public policy and practice. (Dye, 2008, p. 243)

Theoretically, these constitutional amendments gave African-American men the right to vote. In practical terms, particularly in the South, local rules and regulations made it impossible for most former slaves to actually vote. Requirements such as poll taxes and literacy tests were used to bar people from registering to vote. Without paying a tax and passing a literacy test, a man could not register to vote in the South. Without first registering, a man could not cast a vote in any election.

After the Civil War, in spite of emancipation, former slaves who stayed in the South were poor and had little access to education. Southern state and local governments enforced local rules that kept African Americans marginalized by making it impossible for them to obtain adequate educational and financial resources. These local rules and regulations, together with rampant racial discrimination, prevented former slaves from owning land, running businesses, or holding well-paying jobs. Moreover, poll taxes and literacy tests were not the only barriers that kept African Americans from voting. Voter registration was conducted by local officials. When African Americans attempted to register, intimidation and fear tactics were used to discourage them (Polenberg, 1980). Therefore, local laws and practices effectively nullified the impact of the Fourteenth and Fifteenth Amendments.

The impact of these blocking tactics lasted for almost 100 years. This example illustrates how local control and policy setting can be more powerful and effective than federal government rule and move prejudice and discrimination to the level of oppression. In addition, the poll tax and literacy tests are classic examples of **institutional racism,** in which public laws and regulations are used to differentiate and discriminate according to race.

For African Americans in the South, voting did not become a reality until passage of the Twenty-Fourth Amendment in 1964 and the Voting Rights Act in 1965. The Twenty-Fourth Amendment, which barred the use of the poll tax, was reinforced by the congressional passage of the Voting Rights Act. The 1965 Voting Rights Act put an end to literacy tests and made federal registrars responsible for enrolling voters. The impact of these laws was immediate. For example, in Selma, Alabama, one of the cities where civil rights were most strongly contested, on the day of enactment 381 African Americans were registered to vote. That was more than the total number who had registered in the previous 65 years (Polenberg, 1980).

Voting Rights for Women

For women, the legal right to vote was slow in coming. Women activists began their struggle as early as the 1840s to achieve suffrage, the right to vote. Frustration over the denial of women's roles in making public policy decisions prompted women to organize to gain the right to vote. In 1848, Elizabeth Cady Stanton and other early reformers organized the first women's rights conference, the Seneca Falls Convention (Boulding, 1992). This meeting marked the official beginning of the women's suffrage movement in America.

The Civil War shifted reform activities to the abolition of slavery. Women's groups tried unsuccessfully to include sex in the protections of the Fourteenth and Fifteenth Amendments. Abolitionists were concerned that adding women's rights would complicate their efforts (V. Klein, 1984). Thus, women's rights groups, primarily the National Woman Suffrage Association formed by Susan B. Anthony and Elizabeth Cady Stanton, continued to organize and press for the right to vote without the support of other rights movements.

As discussed in Chapter 2, the progressive era came about in response to the social changes wrought by industrialization and urbanization at the turn of the 20th century. Women were deeply affected by these changes. More women had entered the labor force and had become part of other social reform movements. It was the impact of World War I and the large number of women in the labor force, however, that finally influenced the political acceptance of women's suffrage (Axinn & Stern, 2008). The role of women in the war effort made it clear that women were active participants in the nation's economic and political realms. The right of women to vote was finally made law in the Nineteenth Amendment to the Constitution. The amendment was first introduced in 1878 and was reintroduced into every congressional session until 1920, when it was ratified (V. Klein, 1984). It states: "The right of citizens of the United States to vote shall not be denied or abridged by the United States or by any state on account of sex." This marked the culmination of a 70-year struggle. Like all women's issues, it sparked tremendous controversy and met with extreme resistance. Once the amendment was passed, women's rights organizations, which had fought for the right to vote for so long, lost momentum and for the most part remained dormant for the next 40 years.

Voting Rights for Indigenous People

Basic rights for the indigenous populations of this land were nonexistent for hundreds of years. Recognition of citizenship for the people who had long inhabited this country was slow to arrive. The issue of voting rights for Native Americans emerged as other suffrage movements developed and voting rights for freed African-American male slaves were established after the Civil War. To officially control the already established practice of exclusion, Congress passed the Naturalization Act of 1870, which allowed naturalization only for "white persons and persons of African descent" (Axinn & Stern, 2008, p. 89). **Naturalization** is the act of extending citizenship to those who are foreign-born. In the late 1800s, naturalization became an issue because of the growing number of Chinese immigrants who were brought here to work on the railroads. Ironically, Native Americans, who had been born in this country, were considered aliens and therefore were affected by this legislation. Native Americans were denied the right to vote. It was not until after World War I that the right to vote was extended to them. Those who fought in the war were granted the right of citizenship in recognition of their service, and in 1924 all indigenous people became citizens (Day, 2006). However, Native Americans were still officially considered wards of the government, a status that limited the full exercise of their civil rights.

Mexican Immigration and Latino Voting Rights

The major struggle for voting rights for Latino populations centered on the border struggles between Mexico and the United States. For some Latino groups in other parts of the country, legal recognition fell under categories for whites. However, in the Border States, the confrontation rested on racial determinations. Were Mexican Americans whites, or a minority group of color? The conflict officially dates back to the Treaty of Hidalgo in 1848, which ended the Mexican-American War. At that time, the United States acquired the present-day states of California, Arizona, New Mexico, and Texas and parts of Colorado, Nevada, and Utah (Massey, Durand, & Malone, 2003).

A small number of Mexicans entered the United States under the treaty. Most Mexican Americans trace their roots to people who migrated after 1848. For many years, the border was fluid because there was little regulation and populations in the areas were sparse. When the U.S. Border Patrol was created in 1924, the border between the two countries gained official attention (Massey, Durand, & Malone, 2003).

Although the 1848 Treaty of Hidalgo incorporated Mexicans as citizens, they were routinely excluded from the privileges of citizenship, including the right to vote. The vast majority of people of Mexican descent were considered nonwhite, and their racial status was typically determined locally and therefore differed from state to state (Foner & Fredrickson, 2004). The status of nonwhite persons, although not exactly the same as African Americans, severely limited the rights afforded to Mexican Americans. One of the ways that Mexican Americans were legally excluded was to cite their Indian ancestry and categorize them under the Naturalization Act as aliens like Native Americans. When that designation was lifted, the legal grounds for preventing Mexican Americans from voting weakened. However, because local rules were often ignored by federal authorities, recognition of civil rights for Mexican Americans continued to be inconsistent.

PROTECTION FROM DISCRIMINATION AND OPPRESSION

Our nation unfortunately has a long history of hatred and exclusion of people based on their identities, such as race, ethnicity, gender, ability, sexual orientation, and even age. Although discrimination and oppression are ugly aspects of our national legacy, there is also a strong history of government intervention and public policies that have lessened their impact. In fact, the history of civil rights and social justice expressed in social welfare policies presents compelling proof of the power of these policies to improve society and the lives of those most in need.

PROTECTION FROM RACISM

The Civil War was the first time that the federal government intervened to protect people from discrimination based on race. Although the Civil War may have helped to officially end slavery, it did not accomplish much in the way of protecting African-American people from discrimination, harassment, and exclusion based on the color of their skin.

After the Civil War and until the 1960s, race relations were tainted by a sense of racial superiority on the parts of whites (Polenberg, 1980). Discrimination and oppression on the basis of race were present in both the social and the economic spheres. In the South, discrimination through segregation in all facets of life served to keep African Americans and whites separate. Jim Crow laws, which were state rules and regulations that enforced segregation, dominated in Southern states. "Jim Crow" was a minstrel show character who portrayed blacks as childlike, irresponsible, and lazy; this was the image held by Southern whites. The oppression of former slaves was perpetuated through many restrictions, including laws that barred African Americans from many public facilities used by whites, prohibited African Americans from sitting in the front seats of buses, and forced African

Americans to use restricted entrances to buildings. Public law was used to deny African Americans the privileges that whites enjoyed. The Jim Crow system held, and federal intervention and protection from discrimination did not occur until almost 100 years after the Civil War.

In the North, racial discrimination was less overt. African Americans could register to vote, and public facilities were not segregated. There were two areas in which racial discrimination played a significant role, however: housing and employment (Polenberg, 1980). In northern cities with sizable populations of African Americans, neighborhoods were segregated by race and few areas of employment were open to African Americans. Decades after the Civil War, the living conditions of African Americans in the United States were significantly lower than those of white Americans. Even the progressive reforms of the New Deal ignored issues of racial inequality. During the 1940s, groups considered racially different "worked at the hardest jobs, earned the least money, lived in the most wretched homes, and died most frequently of preventable diseases" (Polenberg, 1980, p. 30).

Following World War II, after African Americans had actively participated in defending this country and worked at home in defense plants, awareness of the need for civil rights protections grew. Powerful black leaders such as the Reverend Dr. Martin Luther King, Jr. and the Reverend Ralph Abernathy began their educational training during the postwar years at seminaries and took advantage of the few opportunities to study in the North for their advanced degrees. The life and work of Dr. Martin Luther King, Jr. epitomizes the gradual and painful shift in race relations in this country. Taylor Branch (1988), in his book *Parting the Waters*, thoroughly documents the civil rights struggle through the experiences and work of Dr. Martin Luther King, Jr. Branch provides a history of the civil rights movement interwoven with events from the life of the man most notably involved in the movement, stating that "King's life is the best and most important metaphor for American history in the watershed postwar years" (Branch, 1988, p. xii).

Through civil disobedience and nonviolent efforts such as the Montgomery bus boycott and the sit-ins at lunch counters, public awareness of racial segregation in the South intensified. Public support for civil rights legislation grew as a result of the efforts of charismatic and visionary leaders such as Dr. King, growing political activism within the black community, increased media coverage, and backing from church groups. What further propelled the movement was a shift in the support of the courts. The Supreme Court, with changes in membership, began to broaden "the constitutional rights of citizens and, at the same time, to sanction governmental efforts to remove barriers to social equality" (Polenberg, 1980, p. 177). Through court decisions, public universities were integrated and military forces were used to ensure the right of African-American students to attend. The mood in the country had shifted. Propelled in part by the public's growing sense of civil fairness and in part by their fear of what might happen if civil rights protections were not extended, legislators enacted public policy to protect the civil rights of all citizens regardless of race.

In 1964, legislation drafted by the Kennedy administration and passed under Johnson's presidency guaranteed federal protection for the civil rights of African Americans. The Civil Rights Act of 1964 (P.L. 88-352) prohibited racial, sexual, or ethnic discrimination in employment (Axinn & Stern, 2008). The law required desegregation of public facilities and prohibited institutions that received federal funds from discriminating in the hiring of employees. This legislation also created the Equal Employment Opportunity Commission (EEOC), charged with implementation and, later, enforcement of the act (Jansson, 2009).

Changes took place gradually as the new policies were enforced. Resistance was great because the changes represented a major social shift in American culture. Even though there are public laws on record protecting people's civil rights, has racial discrimination been eradicated in America? Although racism and oppression are not as blatant today as in the years preceding the civil rights movement, many people are faced with racial discrimination. Actions such as racial profiling by law enforcement agencies and racial slurs are still widely reported, as are more subtle forms of racial intolerance, including poor services and lack of respect. According to research conducted in 2001 (Morin & Cottman), nearly 4 out of 10 African Americans reported being unfairly stopped by police, as did 1 out of 5 Hispanic respondents. Only 4 percent of whites reported having experienced such action. Over 80 percent of African-American respondents and two thirds of Latinos and Asians say they regularly experience intolerant acts (Box 5.3 provides more detail).

On the other hand, civil rights have been expanded and progress has been made. Leon Wynter (2002) makes a compelling argument that commercialization and American popular culture are changing the face of the American dream, and it now includes people of color. He credits the civil rights activism of the 1960s for creating the foundation for change, but he argues that we are moving toward a "transracial America" through the marketplace. The presidential election of

---

BOX 5.3 | **CONSIDER THIS ...**

During the last ten years, have you experienced discrimination because of your racial or ethnic background?

	Yes	No
Black	46%	53%
Hispanic	40%	60%
Asian	39%	58%
White	18%	81%

Have you ever been unfairly stopped by police because of your race or ethnic background?

	Yes
Black	37%
Hispanic	20%
Asian	11%
White	4%

Have you ever been physically threatened or attacked because of your race or ethnic background?

	Yes
Black	17%
Hispanic	13%
Asian	15%
White	9%

Source: Morin & Cottman, 2001

Agree that the main reason many blacks can't get ahead is due to racial discrimination:

Blacks	30%
Hispanics	24%
Whites	15%

Source: Pew Research Center, 2007

Barack Obama demonstrates the change—a man born to a black father and a white mother has achieved the highest elected position in the United States, that of President. Obama's election marks an historical moment. However, racial discrimination and oppression are still social problems in America. The experience of race still differs greatly in this country. When asked about racial discrimination, 67 percent of African Americans reported discrimination in applying for a job and 65 percent find blacks face discrimination in housing. The perception held by whites about African Americans' experiences is sharply different. Only 20 percent of white respondents perceive that blacks face discrimination in applying for jobs and 27 percent say blacks encounter discrimination when renting or buying a home (Pew Research Center, 2007). The differences between black and white peoples' experiences mean that policy makers must be vigilant to ensure that hard-won civil rights gains are not lost and further progress is made.

HATE CRIMES LEGISLATION

Racial, ethnic, and identity discrimination still occurs in this country, in spite of laws prohibiting it. **Hate crime laws** have been passed in recent years to both track the occurrence of illegal discriminatory acts and create stricter punishments than those for crimes not motivated by discrimination. Hate crimes are those motivated by prejudice based on race, ethnicity, religion, or sexual orientation. Initial federal legislation was concerned only with documentation of hate crimes. The Hate Crimes Statistics Act of 1990 began the process of acknowledging and documenting the existence of hate crimes. Two highly publicized cases in 1998 fueled the fight for passage of hate crimes legislation. In Jasper, Texas, James Byrd, Jr., an African-American man, was beaten and dragged behind a truck by three white supremacists, until he died. That same year, a young gay college student, Matthew Shepard, was beaten and tied to a fence and left to die. His assailants testified that they were outraged because he was gay. Although these were not the first such acts in American history, they occurred at a time, the late 1990s, when social movements had come together with crime victim advocacy, and publicity about the cases mobilized legislators to respond (Jenness & Gratett, 2001). The impact of these horrible crimes impelled Congress to pass the Hate Crimes Prevention Act in 1998. The act expanded federal responsibility and provided funding for programs to reduce hate crimes.

From 1991 to 2006, the incidence of reported hate crimes grew from 4,558 to 7,722 (although that was a decrease from a high of 9,730 incidents reported in 2002, the number has held steady since then). Half of the 2006 reports were based on race, 19 percent were based on religion, and about 16 percent were based on sexual orientation (Federal Bureau of Investigation, 2007). The public sense of progress deterring hate crimes was jolted with an incident in Jena, Louisiana, that began in 2006. Several African-American students at the local high school asked their principal for permission to sit under a tree where typically white students gathered. The principal told them "sit wherever you want" (Tatum, 2007, p. 26). The next day, three nooses (the historical symbol of lynching) were found hanging from the tree. The message sent by those nooses to the African-American students was hostile and threatening, reminding them that they should "know their place." The incident escalated into racially motivated fights and was exacerbated by severe charges filed against the African-American students, and lesser charges filed against the white students. News of these events spread through the Internet and media, and in 2007, 20,000 protestors from around the country marched on the town of Jena demanding equal justice. The publicity and outrage over the event drew vivid attention to the continued incidence of hate crimes and racial tensions. It highlighted the need for further social policy aimed at diminishing hate crimes and discrimination.

AFFIRMATIVE ACTION

One effect of the civil rights movement was the development of policies supporting affirmative action. **Affirmative action** involves efforts to correct historical imbalances in opportunities based on race and sex. These policies have drawn a tremendous amount of public attention and serious reconsideration.

The provisions of the Civil Rights Act prohibited discrimination in hiring based on race, gender, national origin, or religion, and also stated that hiring should not involve preferential treatment to equalize prior existing imbalances. As a public policy, affirmative action grew out of federal regulations, presidential executive orders, and the courts, not directly out of the Civil Rights Act of 1964. Over the next 15 years, affirmative action primarily evolved out of federal regulations attached to federal contracts.

Affirmative action regulations called for efforts to equalize racial and gender imbalances through hiring practices. For example, in 1968, the Labor Department required affirmative action plans as a condition of receiving a federal contract. The Supreme Court indirectly supported this practice in 1971 by prohibiting labor practices that maintained the status quo of racial imbalances. By 1972, federal regulations required colleges and universities to institute affirmative action plans

---

BOX 5.4 | **CONSIDER THIS ...**

Excerpts from the comments that Dennis Shepard made at the conclusion of the trial against the murderers of his son, Matthew Shepard:

Yes, this was a hate crime, pure and simple, with the added ingredient of robbery. My son, Matthew, paid a terrible price to open the eyes of all of us who live in Wyoming, the United States, and the world to the unjust and unnecessary fears, discrimination, and intolerance that members of the gay community face every day ... How do I talk about the loss that I feel every time I think about Matt? How can I describe the empty pit in my heart and mind when I think about all the problems that were put in Matt's way that he overcame. No one can understand the sense of pride and accomplishment that I felt every time he reached the mountaintop of another obstacle. No one, including myself, will ever know the frustration and agony that others put him through, because he was different ... my son has become a symbol—a symbol against hate ... a symbol for encouraging respect for individuality, for appreciating that someone is different, for tolerance. I miss my son but I'm proud to be able to say that he is my son.

Source: Court proceedings, November 4, 1999

(Polenberg, 1980). Affirmative action plans require proof of efforts to ensure that qualified people of color and women are part of applicant pools and that efforts are made to improve representation in schools and employment.

Questions about the effectiveness and fairness of affirmative action policies gained public attention during the mid-1990s. In many areas of employment, affirmative action policies seem to have made a difference. For example, from 1970 to 1990, the number of African-American police officers increased almost threefold, and African-American representation in fire departments rose from 2.5 percent to 11.5 percent (Taylor, 1995). In many other areas of employment, however, gains have been minimal.

Preferential treatment and quotas have drawn unfavorable public attention to affirmative action. As designed, affirmative action policies are not to set quotas, but rather are meant to require institutions:

> to develop plans enabling them to go beyond business as usual and search for qualified people in places where they did not ordinarily conduct their searches or their business. ... The idea of affirmative action is *not* to force people into positions for which they are unqualified but to encourage institutions to develop realistic criteria for the enterprise at hand and then to find a reasonably diverse mix of people qualified to be engaged in it. (Wilkins, 1995, p. 3)

Although this definition seems clear, the interpretation of affirmative action has varied greatly. Federal regulations developed during the 1970s expanded the use of affirmative action, but conflicts arose during the next decade. Many employers argued that qualified women and minority candidates did not exist.

For example, Harvard Law School made this argument in 1990. In response to demands that the law school practice diversity and hire an African-American woman, the official response was that in order to do so the school would have to, in the words of the associate dean, "lower its standards" (Williams, 1991). It seems difficult to believe that a school such as Harvard University did not have the resources, contacts, or know-how to find and recruit one qualified African-American woman to teach in its law school. The assertion that there were absolutely no African-American women qualified to take such a role illustrates precisely the attitude that makes affirmative action policies necessary.

By the late 1980s, a more conservative Supreme Court ruled against the use of affirmative action to remedy past racial imbalances and discrimination (Axinn & Stern, 2008). In response to these restrictions, Congress passed the Civil Rights Act of 1991. The act reaffirmed the right of employees to bring suits alleging discrimination against employers (Jansson, 2009).

Public sentiment of the 1990s reflected criticism of affirmative action. States passed laws to minimize the impact of affirmative action. For example, in 1996 the state of California passed legislation removing the requirement for affirmative action from state government programs. Immediately following the election, affirmative action supporters filed suit in federal court and won a restraining order so that the law could not take effect.

Recent legal challenges have reaffirmed parts of affirmative action but shifted its emphasis. In 2003, two affirmative action cases involving admission standards at the University of Michigan reached the Supreme Court (Foner & Fredrickson, 2004).

One case involved the law school's practice of including race as a factor in admissions, and the second involved a bonus point system used in undergraduate admissions for students of color. In the first case, the practice of including race was deemed acceptable by the Supreme Court justices because the law school representatives argued convincingly that considering the race of an applicant improved diversity, which enriched the educational system. In the second case, the bonus point system was perceived as being a quota system, which did not consider individually each admissions case. Although in the end affirmative action was upheld, the purpose seems to have shifted from correcting historical imbalances to ensuring diversity.

The fight over affirmative action and university admissions continued in Michigan through a citizen-initiated proposal placed on the statewide ballot in 2006. The proposal passed and amended the state's constitution to end affirmative action that gave preferential treatment in university admissions. So while the Supreme Court's ruling that improving diversity allowed for affirmative action efforts, the state constitutional amendment reinforced the interpretation that using race as a standard to give admission precedence was not allowable. The Michigan state law was appealed through the Michigan state courts, and was upheld in 2008.

Although there have been implementation problems with affirmative action, the principles of protecting civil rights and recognizing past imbalances due to race and sex remain important issues today. The Supreme Court decision in 2003 has given the policy continued support, although with some limitations. Affirmative action's contributions to social justice and civil rights have been vital, and will continue to need attention by policy makers and social reformers.

WOMEN'S RIGHTS

As discussed earlier in the chapter, the major accomplishment in expansion of rights for women was passage of the right to vote in 1920. Since that time, there have been numerous other policy debates regarding the civil rights of women.

Equal Rights Amendment   The most frequently mentioned struggle for women's rights was the fight to pass the **Equal Rights Amendment (ERA)**. This constitutional amendment was written to extend civil rights protections for women and to prohibit discrimination based on sex.

Extending the civil rights coverage of the Constitution is not a new issue. Suffragists as far back as the mid-1800s proposed an equal rights amendment. As already discussed, efforts to include women's rights as part of the Fourteenth Amendment met with failure. Even securing the right to vote did not provide enough public policy momentum to secure an equal rights amendment. Four decades later, however, the reform atmosphere of the 1960s and women's growing involvement in political movements ignited another wave of interest in an equal rights amendment. In 1972, after 49 years of attempts, Congress passed the ERA by an overwhelming margin (E. Klein, 1984). Before an amendment to the Constitution can become law, it must be ratified by a majority of state legislators in three-fourths of the states. During the first year, ratification was secured in 22 states. Through legislative extension, the ERA had a 10-year limit on securing those ratifications.

The obstacle in passing the ERA was in getting state legislators in the remaining states to agree to support the amendment.

Time and resources ran out, and negative publicity efforts prevailed. Although supporters felt that the ERA simply represented an extension to women of the rights that all men and racial groups already possessed, opponents felt that it would create a radical change in the social structure of America. In the end, although a majority of Americans supported the ERA, there were not enough state legislators willing to vote for it (Freeman, 1984). In 1982, when the deadline arrived, the ERA was still 3 states short of the 38 needed for ratification (E. Klein, 1984).

The defeat of the ERA may have been caused, in part, by a shift in political sentiment. The mood of the nation in regard to civil rights and public responsibility shifted from the 1970s to the 1980s, leading to reduced legislative support for the ERA. The amendment was also a victim of the rise in political organization of anti-ERA groups, mobilization of Christian fundamentalist groups, and differing priorities among women's groups (Mansbridge, 1990).

Animosity toward the ERA and women's rights groups continued. In his campaign for the election of a Republican president in 1992, Pat Robertson, a leader of the Christian Coalition, warned that the ERA was part of a "feminist agenda" that represented "a socialist, anti-family political movement that encourages women to leave their husbands, kill their children, practice witchcraft, destroy capitalism, and become lesbians" (Wicker, 1992, p. E3). Although the defeat of the ERA took a tremendous toll on the women's movement, numerous women's groups gained valuable political experience that helped them to advocate for public policies promoting the civil rights of women.

Equality in Education: Title IX Enactment of the right to vote and protection from discrimination in employment granted by the Civil Rights Act of 1964 were significant gains for women. Nevertheless, the American political system has provided limited legislative support for the enactment of policies designed to ensure *equality* based on gender. Although the two concepts are related, there is a difference between **nondiscrimination** and **equality**. People can be protected from discrimination but still lack equality. For example, if a school system guarantees nondiscrimination, it can guarantee schools for all children by creating separate schools for boys and girls. The schools may not be similar or equivalent. On the other hand, equality requires that those schools provide equivalent services and resources. Thus, equal rights is a broader concept than protection from discrimination.

A significant piece of legislation that did support gender equity was Title IX of the Education Amendments to the Civil Rights Act, passed in 1972. The legislation stated that:

> No person in the United States shall, on the basis of sex, be excluded from participation in, be denied the benefits of, or be subjected to discrimination under any educational program or activity receiving federal financial assistance.

The implementation and enforcement of Title IX has been fraught with problems since passage. The greatest resistance to implementation of the policy has centered on the provisions related to academic institutions and athletics. Those provisions:

> ...which sought equalization of sport opportunity and rewards ... engendered the most extreme, organized, and concerted lobbying pro and con, generated the most impassioned pleas, and garnered the most extraordinary claims about the benefits or pending disasters that will befall society if the legislative mandates are implemented. (Boutilier & SanGiovanni, 1983, p. 171)

Interpretation of the legislation meant that elementary and secondary schools and universities that had traditionally committed the vast majority of their resources to sports programs for male students would now be required to equally support programs for female students. Supporters fought for even greater commitment, and detractors complained that such equality would be impossible to achieve and that attempts to achieve it would ultimately dilute the athletic accomplishments and reputations already made by institutions.

Title IX has had a significant impact on the lives of girls and women. Between 1972 and 2002, the number of high school girls who participated in athletics increased from just under 300,000 to 2.78 million (National Women's Law Center, 2002). In 1984, however, the scope of the legislation was significantly narrowed through the Supreme Court ruling in favor of Grove City College (*Grove City College v. Bell*). The court decision stated that Title IX covers only specific programs in institutions of education. This meant that if a specific program did not directly receive federal funds, it was not covered by Title IX protections (Terpstra, 1984). Institutions were able to demonstrate that not all programs, such as athletics, benefited directly from federal funds. Therefore, these programs were not under Title IX. This court decision had ramifications for other civil rights laws as well.

In 1988, the tide turned. Congress overrode President Reagan's veto and passed the Civil Rights Restoration Act. The act restored the original intent of Title IX and protected other civil rights laws from dilution (Congressional Quarterly, 1988). The 1988 legislation defined "program" or "activity" to include an entire institution that received federal funds and thus brought back the original intent of Title IX. The rocky history of Title IX demonstrates the difficulty in protecting and expanding rights that promote gender equality. It also demonstrates the difficulty of protecting the positive impact of such civil rights legislation. For example, the 1996 Summer Olympics showcased numerous American women who were of the first generation to grow up under Title IX. For these women, equal rights to compete athletically seem normal (Kuttner, 1996).

By 2000, almost 30 years after passage of Title IX, the expansion of opportunities for women as a result of this legislation had been documented. A report by the General Accounting Office concluded that since Title IX's enactment in 1972, women's participation in higher education programs and on the playing field had increased significantly (GAO, 2000). However, after 35 years, although females were 57 percent of the students in colleges and universities, they were only 43 percent of the athletes and female collegiate athletes received only 37 percent of sports operating dollars. Furthermore, women and girls are largely absent from traditionally male courses and academic positions. Although women comprise 79 percent of public school teachers in this country, only 44 percent of the principals are female, and women represent less than one in five faculty members in science, technology, and mathematics (National Coalition for Women and Girls in Education, 2008). Title IX provides an excellent example of the power of federal policy and government enforcement in improving opportunities for girls and women in educational institutions, but that constant attention needs to be focused on the implementation and progress over time of public policy.

The Abortion Controversy   Another issue that has sparked tremendous public debate is abortion and who has the right to control the use of the procedure. The controversy surrounding the right of a pregnant woman to choose whether she has an abortion is still unresolved. The controversy is complex. For those who are "pro-choice" (who believe a woman should be allowed to make her own decision), access to legal abortions is a civil right that should be protected by law. For those who are opposed to legal abortion, the issue is a moral one of preserving life by protecting the fetus. Susan Faludi (1991), in her comprehensive analysis of the state of women's issues in America, challenged these differences. She argued that the issue was not the rate of abortions, which in fact decreased during the 1980s, nor was it "protection of the unborn." Rather, for the antiabortion movement, whose leaders were predominantly young men:

> The real change was women's new ability to regulate their infertility without danger or fear—a new freedom that in turn had contributed to dramatic changes not in the abortion rate but in female sexual behavior and attitudes...Women also became far more independent in their decisions about when to have children, under what marital circumstances, and when to stop ... to many men in the antiabortion movement, the speed with which women embraced sexual and reproductive freedom could be frightening ... this revolution in female behavior had invaded their most intimate domain. (pp. 403–404)

The social upheaval implied by the right of women to choose whether to have an abortion is a major component of the conflict. For many people, legal abortion represents a threat to the traditional family. It is believed to lead to premarital sex, divorce, and use of contraceptives, and it touches on a deep social anxiety about what the consequences might be if women are free to control when and if they choose biological motherhood (Gelb & Palley, 1987). These social concerns make the issue of legalized abortions a heated and controversial political and social welfare issue.

Abortions were legal in early America. They did not become illegal until the mid-1800s. For almost 100 years, abortions were illegal and difficult to obtain. In 1973, the Supreme Court decision in *Roe v. Wade* stated that a woman's right to privacy permitted her to make the choice of whether to have an abortion, that states could only intervene during the second trimester to ensure the mother's health, and that abortions could only be prohibited after the sixth month of pregnancy (Biskupic, 1993).

As was true during the previous century, antiabortion movements arose in response to the growth in women's rights organizations. Although Congress has not been able to overturn the legality of abortion, it has restricted it through legislation. Limits on the use of federal dollars to pay for abortions, waiting periods, and educational resources opposing abortion have all become law through Congressional action. The Supreme Court, which has become more conservative since *Roe v. Wade*, has also put limitations on access and availability. In spite of restrictions that vary from state to state, abortions are still legal in this country.

The anger surrounding the right to a legal abortion escalated to dangerous levels. In 1990, 74 violent incidents were reported, and by 1993 that number had jumped to 452 (National Abortion Federation, 2008). In Florida, in 1993, a member of an antiabortion group shot and killed a clinic doctor, and in 1994 clinic workers were killed by a protester in Boston. These escalations and murders prompted federal action in passing the Freedom of Access to Clinic Entrances Act (FACE) in 1994, which limits the extent of protesting that antiabortionists can engage in at abortion clinics. Data reveal that the FACE Act was an effective piece of federal social welfare policy. In 1996, the number of violent incidents against clinics dropped to a low of 112, and, with the exception of a surge in anthrax threats following the 9/11 terrorist attack, remained below the 1993 level until 2005. In the past few years, incidents of trespassing have surged, but murder, attempted murder, bombing, arson, and invasion have all declined over the years following the FACE Act (National Abortion Federation, 2008). Since adoption in 1994, the FACE Act has served as an example of public policy changing behaviors and deterring violence.

Although clinic violence has not grown markedly in recent years, the issue of a woman's right to have an abortion is far from settled. Voters have mixed feelings, and many politicians are reluctant to deal with the issue directly. In 2003, legislators were successful in limiting the scope of *Roe v. Wade*. Congress passed the "Partial Birth" Abortion Ban, the first federal ban on any abortion procedure. The passage of this legislation revealed the complexity of the abortion issue. It involved legal, medical, religious, and civil concerns. Box 5.5 illustrates the controversial nature of the policy.

Members of Congress continue to introduce legislation that would narrow the scope of *Roe v. Wade*. Opponents of abortion have been working for more than 35 years to reverse *Roe v. Wade*. Major women's rights organizations have been supporting legal abortion for more than a century. It is likely that this dispute will continue for years to come.

The area of reproductive rights seems to be one of the most controversial of civil rights issues. It seems to cut across race, class, and religious boundaries because it touches on values and beliefs that are integral to so many parts of our lives. The rights of women affect our families, homes, workplaces, and every sphere of our personal lives. Because of the highly personal nature of sex roles and gender identities, it would seem that issues such as abortion and equal rights, which have been highly politicized and unresolved for 150 years, will continue to be major public policy concerns.

Violence Against Women   The likelihood that a woman will be beaten, forced to have sex, or abused over her lifetime is one in three and most often the person responsible for the abuse is a member of her own family (Population Information Program, 1999). Research has found that 1 in 4 women suffers physical or emotional violence by an intimate partner, and the rate is higher (36 percent) in low income

| **CONTROVERSIAL PERSPECTIVES ...**

Should it be legal to perform abortions? Are there forms of abortion that should be illegal?

In 2003, Congress passed and the President signed into law legislation that outlawed a procedure commonly referred to as "partial birth abortion" and medically known as "D & X," or "dilate and extraction," procedure. The procedure is usually performed in the fifth month of pregnancy or later. Opponents of the procedure argued that it is gruesome and not medically necessary. Those who did not want to outlaw the procedure argued that this procedure was a medical decision and a procedure that might be needed when the life or health of a mother is at risk. The incidence of this procedure is difficult to ascertain. Estimates place the total annual number somewhere between 3,000 and 4,000 per year, but an accurate count is impossible to determine because national records do not exist.

Who is right? Should the government legislate this procedure? Or should doctors and their patients make the decision? What if the life of a woman is compromised by a pregnancy? What if a woman is 20 weeks pregnant and medical tests determine that the fetus has severe birth defects and minimal viability? Should medical personnel have the legal protection to perform this procedure, or should they be sentenced to prison if they perform this procedure?

Whose values and beliefs dominate this issue? Whose values and beliefs should dominate this issue? Legislators? Doctors? Pregnant women? Biological fathers? Religious organizations? Presidents? Political organizations? Human rights groups?

Can you answer this question?

http://womensissues.about.com/od/partialbirthabortion/i/ispartialbirth.htm. Retrieved 2/28/2005

http://www.religioustolerance.org/abo_pba1.htm. Retrieved 2/28/2005

households (Centers for Disease Control, 2008). Gender-based violence stems from two strong traditions. The first is that women have had a subordinate role historically in our society, and the second holds that the privacy of the family is primary. The combination of these two beliefs has contributed to the existence of intimate violence. Socially, and until recently legally, violent acts that men have directed at women in the privacy of the home would be punished if they were directed at an employer or neighbor. Because of this dual standard, for generations women were treated abusively by intimate relations without any protection of the law.

Although crimes based on gender have a long history, the incorporation of gender crimes into hate crime legislation and civil rights was slow in coming. Growing awareness of hate crimes coupled with recognition of the severity of domestic violence helped to propel the legislative response to civil rights protection based on gender (Jenness & Grattet, 2001). With relatively little opposition, Congress passed the **Violence Against Women Act (VAWA)** in 1994 as part of larger crime control and law enforcement legislation. The law includes protections for women both outside the home and within, and protects their civil rights. After initial passage, the need for even stronger legislation became apparent. In 1998, one out of nine murders was an intimate partner homicide, and at least one out of five victims of violence feared reprisal and therefore did not report the victimization to police (Rennison & Welchans, 2000). Because of the privacy of intimate relationships, statistics are probably lower than the actual occurrences. For many victims, fear keeps them from making reports, and the internalized belief that what goes on between a man and a woman is private and should be separate from the state also contributes to the silencing of victims of abuse. Therefore, advocates pushed for even greater legal protections than those provided under the original 1994 legislation.

Since its inception, the law has grown and provided funding for numerous programs designed to ameliorate violence against women. In 2000, the law was reauthorized and greatly expanded. Dating violence was defined and added to programs; stalking laws were expanded; new initiatives were created; protection of battered immigrants was added; and provisions to combat the trafficking of people were included (P.L. 106-386). The legislation seems to have been effective in responding to the need. In 2001, there were more than half a million violent acts committed by intimate partners against females. Although alarming, this number was down significantly from a high of 1.1 million violent acts in 1993 (Rennison, 2003). Overall, the rate of intimate violence since the inception of the Violence Against Women Act has declined by 49 percent. This decrease suggests that even in arenas where there is tremendous resistance to state intervention, the protective power of federal legislation can be very effective.

RIGHTS OF PEOPLE WITH DISABILITIES

How society defines disability and how many people fit that definition are subject to great debate. Estimates of how many people live with disabilities in this country differ because there is variability in what it means to have a disability. According to the U.S. Census Bureau (2007), 51 million people live with a long-lasting physical, mental, or emotional condition that made it difficult for them to do activities. These activities included leaving the house alone or working at a job or business. Although the highest rate of disability affects people over 80 years of age, 12 million 16–64 year olds have a medical condition that impacts their ability to find and retain employment.

For people with disabilities, unemployment and economic stress are major concerns. Although 82 percent of the general population is employed, only 52 percent of working-age people with disabilities are employed, and only 26 percent of people with severe disabilities (National Center on Workforce and Disability, 2002). The major reasons for this exclusion are employers' attitudes, inaccessible workplaces, and inadequate levels of education. Public policy to address inequities in employment and access for people with disabilities was a long time in coming.

The **Americans with Disabilities Act of 1990 (ADA)** (P.L. 101-336) was the first significant piece of legislation providing civil rights protection for people with disabilities. The act prohibits discrimination against people with disabilities in the areas of employment, public accommodations, transportation, and public services. The law includes the mandate that workplaces and public facilities provide "reasonable accommodation" for people with disabilities. In addition, all new buildings that provide public services must be fully accessible (U.S. Department of Justice, 2000).

The impact of the ADA is significant. For example, reasonable accommodation in the workplace may mean physical changes to existing facilities, sign language interpreters, special training and written materials, or time off for treatment for a disability. The goal of the law in terms of employment is to ensure changes to the workplace so that people with disabilities can apply for jobs, perform job functions, and have equal access to benefits available to others in the workplace (U.S. Justice Department, 2000). Overall, the purpose of the law is to enable people with disabilities to participate fully in all aspects of social life. The provisions of the ADA have successfully removed long-standing barriers to many places for people with disabilities.

LESBIAN, GAY, BISEXUAL, AND TRANSGENDER RIGHTS

Civil rights protections by the federal government cover race, gender, ethnicity, religion, and ability. One group that has actively campaigned for civil rights legislation without success is the lesbian, gay, bisexual, and transgender community (LGBT). Sexual orientation and gender expression—whether a person is defined as homosexual, heterosexual, bisexual, or transgender—is far from accepted as a right to be protected. In large part this results from disagreement over whether homosexuality is a legitimate part of a person's identity. For many people, homosexuality cannot be accepted due to personal values. Although this belief is a personal right, is it sufficient reason to deny lesbian, gay, bisexual, and transgender people federal protection from discrimination?

For the vast majority of gay, lesbian, bisexual, and transgender people in America, discrimination is a significant part of their daily lives. Fear of revealing one's sexual orientation or gender identity is based on the life experiences of most LGBT people. In a 1990 national study covering eight U.S. cities, 94 percent of the gay men and lesbians surveyed reported having experienced some type of victimization due to their sexual orientation (Berrill, 1990). Even following the implementation of hate crimes legislation, violence against LGBT people occurs regularly (Human Rights Campaign, 2003b). For youth, it is particularly dangerous. Hostile climates in schools exist for 75 percent of youth (GLSEN, 2006), and violence against LGBT students is widespread (Cianciotto & Cahill, 2003). Almost two thirds of LGBT youth experience harassment and violence in school and feel that school personnel do not respond adequately (GLSEN, 2006).

Lack of civil rights protections means that if an employer discovers that an employee is gay, the employer can fire the worker and the employee has no legal recourse. If a landlord refuses to rent an apartment to a gay person, or a bank refuses to give a mortgage to buy a house, again the person is not protected. If a young person is harassed in school, there are no civil rights protections to legally stop the perpetrators.

Civil rights struggles by LGBT advocates date back to the 1960s and 1970s. Early public demonstrations began with the Stonewall riot in 1968, when a group of drag queens refused to be harassed by police officers in New York City. The patrons argued that police regularly came into bars and arrested and abused patrons and demanded financial protection monies from them. The group barricaded themselves for days and created a small riot, which is considered the beginning of the gay civil rights movement. Early civil rights efforts centered on acceptance and an end to harassment. The AIDS epidemic brought to light the lack of legal protections for gay couples and the need for medical and domestic benefits. Advocates began to focus on specific issues that might afford policy progress.

Efforts in 1993 centered on passing legislation that would prohibit the military from asking about a person's sexual orientation. Although this was a far cry from full civil rights, it was regarded as an entry point from which to gain momentum and push for full civil rights. The legislative effort failed, and advocates focused on presidential intervention. Although President Clinton promised to change the regulations as part of an Executive Order, Congress prevailed and blocked the change.

Gay rights advocates shifted their strategy and moved to push for civil rights protections in the area of employment. In 1994, the Employment Non-Discrimination Act was first introduced to Congress. It has been reintroduced in every subsequent congressional session. The bill would prohibit employers, employment agencies, and labor unions from using an individual's sexual orientation as the basis for employment decisions, including hiring, firing, promotion, or compensation and it would also protect people from discrimination based on sexual orientation (Human Rights Campaign, 2003a). In 2007, the bill passed the House of Representatives. This vote was the first time that either chamber of Congress had passed any kind of employment protection legislation related to sexual orientation.

With a Republican majority in Congress after the 1994 election, passage of gay civil rights in any form was unlikely. In fact, Congress moved to block LGBT rights. As a response to possible state legislation that might legalize gay marriages in Hawaii, the Congress passed the Defense of Marriage Act of 1996 (DOMA). This law does not actually ban gay marriages; rather it permits states to not recognize as legal such action by another state (Schmitt, 1996). Since then gay marriage has become the focus of both advocates and opponents of LGBT civil rights protections.

In an effort to understand the impact of DOMA, the General Accounting Office conducted a study to identify those federal laws in which benefits, rights, and privileges are only available to those who are legally married. The GAO found 1,049 federal laws in which marital status is a factor (GAO, 1997). This finding documented the extent of exclusion that not being allowed to marry presented to the LGBT community. It helped fuel the ongoing fight for civil rights, focusing on marriage as the key issue.

Legal recognition of same-sex relationships has been argued at local, state, and federal levels. With DOMA, the federal government has taken a stand. Because the federal government does not regulate marriage, states do, this was as far as Congress could go without amending the U.S. Constitution to cover marriage. Therefore, advocacy efforts have focused on state levels. For example, the state of Vermont legally recognized "civil unions" in 2000, and in 2004 the Massachusetts Supreme Court ruled that the state must legally permit same-sex marriage. In California the legalization of gay marriages was fought through executive actions, ballot initiatives, and numerous court cases. In 2008, the California Supreme Court ruled that it was unconstitutional (in regard to the state of California constitution) to prohibit same-sex couples from marrying (National Center for Lesbian Rights, 2008). The decision could not be appealed to the Supreme Court because the California Supreme Court has the final say on the California State Constitution. Following this ruling, organizers opposed to legalizing gay marriage placed an initiative on the November 2008 ballot that would overrule the California Supreme Court Decision. It passed, amending the state constitution to identify a marriage as only between a man and a woman. The State of California still legally recognizes domestic partner relationships, which provide some rights typically accompanied by marriage, but does not allow gay marriage. The publicity and cost of this issue has dominated many state elections. Gay marriage has been actively debated in the policy arena and will likely be revisited at the federal level in upcoming congressional sessions.

Although some states and local governments have passed policies that outlaw discrimination based on sexual orientation, federal protection of LGBT civil rights is still lacking. In addition, 433 of the Fortune 500 corporations have nondiscrimination policies that include sexual orientation and over half provide domestic partner benefits (Human Rights Campaign Foundation, 2008). Hundreds of city and county governments have nondiscrimination policies that include sexual orientation. Advocates for gay rights have included in their fight the protection of gender expression, which covers the transgender community. Many nondiscrimination policies have been amended to include this coverage. State and private actions represent progress toward ending discrimination based on sexual orientation and gender expression, but there is still more to be done to ensure equality.

NATIVE AMERICANS AND CIVIL RIGHTS

Recognition of the rights of Native Americans has been slow to occur in this country. The earliest European settlers were insensitive at best, and hostile at worst, to the rights and needs of the peoples who were already living in North America. The history of protected rights for Native Americans is replete with promises never kept and treaties broken. It is a history that spans more than 500 years.

Traditionally, the Native American populations lived under different cultural rules and had very different ways of life compared with the white settlers. These differences were deemed inferior by white European settlers. Race played a significant role in this viewpoint, because the superiority of white culture was already assumed based on relationships with other populations, particularly African slaves. The key to understanding the poor treatment of Native Americans by whites is knowledge of the cultural differences.

Native American tribes lived communally and regarded the land as belonging to all, people and animals alike. The idea of private ownership of land was foreign. White settlers, ignoring or misunderstanding these beliefs, assumed the superiority of their own system of land ownership and disdained the communality of tribal life. These differences, coupled with the driving colonial forces demanding that early settlers stake out land on behalf of their home country, created irreconcilable differences between whites and indigenous people. The colonists had come to America to stay, and they "had little use for Indians. The Indians were 'savages' (being hunters) and 'devil-worshippers' (not being Christians); they were nuisances who blocked the growth of this new English-speaking colonial world" (Nabakov,

1992, p. 20). Ethnocentric and racist attitudes dominated relations between settlers and Native Americans, and the consequences of these feelings remain today.

Prior to the widespread development of farms and ranches in the West, large-scale public policies concerning Native Americans did not exist. Early settlers drove tribes westward, and local treaties were used to contain tribes. Most public policies were handled through the Bureau of Indian Affairs, which dates back to 1824. The bureau was, and still is, under the Department of the Interior. It was created to provide a link between the federal government and American Indian tribes. The early role of the bureau was to assist in containment and control of tribes.

Accelerated westward expansion made it necessary for white settlers to gain lands occupied by Native Americans. These lands had already been promised to tribes in exchange for lands in the East. During the 1870s, an organized movement arose to contain American Indian tribes and control tribal ownership of land. In 1886, the Supreme Court ruled that American Indian tribes were "wards of the nation" dependent upon the United States (Nabakov, 1992). This clearly denied Native Americans sovereign rights and citizenship. In 1887, Congress enacted the Dawes Act, which limited to 160 acres the amount of land each head of a family could receive and pushed Native Americans to live on smaller and smaller plots of land (Jansson, 2009). These two pieces of public policy effectively contained and controlled all aspects of American Indian life.

Civil rights protection for Native Americans was largely ignored by public policy makers. In 1924, citizenship was granted to American Indians who had performed military service in World War I. In periods of social reform, such as the progressive era and the New Deal era, little was achieved in the way of guaranteeing rights for Native Americans. The Dawes Act had legalized ways for whites to acquire Indian land, and from 1887 to 1934, 90 million acres out of the original 140 million were transferred to whites (Day, 2006).

Although Native Americans fought in World War II, they still could not vote in many states. Their rights to own property were curtailed, and the Bureau of Indian Affairs handled all their economic, social, and educational affairs. Sovereignty, the right of self-determination, blossomed with the social reforms of the 1960s. Demonstrations including land takeovers, roadblocks, and armed defense brought to light the anger and resentment of the majority of Native American people. The most publicized event was the 1973 armed takeover of the town of Wounded Knee, South Dakota, by the American Indian Movement (AIM) (Nabakov, 1992). Using the media coverage and events that followed to publicize the historical treatment of Native Americans, the movement was able to tap into the social reform mood of the country.

Some gains have been made in the current status of Native American rights, but some deficiencies need to be addressed. All Native Americans are now U.S. citizens who can vote and own land; however, economic and social rights are still lacking. Poverty statistics on Native Americans are not regularly published by the Bureau of the Census, but local censuses done on reservations often find that most residents' incomes are below the poverty line. Tribal governments struggle to maintain sovereignty while also trying to find economic ways of integrating into the dominant American culture.

One of the most controversial issues today is gaming enterprises on Indian reservations. Sovereign rule allows tribal governments to open their land to gambling, but many worry that the social costs will be enormous. We can argue the merits of gambling and whether building casinos on tribal land is wise, but for some tribes the financial gain has been significant (Gerdes, et al. 1998). And unlike gaming under for-profit corporations as you might find in Las Vegas or Atlantic City, the Indian Gaming Regulatory Act of 1988 requires revenues from gaming to be used for tribal government operations, or to provide for the general welfare of tribal members, or promote tribal economic development (General Accounting Office, 1997). Indian gaming has grown, and by 2006 there were 423 gaming facilities run by 228 tribes in 28 different states with total revenues of almost $26 billion, which accounted for more than 700,000 jobs and almost $12 billion in federal, state, and local tax revenue (Meister, 2007). While gaming on tribal land is still controversial, the economic impact has been considerable and will likely result in expansion of the industry.

CIVIL RIGHTS AND IMMIGRATION

Another civil rights issue that has gained public attention is the rights of immigrants. Immigration has a long history in this country, with the vast majority of Americans tracing their roots to earlier generations of immigrants. At times we have glorified the idea of immigrants coming to this country with nothing and prospering. At other times we have regarded immigrants as taking jobs away from legal citizens and draining public social welfare services. However, research suggests otherwise:

> In contrast to public perception, immigrants do not increase unemployment by taking jobs held by Americans, nor do they drain increasingly scarce public revenues through [social] welfare programs. Quite the contrary—the evidence demonstrates that immigrants create more jobs than they take, and they contribute more in taxes than they consume in social program benefits. (Stoesz, 1996, p. 161)

Quantifying the impact of immigration is difficult and includes weighing the costs and benefits of numerous variables. The infusion of new groups of young workers can benefit the economy, especially if they are producing significant labor hours for low wages, but the long-term impact is difficult to assess (Congressional Budget Office, 2005). There can be increases in social welfare costs, as well as increased contributions to social programs such as social security.

Immigration, particularly undocumented or illegal, raises a number of issues related to civil rights. During the 1990s, in states with significant numbers of recent immigrants, particularly poor immigrants, negative public attitudes have come to the forefront. The focus of that negative attention has been on the legal status of immigrants. Poor economic conditions in Mexico and military hostilities in Central America during the 1980s and 1990s brought thousands of legal and illegal immigrants to this country. Large numbers of these immigrants settled in Border States such as California, Arizona, and Texas. Anti-immigrant sentiments have grown in these regions, and states have reacted through the policy arena. For example, in an effort to discourage immigrants from coming to this country, particularly illegal immigrants from Mexico and Central America, California voters in 1994 passed Proposition 187, which terminated public social services to illegal immigrants living in California. The services terminated included schooling for children, food assistance, and medical care. The legislation was immediately challenged through the court system. For several years the issue was being debated through the courts, with arguments against the legislation citing the civil rights of receiving public education and human services. With a change in the governor of California in 1998, the appeals process was dropped which effectively killed the measure. Proposition 187 was the beginning of numerous state attempts to limit services and resources for undocumented immigrants.

A federal law was also passed limiting public social welfare services for legal and illegal immigrants. The Personal Responsibility and Work Opportunity Reconciliation Act of 1996 bans legal immigrants from receiving Food Stamps and Social Security Insurance (SSI), and states have the option of banning Medicaid and Temporary Assistance for Needy Families (TANF) until they receive citizenship. Illegal immigrants are completely banned from these programs.

In recent years there have been numerous state initiatives to address the growing numbers of people who come to the United States either without any legal documentation or overstay visas. In Arizona, the Legal Arizona Workers Act took effect in 2008. This is the first state law to penalize businesses for knowingly hiring unauthorized immigrants. More on the economic and social impact of immigration legislation is discussed in Chapter 13.

Attention to immigration increased following the events of 9/11 and the finding that some of the terrorists had remained in this country after their visas had expired. Under the new Department of Homeland Security, illegal entry into the United States took on added significance and fell under anti-terrorism efforts. However, immigration advocates argue there are significant differences between the poor, young worker hoping to find better employment opportunities in America and a terrorist intent on destruction. America has always been a country of immigrants, so for those who want to make a better life for themselves, and for the businesses that hire immigrants, immigration advocates argue for humane legislation that will find a way to allow people the economic opportunities they seek without compromising American security.

Conflicting public attitudes toward immigrants reflect the contradictions between nativist tradition, which emphasizes "pure" Americans, and the reality that this is a country of people whose families came here from elsewhere. In fact, American employers rely on imported labor. Prosecution of employers who hire millions of undocumented people in this country will affect whole sectors of the U.S. economy. Recent cases of raids and arrests at meat-packing plants, retail stores, and factories raise issues of people's rights to a fair trial and defense representation, even if they are not documented. The American Civil Liberties Union has filed numerous cases against immigration authorities for dangerous and inhumane conditions in prisons used to hold undocumented workers and the backlog in conducting the civil hearings to determine people's status (ACLU, 2007). Congress has discussed the need for immigration legislation yet has not been able to come to any agreement. Therefore, issues involving immigration will continue to be debated in social welfare policy circles and will face the next Congress as a critical area needing federal intervention.

CONFLICTING VALUES AND BELIEFS

Values and beliefs strongly influence discussions of civil rights and social justice. The strongest belief influencing social justice and civil rights is whether we are comfortable with providing aid to strangers. When we know someone, we understand them and typically share characteristics with them. Strangers are foreign to us, and, hence, we are less likely to understand them. Even though we live in a country full of diversity, we do not necessarily come in contact with that diversity. Many of us live in neighborhoods and go to work or school with people like ourselves. So when we are asked to care about the needs of strangers, we are trying to understand people we do not know. Lack of understanding, experience, and knowledge are often the roots of prejudice and discrimination. The struggle for social justice hinges on fairness to all, regardless of how different they may seem based on race, ethnicity, gender, religion, sexual orientation, gender expression, ability, nationality, or age. In fact, our seeming diversity may be more of a social construction than a biological fact. People are genetically 99.9 percent exactly the same, according to the Human Genome Project, a major scientific collaborative project to map the biological composition of human beings (Weiss, 2001). For example, through advanced sequencing of the human genome, there is scientific evidence that racial groups are not genetically discrete. In spite of scientific research, racism rooted in the belief that there are biological racial differences resulting in superiority and inferiority between races is socially constructed, and therefore a very real social problem (Smedley & Smedley, 2005). If we can use social construction to create "differences," then we can also use social construction to form a just society with civil rights protections for all people.

FINAL THOUGHTS ON SOCIAL JUSTICE AND CIVIL RIGHTS

Until the 1960s, federal involvement was minimal in securing the rights of different population groups. State and local control dominated the political, social, and legal arenas. Local barriers such as poll taxes could be used to override the impact of federal efforts to provide voting rights for people. Political shifts that occurred during the 1960s changed the structure of government.

Two significant trends emerged during the 1960s (Melnick, 1994): (1) expansion of federal responsibilities for public well-being, and (2) increasing fragmentation of power at the national level. During the 1960s and 1970s, federal involvement in protection of people's civil and economic rights expanded greatly. The federal government took the leading role in securing civil rights for African Americans, began the War on Poverty, created new social welfare programs such as Medicare and Medicaid, expanded social insurance coverage and benefits, and took leadership roles in promoting gender equality and civil rights for people with disabilities.

At the same time that the federal role expanded, the power of federal agencies became more fragmented. The strength of political parties lessened, interest groups proliferated, presidents became less powerful, and Congress became more divided. To achieve the lofty goals of so many programs and policies aimed at opening opportunities for people, more and more federal agencies had to be created and developed.

The expansion of the federal role and the fragmentation of federal control were accompanied by an increase in federal spending for social welfare services. The increased spending allowed for greater federal control. Control was developed through the creation of federal regulations and stipulations that accompanied the receipt and use of federal monies. One of the outgrowths of this increased control was federal influence in the expansion of civil rights and public opportunities.

Affirmative action is an example of how federal government funding of state and local programs can influence the course of social welfare policy and civil rights. In order for any public or private organization to receive federal funds, each agency must have in place a policy of nondiscrimination and make concerted efforts at giving access to opportunities for groups who have historically been disadvantaged. Making efforts to open opportunities to groups who have historically been outside is the intent of affirmative action. Because the federal government provides funds contingent upon these efforts, organizations are forced to either follow the provisions or forfeit federal funding.

Although the expansion of federal legislation and enforcement has had the greatest impact on advancing civil rights in America, changes in the federal role could prove to diminish those protections. In recent years the goals of Congress have been to remove federal government sanctions from state and private concerns, as evidenced by DOMA. Efforts to give states more control and fewer federal restrictions could have the effect of lessening the protection of civil rights. If each state is free to decide whether to protect people's rights, we could see a return to the conditions that originally brought the federal government into the role of enforcer of civil rights. Historically, left to their own, most states have not acted as champions of civil rights. A handful of states have been proactive in guaranteeing civil rights, making social justice variable across the nation, which one could argue violates the premise of the Constitution. Voting rights, protection from discrimination and racism, access to legal abortions, affirmative action, and other personal rights were attained only through federal intervention. If more governing turns back to state rule, it may include a turning back of civil rights. Although some states have been at the forefront of civil rights struggles, equalizing treatment across the entire nation has only been accomplished through federal intervention.

Key Terms

civil rights

social justice

prejudice

discrimination

oppression

human rights

Bill of Rights

institutional racism

naturalization

hate crime laws

affirmative action

Equal Rights Amendment (ERA)

nondiscrimination

equality

Violence Against Women Act (VAWA)

Americans with Disabilities Act of 1990 (ADA)

Questions for Discussion

1. How are social justice and civil rights related? Can you have one without the other?
2. What are the differences between prejudice, discrimination, and oppression? How does one lead to the others?
3. Why do you think the right to vote was so difficult to achieve for certain groups in this country?
4. Do you believe we still need affirmative action policies in the United States? Why or why not?
5. What additional civil rights protections would you like to see? Why?

Excercises

1. Find out how to register to vote in your community. Identify all the necessary forms and document the steps one needs to take in order to register for the next election. Is it a simple process? Are there barriers you can identify that might make it difficult for some people to register? How might the process be improved?
2. Divide into small groups and choose a national civil rights group, such as the NAACP, NOW, the Anti-Defamation League, or the Human Rights Campaign, and find out if they have a local chapter. Visit the local office and ask for materials describing the group's mission and current efforts. Share and exchange the information in class. If there are no local civil rights groups, find information on the Internet.
3. Identify one social movement and find a book about it written by a person with first-hand experience. For example, *Parting the Waters* by Taylor Branch, which discusses the civil rights movement of the 1960s; *Stonewall* by Martin Duberman, which discusses the gay rights movement; and *No Pity* by Joseph Shapiro, which discusses the fight for rights for people with disabilities, are good examples. What can we learn from reading an experiential account of fighting for civil rights? What did you learn?
4. Find out if you have a local office of the Federal Immigration and Customs Enforcement agency (ICE). See whether you can visit the office and meet with a staff person. Ask about what the most pressing issue for the agency is in your community. What are the services and activities the agency performs in your community? Are these efforts different in your region of the country compared to other parts of the country? If so, how?

References

American Civil Liberties Union. (2007, January 24). *ACLU sues U.S. immigration officials and For-Profit Corrections Corporation over dangerous and inhumane housing of detainees* (press release). New York: Author.

Axinn, J., & Stern, M. J. (2008). *Social welfare: A history of the American response to need*, 7th ed. Boston: Allyn and Bacon.

Berrill, K. T. (1990). Anti-gay violence and victimization in the United States. *Journal of Interpersonal Violence* 5(3):274–294.

Biskupic, J. (1993). Argument without end. *The Washington Post National Weekly Edition* 10(14):10–11.

Boulding, E. (1992). *The underside of history*. Vol. 2. Newbury Park, CA: Sage Publications.

Boutilier, M., & SanGiovanni, L. (1983). *The sporting woman*. Champaign, IL: Human Kinetics Publishers.

Branch, T. (1988). *Parting the waters: America in the King years, 1954–63*. New York: Simon & Schuster.

Centers on Disease Control. (2008). *Morbidity and mortality weekly report, Volume 57*, pp. 113–117.

Cianciotto, J., & Cahill, S. (2003). *Education policy: Issues affecting lesbian, gay, bisexual, and transgender youth*. Washington, DC: National Gay and Lesbian Task Force Policy Institute.

Congressional Budget Office. (2005). *The role of immigrants in the U.S. Labor market*. Washington, DC: Congress of the United States.

Congressional Quarterly. (1988). Grove City bill enacted over Reagan's veto. *CQ Almanac* 44:63–68. Washington, DC: Author.

The Constitution of the United States. (1986). Washington, DC: BiCentennial Productions.

Day, P. J. (2006). *A new history of social welfare*, 5th ed. Boston: Allyn and Bacon.

Dye, T. R. (2008). *Understanding public policy*, 12th ed. Upper Saddle River, NJ: Pearson Prentice Hall.

Faludi, S. (1991). *Backlash: The undeclared war against American women*. New York: Crown Publishers.

Federal Bureau of Investigation. (2007). *Uniform crime report: Hate crime statistics, 2006*. Washington, DC: US Department of Justice.

Foner, N., & Fredrickson, G. M. (eds.). (2004). *Not just black and white: Historical and contemporary perspectives on immigration, race and ethnicity in the United States*. New York: Russell Sage Foundation.

Freeman, J. (1984). The women's liberation movement: Its origins, structure, activities, and ideas. In J. Freeman (ed.), *Women: A feminist perspective*, 3rd ed. pp. 543–556. Palo Alto, CA: Mayfield.

Gelb, J., & Palley, M. L. (1987). *Women and public policies*. Princeton, NJ: Princeton University Press.

General Accounting Office. (1997). *Defense of Marriage Act*. GAO/OGC-97-16. Washington, DC: Author.

General Accounting Office. (2000). *Gender equity: Men's and women's participation in higher education*. GAO-01-128. Washington, DC: Author.

Gerdes, K., Napoli, M., Pattea, C.M. & Segal, E.A. (1998). The impact of Indian gaming on economic development. *Journal of Poverty, volume 2*, number 4, pp. 17–30.

GLSEN (2006). *2005 National school climate survey*. New York: Gay, Lesbian and Straight Education Network.

Human Rights Campaign. (2003a). *Employment Non-Discrimination Act action alert*. Washington, DC: Author.

Human Rights Campaign. (2003b). *Hate crimes*. Washington, DC: Author.

Human Rights Campaign Foundation. (2008). *GLBT equality at the Fortune 500*. Washington, DC: Author.

Jacobson, G. C. (1987). *The politics of congressional elections*, 2nd ed. Boston: Little, Brown.

Jacoby, T. (2004). Borderline sanity on immigration enforcement. *Washington Post National Weekly Edition* 21(34):27.

Jansson, B. S. (2009). *The reluctant welfare state*, 6th ed. Belmont, CA: Brooks/Cole, Cengage Learning.

Jenness, V., & Gratett, R. (2001). *Making hate a crime: From social movement to law enforcement*. New York: Russell Sage Foundation.

Klein, E. (1984). *Gender politics*. Cambridge, MA: Harvard University Press.

Klein, V. (1984). The historical background. In J. Freeman (ed.), *Women: A feminist perspective*, 3rd ed. pp. 519–532. Palo Alto, CA: Mayfield.

Kuttner, R. (1996). Fair play for female athletes. *Washington Post National Weekly Edition* 13(14):5.

Mansbridge, J. J. (1990). Organizing for the ERA: Cracks in the facade of unity. In L. A. Tilly & P. Gurin (eds.), *Women, politics, and change*. New York: Russell Sage Foundation.

Massey, D. S., Durand, J., & Malone, N. J. (2003). *Beyond smoke and mirrors: Mexican immigration in an era of economic integration*. New York: Russell Sage Foundation.

Meister, A. (2007). *The state of Indian gaming*. Boston: Analysis Group, Economic, Financial and Strategy Consultants.

Melnick, R. S. (1994). *Between the lines: Interpreting welfare rights*. Washington, DC: Brookings Institution.

Morin, R., & Cottman, M. H. (2001). The invisible slap. *Washington Post National Weekly Edition* 18(36):6–7.

Nabokov, P. (ed.). (1992). *Native American testimony: A chronicle of Indian-white relations from prophecy to the present, 1492–1992*. New York: Penguin Books.

National Abortion Federation. (2008). *Violence and disruption statistics*. Washington, DC: Author.

National Center for Lesbian Rights. (2008). *Marriage for same-sex couples in California*. San Francisco: Author.

National Center on Workforce and Disability. (2002). *Basic facts: People with disabilities*. Boston: Author.

National Coalition for Women and Girls in Education. (2008). *Title IX at 35: Beyond the headlines*. Washington, DC: American Association of University Women.

National Women's Law Center. (2002). *The battle for gender equity in athletics: Title IX at thirty*. Washington, DC: Author.

Oleszek, W. J. (2007). *Congressional procedures and the policy process*, 7th ed. Washington, DC: Congressional Quarterly, Inc.

Pew Research Center. (2007). *Optimism about black progress declines: Blacks see growing values gaps between poor and middle class*. Washington, DC: Author.

Polenberg, R. (1980). *One nation divisible: Class, race, and ethnicity in the United States since 1938*. New York: Penguin Books.

Population Information Program. (1999). Ending violence against women. *Population Reports* XXVII(4).

Rennison, C. M. (2003). *Intimate partner violence, 1993–2001*. NCJ 197838. Washington, DC U.S. Department of Justice.

Rennison, C. M., & Welchans, S. (2000). *Intimate partner violence*. Washington, DC U.S.: Department of Justice.

Schmitt, E. (1996, September 11). Senators reject gay marriage bill and job-bias ban. *New York Times*, pp. A1, A11.

Smedley, A., & Smedley, B. D. (2005). Race as biology is fiction, racism as a social problem is real: Anthropological and historical perspectives on the social construction of race. *American Psychologist* 60(1):16–26.

Stoesz, D. (1996). *Small change: Domestic policy under the Clinton presidency*. White Plains, NY: Longman.

Tatum, B. D. (2007, October 1–7). Still no refuge: Fifty years after Little Rock, it's the same old story in Jena today. *The Washington Post National Weekly Edition* 24(50):26.

Taylor, W. L. (1995). Affirmative action: The questions to be asked. *Poverty & Race* 4(3):2–3.

Terpstra, J. (1984). Grove City: Dead end or detour? *Title IX Line* 4(3):2–4.

U.S. Census Bureau. (2007). *Facts: Americans with Disabilities Act*. Washington, DC: Author.

U.S. Department of Justice. (2000). *A guide for people with disabilities seeking employment*. Washington, DC: Author.

Weiss, R. (2001). Breaking the human code. *Washington Post National Weekly Edition* 18(17):6–7.

Wicker, T. (1992, August 30). The Democrats as the devil's disciples. *The New York Times*, p. E3.

Wilkins, R. (1995). Racism has its privileges. *Poverty & Race* 4(3):3–5.

Williams, A. J. (1991). *The alchemy of race and rights*. Cambridge, MA: Harvard University Press.

Wynter, L. E. (2002). *American skin: Pop culture, big business and the end of white America*. New York: Crown Books.

6 | ANALYZING AND RESEARCHING SOCIAL WELFARE POLICIES

Geoff Crimmins/Moscow-Pullman Daily News/AP Photo

Developing a working knowledge of the social welfare system includes learning how to analyze public policy. Social welfare policy analysis has often been thought of as the domain of political scientists, economists, or government officials. Social service professionals, however, bring a unique perspective to the critical analysis of social welfare policies: knowledge of the personal experiences of people who are affected by policies. All too often, policy decisions have been made on the basis of economic and political considerations, whereas the experiences of those directly affected by those decisions have been given little attention.

Even though social welfare policy analysis seems to belong to the domain of other disciplines, social work practitioners are often called upon to provide insight into programs and policies. Because social work is the delivery of social services, other professionals and the public often assume that practitioners can explain the purposes and rationales of social programs. For example, if a local zoning board is trying to decide whether to allow a children's group home to be placed in a residential neighborhood, board members might ask a social worker in the field of children's services to present testimony. The worker might explain the needs of today's youth and describe what is involved in establishing a group home. For workers to adequately explain the needs of clients, it becomes a *professional requirement* for workers to be capable of conducting some level of social welfare policy analysis (Gilbert, Specht, & Terrell, 1993).

To successfully analyze policy, we need to follow the policy process and access resources to help explain the background and content of those policies. This chapter presents theories concerning the development and implementation of public policy, approaches to policy analysis, models that can be used to analyze a social issue, and resources to help track the policy process. Examples of the models' application are also presented.

WHAT IS POLICY ANALYSIS?

In a general sense, social welfare policy analysis is investigation and inquiry into the causes and consequences of public policies (Dye, 2008). **Public policy** is the general term for decisions, laws, and regulations put forth by governing bodies. Typically, social welfare policy analysis is carried out to provide guidance and direction for policy makers (Dobelstein, 2003) and to supply solutions for social problems (Dunn, 1994). Information gained through analysis of public policies can be used to develop policy alternatives for the future, assess existing or previous policies, or explain public problems and social phenomena.

When workers prepare to debate public policy makers and participate in the development and assessment of policies, they need to be versed in social welfare policy analysis. Before discussing techniques of analysis, it is helpful to consider how public policy is created and put into operation.

THE DYNAMICS OF SOCIAL WELFARE POLICY DEVELOPMENT

As discussed previously, values and beliefs influence the content and structure of social welfare policy. Looking at values and beliefs does not, however, explain how policy actually is developed and put into place. Why did "welfare reform" become such an important issue in 1995? Why were Medicare and prescription drug coverage so important in 2003? Will homeland security, which became critical following the 9/11 terrorist attacks, continue to be an important public policy concern? How do social workers get policy makers to pay attention to issues that are important to them? A number of theories attempt to explain how social problems receive recognition and become the objects of debate and legislation. No one theory is clearly the best. When the theories are studied together, however, they provide a framework for analyzing the current social welfare system. They can also help practitioners to recognize opportunities for presenting positions and thereby to influence the policy decision-making process.

RATIONALISM IN POLICY MAKING

The most common assumption made by those who begin to study social welfare policy is that public policy represents the culmination of a rational evaluation of a social problem and all possible solutions. Closer examination shows that this is not the case. **Rational policy making** requires knowledge about values in all segments of society and about all possible alternatives, their consequences, and their costs and benefits. Needless to say, this knowledge is often hard to come by (Dye, 2008). Although rational policy making is the ideal, it is not realistic. Public policies reflect numerous values and competing interests. It is impossible to fully assess all values, alternatives, and consequences and adequately weigh their costs and benefits. Furthermore, rational policy analyses "often neglect the root causes of a problem" (Brewer & deLeon, 1983, p. 85). The more complex aspects of social conditions and structures that give rise to values are not explored. Also, most competing values cannot be weighed without some degree of bias entering into the equation.

Newcomers to government positions are often warned that the policy-making process does not work the way it may be described in a civics class. Policy making is usually messy, not logical or rational. Numerous factors interfere with rationality, such as competing values, interest groups with varying resources, lack of time to weigh all possibilities, and lack of adequate information. Instead, many forces influence the development and implementation of policies, and the influences vary at different times in history.

As discussed in Chapter 1, social issues arise from competing values that impede rationality. The legislative and social fight over abortion exemplifies how difficult rational policy making can be. When weighing the legislative options related to abortion, one must consider religious beliefs, social mores, civil rights issues, and personal needs of the mother, father, and fetus. All these factors complicate the policy-making process.

INCREMENTALISM IN POLICY MAKING

In 1959, Charles Lindblom published an article in which he attempted to explain how public policy is developed. He was responding to the prevailing theory that public policy decisions were made in a rational way, with policy makers considering all available options and then choosing the best course of action. In his article entitled "The Science of Muddling Through," he introduced the theory of **incrementalism**, which states that public policy is developed through small changes to existing policies.

The theory of incrementalism suggests that there is never enough time to consider all the information, that information on all possible choices is not readily available, and that it is easier to make small changes to existing policies than to create something entirely new. Often, great investments have been made in current programs, and it is extremely difficult to dislodge systems that have been in existence for a long time.

Consider the attempts to downsize the U.S. Defense Department. Immediately following the fall of the Berlin Wall in the late 1980s and the "end of the Cold War," proclamations were made about the anticipated savings from the newfound peace (often referred to as the peace dividend). Several years passed, and only small changes were made in the Defense Department. Attempting to close some military bases throughout the country caused tremendous political disagreement. The return to increased military involvement in recent years has reinforced the belief in incremental change: If the nation's military had been downsized, it might not have been ready for the increased U.S. military involvement overseas after the 9/11 attacks. The incremental approach allows for adaptation to occur over time.

The **Social Security Act** is another example of incrementalist policy making. It took 20 years of legislative activity before the act became law in 1935. Through incremental change, the program gradually expanded. Initially it was designed to provide income for workers after retirement and coverage for family members whose main breadwinner had died. In 1956, disability coverage was added. In 1965, health insurance was added through the Medicare program. In 1972, the Supplemental Security Income program was developed to consolidate and expand services for low-income seniors and low-income people with disabilities. In 1996, the control of the Aid to Families with Dependent Children (AFDC) program was shifted from the federal government to the state governments, and the program was changed to the Temporary Assistance for Needy Families (TANF) program. In 2003, the Medicare program was expanded to include prescription drug benefits. In addition to these major programs, hundreds of amendments have been passed and legislative changes made since passage of the Social Security Act 75 years ago.

WINDOW OF OPPORTUNITY IN POLICY MAKING

Most policies in today's social welfare system were being debated long before they actually became law. For example, the debate concerning national health insurance dates back more than 100 years. Also, when this country began to consider social insurance during the Great Depression, it was already in place in most Western European countries. It was not a new idea, but an idea whose time had come. Why? What makes an idea unacceptable at one time, and acceptable at another?

Kingdon (1984) refers to the timing of a public decision as the opening of a policy **window of opportunity**. Political and social events or a change in personnel can open the way for an opportunity, and advocates stand ready with their ideas. Policy windows do not stay open long. Events and personalities change, and public interest in a matter can be short-lived. The likelihood of an idea becoming policy relies on timing and a combination of other factors. Three elements must be present for success: a compelling public problem, a solution, and political support. When these three elements come together, an idea has a high likelihood of becoming policy.

During the 1930s, the three elements came together to culminate in the Social Security Act. The timing was right, as the Great Depression brought significant attention to economic hardship. The solution of social insurance had been debated by political leaders and advocates for years, and the change in presidential leadership from Herbert Hoover to Franklin Delano Roosevelt gave the idea political support both within government and from voters. Those who favored inclusion of medical care in the 1930s were not successful and had to wait for the window of opportunity to open again 30 years later when in 1965 Medicare and Medicaid were added. And those who favored prescription drug coverage as part of the medical care coverage had to wait almost 40 more years for it to be added in 2003. This demonstrates the short-lived nature of the policy window of opportunity.

Magnitude in Policy Making

Sometimes major events or crises prompt the creation of public policy. The **magnitude** of a social event comes into play, causing a policy to be made in response. This is a variation of the window of opportunity theory. The magnitude theory posits that the more dramatic the event, the more significant the policy response. The terrorist attack of 9/11 was the most powerful event to happen on American soil in decades. Its magnitude resulted in major policy shifts: An entirely new federal department, Homeland Security, was created; the agency head was made a member of the President's Cabinet; the Patriot Act was speedily passed, changing the way law enforcement operated; immigration laws were changed; and the federal government took over airport security, creating another new federal agency. The waging of war in Iraq was tied to this event as well. Policy makers continue to cite this event when making and changing social welfare policies. Magnitude theory posits that the greater the impact of the event, the greater the change in policy.

Critical Analysis of Social Welfare Policy

In Chapter 3, critical theory and critical analysis are discussed. **Critical theory** focuses on power: who has it and who does not, and the political, social, and economic outcomes of power imbalance. Applied to the analysis of policy development, critical theory suggests that social welfare policy is debated and developed in a context of power struggles. For example, the argument that social programs are expanded when poor people organize for change reflects the impact that a power imbalance may have. A tax cut that favors people with higher incomes who also have more access to politicians suggests that a policy has been affected by the imbalance of power or access. The relationship of power to the development of social welfare policy is demonstrated in the critical theory model described later in this chapter.

Social construction can help explain the differences in power and the impact on policy and therefore provides the larger paradigm in which to view critical analysis of social policy. Schneider and Ingram (2005) explain the relationship:

> … in the governance process, groups are identified and constructed as deserving and undeserving. These constructions (whether or not they already are part of popular culture) gain legitimacy. Differences become amplified, and, perhaps institutionalized into permanent lines of social, economic, and political cleavage (p. 3) … policy is the dynamic element through which governments anchor, legitimize, or change social constructions (p. 5).

Critical analysis of policy requires understanding the differences in power, and how those differences developed. Those with control have power to both create policies and define the characteristics of groups affected by the policy. This can be done to curtail people's rights, such as the institution of slavery against blacks, or to enhance people's rights, such as the abolition of slavery and desegregation. These policies defined group characteristics, changing over time from one position to another. The shift was achieved via social construction through public policies, reflecting power imbalances and fights for power based on race. Using critical theory as the basis for policy analysis can help explain the fights for social, political, and economic rights that have been a part of the social welfare arena since the founding of this nation.

IMPLEMENTATION OF POLICIES

What develops as a policy and what actually gets implemented as a program or service will often differ. **Implementation** of public policy is an evolutionary process, and policy changes when it is implemented (Pressman & Wildavsky, 1984). Early proposals for policies are seldom actually implemented. Politicians often reach a vague general consensus or write a complicated first draft because their many differing views must be satisfied. Those who devise the policy are not the same people responsible for actually putting the idea into practice. The process has room for different interpretations and values; especially in the social welfare arena. What makes political sense when passed by Congress, a state legislature, or a local board may not fit all communities or population groups. Therefore, it is important to understand the difference between what was planned through public policy and what actually happened. For example, planners of public housing struggling to develop economical and efficient ways to house low-income people did not intend that public housing complexes would become dangerous, uninhabitable places. Historical analysis reveals that poor planning, misjudged social events, and restricted funding resulted in a program very different from the one original planners had envisioned.

STREET-LEVEL BUREAUCRATS

Not all developments in public policy occur on the political policy-making level. Michael Lipsky (1980) focuses on what happens *after* policy is implemented. He describes the power that public service workers have in shaping policy. Service workers are described by Lipsky as **street-level bureaucrats**. They occupy the lowest levels of the social welfare system but exert a tremendous amount of control over how public policy is implemented.

Street-level bureaucrats have significant control over peoples' lives. They make decisions about which people get what, how quickly, and under what circumstances. Because of the bureaucratic nature of social service agencies, workers tend to have quite a bit of discretion and performance is difficult to measure. As long as certain regulations are followed, workers control interactions with clients. Policy makers and analysts must understand that what was designed as a general public policy may not be what is delivered. Part of the challenge for policy makers is to keep in mind the impact of street-level workers. Planners must try to foresee the role of those delivering the service; otherwise, implementation may alter the design of the intended policy.

Actions affecting policy can be as simple as how quickly applications are processed or whether phone calls are returned. For example, if workers in an employment placement and training office are understaffed and feel overburdened, they will not have sufficient time or energy to investigate job opportunities in the community. The support and information they can offer clients will be minimal. The intent of the policy, which is to place people in jobs, is compromised by the resources available for those assigned to carry it out. This brings into question the entire implementation process.

MODELS OF SOCIAL WELFARE POLICY ANALYSIS

Analysis of social welfare policy must involve more than one theory. The policy arena has diverse and numerous interests. The political scientist Aaron Wildavsky (1979) describes policy analysis as both an art and a craft. It requires creativity and technical skills. Many policy analysts posit models designed for assessing public policy. Some are prescriptive and culminate in suggested policy directions (Magill, 1986), whereas others provide explanation only (Dye, 2008; Gil, 1992). The purpose of this book is to explain social welfare policy and give direction for future proposals. Therefore, two models of social welfare policy analysis are presented: the sequential model and the critical theory model. These models are explained and illustrated with examples, and guidance for directives is given.

SEQUENTIAL MODEL OF ANALYSIS

Most analyses of social welfare policy have a linear flow. The sequential model is presented here to show the common flow of policy and for purposes of explanation. However, the creation and operation of social welfare policies are dynamic, and the process is best viewed as a whole. This model has multiple layers, reflecting the complexity of the system in which policy is formulated. Figure 6.1 outlines the model. Applying the model requires the use of numerous questions to analyze the evolution and application of social welfare policy. The accompanying list of questions in Table 6.1 will help the worker to structure his or her social welfare policy analysis.

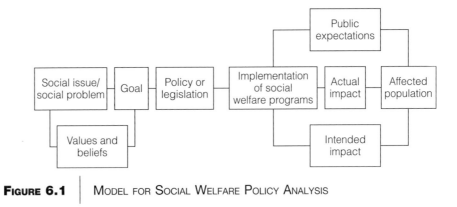

FIGURE 6.1 | MODEL FOR SOCIAL WELFARE POLICY ANALYSIS

SOCIAL PROBLEM:

What is the problem?

What are the definitions of the problem?

What is the extent of the problem?

Who defines this as a problem?

Who disagrees?

What are the conflicting social values and beliefs?

What are the underlying causes or factors?

GOAL:

What is the general goal?

Are there subgoals?

Do the subgoals conflict?

POLICIES, PUBLIC LAWS, OR ADMINISTRATIVE RULES:

What are the relevant public policies?

If there are no public policies, why?

What are the objectives of the policies?

Are there hidden agendas?

Who supports the policies?

Who opposes the policies?

IMPLEMENTATION OF SOCIAL WELFARE PROGRAMS:

What social programs are implemented as a result of the policies?

Are the programs effective?

What are the strengths and weaknesses?

Who is primarily served by the programs?

Who has oversight for the program?

ACTUAL IMPACT:

What are the costs and benefits?

Is the social problem changed?

If so, how?

Are there unintended results?

LEGISLATIVE INTENDED IMPACT:

What was supposed to be the result?

Who was supposed to be affected?

How was the social problem supposed to be changed?

PUBLIC EXPECTATIONS:

Did the social problem decrease?

Are things better now?

Who is satisfied with the outcome?

Who is dissatisfied with the outcome?

AFFECTED POPULATIONS:

Who is touched by the policy and programs?

Are there positive effects?

Are there negative effects?

TABLE 6.1 | QUESTIONS FOR SOCIAL WELFARE POLICY ANALYSIS

The first component of the model is investigation of the social issue or problem. A number of questions should be posed to clarify the issue. For example, what is the definition of the problem? Are there competing and conflicting definitions, or is there general agreement? What is the extent of the problem? Who is defining it as a social concern at this time, and why? Often, social conditions are viewed as a problem by some, but not all, members of society. An issue gains acceptance as a social concern when more and more people, social groups, and policy makers define it as a social problem. Although there may be strong agreement in general, specific values and ideological leanings color how the issue is viewed. For example, homelessness is recognized by many as a social problem, but people may define the problem differently. Some may define it as a problem of poverty; others as discomfort when they see people living on the street; and others as the lack of adequate treatment for people with mental illness.

If enough people agree that an issue warrants social concern and attention, then goals may begin to emerge. Goals for solving the problem may be formulated first. These general goals, when shared by enough people, can gain momentum and draw the attention of policy makers. At this stage, goals are further analyzed, and subgoals may emerge. The details of subgoals may diverge greatly. Using the issue of homelessness again, there may be general agreement that the goal is to end homelessness. If it is viewed as a problem of poverty, subgoals may be to increase employment or public assistance. If it is viewed as individuals living on the streets, publicly mandating stays in shelters could be the means for achieving the goal. If it is viewed as an issue of mental illness, community centers for treatment may be needed. Needless to say, these are different approaches to the goal of ending homelessness.

Although the entire policy process is influenced by values and beliefs, this is particularly true at the stage of identifying and defining social problems and setting goals. Social values and divergent views are played out in the policy-making process. Public policy makers are charged with making policies or legislation to carry out social goals. They are individuals with their own value and belief systems, but at the same time they occupy public positions in which they try to carry out the wishes of citizens and groups who elect or appoint them. Conflict in values and beliefs is frequently the reason why social welfare policy is difficult to develop. Social welfare policies that are passed usually include compromises and have numerous pieces that do not fit together. Most major public policy programs are not exactly what any one person wants but instead have something for a lot of different people. Gaining the consensus of so many different interests often creates vague legislation or policies that are lengthy and complicated.

Assuming that a social issue gains enough attention to warrant public concern and development of a policy, the policy must then be implemented. Program implementation, which is first outlined broadly through public policy, is usually developed in detail within the agencies assigned management responsibility. During the implementation process, the programs authorized by the policies are likely to change. The programs actually implemented often do not look like what the planners and advocates envisioned. Social programs "frequently approach the problems they are meant to solve from an oblique angle, and provide only partial solutions. Valid and realistic standards for judging them are critically lacking. Implemented in an environment charged with emotional and political disagreement and subject to a number of uncontrollable variables, the programs defy careful and systematic evaluation" (Levitan & Wurzburg, 1979, p. 9).

There are occasions when a social welfare policy is passed but not implemented. In such cases, funding and economics may play a part. A policy plan may be endorsed, but when it comes time to fund the effort there is little or no money allocated. The creation of social welfare policy may not be matched by economic commitment. Politics can also play a part. A majority vote may pass a policy, but there may not be a strong enough consensus to actually carry through on the implementation or development of programs. Timing also plays a role. For example, a Democratic Congress may pass legislation to be enacted, but before the process can begin, there is a change in leadership and a new Republican majority forms. The new majority may have different priorities and neglect to develop or implement the policies of the previous majority. Such was the case after the 1994 election. The Congress of 1992 had been controlled by Democrats. Programs enacted had not received funding by the time the next Congress, controlled by Republicans, took office in 1995. It is important to remember that passage of a public policy does not guarantee implementation.

Comprehensive policy analysis also includes consideration of the results of implementation. Once a program is implemented, some impact is made. A complete social welfare policy analysis examines three areas of impact: the intended impact, the actual impact, and a follow-up impact on those who have been affected by the policy and its subsequent programs. It may seem clear at first who will be affected by a program, but over time analysts may see that those actually affected are not those who were intended to be affected. For example, the deinstitutionalization of people with mental illness that occurred during the 1970s initially appeared to concern only those released from institutions and their families. Over time, however, the impact has been much greater. Community services were not adequate to care for persons who were deinstitutionalized, and social services were hard pressed to fill the void. Many people with mental illness were left without services and without a residence, further increasing the number of homeless people. Other instances of the unintended consequences of social welfare policy can be found throughout our social welfare system. Let us look at another example to emphasize this point.

Analysis of the high cost of medical care suggests that the expense may be an unintended outcome of public policy. When the federal government introduced Medicare in 1965, it became a funder of medical services. The initial structure of the program allowed medical providers, such as doctors and hospitals, to set the fee for service. The government would then reimburse the providers for services rendered. Prices set by medical providers increased dramatically during the 1970s. Therefore, by 1983, the federal government passed legislation to regulate reimbursement. Some medical providers felt that the reimbursement was not enough and began to charge higher prices, which had the unintended consequence of implying that more expensive services were better services. Also, providers of new health care procedures and technologies were frequently not covered immediately under government reimbursements. Private individuals with financial means were able to pay higher prices for new services, as were many private insurers. Over time, the public demanded access to these new and "better" services, so the government expanded coverage and increased reimbursements. The cycle of expanding reimbursement and limiting reimbursement continued, and the goal of cost containment for medical services has not been realized. One of the unintended impacts of public health care policies has been an inability to halt the escalating costs of medical services.

Ideally, if a social welfare policy is well conceived, it will be passed and implemented and the actual impact will reflect the goal. If the outcomes are vastly different than the goal, then one may conclude that the policy or its implementation, or both, were flawed. Such assessment of social programs is the primary purpose of policy analysis for social service practitioners.

Public expectations play a key role as well. Often new legislation is enacted with a great deal of public attention and political fanfare. The signing of major legislation is often done with media coverage. This publicity leads people to believe that the problem is being addressed and will be "solved." The level of public expectation can lead to disappointment and even backlash when a social problem does not improve. Public awareness and an open policy process are important. When a social problem does not improve, however, negative perceptions of the ability of public policy and policy makers to improve social welfare can result. One of the challenges is not raising public expectations too high but at the same time citing the positive impact hoped for by enactment of the new law.

CRITICAL THEORY MODEL OF ANALYSIS

When analyzing a social problem, one may find that no social policy exists to address it. For example, as discussed before, AIDS was documented as a serious infectious disease throughout the 1980s but there was no federal legislation to address the issue until 1990. As mentioned in Chapter 1, the absence of legislation is a form of public policy. In such instances, it is important to analyze why there has not been any public policy. Are those most directly affected by the social issue powerless or disenfranchised? Is there a lack of consensus about whether an issue is worthy of social concern and public policy? Are conflicting values keeping the issue from the agenda of policy makers? To understand the impact of power imbalances on the development of social welfare policy, an alternative model for analysis is offered. This model serves particularly well when one analyzes a social problem that has not received any major public policy response.

The **critical theory model** is also useful in analyzing who is making policy decisions, who benefits, and who does not benefit. This model considers power and whether race, ethnicity, gender, class, sexual orientation, ability, or other characteristics play a part in the identification of a social issue. This model questions whether these characteristics affect the process of development and implementation. Those with power are viewed as exercising tremendous influence over the social constructions that permeate public policies. Therefore, in order to understand the historical development of policy responses to social issues, it is important to understand the views held by those with power and the way those views shape our culture and our social welfare policies and programs. Figure 6.2 outlines the model. There are also questions that help to apply the model (see Table 6.2).

THE IMPACT OF VALUES AND BELIEFS ON SOCIAL WELFARE POLICY

Values and beliefs constantly affect the entire policy-making process. Both models presented are affected by the values and beliefs of constituents, legislators, regulators, service providers, and recipients. All of the conflicting beliefs outlined in Chapter 1 play a role in the development and implementation of social welfare policy. For example, if one believes in individual responsibility over social responsibility, one will be more likely to oppose government-sponsored social welfare programs. The belief in individual responsibility is often supported by beliefs in self-sufficiency rather than social support and in individual change rather than social change.

Disagreements over policy often rest on disagreements over beliefs. Although it would be better for policy makers to debate underlying beliefs than to fight over the details of each policy, beliefs are personal convictions and as such are difficult to debate. Identifying conflicting beliefs and putting aside one's own beliefs can be the most challenging part of social welfare policy analysis.

SOCIAL WELFARE POLICY AND THE POLITICAL ARENA

Although social welfare policy reflects public input and the values and beliefs of the majority, the political process plays a crucial role. Most public policies are debated and subsequently developed in the political arena. Several key factors come into play when social welfare policy and politics are mixed. The political actors—the president, elected officials, and appointed personnel—and the political environment—timing of elections, interest groups, and lobbying efforts—are important. It is important to consider the actors as well as the social, political, and economic context in order to fully analyze a given policy. It is also important to consider belief systems. Who supports public policy intervention? Who supported it in the past? Who opposes public policy intervention? Who did so in the past? What are

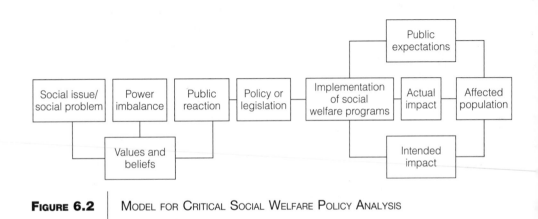

FIGURE 6.2 | MODEL FOR CRITICAL SOCIAL WELFARE POLICY ANALYSIS

SOCIAL PROBLEM:

What is the problem?

What are the definitions of the problem?

What is the extent of the problem?

Who defines this as a problem?

Who disagrees?

What are the conflicting social values and beliefs?

What are the underlying causes or factors?

Who are the groups affected by this problem, and do they belong to a particular race, ethnicity, gender, class, age, ability, sexual orientation, or other special group?

POWER IMBALANCE OR STRUGGLE:

Who loses from this social problem?

Who gains from this social problem?

Who opposes it? Who supports it?

Does race, ethnicity, gender, class, age, ability, sexual orientation, or any other personal attribute play a role in this issue?

Who seems to have power and who does not?

PUBLIC REACTION:

What do voters think?

What do people think who do not typically vote?

What do people with higher incomes think?

What do people with lower incomes think?

How is the media covering and portraying this issue?

What values and beliefs are important?

Whose values and beliefs are dominant?

Whose values and beliefs are minimal?

POLICIES, PUBLIC LAWS, OR ADMINISTRATIVE RULES:

What are relevant public policies?

If there are no public policies, why not?

What are the objectives of the policies?

Are there hidden agendas?

Who supports the policies?

Who opposes the policies?

Who has spoken out in favor of the policies?

Who has spoken out against the policies?

Does race, ethnicity, gender, class, age, ability, sexual orientation, or any other personal attribute seem significant in these policies?

IMPLEMENTATION OF SOCIAL WELFARE PROGRAMS:

Which social programs have been implemented as a result of the policies?

Are the programs effective?

What are the strengths and weaknesses?

Who is primarily served by the programs?

Who has oversight for the programs?

Is there a disproportionate involvement of any one group based on race, ethnicity, gender, class, age, ability, sexual orientation, or any other personal attribute?

ACTUAL IMPACT:

What are the costs and benefits?

Is the social problem changed?

If so, how?

Are there unintended results?

LEGISLATIVE-INTENDED IMPACT:

What was supposed to be the result?

Who was supposed to be affected?

How was the social problem supposed to be changed?

PUBLIC EXPECTATIONS:

Did the social problem decrease?

Are things better now?

Who is satisfied with the outcome?

Who is dissatisfied with the outcome?

AFFECTED POPULATIONS:

Who is touched by the policy and programs?

Are there positive effects?

Are there negative effects?

Are those affected disproportionately from a particular population?

TABLE 6.2 | QUESTIONS FOR A CRITICAL MODEL FOR SOCIAL WELFARE POLICY ANALYSIS

their values? How important is the timing of events? Is it during a campaign year? Is it late in a congressional cycle? Is it a time of recession or a period of economic expansion? These questions all become part of a full social welfare policy analysis.

THE DYNAMICS OF SOCIAL WELFARE POLICY: APPLICATION OF THE MODEL

Social welfare policies exist at all levels of government as well as within social service settings. Social service providers are confronted by social welfare policies in their work all the time. Not all policies originate at the federal level, but they usually flow from the macro to the micro level.

Typically, the federal government passes legislation that either mandates rules and regulations or offers funding that has attached requirements. State governments then are either required to follow those mandates or choose to apply for funds and agree to abide by certain rules if those funds are granted. State governments replay the federal role with local governments and communities who provide services. The local government is most likely to actually implement the programs and directives of federal social welfare policies. Social service agencies, workers, and clients are those most closely involved with the application and impact of policies.

SEQUENTIAL MODEL APPLIED—WELFARE REFORM

In this section there is an example of the policy analysis model applied to a piece of social welfare legislation (see Figure 6.3). In 1996, Congress created the Temporary Assistance for Needy Families (TANF) program as part of the Personal Responsibility and Work Opportunity Reconciliation Act (P.L. 104-93) to replace the public assistance program Aid to Families with Dependent Children (AFDC). One of the many legislated changes required all TANF adults to begin working within two years. Furthermore, 50 percent of TANF recipients had to immediately become involved in work-related activities for 30 hours per week. This change differed from previous legislation by requiring all adults with children, regardless of how young those children may be, to work or attend employment training programs. There are numerous aspects to this policy that could be analyzed. Chapter 8 provides more details of the TANF program. For this analysis, we will focus on a key aspect of the TANF program, the expectation for all adults to become employed, even if they are the single head of the household with young children. Required employment means child care is very important.

Figure 6.4 demonstrates how this social welfare policy change created a chain of events affecting local communities, workers, and clients. The changes made in the legislation meant that more adults with small children would be out of the home to participate in work-related activities. It also meant that those participants would need additional child care. However, in the years following enactment, states did not receive sufficient federal or state money to increase the supply of child care. Although caseloads went down at first, as the impact of the recession of 2001 hit those on public assistance, the need for child care increased. Because of reduced state revenues and no increase in federal support, states reduced the

SOCIAL PROBLEM: PUBLIC ASSISTANCE DEPENDENCY

The belief and perception that too many able-bodied adults are not working to support themselves and their families.

Values of individual responsibility and work ethic are key.

Belief by majority that the cost for public assistance is too great.

GOAL: ECONOMIC SELF-SUFFICIENCY

Subgoals vary from a genuine desire to help the poor become self-sufficient to dislike of those who are poor and not wanting to be responsible for the economic well-being of others.

Conflict between subgoals.

POLICY/LEGISLATION: PUBLIC LAW 104-93

TEMPORARY ASSISTANCE FOR NEEDY FAMILIES

Increase the number of adults who must participate in work-related activities.

IMPLEMENTATION:

Programs to prepare adult recipients for work and decrease the number of people on the welfare rolls.

ACTUAL IMPACT:

Lack of sufficient child care assistance to meet increased need.

Lack of adequate entry-level jobs to lift a family to economic self-sufficiency so there is no child care need.

LEGISLATIVE-INTENDED IMPACT:

Self-sufficiency for public assistance recipients through employment.

Dollar savings from decrease in public assistance funding.

PUBLIC EXPECTATIONS:

Problem of welfare dependency will be solved.

All able-bodied adults will be employed.

AFFECTED POPULATIONS:

TANF recipients

Employment training providers

State budgets

Taxpayers

Existing child care systems

FIGURE 6.3 | EXAMPLE OF SEQUENTIAL SOCIAL WELFARE POLICY ANALYSIS: TEMPORARY ASSISTANCE FOR NEEDY FAMILIES PROGRAM

availability of child care assistance during the early 2000s (General Accounting Office, 2003). By 2004, only one of every seven eligible children actually received child care assistance (Mezey et al., 2004). The lack of adequate funding continued. TANF dollars for child care assistance declined by 21 percent from 2000–2006, leaving 17 states with waiting lists for child care assistance applicants in 2007 (National Women's Law Center, 2007).

Child care is critical to the success of welfare reform. However, funding has not been sufficient to accompany need in the TANF program. The result is that women on public assistance must either find unsuitable child care arrangements while they fulfill the 30-hour requirement or risk being expelled from the program for noncompliance. Policy makers fulfilled their political promise to ease reliance on public assistance and promote employment, but the actual result has been quite different. There has been a strain on state budgets and child care has been insufficient. Most of the people who left TANF for employment are not better off

FEDERAL LEGISLATION:

"Welfare reform" through mandatory enrollment in work-related activities for 30 hours per week.

STATE:

Need to provide state funding for child care assistance for TANF recipients.

COMMUNITY:

Increased demand for child care services.

AGENCY:

Greater demand for provision of support services, particularly child care.

Possibility that people would be terminated from TANF if they failed to comply with work activities requirement.

WORKER:

Greater service demand and caseload. More rules and regulations to consider. Requirements to sanction recipients for noncompliance adds tension to worker-client relationship.

CLIENT:

Tighter requirements and possible sanctions for not participating. Promise of greater economic opportunity. However, if community cannot respond with child care assistance, frustration and anger with new requirements and what may appear to be decrease in services. Ultimate possibility, sanction and removal from TANF program.

FIGURE 6.4 | FLOW OF IMPACT OF THE TEMPORARY ASSISTANCE FOR NEEDY FAMILIES PROGRAM

---

financially. Chapter 8 provides greater detail on the policy struggle to reform public assistance programs and the outcome of changes in TANF.

The mix of public expectations for change and the reality of the policy outcome most directly affect the recipients themselves. When policy makers and the public perceive that they have taken action to correct a social problem and it is not solved, attention often focuses on the recipients. The public asks why they are still in need of income support. Because so much of our value system rests on the individual, the public perception is that people in need must have done something "wrong." Individual responsibility is elevated over social responsibility and, hence, personal failure over system failure.

CRITICAL ANALYSIS MODEL APPLIED—WELFARE REFORM

A second example that uses the critical theory model demonstrates the perspective that power imbalances can play on the development and implementation of social welfare policy (see Figure 6.5). Much of the analysis is the same as in the prior example. However, the critical analysis model stresses the impact of power imbalances and diversity. In terms of welfare reform, there is a vivid split between those who are making policy and those who are directly affected by the policy. Most policy makers are affluent white men and most TANF recipients are poor single women of color who are heads of households. Analysis of welfare reform debates revealed the disparities between those with the power to make decisions and those for whom the policy was devised (Segal & Kilty, 2003). The membership of Congress behind the development of TANF in 1996 demonstrates the power and

SOCIAL PROBLEM: PUBLIC ASSISTANCE DEPENDENCY

The belief and perception that too many able-bodied adults are not working to support themselves and their families.

Values of individual responsibility and work ethic are key.

Belief by majority that the cost for public assistance is too great.

POWER IMBALANCE:

Policy makers are all employed in powerful political positions. People directly affected by the policy are low-income families, primarily headed by single women.

Policy makers are disproportionately white males, and program recipients are disproportionately women of color.

PUBLIC REACTION:

Voters are tired of welfare problem.

Media highlights dependency and problems with not working.

Public opinion is to help people but not foster dependency.

POLICY/LEGISLATION: PUBLIC LAW 104-93

TEMPORARY ASSISTANCE FOR NEEDY FAMILIES

Increase the number of adults who must participate in work-related activities.

IMPLEMENTATION:

Programs to prepare adult recipients for work and decrease the number of people on the welfare rolls.

Almost all adult recipients are poor women heads of household, so program is primarily targeted to these families.

ACTUAL IMPACT:

Lack of sufficient child care assistance to meet increased need.

Lack of adequate entry-level jobs to lift a family to economic self-sufficiency so there is no child care need.

Employment opportunities for women tend to be low-paying jobs without health insurance or benefits.

LEGISLATIVE-INTENDED IMPACT:

Self-sufficiency for public assistance recipients through employment.

Dollar savings from decrease in public assistance funding.

PUBLIC EXPECTATIONS:

Problem of welfare dependency will be solved.

All able-bodied adults will be employed.

AFFECTED POPULATIONS:

TANF recipients, predominantly poor women of color and their children

Employment training providers

State budgets

Taxpayers, most of who are employed

Existing child care systems

FIGURE 6.5 | EXAMPLE OF CRITICAL SOCIAL WELFARE POLICY ANALYSIS: TEMPORARY ASSISTANCE FOR NEEDY FAMILIES PROGRAM

resource differences between the policymakers and the group affected most by the policy. Congress at the time of passage of welfare reform was 86 percent male, with an average age of 55 years, 87 percent white, with 93 percent educated beyond high school and almost 30 percent of whom were millionaires. TANF recipients were 90 percent female, with an average age of 31 years, 32 percent white, with only 3 percent educated beyond high school and 100 percent of whom were in poverty before receipt of TANF. Critical analysis examines the vastly different characteristics of those making the policy compared to those targeted by the policy—in the case of TANF we see that older, educated, wealthy white men decided what was the best public policy for young, uneducated, poor women of color. Application of the critical model illuminates the differences that often exist between those making decisions and those affected by decisions.

Underlying these policies are social constructions that both influence the policy and are in turn influenced by the policy. In the case of TANF, much of what prompted the efforts to reform welfare was the claim that welfare promoted dependency and a lack of commitment to work. Single female-headed families with lots of children were staying on welfare forever. This dependency was costing large amounts of tax dollars. Implicit in this view was the distinction that welfare recipients were not deserving because they were not participating positively in the economy. This belief guided the changes in welfare and the replacement of AFDC with TANF. However, data on the make-up of welfare recipients showed a different reality (Office of Human Services Policy, 1998). Before the changes in 1996, AFDC caseloads were relatively constant for 25 years. Fluctuations reflected national economic conditions with increases during recessions and times of increased unemployment and declines during times of economic growth and higher employment. In fact, over the three years prior to enactment of welfare reform in 1996, the total number of families receiving AFDC had been declining, falling almost 13 percent. The effort toward economic security was focused on the employment of adult recipients. What was never clearly articulated was that almost 70 percent of AFDC recipients were children, on average a little less than 2 per family, and 1 out of 5 cases included no adult recipient, they were children-only cases. Family size of cases had been dropping steadily since the 1960s, declining from an average of 4 recipients per case in 1963 to 2.8 recipients in 1996. Also, the children on AFDC were young. During this period, the median age of children dropped as well, from 8.5 years of age to 7 years of age. Over the 20 years prior to reform, the racial distribution remained constant, with a very slight drop from 37 percent to 36 percent white parents. Even the costs had dropped. From 1990 to 1996, real average benefits per family declined by 17 percent, and real average benefits declined by 20 percent. Total federal expenses for AFDC accounted for less than 1 percent of the federal budget in 1996 (author calculations from Office of Management and Budget, 2008). Twelve percent of female heads of AFDC households worked and almost 80 percent of AFDC families were recipients for five years or less, more than 50 percent for two years or less.

The data provide an interesting picture of welfare prior to the political outcry for welfare reform. Most welfare recipients were young children living in single-headed households with mothers who had very little education, worked some, and overall stayed on welfare for a few years. Public expenses and caseloads for AFDC had been declining. Yet the public image was very different. Instead, the perception was of single women with lots of children spending decades on the public dole, costing more and more public dollars. The difference between the actual data and the public image was in part due to social construction and the influence of those in power to entrench those perceptions through new policy, the welfare reform legislation of 1996. Critical policy analysis reveals this impact.

Although much of social welfare legislation is national and passed through Congress, the impact ultimately can be personal and local, as shown by the previous examples. This is typical of the flow of public policy. Federal government mandates start a chain of events that ultimately affects individuals on a personal level. Although states accept federal mandates or funds, community agencies often provide actual services, involving social service workers and their clients. These examples demonstrate how national decisions affect all levels of social services (see Box 6.1).

SOCIAL WELFARE POLICY RESEARCH

The best way to stay informed about social welfare policy is to follow current events and track public policy resources. This means developing skills in policy research. Social welfare policy analysis is one form of policy research. Because there is tremendous overlap, research and analysis are often regarded as the same process. Although the terms are used interchangeably, social welfare policy analysis can be described as more theoretical, whereas social welfare policy research is more applied. Social welfare policy research uses analysis "to provide policy-makers with pragmatic, action-oriented recommendations for alleviating the problem" (Majchrzak, 1984, p. 13). It is a catchall term for the gathering and processing of information that influences the making of public policy (Haas & Springer, 1998). Policy research informs policy analysis. Good policy analysis demands up-to-date and accurate information. Therefore, it is valuable to discuss how to conduct policy research and some of the best resources that are available.

BOX 6.1 | **CONTROVERSIAL PERSPECTIVES...**

Can we really analyze public policy?

Public policies that are meant to respond to social needs are, because of the nature of human concerns, constantly shifting and subject to varying values and beliefs. Can we really analyze all the variables related to public policy? Consider analyzing the newest presidential cabinet–level agency, the Department of Homeland Security. Born out of the events of 9/11, the department's main function is to respond to international terrorism. However, the agency is also responsible for immigration, a major concern of southwestern states that border Mexico. There was little publicity about this responsibility before passage of the legislation creating the department. In addition to these different yet related concerns, the department also took on the function of dealing with domestic disasters; the Federal Emergency Management Agency (FEMA) became part of the department. FEMA was caught unprepared for the devastating flooding caused by the aftermath of hurricane Katrina in New Orleans in 2005.

Can policy analysts adequately assess a public policy that is as far-reaching as the creation and implementation of the Department of Homeland Security, or can they only react to events after they occur? Clearly, the position of this book is that analysis *can* inform policy makers. The bigger question is whether analyses are heeded by those with the power to make policies.

The techniques for conducting social welfare policy research follow the general process of gathering relevant reliable information to inform decision making. However, information that is most helpful for policy research can be difficult to find if one is not familiar with policy-related sources. There are several categories under which policy sources can be found. With the Internet, sources are easily accessed and consequently policy research has become easier to do. There is a comprehensive list of sources at the end of the chapter, many of which are referenced in the following sections.

DATA AND STATISTICS SOURCES

Policy makers are very concerned about the extent of a problem. Is there a great enough need to direct precious spending on the problem? How many people are affected? Having data that can document the need or extent of a social problem is very important. The best national source is the *Statistical Abstract of the United States*. Published annually by the U.S. Census Bureau since 1878, it is a compilation of statistics from government and private sources. There are 30 sections, including topics such as population, health, education, law enforcement, elections, employment, social insurance, and human services. Each section includes numerous tables of data. Each table has the source or sources listed at the bottom, often with web site addresses so you can go to the original source and get more details.

The *Statistical Abstract* is an excellent place to start any policy research to view background data. The entire book is also available online through the Census Bureau web site. If you are not familiar with the book, it can be difficult to use online as there are more than 1,300 tables with data. Most libraries have hard copies as part of their reference materials and a copy can be easily purchased through the Census Bureau or the Government Printing Office.

Many states have their own versions of statistical abstracts, although they are often not kept up annually. For example, the state of California offers its statistical abstract through the state Department of Finance. In 2008 they discontinued printing hard copies and it is only available online. Most states now offer statistical information only online. A guide to state statistical abstracts can be found in the appendix of the *Statistical Abstract of the United States*.

An excellent source for data on health, injuries, morbidity, and mortality is the Centers for Disease Control and Prevention. This federal agency tracks all the statistics related to health and epidemiology in the United States. It includes information on best health practices and leading issues related to health in America. Each year it publishes the National Health Report, which is in hard copy and available online. The book is titled *Health, United States, with Chartbook on Trends in the Health of Americans*. It too is large, with almost 600 pages and hundreds of tables with data, all indexed. Much of the data from the CDC is reprinted in the *Statistical Abstract*, but the National Health Report provides additional information and more detailed data related to health in the United States.

The U.S. Census Bureau provides data on states and localities based on the decennial census. The Constitution mandates that a census be taken every ten years. The data gathered on the population are used to determine voting apportionments and for government funding, and are used by states and localities as well. The breakdown of data is from the national to the local levels. The data are now so user-friendly that one can access data by Zip Code, all very quickly online. To find local community data, go to the U.S. Census Bureau home page (www.census.gov) and go to American Community Survey. This section will have the **American FactFinder** and you can type in any Zip Code to get data about the community (http://factfinder.census.gov). You can even see the data mapped onto the community. Again, much of the general data are reprinted in the *Statistical Abstract*. However, there are many other collections of data organized by the Census Bureau and identifying data by local communities can be done through the web site. With advances in technology, the information is continually growing and becoming more accessible for use. For policy research, it is helpful to spend some time visiting the U.S. Census Bureau web site to become familiar with the breadth and depth of data available.

GOVERNMENT AGENCIES

Every government agency keeps track of information and data relevant to its domain. The agencies also track legislation and the policies and programs that fall under their purview. If you are looking for information and data on a specific topic, you should determine the agencies most likely to be involved in policies and programs related to your topic. For example, if you are looking at an issue related to health care, you might want to visit the web site of the federal Department of Health and Human Services. From there you can be more specific as there are numerous divisions that might fit for your research topic. Box 6.2 provides a list of the major agencies within the Department of Health and Human Services.

Information on social welfare programs that fall under the auspices of the agency or division can be found through that department. For example, if you wanted information on the TANF program, you would find it under the Administration for Children and Families, which is responsible for the management of the program at the federal level. You may need to do some research on the federal agency responsible for a program so you can find the relevant information. The Food Stamp program is a vital source of support for low-income people and therefore one might think it would be found with other programs related to income support. However, the Food Stamp program falls under the authority of the Department of Agriculture and can be found under that department's information.

| BOX 6.2 | MORE ABOUT THE DEPARTMENT OF HEALTH AND HUMAN SERVICES |

Major Agencies under the Department of Health and Human Services

Administration for Children and Families (ACF)
Administration on Aging (AoA)
Centers for Medicare and Medicaid Services (CMS)
Centers for Disease Control and Prevention (CDC)

Food and Drug Administration (FDA)
Indian Health Services (IHS)
National Institute of Health (NIH)
Substance Abuse and Mental Health Services Administration (SAMHSA)

Therefore it is necessary to establish the authority for any social welfare programs being studied and examine relevant information through that agency. Under each federal department are numerous major agencies, all with their own web sites, research, and data. Each agency will also track relevant legislation and social programs. Information on the policies and programs relevant to the agency can be found through their web sites.

GOVERNMENT RESEARCH SOURCES

In addition to government agencies, there are government research centers dedicated to conducting policy research to inform policy makers. Much of the information is available to the public. The most significant agencies are the U.S. Government Accountability Office (GAO), the Congressional Budget Office (CBO), and the Congressional Research Service (CRS). These three agencies provide detailed information on government policies and programs. The GAO serves the U.S. Congress and is the investigative arm of the Congress. Members of Congress request information or investigation on policies, programs, or procedures that fall under the domain of the government. Every month the GAO publishes the reports and testimonies that are available for review. Hundreds of reports are prepared every year and cover all the domains of the federal government. You can subscribe to the monthly listing and receive an email alert and summaries of all the reports that are available (http://www.gao.gov/subscribe/index.php).

The Congressional Budget Office (CBO) also serves the U.S. Congress. It is responsible for providing objective and nonpartisan analyses of economic and budgetary issues to help legislators make policy decisions on the multitude of programs covered by the federal budget. This information is used by CBO to provide the information and estimates required for the Congressional budget process. The public has access to CBO information including economic forecasts, productivity data, budget projections, and policy analyses related to federal spending. It has special collections on a wide variety of topics including Social Security, Medicare, immigration, climate change, health, natural disasters—all topics are analyzed from a budgetary perspective.

The Congressional Research Service (CRS) serves Congress as its policy research service. It was established in 1914 as a separate department within the Library of Congress. It was charged with supporting the legislative needs of Congress. Over the years it has expanded and today it is a comprehensive research agency that provides confidential, objective, and nonpartisan information and analyses on a wide range of public policy issues. CRS reports are not publicly disseminated and are supposed to be developed for the use of members of Congress in a confidential format. The purpose of this format is to allow members of Congress open access to information and a way to process policy alternatives without bringing in politics. However, with the Internet and the access of CRS materials through many of the users, the reports can be found online and even through university library systems. Those who have organized CRS materials into available formats argue that public funds finance the agency and as such it should be available to the public. CRS's mandate of confidentiality to serve Congress has been interpreted as the reason for not allowing public dissemination of the reports. For policy analysts, CRS reports can be the most in-depth and detailed information on pressing issues of legislative concern. CRS reports can be requested through members of Congress, and it is legal for them to distribute reports to their constituents upon request.

The Executive branch also has agencies to conduct research. The Office of Management and Budget (OMB) provides data on economic and budgetary issues, similar to the CBO. However, as it serves the office of the president, it tends to be partisan. What is valuable to policy researchers are the reams of data on actual budgetary expenses and reported economic conditions. Each year OMB is responsible for producing the Annual Budget of the United States that the president presents to Congress. This volume contains data on all the expenditures and receipts of the federal government. Also available is a historical compendium that provides decades of data. Both documents as well as other budget information can be accessed at www.budget.gov/budget. The president also releases the *Economic Report of the President* annually, and this book includes numerous tables with economic data.

LEGISLATIVE INFORMATION

Legislative tracking can be helpful in understanding the history of a particular policy. It is also a difficult process as one needs to understand the legislative process and terminology specific to public lawmaking. Details on the legislative process are found in the last chapter of this book. More details on legislative tracking can be found in those sections. For now be aware that there are two major sources for legislative tracking that are available online. THOMAS (www.thomas.gov) is the official web site of the federal government for legislative information and it is run by the Library of Congress. It is free and completely open to the public. This site allows one to search for public laws, and the bills introduced to Congress. It provides background information and legislative histories of all the bills and laws introduced and passed by both chambers of Congress. The site also provides access to the *Congressional Record*, which is the daily digest of discussions on the floors of the House of Representatives and the Senate. Committee reports are available and links to other sources of information related to the legislative process can also be found.

A similar source is LexisNexis, a very comprehensive data base with legislative information similar to THOMAS. However, LexisNexis is a private, for-profit organization and its services are only available through subscription. Most major libraries subscribe, so access can be obtained. For example, university libraries often have a subscription so all faculty and students can access the LexisNexis database. It can be a little more difficult to use, as it is geared toward the legal profession and therefore can seem more technical and use legal terms that may not be familiar to the average person.

States also have their own legislative sites on which it is possible to track legislation and find information on pending bills and policy topics. You can find links to all the state legislatures through http://www.ncsl.org/public/leglinks.cfm hosted by the national organization National Conference of State Legislatures. Or, you can simply Google the state you are interested in, followed by "Legislature" and that should take you to the home page of that state's legislative body. The site typically will include listings of all the state-elected officials and information on the policy process in the state.

General legislative information about federal policy-making is also available through a number of publications of the Congressional Quarterly Press, which publishes books, periodicals, directories, and general information on the American government, politics, and currents events. CQ Press is a private, nonpartisan, independent publisher that has been providing Congressional coverage since 1945. Most of its products are for sale to the public, and some of its subscription series are held by libraries. The *CQ Weekly Report* is a weekly news periodical covering legislation and the social issues related to pending bills and enacted laws.

C-SPAN (the Cable-Satellite Public Affairs Network) televises the proceedings of the House of Representatives and the Senate as well as committee hearings and other public policy events. C-Span can be found on cable television channels so you can directly watch the U.S. Congress in action. The web site also provides an archive of video clips and background information on the workings of Congress. The Supreme Court and campaign and election activities are also covered.

ADVOCACY GROUPS

Nowadays almost all national groups have a web page and are accessible to the public. Advocacy groups can be rich sources of policy-related information. The challenge for policy analysis is to be sure the source is a credible and well-respected group with accurate information. Organizations that have a long history and are well known are usually respected sources for information. Of course these organizations do take positions and therefore can be biased in their approach to a policy issue. One way to enhance your policy research is to find organizations that take different perspectives and access the information on an issue from the multiple sources. That way you can analyze the issue from a number of angles and discover the underlying values and beliefs that impact the perspectives.

The topic of immigration has become a hotly contested issue in recent years. There are several national organizations that provide analyses and information on the topic. Two very thorough organizations with slightly different perspectives are the Pew Hispanic Research Center and the Center for Immigration Studies. Careful reading of the materials demonstrates slightly different perspectives on immigration. The Pew Hispanic Research Center focuses primarily on Latino immigration and does not take a position pro or con, whereas the Center for Immigration Studies identifies itself as pro-immigration but seeks to lower the rate of immigration and especially close access for undocumented immigrants. It is important to remember that although advocacy groups can provide valuable information, these groups often operate with a mandate that prescribes a certain position. Good policy analysis requires that you are aware of their position and can articulate the alternative positions as well.

STATE AND LOCAL SOURCES

There are also valuable state and local sources for policy analysis and research. Two national organizations that are non-partisan and highly respected are the National Conference of State Legislatures (NCSL), cited earlier as a source for state legislatures, and the National Association of Governors (NGA). Both organizations track national public policies and the impact the legislation might have on states and localities. The Unites States Conference of Mayors is a nonpartisan organization that represents cities with populations of 30,000 or more. In 2009, that covered more than a thousand municipalities. Part of its mission is to provide information for and about urban/suburban communities and strengthen relationships between federal and city governments. They also produce reports and data on public policy topics related to cities.

Through the Internet you can find the web sites for numerous organizations and government agencies that will help you to conduct social welfare policy research. Web sites change often, so some may not be available over time. The sources discussed previously all have long histories and will likely be excellent sources for decades to come. With the Internet, policy resources are abundant, and easily accessible. A mere 15 years ago, most of these resources were available in hard copy only and required hours and hours of in-person library research. The best policy data sources were only accessible with intimate knowledge of government agencies and contacting those agencies directly for copies. Today, policy analysis is accessible to anyone anywhere with an Internet connection and often provides more information than time to use permits. Good policy analysis will require finding the most beneficial sources and dismissing the multitude of sources that are more commentary on topics than resource data. Be mindful of this explosion in accessible information.

FINAL THOUGHTS ON SOCIAL WELFARE POLICY ANALYSIS

The questions and guidelines for social welfare policy analysis as outlined in this chapter serve as a technical framework. These are the tools of the craft. The art of social welfare policy analysis comes in applying these techniques. Creativity comes into play as an analyst focuses on a social issue and analyzes all the diverse components that have an impact on a social problem. The key is to ask many questions without losing focus on a particular social issue. Diagrams can help us to visualize the multiple dimensions that influence the evolution of social welfare policy. Invariably, policy-making is not a neat and precise process. All social welfare policies evolve differently and with different players. Advocates of one policy may be opponents of another. Effective analysis requires staying focused on an issue and keeping the issue central to the analysis.

Key Terms

social welfare policy analysis	rational policy making	window of opportunity	street-level bureaucrats
public policy	incrementalism	magnitude	policy research
		implementation	

Questions for Discussion

1. Can you think of policy examples that have been instituted incrementally?
2. Identify an event that might create a window of opportunity for changing social welfare policy. What impact might this event have on social change?
3. What are the key questions to ask when analyzing policy? Explain the significance of each.
4. Give an example of a power imbalance in society. How do you think this affects social welfare policies and programs?
5. What role does social construction play in policy-making?

Excercises

1. Choose a social problem. Describe a rational approach to the problem. Develop incremental steps to change policies that address the problem.
2. Identify a policy or rule in your school, job, or field practicum. Try to chart the flow of this policy. Where did it originate, and on what or whose authority? What steps does it follow as it is applied? Are there unintended consequences of the policy? Who is directly affected? Who is indirectly affected? Does the actual impact reflect the original goal?
3. Using the same policy as in Exercise 1, identify the key players in the development of the policy. Are they still at the organization? If they are, would the policy still be in effect if they were gone? If they are no longer there, why has the policy endured? How much of an impact did personalities play in the development and implementation of the policy?
4. Visit your university library or local public library and familiarize yourself with the resource documents available. Which of the sources listed in this chapter are in the library? List and describe five sources that are not listed in this chapter but would be helpful when analyzing social welfare policies and programs.
5. Find C-SPAN on television. Spend an hour watching coverage of the House of Representatives or the Senate. What are your impressions? Was it easy to follow? What information would be helpful to enhance your understanding of the proceedings?

References

Brewer, G. D., & deLeon, P. (1983). *The foundations of policy analysis*. Homewood, IL: Dorsey Press.

Dobelstein, A. W. (2003). *Social welfare policy and analysis*, 3rd ed. Pacific Grove, CA: Brooks/Cole.

Dunn, W. N. (1994). *Public policy analysis*, 2nd ed. Englewood Cliffs, NJ: Prentice Hall.

Dye, T. R. (2008). *Understanding public policy*, 12th edition. Upper Saddle River, NJ: Prentice Hall.

General Accounting Office. (2003). *Child care: Recent state policy changes affecting the availability of assistance for low-income families*. GAO-03-588. Washington, DC: Author.

Gil, D. (1992). *Unraveling social policy*, 5th ed. Rochester, VT: Schenkman Books.

Gilbert, N., Specht, H., & Terrell, P. (1993). *Dimensions of social welfare policy*, 3rd ed. Englewood Cliffs, NJ: Prentice Hall.

Haas, P. J., & Springer, F. (1998). *Applied policy research*. New York: Garland Publishing.

Kingdon, J. W. (1984). *Agendas, alternatives, and public policies*. Boston: Little, Brown.

Levitan, S. A., & Wurzburg, G. (1979). *Evaluating federal social programs: An uncertain art*. Washington, DC: The Brookings Institution.

Lindblom, C. E. (1959). The science of muddling through. *Public Administration Review* 19:79–88.

Lipsky, M. (1980). *Street-level bureaucracy*. New York: Russell Sage Foundation.

Magill, R. S. (1986). *Social policy in American society*. New York: Human Sciences Press.

Majchrzak, A. (1984). *Methods for policy research*. Newbury Park, CA: Sage Publications.

Mezey, J., Parrott, S., Greenberg, M., & Fremstad, S. (2004). *Reversing direction of welfare reform: President's budget cuts child care for more than 300,000 children*. Washington, DC: Center on Budget and Policy Priorities and Center for Law and Social Policy.

National Women's Law Center. (2007, September). *Issue Brief - State child care assistance policies 2007: Some steps forward, more progress needed*. Washington, DC: Author.

Office of Management and Budget. (2008). *Historical tables: Budget of the United States Government*. Washington, DC: U.S. Government Printing Office.

Office of Human Services Policy. (1998). *Aid to Families with Dependent Children: The baseline*. Washington, DC: U.S. Department of Health and Human Services.

Pressman, J. L., & Wildavsky, A. (1984). *Implementation*, 3rd ed. Berkeley, CA: University of California Press.

Schneider, A. L. & Ingram, H. M. (2005). Public policy and the social construction of deservedness. In Schneider, A. L. & Ingram, H. M. (eds.), *Deserving and entitled: Social constructions and public policy* (pp. 1–28). Albany, NY: State University of New York Press.

Segal, E. A., & Kilty, K. M. (2003). Political promises for welfare reform. *Journal of Poverty: Innovations on Social, Political, and Economic Inequalities* 7(1 and 2):51–68.

U.S. Census Bureau. (2007). *Statistical abstract of the United States: 2008*, 127th edition. Washington, DC: Author.

Wildavsky, A. (1979). *The art and craft of policy analysis*. Boston: Little Brown.

SOCIAL INSURANCE

CHAPTER 7

Scott J. Ferrell/Congressional Quarterly/Getty Images

Very few social programs in the United States fall under the typology of an institutional social welfare structure. As described in the first chapter, institutional social welfare programs are built into the social and economic structure of our society and are a normal and expected part of our social system. All persons, regardless of their incomes or special needs, are considered part of the program. It is based on the value of collective responsibility for social well-being. The social insurance program in the United States is the closest example we have of an institutional social welfare program.

WHAT IS SOCIAL INSURANCE?

The concept of **social insurance** was introduced in Chapter 2. Social insurance is a collectively funded program for workers and their dependents that provides economic resources at the conclusion of employment. The key national social insurance program in the United States is Social Security. The Social Security program is *social* because it covers almost every employed person in this country, and it is *insurance* because all payments into the program are pooled to cover all citizens collectively. It is the purest institutional social welfare program in the nation. Regardless of one's needs, if one pays into the system, one is eligible to receive benefits. A millionaire can collect Social Security benefits just as an impoverished person can. The institutional and universal characteristics of the program make it the most accepted and protected social welfare program in our country. The evolution of Social Security represented a political transformation in social welfare policy in the United States.

HISTORY OF SOCIAL SECURITY

Today the most well-known social welfare program is the **Old-Age, Survivors, and Disability Insurance Program (OASDI)**, commonly referred to as **Social Security**. Its creation and enactment into law were a direct result of the social and economic upheaval of the Great Depression. In the 1920s, economic instability and unemployment were not social welfare concerns. The "Roaring Twenties" were for some people years of economic prosperity and extravagant living (see Chapter 2). Although there were impoverished people, they tended to live in areas secluded from the view of policy makers and the mainstream public. The poverty of the years following World War I was concentrated among rural populations and immigrants, groups that were often ignored by politicians. Those who benefited economically from the business activities of the 1920s could easily be oblivious to the needs of the poor. Many of the people benefiting from the economic progress of the time were living beyond their means, buying on credit, and saving little or nothing. Stock market speculation and illegal business deals were common. The shrewd business person who could earn sums of money in a short time was idealized. Therefore, the attitude of the time was that anyone could succeed economically.

The stock market crash of October 24, 1929, changed political, social, and economic beliefs. It demonstrated that the market system was not perfect. The economic depression that followed revealed the uneven prosperity of the 1920s. The result of years of extended credit, little savings, and market speculation was economic upheaval on a scale never before experienced in this country. The existing network of social and charitable supports was insufficient to provide for the need created by the Great Depression.

The magnitude of the Great Depression was a catalyst for social change. It gave impetus to the development of the **New Deal**. The New Deal was a set of legislative reforms put forth by President Franklin Delano Roosevelt that set a new legislative tone for the country. These new programs were designed to employ people and return the economy to working order (see Chapter 2). The first social welfare efforts following the start of the Great Depression were loans and grants to states to pay for direct relief and create work programs. However, state efforts were not enough. Prior to 1935, some states had been moving toward worker protection; however, there was no national system to protect workers from the economic consequences of job loss or old age. In 1934, President Roosevelt created the Committee on Economic Security, chaired by Secretary of Labor Frances Perkins, and charged it with the task of studying the problem of economic insecurity and making legislative recommendations on it. Drawing on state experiments and European models, the committee developed a plan that was endorsed by the President and sent to Congress. After months of debate, the Social Security Act was passed. It was signed into law on August 14, 1935 (Social Security Administration, 2000).

The political and social dimensions of the New Deal transformed the way that social well-being was addressed in the United States. The programs that were part of the New Deal, particularly the Social Security system, represented a new governing philosophy that redefined 20th-century public policy and, in the words of one of the master architects of the New Deal, Harry Hopkins, it "made America over" (Milkis & Mileur, 2002, p. 2). The impact of the New Deal was significant for social welfare policy in America because it firmly placed the federal government at the head of social welfare support and it contributed to the return of economic stability. Although the New Deal was significant, it did not displace capitalism. For some, the reforms did not go far enough:

> The rich still controlled the nation's wealth, as well as its laws, courts, police, newspapers, churches and colleges. Enough help had been given to enough people to make Roosevelt a hero to millions, but the same system that had brought depression and crisis—the system of waste, of inequality, of concern for profit over human need—remained. (Zinn, 2003, pp. 403–404)

Although the New Deal did not radically alter the underlying economic system, it did make significant changes and established permanent safeguards through federal legislation. The New Deal transformed America, and still affects our lives today. When 48 million people receive their monthly Social Security checks, or millions of Americans deposit money in a federally insured bank, visit one of the thousands of public buildings such as post offices, college dormitories, public schools, public hospitals, and museums constructed during the 1930s, collect unemployment insurance, join a labor union without threat, or are guaranteed a minimum wage and set working hours for employment, they are reaping the benefits of the New Deal. Familiar landmarks such as the Lincoln Tunnel and Triborough Bridge in New York; the port of Brownsville, Texas; Coit Tower in San Francisco;

and the Link from Key West to the Florida mainland were all built as part of the employment initiatives under the New Deal (Leuchtenburg, 1963).

Social insurance was the keystone to the reforms of the New Deal. The Social Security Act codified a more universal and institutional approach to social welfare policy. It has permanently transformed our social welfare system. Box 7.1 outlines the original parts of the policy and the current version of the act. The act has been amended greatly over its 75-year history.

The focus in this chapter is on the social insurance programs of the Social Security Act. The numerous other programs that are now part of the act are covered elsewhere in the book. When reviewing Box 7.1, keep in mind all the programs that have grown out of the Social Security Act that are critical to social well-being today, such as the Medicare and Medicaid health programs, the Temporary Assistance for Needy Children public assistance program, and child welfare services for adoption, foster care, and child support enforcement. These programs are discussed later in the book.

THE TWOFOLD PURPOSE OF THE SOCIAL SECURITY ACT

The two components of the Social Security Act, social insurance and public assistance, were seen as complementary but not equal. The overall intent was to create a program that would respond to the immediate crisis of unemployment and loss of savings, and also lay a firmer economic foundation so that no future economic upheaval would have the same impact on the populace. Public assistance was designed to be temporary and take care of the immediate economic crisis. Once the crisis had passed and people were employed again, the social insurance programs would cover all future economic downturns and make public assistance unnecessary. Even President Roosevelt was cautious about the public assistance aspects of social welfare policy:

> The Federal Government must and shall quit this business of relief . . . I am not willing that the vitality of our people be further sapped . . . We must preserve not only the bodies of the unemployed from destitution but also their self-respect, their self-reliance and courage and determination. (President Franklin D. Roosevelt, Annual Message to Congress, January 3, 1935, cited in Axinn & Levin, 1975, p. 179)

The reluctance to rely on relief, or direct cash assistance, was evident in the development of the Social Security Act. The goal of the legislation was to create a system attached to the employment market. Over time the program would cover all people, either as workers or as the survivors or dependents of workers. This coverage would displace the immediate need for cash relief as outlined in the public assistance programs of the Social Security Act. For example, a poor widow who was raising her children alone would need public assistance. However, if the Social Security program had existed, her husband would have paid into it, and the woman and her children would be taken care of through the program's survivor and dependent coverage, making the public assistance program unnecessary. The original public assistance components were old-age assistance, aid to dependent children

BOX 7.1	MORE ABOUT THE SOCIAL SECURITY ACT*

The Social Security Act of 1935	The Social Security Act in 2009
Title I: Grants to States for Old-Age Assistance	[Grants to States for Old-Age Assistance]*
Title II: Federal Old-Age Benefits	Federal Old-Age, Survivors, and Disability Insurance Benefits
Title III: Grants to States for Unemployment Compensation Administration	Grants to States for Unemployment Compensation Administration
Title IV: Grants to States for Aid to Dependent Children	Grants to States for Aid and Services to Needy Families with Children and for Child Welfare Services
Title V: Grants to States for Maternal and Child Welfare	Maternal and Child Health Services Block Grant
Title VI: Public Health Work	Temporary State Fiscal Relief
Title VII: Social Security Board	Administration
Title VIII: Taxes with Respect to Employment (for Old-Age Insurance)	Special Benefits for Certain World War II Veterans
Title IX: Tax on Employers of Eight or More (for administration of unemployment compensation)	Miscellaneous Provisions Relating to Employment Security
Title X: Grants to States for Aid to the Blind	[Grants to States for Aid to the Blind]
Title XI: General Provisions	General Provisions, Peer Review, and Administration Simplification
Title XII:	Advances to State Unemployment Funds
Title XIII:	[Repealed]
Title XIV:	[Grants to States for Aid to the Permanently and Totally Disabled]
Title XV:	[Repealed]
Title XVI:	[Grants to States for Aid to the Aged, Blind, and Disabled]
Title XVII:	Grants for Planning Comprehensive Action to Combat Mental Retardation
Title XVIII:	Health Insurance for the Aged and Disabled (Medicare)
Title XIX:	Grants to States for Medical Assistance Programs (Medicaid)
Title XX:	Block Grants to States for Social Services
Title XXI:	State Children's Health Insurance Program

*Titles in brackets were either repealed or amended into other titles and are therefore no longer part of the current legislation.

and their mothers, aid to disabled children, aid to the blind, and child welfare services, all of which were thought to be temporary:

> The Bureau of Public Assistance was in charge of a despised program, which, at least in theory, the Social Security Board intended should wither away, whereas the Bureau of Old Age and Survivors Insurance was in charge of a preferred program that was expected to grow until, again in theory, it virtually supplanted the first. (Derthick, 1979, p. 160)

Seventy-five years later, there is still a need for the public assistance programs of the Social Security Act. Those public assistance programs are covered in detail in the next chapter. Since the original Social Security Act was passed, it has been amended to include numerous other social programs. Most of the key social welfare support services of today are found under the Social Security Act. Box 7.2 lists the current programs that fall under the two parts of the Social Security Act.

Social Insurance

The original social insurance provisions were a federal system of old-age benefits for retired workers and a federal-state partnership for unemployment insurance. The system of old-age benefits was called the **Old-Age Insurance** program. It provided benefits for retired workers who had paid taxes into the system while employed in industry and commerce. The program was to begin collecting taxes in 1937 and pay out benefits to retired workers starting in 1942. Before full enactment of the law, it was expanded in 1939 to cover workers' survivors and dependents. Survivors' provisions meant that if a worker died, dependent family members would continue to receive benefits. Benefits became payable in 1940 instead in 1942, as originally planned.

Disability insurance was added in 1956 to provide cash benefits for disabled workers. Throughout the 1950s, disability coverage was expanded to include benefits for dependents of disabled workers and for adult disabled children of deceased or retired workers. Retirement, survivor, and disability coverage reflect the major provisions of the **Old-Age, Survivors, and Disability Insurance (OASDI)** program today.

| BOX 7.2 | MORE ABOUT THE SOCIAL SECURITY ACT PROGRAMS OF 2009 |

Social Insurance Programs	Public Assistance Programs
Old Age Survivors Disability Insurance	Temporary Assistance for Needy Families
Unemployment Insurance	Supplemental Security Income for the Aged, Blind, and Disabled
Workers Compensation	Medicaid
Medicare	Block grants to states
	State Children's Health Insurance Program
	Child welfare services

The second major social insurance program enacted as part of the Social Security Act made benefits available in the event of unplanned unemployment. **Unemployment Insurance (UI)** is provided through federal-state partnerships that give benefits to regularly employed members of the labor force who become involuntarily unemployed. Unemployment benefits are provided as a right. Recipients are not required to take a means test. These aspects make the program a social insurance program. The importance of the Unemployment Insurance program for economic security is discussed in Chapter 9.

The driving force behind the creation of the UI program was the overwhelming unemployment of the Great Depression. With millions out of work, it became clear that instead of dismantling the economic system, the government needed to create a safety net for times when businesses, for their survival, had to lay off employees. The UI program is designed to help a person who has been regularly employed and, through no fault of his or her own, loses that employment. He or she is eligible to receive weekly benefits to supplant some of the lost wages. The Social Security Act offers employers tax credit incentives to participate in the program and authorizes federal grants to cover the administrative costs. The UI program is financed through an employer tax that entitles the employer to receive a tax credit. Under the guidance of federal standards, each state decides the amount and duration of benefits, coverage, contribution rates, and eligibility requirements. State regulations vary greatly, but all follow the major federal guidelines in determining program eligibility within the state's jurisdiction (Social Security Administration, 2008).

All taxes collected from employers are deposited in the **Federal Unemployment Trust Fund**. The fund is invested as a whole, but each state has a separate account from which to pay benefits. The states directly administer the programs. Benefits are calculated according to the worker's past wages within limits set by each state. Since 1949, the program has been administered under the Department of Labor.

PUBLIC ASSISTANCE

The original **public assistance** provisions were a group of grants to states for means-tested programs for poor elderly persons, people who were blind, and mothers and children who needed health and welfare services. The next chapter presents the public assistance programs of the Social Security Act in detail. To understand the importance of social insurance as a social welfare approach, it is informative to highlight some of the differences between it and public assistance. As stated previously, the public assistance provisions were considered necessary but temporary, and were not at all favored by those charged with administering the program. The strong belief in individual responsibility and the value of work made the social insurance program preferable to public assistance. Public assistance was not seen as reinforcing the American work ethic and was therefore less desirable. These negative beliefs were present at the inception of the program and continue today. Social insurance was built on employment and individual effort, with a shared overall commitment. The negative beliefs surrounding public assistance are presented in more detail in the next chapter. The contrast between the two approaches has made Social Security a publicly supported program and public assistance a program plagued by public disfavor.

How the OASDI Program Works

The structure of the OASDI program requires people who are young and working to pay into the system. About 96 percent of the American workforce is covered by OASDI (Social Security Administration, 2008). Those not covered include civilian federal employees hired before 1984; railroad workers, who are covered by the federal railroad retirement system; and some state and local government employees, who are covered under their employers' retirement systems. The design of the program is that each covered person contributes either through payroll taxes or self-employment taxes. The law that mandates the payment for employees is the **Federal Insurance Contributions Act (FICA)**. The amount deducted for FICA is shown on workers' paychecks. Employers match the employee contribution, and self-employed workers pay both the employee and the employer taxes. The tax applies to a set amount of earnings, for which there is a ceiling. The upper limit increases annually to account for inflation. Initially, the program was set to tax the first $3,000 of earnings at a rate of 1 percent for the employee, matched by 1 percent by the employer (Meyers, 1985). From 1937 to 1949, this amounted to a maximum total of $30 for each covered employee. Over the years, the tax rate and the upper limit on earnings have increased to accommodate the funds necessary for benefits.

The accompanying tax rate schedule, in Box 7.3, lists the percentages of income paid for OASDI and Medicare in 2009. Each worker's employer matches the amount and pays it directly to the federal government. If a person is self-employed, he or she is responsible for paying both portions. The amount paid in is a set percent, 7.65 percent as of 2009, for OASDI and Medicare together, up to a certain amount of the overall salary. In 2009, Social Security taxes had to be paid on all income up to $106,800. Any income exceeding that amount was taxed only for the Medicare portion (1.45 percent). Therefore, because of the cap, as a person's salary rises, a decreasing percentage of income is withheld. Some argue that this is unfair, because people with lower incomes pay a larger percentage of their salary. For example, in 2009 a person who earns $30,000 pays $2,295 in Social Security and Medicare taxes, or 7.65 percent of total income. A person who earns $150,000 pays $8,797, or 5.86 percent of overall salary, and a person who earns

| BOX 7.3 | MORE ABOUT SOCIAL SECURITY TAX RATE SCHEDULE FOR OASDI AND MEDICARE |

2009 Tax Rate Percent* on Employee Earnings			2009 Tax Rate Percent on Self-employed Earnings		
Total	OASDI**	Medicare	Total	OASDI**	Medicare
7.65	6.2	1.45	15.3	12.4	2.9

*Employers also contribute these amounts.
**OASDI tax applies to first $106,800; there is no cap for Medicare.

$300,000 pays $10,972, a total of 3.66 percent of overall salary. So although the higher-salaried person paid more in tax dollars, the proportion of the tax was less. This disparity makes the Social Security tax a **regressive tax**, one that is proportionately greater for people with low incomes than for people with higher incomes.

The federal government holds the money in a special account, the **Social Security Trust Fund**. Money in the trust fund can be used only for the OASDI program in the form of monthly benefits, vocational rehabilitation services for disabled beneficiaries, administrative costs, and lump-sum death payments for eligible survivors (Social Security Administration, 2008). Therefore, money in the trust fund cannot be used for any other government purpose. FICA revenues that exceed the outlays for a given year are invested in interest-bearing Treasury Bonds that are assets of the trust fund to be used when needed to cover Social Security costs.

Eligibility requirements include working for at least 40 quarters (10 years) in covered employment and reaching the retirement age of 65 years (and by the year 2022, the retirement age of 67 years). Spouses and children of workers who have died are eligible for survivorship benefits. There are some exceptions and variations to these rules, and the specifics change from year to year. In order to be absolutely certain of eligibility, each person should check with a local Social Security Administration office. The details of the program are also available in book format from the Social Security Administration or on the Internet (www.ssa.gov).

The Social Security Administration keeps track of the contributions made by each worker and that person's employer. This amount is used to calculate how much a retiree receives per month in benefits when he or she becomes eligible. The average monthly benefit for a retired worker in 2007 was $1,082 and for a disabled worker was $1,004 (Social Security Administration, 2008).

Most women who receive Social Security benefits do so as wives or survivors of eligible workers. A wife or widow can choose to receive benefits based on her own work history or based on the earnings of her spouse. For most women, monthly benefits are greater if based on the earnings of their husbands. A woman still living with her husband receives 50 percent of his entitlement. Therefore, a married couple typically receives 150 percent of the husband's benefits. If a woman becomes a widow, she is entitled to 100 percent of her late husband's benefits. In 2007 the average survivor benefit was $1,023 per month (Social Security Administration, 2008).

BOX 7.4 | **CONSIDER THIS . . . THE EARLY YEARS OF SOCIAL SECURITY**

The lowest number ever issued was SSN 001-01-0001.

The smallest payment ever made was for 5 cents.

The first monthly retirement check was issued to a retired legal secretary, Ida May Fuller of Vermont, for $22.54. She lived to the age of 100 and during her 35 years as a beneficiary, she received over $22,000 in benefits.

Source: Social Security Administration, 2000.

PUBLIC PERCEPTIONS OF SOCIAL SECURITY

Advocates and opponents of Social Security battled openly over passage of the program. Today, although there are varying views on how to best strengthen the Social Security program, it enjoys bipartisan support. Conservatives and liberals alike claim to support the program, albeit with variations on how to best structure certain parts of it.

Overwhelming support was not always present. Opposition to the Social Security Act during the 1930s included accusations of socialism and concerns about dependency. New Jersey Senator A. Harry Moore said that "It would take all the romance out of life. We might as well take a child from the nursery, give him a nurse, and protect him from every experience that life affords." Racism was evident in some views, as exemplified in this quote from the Jackson (Mississippi) *Daily News*: "The average Mississippian can't imagine himself chipping in to pay pensions for able-bodied Negroes to sit around in idleness on front galleries, supporting all their kinfolks on pensions, while cotton and corn crops are crying for workers to get them out of the grass" (Leuchtenburg, 1963, p. 131). Today such criticisms seem unthinkable, but during the 1930s, the passage of Social Security was seen as a major social welfare initiative and met with stiff resistance from many quarters.

From the beginning, the social insurance provisions of the Social Security Act have been viewed differently than the public assistance programs. In order to maintain public support, the administrators and supporters of Social Security publicized the insurance aspect of the program:

> Because insurance implied a return for work and investment, it preserved the self-respect of the beneficiaries; because it implied a return in proportion to investment, it satisfied a widely held conception of fairness; and because it implied the existence of a contract, it appeared sound and certain. (Derthick, 1979, p. 199)

The concepts of insurance, fairness, and entitlement, which are firmly ingrained in the popular perception of the program, have solidified public acceptance of the program. Social Security is the most widely supported social welfare policy in our country. The public support is well warranted. The Social Security program plays an important role in improving the social well-being of our country.

HOW IMPORTANT IS SOCIAL SECURITY?

Monthly Social Security benefits are vital for millions of seniors. The Social Security program directly touches most seniors' lives. Ninety-one percent of people aged 65 and older receive Social Security benefits (Social Security Administration, 2008). For elderly persons with low incomes, Social Security provides nearly 90 percent of their retirement income; for those with middle incomes, 75 percent of their retirement income; and for those with high incomes, 24 percent of their retirement income (Congressional Quarterly, 2000). Social Security is the main source of income for two thirds of all elderly people (Social Security Administration, 2008). Social Security benefits have reduced the number of elderly people who live in poverty, lifting 13 million seniors age 65 and older above the poverty line (Center on Budget and Policy Priorities, 2005). Almost half of elderly people (47 percent) had incomes below the poverty line before they received Social Security benefits. With monthly benefits, the proportion dropped to less than 9 percent. For 20 percent of those workers who are 65 or older, Social Security is the only source of income, and for 65 percent of all recipients aged 65 and over, Social Security is at least half of their total money income (Social Security Administration, 2005). Without monthly benefits, millions of senior citizens would be in poverty or financially dependent on their children or other family members.

The inequalities of the workplace, particularly racism and sexism, are compounded with age. For many elderly persons, the OASDI program is a safety net that prevents them from falling into poverty after they retire. Over the past 40 years, the poverty rate for the elderly has dropped from 35 percent to less than 10 percent (Binstock, 1990; U.S. Census Bureau, 2007). This decrease in poverty among the elderly is directly related to increases in Social Security benefits and is evidence of the program's effectiveness.

The original design of the program actually benefited the typical woman of the 1930s. Most women did not work outside the home, and the program was designed with that in mind. As spouses, women are entitled to 50 percent of their husband's retirement benefit while he is alive, and 100 percent after he dies. For married women, this structure is very beneficial. Most women on their own would not earn as much as men and, consequently, would not receive as large a payment.

Although the tax structure of the Social Security program is regressive, the benefits are **progressive**, that is, the program redistributes income from those who have higher incomes to those who have less. An example based on data from the trustees report in 2008 demonstrates the progressive nature of Social Security. A worker who earned average wages over his or her career and retired at age 65 years in 2008 received annual Social Security benefits equal to 39 percent of his or her average annual earnings. Social Security would replace 53 percent of the average annual earnings of a low-earning worker, and 32 percent of the average annual earnings of a high-earning worker. So, although high-earning workers receive more money in their monthly Social Security checks, they receive a smaller portion of their earnings (Board of Trustees of the Federal Old-Age and Survivors Insurance and Disability Insurance Trust Funds, 2008).

LIMITATIONS OF SOCIAL SECURITY

Initially, the program had some defects (McElvaine, 1993). The first limitation of the Social Security program was that not all workers were covered. For example, to gain the support of southerners, farm and domestic workers were excluded from coverage. By 2008, coverage had become almost universal, with 96 percent of all work covered by the OASDI program. The second limitation was that the program was funded through payroll taxes as opposed to general tax revenues, as demonstrated in the preceding section. Although this format proportionately taxed lower-income workers more than higher earners, over time it has had the effect of creating universal investment in the program—for people paying in, it is perceived as their program and an entitlement. This relationship has strengthened public support.

There were significant limitations for women and people of color as well. In part, limitations based on gender and race reflected the social and political realities of the 1930s. Women tended to have lower lifetime earnings than men and, therefore, their average benefits were lower. This situation still exists today. Furthermore, the program was based on the family model of married, stay-at-home mothers, a model that is not as pervasive today. A woman who never marries and works her whole life may receive much lower benefits than a woman who married but never worked outside the home or paid into the system. The married woman will be eligible to receive 50 percent of her husband's benefits while he is alive, and 100 percent when he dies. That may be more than the benefits received by a woman who has worked and paid into the system her whole life.

Racism was still significant in employment practices throughout the South in 1935. Initially, farm and domestic workers, the predominant categories of African-American workers, were excluded from the program. Migrant workers were also excluded, as were any workers not paid official wages. It was not until 1954 that farm and domestic workers were added to the program. The level of benefits for women and people of color demonstrates the disparity in earnings and coverage. The average monthly benefit for a white retired worker was $1,065 in 2006, compared with $920 for an African-American retired worker, and $904 for a woman (Social Security Administration, 2008).

Even today, a disproportionate number of women and people of color work for employers who do not, although it is illegal, report workers' wages to the government. Therefore, these workers will not receive benefits from the Social Security program. Employers often justify this practice by saying they can pay more directly to workers if they do not have to take deductions to pay the tax, so workers receive more cash up front rather than having to contribute to FICA. Although this is true in the short term, it penalizes workers as they age. When a person spends years working but not paying FICA taxes and has no retirement provisions, he or she may struggle after retirement. Jobs in areas such as migrant farm labor, domestic cleaning services, landscaping, low-level service work such as dishwashing, and child care are disproportionately populated by women and people of color. When uncovered workers age, even though they may have worked for decades, they are excluded from the retirement coverage of Social Security.

There is a common belief that Social Security is a retirement program, but in reality OASDI benefits are not sufficient to provide a comfortable retirement of leisure and travel. The average benefits are about $12,000 a year—not enough to comfortably support people in retirement. It is important for people to understand that Social Security is an economic safety net meant to keep people from poverty. As such, it is a highly successful social welfare program. However, planning for retirement must include more than Social Security. As people age they need to consider employer pensions and personal retirement savings in addition to Social Security.

Not all older people depend on Social Security. Receipt of Social Security is not linked to economic means. Thus, for some workers it is a monthly check that is not necessarily needed. The universality of the program allows that whether people are rich or poor, as long as they paid into the program, they are eligible to receive benefits. Unlike public assistance, Social Security is regarded as an entitlement program.

People believe they have a right to receive benefits because they have paid into the system. If a person dies before reaching retirement, however, he or she will not receive anything (although the person's eligible survivors will receive benefits). If, on the other hand, a person lives for many years past retirement, the person may receive more money than he or she actually paid into the system. The Congressional Research Service calculated that retirees in 1980 received through monthly benefits the equivalent of all the contributions paid in over their work lives in just 3 years of retirement (Pearlstein, 1993). In 1995, the typical single-earner couple who retired could expect to receive two and one-half times the total amount the earner had contributed (Crenshaw, 1996). Historically, most Social Security recipients received more in benefits than the total amount they had paid in over their working years. With more people living longer and benefits higher, that trend will vary by levels of pre-retirement earnings. For low earners, lifetime Social Security benefits will average twice as much as they paid in, for middle income earners the amount of lifetime benefits will average about what they paid in, whereas for the highest 20 percent of earners, social security will pay out an average of about 65 percent of their lifetime contribution (Congressional Budget Office, 2006). It is important to remember that Social Security is not a retirement program. The comparison of taxes paid in versus benefits paid out is misleading. Those averages include people who paid in but may have died before receiving any benefits, as well as people who far outlived others and received much more than they paid in. Rather than focus on Social Security as an investment—getting more than one paid in—we need to ask whether the millions who receive Social Security each year would have been able to, or been disciplined enough to save that money during their working years. The program emphasizes a social or shared commitment, not reliance on individuals. We all need to ask ourselves whether we would have saved the 7.65 percent taken out of our paychecks diligently, every payday for all our working years, or whether we would have used those dollars for other purposes. Based on American savings rates (which is less than a half percent on average over the past several years), the answer is likely that we would not have saved the money for retirement. Social Security provides the framework to discipline workers to save for retirement.

Demographic changes raise concerns about the financial strength of the Social Security system. Since the system's inception, there have been more workers paying into the system than there have been recipients receiving benefits. In 1960, there were 5.1 workers per beneficiary, and in 2007, there were only 3.3 workers per beneficiary. However, this rate has remained relatively constant, remaining between 3.2 and 3.4 since 1974. By 2030, it is projected that there will only be 2.2 workers per beneficiary (Board of Trustees, 2008). In addition, in about 30 years there will be twice as many older people as there are today. Health care advances are helping people to live longer. With more people living longer, there will be more recipients and hence more dollars will be needed to pay for the benefits. These factors reflect the aging of America, which in turn places a greater demand on the Social Security program.

CHANGES IN THE SOCIAL SECURITY PROGRAM

The solvency crisis is not new to the Social Security program. Over the years, generous benefits were set by Congress based on the amount of money paid into the trust fund each year. This form of redistribution did not take into account changing demographics. During the early years of the Social Security system, there were many more people working than receiving benefits. As the population ages and people live longer, the number of people receiving benefits increases whereas the number of people working and paying into the system decreases. This imbalance led to ominous predictions in the early 1980s that the Social Security system would run out of money. In 1983, policy analysts calculated that the system would be bankrupt in 10 years. Fortunately, the system did not go bankrupt, because lawmakers made legislative decisions to change the program. The key changes were as follows: The retirement age limit was raised from 65 to 67 years, to be phased in over time; cost-of-living increases in benefits were delayed; the withholding tax was increased; and the taxable income ceiling was raised. These legislative changes created a surplus in funds that accumulated to cover the increase in the number of retirees for the next 30 years. The 1983 legislative changes averted the solvency crisis for several decades.

Recent legislative changes have made the program more responsive to current needs. In 2000, the **Senior Citizen's Freedom to Work Act** (P.L. 106-182) was enacted. This legislation removed barriers so that seniors could work without having their benefits reduced. The original design of the program was to keep older people out of the workforce because jobs were desperately needed for young people. As demographics shift, there are fewer workers to support the system, and people who are older still want to work. Prior to the 2000 legislative change, income earned after retirement reduced a person's Social Security benefits. This legislation lifted the cap on earnings. This change is another example of how amending the program ensures its fit with current social welfare needs.

Currently, more than 25 years after the 1983 legislative changes, concern for the financial stability of Social Security is once again receiving political attention. For the past several years, the Board of Trustees of the Federal Old-Age and Survivors Insurance and Disability Insurance Trust Funds has voiced concern over the financial solvency of the Social Security program. In their 2007 report, they projected that without any changes, the trust funds would be exhausted by 2041. There would still be taxes paid in, so the program would not be bankrupt, but it would run out of the surplus accumulated to cover the growing number of retirees. After 2041, the system would be drawing on current contributions. Based on the board's projections, from 2041 to 2082 the current rate of contributions would allow payment of 75 percent of anticipated benefits. Having enough revenue for more than 30 years gives policy makers time for planning. However, the program is so important that policy makers should make changes soon. If they do so, beneficiaries will not have to deal with changes that they did not anticipate.

THE FUTURE OF SOCIAL SECURITY

Social Security seems to be a permanent expectation of Americans of all income levels. To ensure the continuation of the program, some difficult political decisions must be made. Policy makers will have to decide how to keep the system financially solvent as baby boomers grow older and become retirees and as people live longer. The policy choices for maintaining Social Security include cutting benefits, limiting eligibility, raising taxes, or creating other forms of investment for old age. Those choices are typically not supported by voting constituencies, and, hence, elected officials will try to stay away from them for as long as possible. Political urgency and economic urgency sometimes become enmeshed, and it is difficult to understand the true dimensions of the problem of Social Security. Box 7.5 highlights the heated political arguments concerning Social Security that followed President Bush's reelection and his pledge to amend the Social Security program. His attempts failed, and throughout his presidency, Congress took no action to address the Social Security Trust Fund's solvency. With millions of older people currently receiving benefits and most workers paying into the system, all citizens are directly or indirectly affected by the political debate over the system.

BOX 7.5 | ### CONTROVERSIAL PERSPECTIVES

What is the best way to address the future of the Social Security program?
In 2005, President George W. Bush advocated creating a system of private or personal accounts for younger workers that would supplant some of their current contributions. Opponents of the proposal worried that it would be too costly and would not address the problem of solvency.

Yes, it would work:
"Bush aides say that the president's plan would wipe out a long-term structural deficit facing the nation in coming decades and that the transition costs in the next decade or so will ultimately be overshadowed by the benefits" (Weisman & Baker, 2005, p. 10).

No, it would make things worse:
"If Congress were to pass Bush's Social Security plan...the budget deficit would climb steadily to $335 billion by 2015" (Weisman & Baker, 2005, p. 10).

What is wrong?
According to President Bush, "Social Security was a great moral success of the 20th century and we must honor its great purpose in this new century. The system, however, on its current path, is headed toward bankruptcy" (Balz, 2005, p. 6).

According to Democratic representative Rush D. Holt of New Jersey, the Social Security system has been one of the most successful social welfare programs and the president is "overstating the system's long-term problems of insolvency and

proposing a risky solution that would make them worse, not better" (Allen, 2005, p. 11).

Who is right?
According to estimates, it is possible that Social Security could run out of funds, but that would be offset by current contributions so that even in 75 years, there would be enough to pay more than two thirds of the expenses. Imagine looking back 75 years, to the first years of the Great Depression, and trying to estimate what 2005 would look like. It would be impossible to foresee all the events and economic changes. That is not to say that planners should not attempt to ensure the strength of the program with possible changes, but dire warnings of events that might happen in 75 years are wildly speculative.

Robert Ball, the Commissioner of Social Security from 1962 to 1973, writes:

As things stand, the trustees' annual release of their latest 75-year estimates becomes a sky-is-falling media circus. The middle-range estimates are reported as if they were meant to be exact and immutable rather than as one of many possibilities. What is really the trustees' tentative expectation of a possible distant shortfall is transformed into a looming "crisis," prompting millions of Americans to believe, wrongly, that Social Security is doomed unless it gets a radical overhaul. Social Security doesn't require radical "reforms" because it hasn't failed. The system that has served so many so well for so long just needs some timely maintenance work (Ball, 2004, pp. 22–23).

SOLVENCY OF THE TRUST FUND

As stated previously, under the current provisions, the Social Security trust funds are projected to run out of surplus funds by 2041, and only three fourths of the anticipated benefits will be funded by 2082. What does this mean? Threats to the financial solvency, or permanency, of the Social Security program have caused great concern. There are conflicting points of view about the financial strength of the system.

Supporters of the Social Security system argue that although financial solvency is important, the projected situation for the 34-year horizon described by the Social Security Board of Trustees does not constitute a crisis. Two factors are critical: (1) Incremental changes can be made to alter the financial forecast. (2) Demographics are difficult to predict and, therefore, the overall situation may turn out to be positive for the financial health of the system.

Incremental changes include raising the tax rate, raising the ceiling on income taxed, raising the retirement age, or decreasing benefits, or any combination of these changes. These are politically difficult, but structurally easy, choices. All these factors were set by legislators and can therefore be changed by legislators. For example, in 1935 life expectancy was significantly lower than it is today. Just over the past 40 years, life expectancy has increased from 71 years to almost 78 years, and by 2015 it will be approaching 80 years (U.S. Census Bureau, 2007). When the Social Security program was established, 65 years was considered old age, and the average life expectancy was not many years beyond that. Today, if a person retires at 65 years, he or she can expect to live for another 15 to 20 years, if not longer. The legislative changes of 1983 acknowledged this change by gradually raising the retirement age from 65 to 67 years. This issue should perhaps be revisited, and the retirement age raised to 68 or 69 years. It is estimated that a one-year increase in the age for retirement will decrease the average lifetime benefits paid to a worker by 7 percent (Congressional Quarterly, 2000). A change such as that would add years to the financial solvency of the system. Furthermore, as people live longer, they may choose to work longer or work part-time. As the 2000 legislative changes demonstrated, more people want to work while they are retired. This too adds unexpected tax revenue to the trust fund.

Another possible change might be to raise the ceiling for contributions. The cutoff of $106,800 means that all income earned over that amount is not taxed for the retirement portion of the trust fund. What if the ceiling were raised to $150,000? That would amount to about $3,000 more per year for people earning more than the current capped level up to a new level of $150,000. Currently, 84 percent of all U.S. earnings are taxed for the Social Security retirement portion. Raising that amount to 90 percent (which would affect about 9 percent of American workers, all of whom are high earners) would cut the 75 year shortfall in the Trust Fund by almost half (Center for Retirement Research, 2007). Such changes would extend the solvency of the program.

Immigration is another issue related to Social Security. Historically, immigration has added to the numbers of active workers and usually these workers come to this country at a young age. The influx of young workers has added to the numbers of active contributors to the Social Security program, and helped to keep the worker/retiree ratio stable over the past 30 years. If we significantly decrease the rate of immigration, there will be a lower influx of new, younger workers to contribute to the Social Security system.

Economics plays an important part in the projections of solvency. The past few years have been ones of higher unemployment and consequently less income taxed for contributions to the program. If employment increases and wages grow, contributions will also increase. At the same time, if unemployment rises, there will be a decline in worker contributions. The cycle of employment affects the solvency of the program.

It would be foolish not to attend to the solvency concerns of the Social Security program. Even though the decisions are politically difficult, acting sooner rather than later means that the changes will not have to be as great. And in perspective, the 34-year horizon of 2007 is far better than the 10-year horizon of the 1980s. This means we have ample time to amend the system to ensure its financial health for decades to come.

PRIVATIZATION OF SOCIAL SECURITY

One of the most contested ideas for improving the Social Security system is to privatize parts of it. This means that instead of the current system, in which all contributions are collectively held by the federal government, each person could earmark a part of his or her contributions for a private program. Advocates of the privatization of Social Security argue that creating privately invested accounts would encourage more individual responsibility and offer workers the opportunity to earn larger benefits. The idea behind privatization is that a portion of the money an individual would pay into the current Social Security system would be diverted to a private investment account. The growth and returns on the account would accrue to the individual. The performance of the investment would rest with the market and with the savvy of the individual in managing his or her investment.

Critics of the privatization approach worry that those who understand financial markets and investment will do well, but those who do not will be worse off. Private investments would also be subject to more risk, stock market volatility, and high fees for administration of the funds. The premise of the Social Security Act was to find a safety net that would be there when the vicissitudes of the marketplace went awry. The market collapse and economic upheaval of the 1930s demonstrated how unstable the marketplace can be. Privatization would return the system to that unpredictability. Privatization would be a major step away from the principles of the New Deal, which built a guaranteed benefit for the elderly, their survivors, and people with disabilities. Furthermore, critics argue that the option to privatize one's investments is already available and that millions of people choose this option already. They also argue that it is not responsible to risk the savings of those least likely to afford the volatility of the private market, low earners who are disproportionately unskilled in understanding the investment market. The economic downturn and steep stock market decline of 2007–2009 provided further evidence supporting the opposition to privatization of Social Security.

Another option that has elements of privatization is to change the way the trust fund is invested. Currently, trust fund money can be invested only in Treasury Bonds, which are very stable and conservative. Supporters of privatization suggest that a more aggressive investment program for the trust fund would bring in greater revenues. One way to achieve this would be to allow trust funds to be invested in the stock market and other more risky venues. Again, the argument against this centers on security and guaranteed benefits. Allowing the volatility of the market to affect the solvency of the trust fund is risky and contrary to the founding principles of the Social Security program.

The solution to funding Social Security likely rests with a combination of changes, similar to what was done in 1983. For example, the payroll tax rate could be raised by one percent for both employers and employees (making the contribution 8.65% for workers). Such an increase would completely reduce the Social Security Trust Fund shortfall for the next 75 years (Center for Retirement research, 2007). Combining such a payroll tax increase with raising the cap as already discussed would provide a surplus in the Trust Fund over the next 75 years. Shifting other factors such as raising the retirement age or changing the cost of living increase in benefits would add even more. There are numerous options available, the difficulty is the politics of making these decisions.

CONFLICTING VALUES AND BELIEFS

The social insurance programs of the Social Security Act embody the values of social responsibility and social support. There are no guarantees that each of us will live long enough to receive social insurance benefits, but we pay in for that possibility. Our contributions also fund a collective form of care for others. Social insurance was founded during a time when system failure was recognized. People realized that economic need might not be brought on by individual failure as much as failure of the economic structure. It even reflects the value of aiding strangers, as we pool our contributions and ultimately pay for people we do not personally know. People feel connected to the program and entitled to it, further reinforcing its support.

The greatest underlying struggle in supporting the Social Security system is the extent of belief a person has in individual responsibility versus social responsibility. If you hold strongly to individual rights and privacy, then the social aspects of the program will be difficult to accept. If you believe in shared responsibility, even for people you do not know, then the program delivers those values. Most of the arguments about changing the program rest on those divergent beliefs, the value of individual rights versus social responsibility.

In addition, although paying into Social Security is a form of covering one's own needs, it is also a payment for the security of others anonymously. This requires a social commitment to people we will never know. This too is a conflicting value in America, the struggle between taking care of your own and helping strangers.

FINAL THOUGHTS ON SOCIAL INSURANCE

Social Security is our oldest continuing federal social welfare program. It has received support from every president since 1935 (see Box 7.6). It embodies values of universalism and institutionalism, as well as a belief in the importance of social responsibility. As a social insurance program, its risks are shared among the entire population and it offers a safety net to individuals who have less financial means. That it has endured for 75 years is a testament to its acceptance as a key social welfare program. We are all affected by Social Security and need to understand how each of us is a part of the program (see Box 7.7). Although there are concerns about its future, its enmeshment with our social, economic, and political fabric makes it likely to continue for generations to come.

BOX 7.6   **CONSIDER THIS . . .**

Every president since Franklin D. Roosevelt has supported Social Security. Here are some of their statements:

Franklin Roosevelt: "We can never insure one-hundred percent of the population against one-hundred percent of the vicissitudes of life. But we have tried to frame a law that will give some measure of protection to the average citizen and to his family against the loss of a job and against poverty-ridden old age. This law, too, represents a cornerstone in a structure which is being built, but is by no means complete...that will take care of human needs and at the same time provide for the United States an economic structure of vastly greater soundness." (August 14, 1935)

Dwight Eisenhower: "We will... endeavor to administer the disability [program] efficiently and effectively...to help rehabilitate the disabled so that they may return to useful employment...I am hopeful that this new law...will advance the economic security of the American people." (August 13, 1945)

Richard Nixon: "I have today signed [legislation which]...constitutes a major breakthrough for older Americans, for it says at last that inflation-proof Social Security benefits are theirs as a matter of right..." (July 1, 1972)

Jimmy Carter: "The Social Security program... represents our commitment as a society to the belief that workers should not live in dread that a disability, death, or old age could leave them or their families destitute." (December 20, 1977)

Ronald Reagan: "[This law] assures the elderly that America will always keep the promises made in troubled times a half century ago...[The Social Security Amendments of 1983 are] a monument to the spirit of compassion and commitment that unites us as a people." (April 20, 1983)

George H. W. Bush: "To every American out there on Social Security, to every American supporting that system today, and to everyone counting on it when they retire, we made a promise to you, and we are going to keep it." (January 31, 1990)

Bill Clinton: "Social Security...reflects some of our deepest values—the duties we owe to our parents, the duties we owe to each other when we're in different situations in life, the duties we owe to our children and our grandchildren. Indeed, it reflects our determination to move forward across generations and across the income divides in our country, as one America." (February 9, 1998)

George W. Bush: "Social Security is one of the greatest achievements of the American government, and one of the deepest commitments to the American people. For more than six decades it has protected our elderly against poverty and assured young people of a more secure future. It must continue to do this important work for decades to come" (April, 2004)

Source: Social Security Administration, 2000 & 2008

BOX 7.7 | **CONSIDER THIS . . . KEEPING UP WITH SOCIAL SECURITY**

With technology, each person can stay abreast of his or her Social Security contributions and future benefits.

www.socialsecurity.gov Use the Social Security Benefit Calculators to calculate your future retirement benefits.

www.ssa.gov/planners Three planning programs are shown to help you estimate future Social Security retirement benefits.

http:/best.ssa.gov Screening tool to see if you are currently eligible for Social Security, SSI, or Medicare benefits.

www.ssa.gov/applytoretire Online application for retirement benefits.

Key Terms

social insurance

Old-Age, Survivors, and Disability Insurance (OASDI)

New Deal

Unemployment Insurance (UI)

public assistance

Federal Insurance Contribution Act (FICA)

regressive tax

Social Security trust fund

progressive tax

Questions for Discussion

1. Do you think Social Security should continue as a socially shared program, or should it include private investment options?
2. What is an appropriate retirement age? Why?
3. Should benefits be limited for people with high incomes? Why?
4. What changes would you recommend for the future to ensure the strength of the Social Security program?
5. Explain the differences between social insurance and public assistance.

Excercises

1. Make an appointment to visit a local Social Security Administration office. Identify yourself as a student and ask if you can receive information on your status in the system. For how many quarters have you paid in? What benefits are you entitled to? Are you eligible for disability coverage? At what age can you retire and receive full benefits?
2. Divide a sheet of paper into two columns, one for social insurance and another for public assistance. List the characteristics of each program, including eligibility, cover-

age, benefits, and time limits. Also, list public attitudes and perceptions about the programs. How do the programs differ? How are they similar?
3. Identify a person who is receiving Social Security benefits. Ask if he or she might be willing to talk to you about the program. How do they feel about receiving Social Security? What did they think of the program when they were young? Have their opinions changed? How do they think the program could be improved?

4. Visit some web sites about Social Security. Can you find information that supports the program? Can you find information that promotes changing the program? What are the points made by each side? How do they compare?

References

Allen, M. (2005). Mobilizing the opposition: Democrats launch their campaign against Bush's Social Security changes. *Washington Post National Weekly Edition* 22(18):11.

Axinn, J., & Levin, H. (1975). *Social welfare: A history of the American response to need*. New York: Harper & Row.

Ball, R. M. (2004). Just a little maintenance: We can fix Social Security, if we manage the politics. *Washington Post National Weekly Edition* 21(40):22–23.

Balz, D. (2005). Soothing words: Assuring older Americans, Bush makes case for Social Security changes. *Washington Post National Weekly Edition* 22(16):6.

Binstock, R. H. (1990). The politics and economics of aging and diversity. In S. A. Bass, E. A. Kutza, & F. M. Torres-Gil (eds.), *Diversity in aging*, pp. 73–99. Glenview, IL: Scott Foresman.

Board of Trustees of the Federal Old-Age and Survivors Insurance and Disability Insurance Trust Funds. (2008). *Annual report*. Washington, DC: Author.

Center for Retirement Research. (2007). *The Social Security fix-it book*. Boston: Trustees of Boston College.

Center on Budget and Policy Priorities. (2005). *Social Security lifts 13 million seniors above the poverty line*. Washington, DC: Author.

Congressional Budget Office. (2006). *Is Social Security progressive?* Washington, DC: Author.

Congressional Quarterly. (2000). *Issues in social policy*. Washington, DC: CQ Press.

Crenshaw, A. B. (1996). A stock answer to social security worries. *The Washington Post National Weekly Edition* 13(32):22.

Derthick, M. (1979). *Policymaking for Social Security*. Washington, DC: Brookings Institution.

Leuchtenburg, W. E. (1963). *Franklin D. Roosevelt and the New Deal*. New York: Harper & Row.

McElvaine, R. S. (1993). *The Great Depression: America 1929–1941*. New York: Times Books.

Meyers, R. J. (1985). *Social Security*. Homewood, IL: Richard D. Irwin.

Milkis, S. M., & Mileur, J. M. (eds.). (2002). *The New Deal and the triumph of liberalism*. Amherst, MA: University of Massachusetts Press.

Pearlstein, S. (1993). Battling for a slice of the pie: The young challenge their elders. *The Washington Post National Weekly Edition* 10(17):22.

Social Security Administration. (2008). *Annual Statistical Supplement, 2007*. Washington, DC: Author.

Social Security Administration. (2007). *Social Security Bulletin* 67(4):122.

Social Security Administration. (2008). *The Future of Social Security*. Washington, DC: Author.

Social Security Administration. (2000). *A brief history of Social Security*. Washington, DC: Author.

U.S. Census Bureau. (2007). *Statistical abstract of the United States: 2008*, 127th ed. Washington, DC: U.S. Government Printing Office.

Weisman, J., & Baker, P. (2005). What Bush's successor could inherit: Under the president's budget proposal, costs will balloon after he leaves office. *Washington Post National Weekly Edition* 22(16):7.

Zinn, H. (2003). *A people's history of the United States: 1492 to present*. New York: HarperCollins.

CHAPTER 8

POVERTY AND ECONOMIC INEQUALITY

Courtesy of Elizabeth Segal

| BOX 8.1 | CONSIDER THIS... |

How much income is enough for one person? For a family of four? Ask another person for his or her estimates. Do you agree? Why? What are the necessities a person must have to live? What considerations did you bring to your determination?

Do you think a phone is a necessity? Is a television? Is a car? What type of health care is a necessity? Who should decide what the necessities are? Who should be responsible for providing those necessities?

The United States is an affluent country with abundant resources. By most standards, it is the wealthiest nation in the world. In spite of general economic prosperity, millions of Americans lack basic resources and opportunities for advancement. Millions live in poverty. This chapter covers the extent of poverty in America, the reasons why poverty exists, and the social welfare programs designed to address it.

DEFINING POVERTY AND ECONOMIC NEED

There are a number of ways to define poverty. Agreement is lacking on what exactly makes a person poor, although most agree that certain extremes are present. For example, most people agree that not having a place to live or not having plumbing is an aspect of poverty. But most cannot agree on how much living space is enough or what constitutes adequate plumbing. What is poverty to one person may not seem so bad to another.

MEASURES OF POVERTY

There are two measures of poverty: **absolute** and **relative**. An absolute measure of poverty uses a fixed, predetermined amount below which people are defined as poor. A relative measure of poverty uses societal standards to assess the minimum needed for a reasonable living situation, and anything less than that standard is considered poor. In the United States, an absolute measure of poverty is used.

The absolute measure of poverty used today was developed in the 1960s. As poverty emerged as an important social issue, government agencies grappled with ways to define, assess, and respond to it. In 1963, the Social Security Administration (SSA) attempted to define what the necessary minimum income was for a family. At that time, the SSA was responsible for programs designed to address poverty. Two pieces of data were used to determine the official **poverty threshold**, or the dollar amount set for the federal poverty measure. Informally, it is often referred to as the **poverty line**. The first piece of data used to develop the poverty threshold was the amount of money it took to feed a family. The second statistic was the proportion of family income that went toward food. In the words of the creator of the poverty threshold, Mollie Orshansky, then director of the SSA, "The standard itself is admittedly arbitrary, but not unreasonable. It is based essentially on the amount of income remaining after allowance for an adequate diet at minimum cost" (Orshansky, 1965, p. 4).

Food costs were based on the Department of Agriculture's "economy" food plan. This diet itemized the cost for food in temporary or emergency situations. This calculation was developed during the 1950s in response to concerns for disaster planning, particularly in the event of nuclear war. The diet was not meant as a long-term food plan but rather as the minimum needed to get through an emergency. The other statistic available at the time was the Department of Agriculture's assessment that the average family spent one third of their income for food. Therefore, the line was developed using the estimate for the economy food plan and multiplying that by three.

However, absolute and relative costs have changed over the years. Because of growth in other family expenses such as housing and health care, food requires less than one fifth of a typical necessity budget, not one third (Bernstein, Brocht, & Spade-Aguilar, 2000). Figure 8.1 demonstrates this relationship. Consider that a family of four needs $500 a month for food. If the 1960s relationship of one third were used, then the entire family monthly budget would be calculated to equal $1,500 ($500 is one third of $1,500). But if the more current proportion of 17 percent is used, then the entire family budget would equal $2,941 ($500 is 17 percent of were used $2,941). The SSA budget also did not address other needs that are costly today, such as health care, child care, and transportation. In the administrative view of what the typical family of the 1950s and 1960s looked like, there were two parents and the mother stayed at home; therefore, there was no child care cost in dollar terms. Furthermore, most people lived in the cities where factories and businesses were clustered, so they had access to employment and public transportation. Now, many workers live far from viable jobs and need a car to get to work. In addition, health care costs have risen dramatically over the past 20 years and people today pay more out-of-pocket costs than previous generations. Although the cost of food has gone up, other expenses have too, and the proportions for family budgets have changed.

The change in living costs in the almost 50 years following the creation of the poverty threshold means that the absolute line below which people are officially recognized as poor is proportionately much lower than when it was developed. If a new line were to be constructed based on the typical cost of food in relation to the other costs of living, and took into account the dramatic increases in child care and health care, many millions more people would be officially counted as poor in this country.

Another way to examine the validity of the poverty threshold is in comparison to the income of a typical household. The poverty line in the 1960s for a family of four was almost half of the median family income. Today it has dropped to 29 percent (Mishel, Bernstein, & Allegretto, 2007). Changing the poverty line to reflect changes in economics would have an immediate impact on how many people are categorized as poor. For example, if the poverty line were 25 percent higher, 12 million more people would be counted as officially poor, raising the rate more than 4 percentage points (U.S. Census Bureau, 2007). Such an immediate increase is a strong disincentive for policy makers to change the measure.

Why is an absolute measure used instead of a relative measure? Although many assumptions and values go into both determinations, in the end the absolute measure is fixed and less debatable. Viewing poverty from a relative perspective

1963 formula for poverty threshold based on 1960s distribution of income

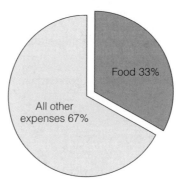

2000 estimates for distribution of income

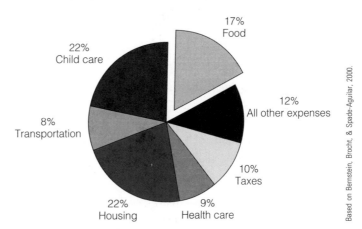

* All other expenses include telephone, clothing, school supplies, personal care supplies, entertainment.

FIGURE 8.1

involves a host of variables. For example, is a telephone a luxury or a necessity? If you have small children or are looking for a job, a phone will most likely feel very much like a necessity. For many parents, a portable cellular phone is a necessity. The knowledge that they can be reached at any time if an emergency should arise feels indispensable. If a cellular phone is a relative necessity, many people would define poverty as the lack of resources to acquire such a phone.

The poverty threshold has been used since the 1960s to measure the extent of poverty in the United States. The threshold has been changed only to reflect inflation and is adjusted for family size. However, it is not the standard used to determine eligibility for social welfare programs. Instead, the Department of Health and Human Services uses **poverty guidelines**. The poverty guidelines are issued each year and "are a simplification of the poverty thresholds for use for administrative purposes—for instance determining financial eligibility for certain federal programs"

BOX 8.2	MORE ABOUT THE POVERTY THRESHOLD

The following dollar amounts were determined to be realistic monthly minimums for a family of four in the following communities in 2005:

	Minneapolis, MN	Johnstown, PA	Denver, CO	Boston, MA
Food	587	587	587	587
Housing	928	428	888	1266
Health care	345	338	334	592
Transportation	358	375	358	321
Child care	1364	954	1001	1298
Taxes	588	243	394	824
Other	409	274	398	500
(e.g., telephone, clothing, school supplies, personal care)				
TOTAL	$4,579	$3,199	$3,960	$5,388
Percent of Poverty				
Threshold	287%	200%	248%	338%

These amounts were two to three times higher than the poverty threshold of $1,596.50 per month (or $19,157 for the year).

The poverty threshold is set extremely low in comparison to the minimal expenses of the typical family.

Do you think the above budget is too little, too much, or just right?

How does your family and living situation compare?

Source: Allegretto, 2005

(Department of Health and Human Services, 2008, p. 3971). Although the numbers are not identical, the poverty guidelines closely follow the threshold. Box 8.3 lists the 2008 poverty guidelines.

HOW MANY PEOPLE ARE POOR?

According to the official definition of poverty, in 2007, over 37 million people were below the poverty threshold. This was 12.5 percent of the population, or one in eight people in the United States (DeNavas-Walt, Proctor, & Smith, 2008). The largest single group within the larger group of poor people were children. Thirty-six percent of those who were poor were under the age of 18 years. Almost 10 percent were over 65 years of age. Therefore, almost half the people who are poor in this country are in the vulnerable age categories of youth or the aged. Poverty during the early 1960s, before the major federal social welfare response of the War on Poverty, affected over 20 percent of the population. However, government intervention in the way of cash assistance, in-kind benefits, and prevention efforts seems to have made a difference. As Box 8.4 demonstrates, the poverty rates over the past 45 years decreased following the antipoverty efforts of the 1960s and 1970s, and

| BOX 8.3 | MORE ABOUT THE 2008 HEALTH AND HUMAN SERVICES POVERTY GUIDELINES |

Size of Family	48 Contiguous States and D.C.	Alaska	Hawaii
1	$10,400	$13,000	$11,960
2	$14,000	$17,500	$16,100
3	$17,600	$22,000	$20,240
4	$21,200	$26,500	$24,380
For each additional person, add	$3,600	$4,500	$4,140

Source: Department of Health and Human Services, 2008

rose with the cutbacks of the 1980s. The second half of the 1990s saw an improvement over the previous 15 years, likely as a result of the unprecedented economic growth of that decade. In recent years, the poverty rate has begun to rise, from 11.3 percent in 2000 to 12.7 percent in 2004. It has tapered off a bit, although the impact of the economic downturn in recent years will likely cause the percent to rise. Although the rate is still lower than in the 1990s, the increase raises concerns that the economic downturn of the early 2000s had an impact on those who are poor, and the additional downturn of 2007 and 2008 is resulting in greater numbers in poverty.

WHO ARE THE POOR?

Using the words "the poor" sounds as if there is one group or one identity that shares a commonality, poverty. However, nothing could be further from the truth. Although the poverty threshold identifies who is officially counted as poor according to income, the people who constitute that group vary widely.

The Working Poor One might assume that poverty is a result of lack of work. In fact, there is a strong national belief that hard work is rewarded with economic gain. Furthermore, the harder one works, the more one can achieve. Although this is true for some, it is not true for all. Consider the experience of Barbara Ehrenreich (2001), a successful author, well-renowned scholar, and holder of a Ph.D. Ehrenreich joined the ranks of service workers and documented her attempts at working full-time and earning enough to support herself. She visited three different cities and held various entry-level service jobs. "You might think that unskilled jobs would be a snap for someone who holds a Ph.D ... not so. The first thing I discovered is that no job, no matter how lowly, is truly 'unskilled.' Every one of the six jobs I entered into in the course of this project required concentration, and most demanded that I master new terms, new tools, and new skills..." (p. 193). Ehrenreich found that only if she worked two jobs, 7 days a week, could she afford the most basic of necessities, and she was supporting only herself. Ehrenreich had joined the ranks of the working poor, those who live in poverty despite

BOX 8.4 | MORE ABOUT THE DISTRIBUTION OF PEOPLE IN POVERTY

Author calculations based on data in Proctor & Dalaker (2003); DeNavas-Walt, Proctor, & Mills (2004); and DeNavas-Walt, Proctor, & Smith (2008).

Persons in Poverty		Children in Poverty	
1960–1964	20.72%	1960–1964	24.72%
1965–1969	14.22%	1965–1969	16.96%
1970–1974	11.86%	1970–1974	15.06%
1975–1979	11.76%	1975–1979	16.32%
1980–1984	14.32%	1980–1984	20.80%
1985–1989	13.36%	1985–1989	20.12%
1990–1994	14.42%	1990–1994	21.84%
1995–1999	13.06%	1995–1999	19.40%
2000–2004	12.06%	2000–2004	16.92%
2005	12.6%	2005	17.6%
2006	12.3%	2006	17.4%
2007	12.5%	2007	18.0%

employment. "The term by which they are usually described, 'working poor,' should be an oxymoron. Nobody who works hard should be poor in America" (Shipler, 2004, p. ix). In spite of that observation, the fact remains that there are millions of working poor in America.

During the late 1990s, 5.2 million families with children had incomes that placed them below the federal poverty line, yet 76 percent had one or more working parent and 31 percent had a worker employed year-round full-time (Tenny & Zahradnik, 2001). These statistics were recorded during a period of strong economic growth. Since then, the economy experienced a recession, bounced back for a few years, and has fallen again. Unemployment has climbed, and those hardest hit have been low-income workers and families. For people already on the margin economically, recession and unemployment portend worse economic conditions. One of the trends that has contributed to the depth of poverty even for those who are working is the income disparity in this country. Economic growth over the past 25 years has not benefited all workers. As Box 8.5 outlines, income growth has benefited those who already were economically well off. The top 20 percent of households in this country realized an increase of almost 50 percent (over inflation) or $56,576 in their annual household incomes, while the bottom 20 percent of households realized an increase of 12 percent or $1,225 in income. With all the economic growth of the past 30 years, those at the top benefited more than those at the bottom. One theory is that this inequity may be because the "growing power of technology and the increasingly competitive economic climate seem to be pushing toward declining rewards for less-skilled workers and greater pay for

BOX 8.5	MORE ABOUT DISTRIBUTION OF HOUSEHOLD INCOME (IN PERCENT)

	2007	2000	1990	1980	1970	1960	1950	1941	1935
Highest 20%	49.7	49.6	46.6	43.7	43.3	45.4	46.1	48.8	51.7
Fourth 20%	23.4	23.0	24.0	24.9	24.5	22.7	22.1	22.3	20.9
Third 20%	14.8	14.8	15.9	16.9	17.4	16.4	16.1	15.3	14.1
Second 20%	8.7	8.9	9.6	10.3	10.8	10.9	10.9	9.5	9.2
Lowest 20%	3.4	3.6	3.9	4.3	4.1	4.6	4.8	4.1	4.1

Source: DeNavas-Walt, Proctor, & Smith, 2008; DeNavas-Walt, Proctor, & Mills, 2004; U.S. Census Bureau, 2001; McElvaine, 1993

Mean Household Income (income held in constant 2007 dollars)

	2007	2000	1990	1980
Highest 20%	167,971	171,297	134,006	111,395
Fourth 20%	79,111	79,049	69,053	62,477
Third 20%	49,968	50,850	45,799	42,408
Second 20%	29,442	30,535	27,728	25,700
Lowest 20%	11,551	12,229	11,020	10,326

Source: DeNavas-Walt, Proctor, & Smith, 2008

Percent Change from 1980–2007 (in constant dollars)

	Percent change	Dollar change
Highest 20%	+ 52%	+ $56,576
Fourth 20%	+ 27%	+ $16,634
Third 20%	+ 18%	+ $7,560
Second 20%	+ 15%	+ $3,742
Lowest 20%	+ 12%	+ 1,225

(author's calculations)

more-skilled workers" (Ellwood et al., 2000, p. 31). Other reasons may include business and economic growth and tax breaks that favored high earners over low earners. The economic climate includes the closing of factories and manufacturing plants in this country, which typically offered better-paying jobs. These jobs have been replaced by growth in the service sector, which offers lower-paying jobs. The result of this shift is greater economic imbalance between those at the top and those at the bottom, and more people who fall into the category of working poor.

Women and Poverty   Gender is a critical component of poverty. Women are more likely than men to be among those who are poor. This phenomenon was identified as the **feminization of poverty** (Pearce, 1978). On average, women earn 78 cents for each dollar men earn (DeNavas-Walt, Proctor, & Smith, 2008). Although this ratio is an improvement over the ratio of female to male earnings during the 1970s and 1980s, it has been stagnant since 1996. By the year 2007, the median income for women working full-time, year-round in the United States was $35,102 compared with $45,113 for men. Even when comparing equal work status and education, men fared better than women. For example, for men who worked full-time and had a bachelor's degree or better, the average annual income in 2005 was $87,777. For comparable women, the average income was $55,222 (U.S. Census Bureau, 2007).

Children and Poverty   As outlined in Box 8.4, children are the most likely group to live in poverty. This trend grew during the 1980s, and was identified as the **juvenilization of poverty** (Segal, 1991; Wilson, 1985). In spite of recent progress in decreasing the rate of poverty, children are still poor in greater proportions than any other age group. The social implications for millions of children raised in poverty are significant. Childhood poverty is linked to poor health, lower educational attainment, dangerous living situations, and a higher likelihood of experiencing disadvantaged life outcomes.

In addition to a moral imperative to provide a safe and healthy upbringing for children, there is a strong economic rationale. Research documents the relationship between childhood poverty and lower lifetime earnings, poor health, and a propensity to commit crime. The costs to the U.S. economy are significant. Focusing on lost productivity, each year childhood poverty reduces the Gross Domestic Product by almost 1.3 percent, raises the cost of crime by 1.3 percent of GDP, and raises health expenditures 1.2 percent of GDP. Together the costs related to childhood poverty are about $500 billion a year (Holzer et al., 2007). Therefore, for moral and economic reasons we should concentrate on reducing the level of poverty among children.

Race and Poverty   In 2007, the median income for white households was $54,920 compared with the median income of $33,916 for black families and $38,679 for Hispanic families (DeNavas-Walt, Proctor, & Smith, 2008). Thirty-six percent of whites earned $75,000 or more compared to 18 percent of blacks and 20 percent of Hispanics. The significantly higher earnings of white families can be traced back in part to historical racism and discrimination. African Americans, who have long been excluded from earning opportunities—first by hundreds of years of slavery and then by deliberate policies of exclusion—have experienced a legacy of income disparity. Many Hispanic people, who have come to the United States as undocumented persons unable to speak English, have been placed in a secondary class of employment, low-paying jobs that do not require English or legal documentation. Consider the data in Box 8.6.

Possibly the most impoverished people in the United States are Native Americans. The indigenous people have been systematically moved or destroyed since the time of the colonization of America by white Europeans. Today most Native Americans live

BOX 8.6	MORE ABOUT RACE AND POVERTY

2007 Poverty by Race	White	African American	Latino
All persons	8.2%	24.5%	21.5%
Families below poverty	6.0%	23.8%	20.6%
Female-headed families below poverty	21.4%	39.7%	39.6%
Children below poverty	10.1%	34.5%	28.6%

Source: DeNavas-Walt, Proctor, & Smith, 2008

on reservations, which are some of the most concentrated areas of poverty in the United States. For example, almost 50 percent of the Navaho Nation lives in poverty and about 26 percent of all American Indian and Alaska natives live in poverty (U.S. Census Bureau, 2007).

Asian immigrants to the United States have done better economically than others. However, their experiences have also been hampered by racism and discrimination. Poverty rates for Asian Americans, though better than for other groups, are still higher than those of white Americans. Poverty varies by nation of origin, with very high rates among some Asian groups, particularly those who came as refugees (Segal, Kilty, & Kim, 2002).

Homeless People   Possibly the most severe form of poverty is to be **homeless**, living without a permanent residence. Estimates of the number of people who are homeless vary widely. Because the nature of homelessness is transiency and impermanent housing, finding and counting people who are homeless becomes difficult. Many estimates are based on the numbers of people who use shelters and other services designed for people who are homeless. Although this may document the provision of services, it does not account for people who do not use services or are temporarily living with friends or family members but lack a permanent place of their own.

One of the biggest contributors to homelessness in this country is the lack of affordable housing. Many poor individuals and some families relied on rental of single rooms, often in former hotels that lacked kitchen facilities. These rooms, commonly referred to as **single room occupancies (SROs)**, offered affordable housing, albeit not ideal. However, due to urban development and efforts to "clean up" urban centers, one million SROs disappeared between 1960 and the mid-1980s (U.S. General Accounting Office, 1992). During the 1990s, the number of affordable apartments decreased by almost 25 percent. In 1991, there were 47 affordable rental units per every 100 low-income families, but in 1997, only 36 (U.S. Department of Housing and Urban Development, 2000). The decline in affordable housing greatly affected low-income workers and has contributed to the increase in the numbers of homeless people. Although difficult to assess, studies suggest that approximately one percent of the U.S. population experiences homelessness each year, which is about 3.5 million people (National Coalition for the Homeless, 2007). These numbers represent some of the poorest members of our society, and it is likely that almost 40 percent of them are children.

Each year the U.S. Conference of Mayors (2008) surveys major cities to assess the extent of homelessness in America. In 2008, 83 percent of the cities reported an increase in homelessness. As a consequence of economic conditions, 63 percent reported an increase in homelessness due to the home foreclosure crisis. Ninety-five percent reported increases in requests for emergency food assistance, and almost all the cities expected the demand for food assistance to increase in 2009. Another study found that more than three fourths of emergency shelters turn people away because they lack enough space (National Student Campaign Against Hunger and Homelessness, 2005). The economic crisis and increase in job losses will contribute to the growing number of people who find themselves homeless, with significant numbers of children among them. The issue of homelessness is becoming a reemerging policy concern.

WHAT CAUSES POVERTY?

The cause of poverty has probably been the subject of debate for as long as there have been people who are poor. If we could easily determine the cause of poverty, we could effectively respond to it. However, values and beliefs play a role in how we view poverty and, consequently, what we view as the underlying reasons for poverty in our society. Chapter 3 discussed the ideas of the culture of poverty and blaming the victim. These two perspectives take a personal or individual view of the cause of poverty. A structural perspective views poverty as a consequence of our economic, social, and political systems. And within these two categories are numerous theories to explain the cause of poverty. Some of the leading theories cited to explain poverty include the following (Jennings, 1999):

Human capital: People are poor because they lack education, training, or job skills.

Unfortunate circumstances: Unforeseen mishaps greatly disadvantage some people and lead to impoverishment.

Macroeconomics: Shifts in the employment sector have created permanent low-wage jobs that do not allow for advancement.

Racism, discrimination, and segregation: People are excluded from the mainstream economic system through prejudice, discrimination, and oppression.

Dependency: People become accustomed to receiving assistance and have no desire to work.

Lack of political power: Some groups are excluded from policy-making and, without wealth and privilege, these groups continue to be excluded.

The difficulty in determining the cause of poverty is that for every individual or family, there could be one or several of the listed reasons for economic distress. Some of the reasons are individual and some are social, and usually there is a combination of these forces. The difficulty in creating social policies that respond to poverty is in part because of the complexity of factors that contribute to it but also because of the values and beliefs that surround our views of people who are poor. The conflicting beliefs about poverty and the cause of it have led to a patchwork of social welfare policies and programs.

ANTIPOVERTY POLICIES AND PROGRAMS

Aiding those in need is not new. As discussed in Chapter 2, assistance for the poor dates back to colonial times. The major social services for people who are poor are cash assistance and in-kind benefits. Cash assistance has been most controversial because of a reluctance to give people money without controlling how it is spent. In-kind programs such as medical care and food coupons have received more public support.

PROGRAMS TO ENSURE ECONOMIC STABILITY

Temporary Assistance for Needy Families (TANF) Variations of local public assistance based on the Elizabethan Poor Laws dominated the public response to poverty among women and children until the 1900s. The first federal effort came in 1920, with passage of the **Mother's Aid** law. This program was narrow in scope. Prompted by the economic devastation of the Great Depression, Mother's Aid was expanded to become the **Aid to Dependent Children program (ADC)** and was passed as Title IV of the Social Security Act in 1935. ADC was viewed as a temporary program to support poor widows and their children. The original plan was that after social insurance became established, women and children who lost working husbands and fathers would be covered by the worker's social insurance as dependents of the deceased worker. They would not need ADC. Additionally, ADC was supported because single mothers and their children were considered a deserving group, and "by devoting themselves to mothering, the female recipients were performing what God, nature, and society intended women to do and doing so, moreover, under difficult circumstances" (Gordon, 2001, p. 17).

However, rather than serve as a temporary program, the demand for ADC expanded and it took on the status of a permanent program. In 1962 it was transformed to **Aid to Families with Dependent Children (AFDC)** to include the single parent, and several years after that it was expanded to include two-parent families if the main earner became unemployed. As the program became further entrenched in the social welfare system, additional efforts to change the program were launched.

Major revisions were enacted into law in 1988 under the **Family Support Act**, and then in 1996 the program was restructured under the **Personal Responsibility and Work Opportunities Act (PRWORA)**. The impetus behind PRWORA stemmed from changing demographics and perceptions of AFDC. The composition of families had shifted since the inception of the program. Women receiving AFDC were no longer predominantly widows but rather were mostly single women, either divorced or never married. At the same time, more women were entering the labor market, and the public perception grew that poor women were allowed to stay at home and receive a government check while other women were forced for economic reasons to work and not stay at home with their children. Statistics demonstrate that in some ways this perception was true, and in other ways it was not. Indeed more women had entered the labor market and were working outside the home. From 1970 to 2006, the percentage of women in the labor force grew from 43.3 percent to 59.4 percent (U.S. Census Bureau, 2007). Indeed, more women were working outside the home. Some of those working women were also recipients of AFDC, or relied on AFDC because they were between jobs or had experienced a major life change, such as divorce. During the 1990s, 72 percent of families that received cash assistance had a parent who worked at least part of the year (Tenny & Zahradnik, 2001).

Although the public perception was that women on public assistance "had it made" because they were receiving a check from the government for doing nothing but stay at home, the reality was different, as discussed in the critical policy analysis in Chapter 6. Most AFDC recipients were in and out of the labor force. Almost all female recipients were single mothers with young children facing barriers to working full-time and raising small children. Prior to passage of PRWORA, the average AFDC family consisted of one adult and two children under the age of 7 years who were receiving about $380 a month for three years or less (Administration for Children and Families, 1995). This amounted to about $2.20 an hour if considered from a full-time working role. Although the amount of AFDC was critical to families, it was not a large sum of money, and it went to the most vulnerable families, those with a single parent and young children with no savings or steady employment. By 1999, although the total numbers of recipients had declined, the characteristics had remained similar. The average TANF family consisted of one adult and two children whose average age was 7.8 years, who were receiving about $360 a month (Administration for Children and Families, 2000).

For 61 years, since its inception, AFDC had been an entitlement program. Any family who was eligible received benefits for as long as their eligibility was maintained. Furthermore, the federal government provided states with a portion of the funding for AFDC. With increased participation, federal spending grew. PRWORA changed the program in major ways. AFDC was replaced with **Temporary Assistance for Needy Families (TANF)**, which was not an entitlement program but rather a time-limited, no-guarantee program. The federal funding changed to an annual block grant. Public assistance for poor families was no longer a given but rather a conditional, time-limited support.

TANF provides temporary cash assistance and work opportunities for participants. Nearly all recipients must work within 2 years of receipt. The provisions of the law required each state to have 40 percent of the families either working or off the program by 2000, and 50 percent by 2002. The work requirements include 30 hours a week for single parents. The work can be unsubsidized or subsidized, on-the-job training, community service, up to 12 months of vocational training, or child care for other parents participating in community service. What is not allowed any longer is staying at home with one's own child, unless that child is under one year of age (Administration for Children and Families, 2004). If states could demonstrate cuts in their caseloads, they were exempt from the work participation rules and quotas. The result was that after ten years, only about one third of TANF recipients worked at least 30 hours a week (Benson, 2007).

In 2005, TANF was reauthorized under the Deficit Reduction Act. This legislation tightened the work requirements by further limiting what activities and which recipients states can count toward work participation. For example, the law now requires states to count as eligible to work, people who are waiting to qualify for disability and denies work credit for students studying at four-year colleges. If states do not meet these new stricter rules, they will lose federal funding through penalties (Parrott & Sherman, 2006).

Families cannot spend more than a lifetime total of five years on TANF. States can make that time limit even shorter or can exempt up to 20 percent of the caseload from the five-year time limit. After the five years, states may continue assistance but will not receive federal support to do so. As part of TANF, families can receive child care services and health care coverage through Medicaid. Child support enforcement is also a key provision of TANF.

Since its inception, TANF has reached its goal of decreasing the numbers of families receiving assistance. In 1996, 4.4 million families with 12.3 million participants received cash assistance under AFDC; by 2005, those numbers had dropped to 2.1 million families with 5.1 million recipients receiving assistance under TANF (Administration for Children and Families, 2004; Department of Health and Human Services, 2007). Research on mothers of young children who were eligible for TANF found that many were disconnected from the welfare system. Forty-five percent were not receiving TANF, and 16 percent had left voluntarily or because their time limits had run out or they had received sanctions. Both those receiving TANF benefits and those not receiving benefits were not doing well. They were experiencing high levels of economic hardship, eviction, hunger, and poor health (Center for Research on Child Wellbeing, 2003). The drop in TANF participation seems to be related to regulation changes and time limits, not eligibility or number of people in need. In the 1990s, 80 percent of families who were eligible received AFDC, compared to 48 percent of eligible families under TANF (Parrott & Sherman, 2006). Much of the caseload decline is due to administration of the program, not a reduction in poverty or economic need. It would seem that the changes in approach from AFDC to TANF, and a growing economy helped to bring down the number of recipients. The data raise this question: Are people better off with TANF, or is it only the government that benefits because caseloads are reduced and less has to be spent on public assistance?

Research findings on those who left TANF are mixed. Although more women are leaving and finding work, they do not seem to be better off. The majority of women who leave TANF have full-time jobs that pay $7 to $8 an hour (Acs & Loprest, 2004; Bazelon, 2002; Parrott & Sherman, 2006). Even with transitional support, eventually these women lose health care coverage from Medicaid and child care assistance. Only about one third of those who work after leaving TANF have employer-sponsored health insurance (Loprest, 2003). Touting the success of TANF in getting adult recipients into the work force, the Administration for Children and Families (2003) reported that average monthly earnings had risen to $686 in 2001. Although this was an improvement over previous years, these wages amounted to an average of $8,232 a year for a family of typically one adult and two children. Therefore, even though more TANF adults were working, their incomes still left them below the poverty line. The result of TANF seems to be that the decrease in caseload numbers is leading to an increase in the numbers of households headed by single women among the working poor.

In fact, among families with income below the poverty threshold, almost half (48 percent) received family income from earnings and only 31 percent of their total family income was from any means-tested programs, including TANF, SSI (discussed next) and food stamps (Department of Health and Human Services, 2007). Most telling in regard to the impact of TANF and welfare reform is the coverage of poor children. From 1988 until 1996, 58–62 percent of children living in poverty received AFDC. After the 1996 legislation, that portion dropped. By 2003, only 31 percent of poor children received TANF (Parrott & Sherman, 2006) and calculations for 2005 reveal that portion dropped further to less than 30 percent (author calculations based on Department of Health and Human Services, 2007 data). The "success" of TANF caseload reductions appears to rest on tighter eligibility and administrative restrictions so that less of the poor receive any assistance while the population of people who are poor has remained rather constant. The unanswered question is, what have poor people who previously would have received cash assistance been doing to survive now that eligibility has been severely reduced? Research is needed to answer this question and explain how poor families have been managing with less since welfare reform.

Supplemental Security Income   The Supplemental Security Income (SSI) program provides cash assistance to any person who is age 65 years or older, is blind, or has a disability and whose income falls below the poverty line. Poor children with disabilities are also covered under SSI. This federal program is an important support for low-income families, particularly those affected by disabilities. This may be either a disabled adult who cannot work or a disabled child who requires extra care. SSI is federally administered under the Social Security Administration, as opposed to TANF, which is state run as a partnership with the federal government. In 2007, 7.2 million people received SSI benefits, with an average monthly amount of $455 (Social Security Administration, 2008). For children under 18 years, the average monthly benefit was higher, at $542. About 15 percent of SSI recipients are children and 28 percent are 65 years of age or older. SSI is a significant antipoverty program for the elderly, covering from 55–60 percent of all elderly poor over the past five years (Department of Health and Human Services, 2007). The support from SSI for poor families with a child who has a disability has been extremely vital to creating a financial safety net for these families. SSI is also discussed in Chapter 12.

Earned Income Tax Credit   The Earned Income Tax Credit (EITC) is a federal program designed to lift families with full-time year-round workers above poverty levels. The program was created in 1975 for families with dependent children in which one or more family members work. Only wage earners qualify for this program. At certain income levels, the family qualifies to receive an income tax credit. This program is handled directly through the tax process, using income tax returns as the forms for calculating the credit. This program bypasses eligibility workers and welfare bureaucracies because it ties into the already existing income tax system. In 2003, one out of every six people filing federal income tax returns claimed the EITC, that is, more than 22 million families and individuals (Greenstein, 2005). In the tax year of 2007, qualifying families with 2 or more children could receive up to $4,716 and families with one child could receive up to $2,853 (Center for Policy Alternatives, 2007). The program calculates a credit based on income and family size, and if it exceeds the total tax owed, the difference is paid to the family as a refund.

Two examples highlight how the EITC works:

> Consider a family of four with a full-time year-round worker earning $6.75 per hour. This results in an annual income of $14,040. This family is entitled to $4,716 in EITC. After subtracting the employee's portion of payroll taxes and allowing for a child care credit, the family would be left with cash income of $17,682. While this is a significant benefit, it would still leave the family below the poverty threshold by more than $3,500.
>
> Now consider a single parent with one child. The parent works nearly full-time, 48 weeks at 38 hours, at the 2009 minimum wage of $7.25 per hour. This family's annual income is $13,224, resulting in an EITC of $2,853. After payroll taxes, the family is left with $15,065, which is more than $1,065 above the poverty threshold.
>
> (EITC credit calculated on Center on Budget and Policy Priorities Earned Income tax Credit Estimator, available at www.cbpp.org/eic2007/calculator/eitcchoose.htm)

Although in both these cases the families benefited from the cash support of the EITC, for the larger family it was not enough to lift them from poverty, but significant for the single parent family. Three fourths of EITC benefits go to families with adjusted gross incomes between $5,000 and $20,000 a year (Greenstein, 2005). The program is a critical support for low-income families lifting millions out of poverty. However, advocates argue that the EITC needs to be raised even further and also that wages, which are far too low, need to be increased.

Minimum Wage   The most productive way that wages can be increased is through raising the minimum wage. The **minimum wage** is the federally mandated lowest hourly wage that employers may legally pay their workers. Minimum wage is not typically thought of as a poverty program but rather as an employment policy. As such, it is discussed in more detail in Chapter 9. Its place in our economic and labor systems is also discussed. However, wages are crucial to low-income workers, so it is important to consider the impact of a minimum wage for low-income earners. In 2006, the minimum wage stood at $5.15 per hour. After years of legislative attempts, the Fair Labor Standards Act, which regulates the minimum wage, was amended. The minimum wage was slated to gradually rise from $5.15 to $5.85 in 2007, $6.55 in 2008, and $7.25 in 2009. Under the minimum wage of $7.25 per hour, at 40 hours a week, for 52 weeks a year, after payroll tax, a worker earns $13,926. Comparing this amount to the chart in Box 8.3, this would lift only one person above the poverty threshold. Raising the minimum wage by two more dollars would provide almost $4,000 more in income. Although a family would still have difficulty on this salary, at least it would begin to match what we officially identify as poverty. A family of four would need more than $10 per hour wage to match the poverty threshold for 2008. It is a policy discrepancy that the minimum wage—the hourly wage that is thought to be the lowest level—is not even enough to keep people out of the official level of poverty. And as previously discussed, that poverty threshold is already unrealistically low. The minimum wage and the EITC are discussed in more detail in the next chapter.

In spite of those limitations, the EITC and the minimum wage have combined to improve economic conditions for the working poor. From 1989 to 1997, expansions in both policies raised the amount of earnings for workers. For a single working mother with one child, earnings (after inflation) increased almost 27 percent, and for the same worker with two children, the increase in earnings was almost 42 percent (Blank, 2000). In 2005, about 4.4 million people were removed from poverty as a result of the federal EITC (Greenstein, 2005). Although working families are still in poverty or very near poverty, without these economic policy interventions, their situations would be far worse.

Other cash assistance programs, falling primarily under social insurance or federal tax exemptions, help to keep some people from falling into poverty. This has been especially true for the elderly over the past 25 years. Social insurance, unemployment insurance, workers compensation, and survivors and disability insurance are examples of other cash assistance programs. However, unlike those discussed here, they do not require poverty as a prerequisite for eligibility. Therefore, these programs are discussed in greater detail in other chapters. It is important to remember that although they are not regarded as antipoverty programs, they play an important part in keeping people out of poverty.

PROGRAMS PROVIDING IN-KIND SUPPORT

Food Stamps/ Supplemental Nutrition and Assistance Program   Social welfare policies for food distribution, developed as part of the New Deal, were originally designed to deal with a surplus of agricultural commodities. Support for government involvement in the purchase of food came from agricultural groups as a way to guarantee price support. With government subsidies through food distribution programs, people were able to purchase needed foods at prevailing prices even with overproduction and during economic depression. The agricultural support of surplus food distribution programs resulted in their administration by the Department of Agriculture. Legislative changes to government food distribution programs in later years shifted the emphasis to an antipoverty program (Finegold, 1988).

In response to the War on Poverty and the push for antipoverty programs, the **Food Stamp** program was enacted in 1964 as a way to assist poor individuals and families in purchasing food. The program was designed as a support, not to supply a family with all the food it needs. To reflect this, in 2008 the name was officially changed from the Food Stamp Program to the **Supplemental Nutrition and Assistance Program (SNAP)**. The benefits are based on a low-cost food plan known as the Thrifty Food Plan, which averages about $1 per person per meal (Jenkins, 2008). Today the program distributes coupons or credit cards with benefits allocated monthly to those who fall below a federally determined level of need. This system allows recipients the discretion to choose what food items they want to buy. Benefits may not be used for alcoholic beverages, tobacco, paper products, diapers, personal care products, or ready-to-eat foods. The program is administered through the Department of Agriculture, with local public aid offices responsible for determining eligibility and allotment of benefits. The Supplemental Nutrition and Assistance Program is funded from federal general revenues for the full value of the recipient's benefits, with administrative costs shared by the states and federal government. It is the largest food assistance program in the country and reaches more people over the course of a year than does any other public assistance program. In 2008, 28.4 million recipients received SNAP benefits, for an average monthly amount of $101.53 (Food and Nutrition Service, 2008). The anti-poverty impact of the program is significant. Ninety-six percent of children in poverty participated in the program, and almost 70 percent of all poor people received some amount of Food Stamp support (Department of Health and Human Services, 2007).

Supplemental Food Program for Women, Infants, and Children   The Supplemental Food Program for Women, Infants, and Children (WIC) is a federal program designed to provide nutrition and health assistance to pregnant and postpartum women, infants, and children up to the age of 5 years. To be eligible, women and their children must be at nutritional risk and have an income below the standards consistent with measuring need in the state. Administered by the Department of Agriculture and distributed through local clinics, the program provides participants with vouchers that can be redeemed for nutritional foods such as milk and eggs. Participants also qualify to receive nutrition education and health services aimed at improving the health of newborn babies and young children.

Public Housing   A number of housing programs are administered by federal, state, and local governments. Almost all are funded with federal money through the Department of Housing and Urban Development (HUD). Low-rent public housing projects, originally developed under 1937 legislation, are federally funded programs managed and administered by local Public Housing Authorities. Families, elderly persons, and people with disabilities usually qualify if their income is below a certain point, typically less than 50 percent of the median income for the area. Rental charges, set by the federal government, are about 30 percent of the recipient's monthly after-tax income.

The Department of Housing and Urban Development also provides rental assistance to poor families. Commonly referred to as the **Section 8 housing** program, the federal government provides rental certificates and vouchers that can be used to subsidize the lease of a privately owned rental unit. Participants pay 30 percent of their income toward rent, and a government voucher pays the rest. For a unit to qualify, its monthly rent cannot exceed a specific amount set by the government.

Since the late 1980s, the federal government has developed additional housing support programs specifically for people who are homeless. Passage of the Stewart B. McKinney Homeless Assistance Act of 1987 (P.L. 100-77) was the first comprehensive federal effort to aid people who are homeless. It was expanded over the years and renamed the McKinney-Vento Homeless Assistance Act in 2000 to reflect the passing of another strong legislative supporter of the program. The housing programs covered by the legislation include grants and funds for emergency shelter and monies to support transitional and permanent housing.

Clearly, a comprehensive and unified institutional approach to services for the poor is lacking in this country. There can be both positives and negatives to our residual approach. On the positive side, local administration can allow programs to be tailored to the unique needs of each community. Federal guidelines can create national minimums so that each citizen is entitled to an equal baseline of services.

Federal funding can equalize the differing financial means of states, thereby not penalizing poorer states and their residents. However, there are risks with such an approach. On the negative side, a piecemeal approach can leave gaps in services and a lack of coordination, leaving many without needed assistance. Funding can be inadequate because of the reluctance by states to contribute, relying only on federal funds instead. The reliance on a residual approach results in programs that are often inadequate in coverage, funding, and support services. Emphasis is placed on responding to poverty once it has occurred. Little is done preventively to address the factors that might lead to poverty in the first place.

RELATIVE POVERTY AND FEELINGS OF ECONOMIC DECLINE

In the beginning of this chapter, the concept of relative poverty was discussed. Although all assistance programs and statistical measures use absolute levels of poverty, many people experience relative poverty. More Americans are feeling economically squeezed. Seventy-nine percent of respondents in a recent annual national survey found it more difficult for people in the middle class to maintain their standard of living than in previous years (Pew Research Center, 2008). A majority felt stuck or falling backwards, the most downbeat assessment in almost 50 years of polling. In real economic terms, as of 2007, median household income had not returned to its 1999 level, making this the longest downturn for middle class earners (DeNavas, Proctor, & Smith, 2008). It seems that middle-income families have kept up over the years through women, particularly wives, entering the paid labor market (Mishel, Bernstein, & Allegretto, 2007). Losses in the housing and financial markets and growing numbers of foreclosures are adding to the distress felt by both those at the bottom and those in the middle.

Today, poverty, low incomes, and economic stress have taken broader meanings. Those people who identify in the middle are feeling poorer and this has an impact on how we approach poverty and government intervention. It may draw attention to the growing economic need for support. For the first time in many years, in 2008 Congress addressed its "moral responsibility to meet the needs of those persons, groups and communities that are impoverished, disadvantaged or otherwise in poverty" through passage of a House Concurrent Resolution (H. Con. Res. 198, 110th Congress, 2nd Session). While mostly symbolic, it may lead to more concrete action on addressing poverty in the United States.

CONFLICTING VALUES AND BELIEFS

Values and beliefs vary greatly and opinions are strong when it comes to discussions of poverty. Research on public opinion suggests that:

> Most Americans see welfare as a necessary and desirable function of government. That is not to say, however, that Americans are particularly happy with the current welfare system. But the source of their unhappiness, indeed the focus of considerable public anger and resentment, is not the principle of government support for the needy, but the perception that most people currently receiving welfare are undeserving. (Gilens, 1999, p. 2)

In recent years, the belief in government responsibility for the poor has grown. Sixty-nine percent feel that "the government should take care of people who can't care for themselves," up from 57 percent in 1994, and 54 percent fell that "the government should help more needy people even if the debt increases," which is up from 41 percent in 1994 (Pew Research Center, 2007). Yet people also feel that "poor people have become too dependent on government assistance," with 69 percent agreeing. However, this was a significant drop from 1994 when 85 percent felt poor people were too dependent.

Thus, in principle, Americans believe that government should play a role in helping people and addressing poverty. Where their support declines is in the belief that those who actually receive assistance are not deserving of that support. "In large measure, Americans hate welfare because they view it as a program that rewards the undeserving poor" (Gilens, 1999, p. 3). Why?

Examination of poverty in American society suggests that it is not a case of disagreement between people with a value of caring for the poor and people who lack that value. Nor is it as simple as recognition that there are people in need as opposed to lack of recognition. What really distinguishes how a person feels about poverty in America has to do with a person's beliefs. And the conflict in dealing with poverty therefore rests in the conflict between competing beliefs.

UNDESERVING VERSUS DESERVING

Most Americans support the idea of helping people in need, as long as that person is worthy of that help. They must be seen as trying hard, willing to work if given the chance, and grateful for any and all opportunities. The values of deserving and undeserving, dating back to the colonial period (1700s), are significant today in discussions of poverty. The early colonial laws considered widows, orphans, elderly people, and people with a physical disability as worthy of assistance. The characteristic they shared was that they were in need through circumstances beyond their control. That view persists today. In political speeches given in the House of Representatives hours before the approval of the welfare reform legislation in 1996, the overriding concern of lawmakers was self-sufficiency and serving the truly needy (Segal & Kilty, 2003). If a person is perceived as able to work but still poor, then the belief is that the person is not worthy of assistance. This value of distinguishing between deserving and undeserving may seem clear and logical, and therefore a reasonable way to distinguish who should receive welfare and who should not. However, other conflicting beliefs influence how we perceive deservedness.

PERSONAL FAILURE VERSUS SYSTEM FAILURE

At first, when we meet a person who looks healthy and is receiving government assistance, we question why the person is not working. It is difficult not to immediately compare our own efforts at holding a job and earning enough to support ourselves and our families with the fact that this person is getting assistance without working. Feelings of unfairness come to us, and we consider the person to be undeserving. However, oftentimes, what is lacking in understanding poverty in

America is the impact of our economic, social, and political systems on access and opportunity. Racism limits people's opportunities. Women are treated differently than men. Companies find it cheaper to close plants and move, leaving hundreds of workers without jobs, and many do not have skills to quickly change to another job. Education is not equally available at high levels, so some people at a young age do not learn the skills that would help them get jobs. Therefore, we must question whether these are instances of personal failure or whether there are flaws in our social interactions, economic policies, or educational systems. This raises the next question: Who is responsible for people's well-being, each individual or society?

SELF-SUFFICIENCY VERSUS SOCIAL SUPPORT

How much responsibility for having enough to eat, a safe place to live, and an education should be placed on the individual, and how much on society? If we view poverty as the result of a person's unwillingness to work hard enough or mistakes the person has made in his or her life, then we are most likely going to focus on individual responsibility. If we view poverty as a consequence of social conditions, then we are most likely going to call for public policies and programs that address poverty through government and societal efforts. For some of us, the value of social responsibility is so strong that it may not matter who is at "fault" for poverty, the individual or society. Rather, our responsibility to others supersedes all, and therefore we must take care of all people, regardless of the cause of their need.

THOSE WE KNOW VERSUS THOSE WHO ARE STRANGERS

One characteristic that seems to pervade American society is the tendency to be more comfortable and more inclined to help people we know, or feel we know, rather than help strangers. With the class differences in American society, people with wealth, or even comfortable means, rarely if ever have contact with people who are poor. What little contact they have is typically not on a personal level but rather through the media or hierarchical relationships where a person of a lower class serves or works for a person of a higher class. Those with means are served in restaurants or have their lawns and homes cared for by those who are barely making ends meet.

SYMPATHY VERSUS EMPATHY

Poverty evokes a lot of emotions, including feelings of sadness and pity. These feelings tend to fall under sympathy. We feel how unfortunate poor people are and how difficult their lives might be. But we do not relate to them as if they are the same kind of people that we are but without financial means. Being empathic would mean that we realize that poverty could happen to any one of us and, therefore, it is not the individual's fault alone. Outside circumstances contribute to poverty, and if we do not address those outside circumstances, we too could someday face being poor. However, this view is rarely held by those who make the decisions regarding poverty-related policies. Consider Box 8.7 and notice how very different those who receive public assistance are from those who vote on the policies that regulate those programs. Viewing poverty from a sympathetic perspective typically means addressing it as an individual problem. When looking at it from an empathic viewpoint, the desire is to change the external factors that contribute to impoverishment.

FINAL THOUGHTS ON POVERTY

Poverty is not a new phenomenon in this country, but it continues to evoke strong responses from policy makers and the public. The debate surrounding what to do about poverty reflects the dilemma of reconciling the level of wealth in the United States with the persistence of poverty among millions of people. "In just a little over two centuries the United States went from being a society born of revolution and touched by egalitarianism to being the country with the industrial world's biggest fortunes and its largest rich-poor gap" (Phillips, 2002, p. xviii).

Recognition that the structure of our economic system results in poverty demands large-scale changes in our market and labor systems. If one holds that the individual is responsible for his or her poverty, then the emphasis is on changing peoples' behaviors. Thus far in American history, neither approach has been implemented effectively. The current trend toward holding individuals completely responsible for their economic conditions means that millions of people, particularly children, will lack proper shelter, sufficient nutrition, adequate education, or access to opportunities. Over time, that approach guarantees the perpetuation of poverty and its consequences in this country.

BOX 8.7	CONTROVERSIAL PERSPECTIVES

How similar are the lives of the people who make policy decisions to the lives of people who are subject to those decisions?

Comparison of TANF Adult Recipients and Members of Congress

	TANF Adults	Members of Congress
Average age	31 years	55 years
Female:	90%	14.4%
White	31.6%	87.1%
Black	38.3%	6.9%
Hispanic	24.9%	4.5%
More than a high school education	3.3%	92.7%
Employment rate	25.3%	100%
Millionaires	0	29.2%

Source: Segal, 2006.

Key Terms

absolute poverty

relative poverty

poverty threshold

poverty guidelines

feminization of poverty

juvenilization of poverty

homeless

Temporary Assistance for Needy Families (TANF)

Supplemental Security Income (SSI)

Earned Income Tax Credit (EITC)

minimum wage

Food Stamp

Supplemental Nutrition and Assistance Program (SNAP)

Supplemental Food Program for Women, Infants, and Children (WIC)

Section 8 housing

Questions for Discussion

1. How much is enough for a person to live on adequately?
2. Define basic needs. Is a telephone a necessity? What if you have young children? Is health insurance a necessity? What kind of shelter is sufficient?
3. What is the impact of poverty on a person's life? How do you think poverty affects people? How does poverty affect our society?
4. Define the term *working poor*. Explain how it is possible for a person to work and still be poor. Does this seem fair? Why or why not?
5. Describe the term *middle class*. What is the difference between lower and middle class? How would you define working class, and where does that group fit in?

Excercises

1. Find the local public assistance office in your community. Spend some time sitting in the waiting room. What does it look like? How many people are there? Can you find information on the programs? How was this waiting room different or the same as other public offices or private offices, such as doctors' or driver registration offices? After you leave, write down your observations and impressions. Compare your experience with your classmates' experiences.
2. Apply for an entry-level job at a local business. How much does the job pay? How does it compare to the poverty level? Does it include health care coverage? What about other benefits, such as sick leave or vacations? Are there other costs involved, such as transportation or uniforms? Could you care for children with the schedule of this job?
3. Call a local public assistance office and identify yourself as a student. Ask if you could get a copy of an application for TANF or food assistance. What information does the application require? Does it seem extensive or minimal? Is it like other applications you have filled out? Why or why not?
4. For one month, record all your living expenses. How much is your monthly budget? What percentage do you spend on food? On housing? How does your budget compare with the poverty line?
5. Go online to the Internal Revenue Service web site, irs.gov, and find out what the income criteria are for the Earned Income Tax Credit program. What income levels qualify, and what are the benefits?

References

Acs, G., & Loprest, P. (2004). *Leaving welfare: Employment and well-being of families that left welfare in the post-entitlement era.* Kalamazoo, MI: W.E. Upjohn Institute for Employment Research.

Administration for Children and Families. (2004). *Welfare: TANF factsheet.* Washington, DC: U.S. Department of Health and Human Services.

Administration for Children and Families. (2003). *TANF Program: Fifth annual report to Congress.* Washington, DC: U.S. Department of Health and Human Services.

Administration for Children and Families. (2000). *TANF Program: Third annual report to Congress.* Washington, DC: U.S. Department of Health and Human Services.

Administration for Children and Families. (1995). *Characteristics and financial circumstances of AFDC recipients FY 1993.* Washington, DC: U.S. Department of Health and Human Services.

Allegretto, S. A. (2005). *Basic family budgets: Working families' incomes often fail to meet living expenses around the U.S. Briefing Paper #65.* Washington, DC: Economic Policy Institute.

Bazelon, E. (2002, June 17–23). A limit that loses sight of the goal: What will happen when welfare recipients reach the five-year cutoff? *Washington Post National Weekly Edition* 19(34):23.

Benson, C. (2007). States scramble to adapt to new welfare rules. *CQ Weekly* (June 25, 2007), p. 1907.

Bernstein, J., Brocht, C., & Spade-Aguilar, M. (2000). *How much is enough? Basic family budgets for working families.* Washington, DC: Economic Policy Institute.

Blank, R. M. (2000). Enhancing the opportunities, skills, and security of American workers. In D. T. Ellwood, R. M. Blank, J. Blasi, D. Kruse, W. A. Niskanen, K. Lynn-Dyson (eds.). *A working nation: Workers, work, and government in the new economy,* pp. 105–123. New York: Russell Sage Foundation.

Center for Policy Alternatives. (2007). *Progressive agenda for the states 2008: Leadership for America.* Washington, DC: Author.

Center for Research on Child Wellbeing. (2003). *Variations in maternal and child wellbeing by TANF eligibility and participation.* Fragile Families Research Brief, Number 19. Princeton, NJ: Princeton University.

DeNavas-Walt, C., Cleveland, R. W., & Roemer, M. I. (2001). Money income in the United States: 2000. *Current Population Reports,* P60-213. Washington, DC: U.S. Census Bureau.

DeNavas-Walt, C., Proctor, B. D., & Smith, J. C. (2008). Income, poverty, and health insurance coverage in the United States: 2007. *Current Population Reports,* P60-235. Washington, DC: U.S. Census Bureau.

DeNavas-Walt, C., Proctor, B. D., & Mills, R. J. (2004). Income, poverty, and health insurance coverage in the United States: 2003. *Current Population Reports,* P60-226. Washington, DC: U.S. Census Bureau.

Department of Health and Human Services. (2008, January 23). 2008 HHS poverty guidelines. *Federal Register* 73(15):3971–3972.

Department of Health and Human Services. (2007). *Indicators of welfare dependence: Annual report to Congress 2007.* Washington, DC: Office of the Assistant Secretary for Planning and Evaluation.

Ehrenreich, B. (2001). *Nickel and dimed: On (not) getting by in America.* New York: Henry Holt.

Ellwood, D. T. (2000). Winners and losers in America: Taking measure of the new economic realities. In D. T. Ellwood, R. M. Blank, J. Blasi, D. Kruse, W. A. Niskanen, K. Lynn-Dyson (eds.). *A working nation: Workers, work, and government in the new economy,* pp. 1–41. New York: Russell Sage Foundation.

Finegold, K. (1988). Agriculture and the politics of U.S. social provisions: Social insurance and food stamps. In M. Weir, A. S. Orloff, & T. Skocpol (eds.). *The politics of social policy in the United States.* Princeton, NJ: Princeton University Press.

Food and Nutrition Service. (2008). *National level annual summary Supplemental Nutrition Assistance Program.* Washington, DC: US Department of Agriculture.

Gilens, M. (1999). *Why Americans hate welfare: Race, media, and the politics of antipoverty policy.* Chicago: University of Chicago Press.

Gordon, L. (2001). Who deserves help? Who must provide? *Annals of the American Academy of Political and Social Science* 557:12–25.

Greenstein, R. (2005). *The Earned Income Tax Credit: Boosting employment, aiding the working poor.* Washington, DC: Center on Budget and Policy Priorities.

Holzer, H. J., Schanzenbach, D. W., Duncan, G. J., & Ludwig, J. (2007). *The economic costs of poverty in the United States: Subsequent effects of children growing up poor*. Washington, DC: Center for American Progress.

Jenkins, C. L. (2008, June 2–8). Food Stamps must stretch even further. *Washington Post National Weekly Edition 25*(3):33.

Jennings, J. (1999). Persistent poverty in the United States: Review of theories and explanations. In L. Kushnick, & J. Jennings (eds.). *A new introduction to poverty: The role of race, power and politics*, pp. 1338. New York: New York University Press.

Loprest, P. (2003). Fewer welfare leavers employed in weak economy. *Snapshots of America's Families*, Series 3, No. 5. Washington, DC: Urban Institute.

McElvaine, R. S. (1993). *The Great Depression*. New York: Times Books, Random House.

Mishel, L., Bernstein, J., & Allegretto, S. (2007). *The state of working America 2006/2007*. New York: Cornell University Press and Economic Policy Institute.

National Coalition for the Homeless. (2007). *How many people experience homelessness? NCH Fact Sheet #2*. Washington, DC: Author.

National Student Campaign Against Hunger and Homelessness. (2005). *Survey of hunger and homelessness in America 2004*. Washington, DC: Author.

Orshansky, M. (1965). Counting the poor: Another look at the poverty profile. *Social Security Bulletin 28*(1):3–29.

Parrott, S. & Sherman, A. (2006). *TANF at 10: Program results are more mixed than often understood*. Washington, DC: Center for Budget and Policy Priorities.

Pearce, D. (1978). The feminization of poverty: Women, work, and welfare. *Urban and Sociological Change Review 11*(1–2):28–36.

Pew Research Center. (2008). *Inside the middle class: Bad times hit the good life*. Washington, DC: Author.

Pew Research Center. (2007). *Trends in political values and core attitudes: 1987–2007*. Washington, DC: Author.

Phillips, K. (2002). *Wealth and democracy: A political history of the American rich*. New York: Broadway Books.

Proctor, B. D., & Dalaker, J. (2003). Poverty in the United States: 2002. *Current Population Reports*, P60-222. Washington, DC: U.S. Census Bureau.

Segal, E. A. (1991). Juvenilization of poverty in the 1980s. *Social Work 36*(5):454–457.

Segal, E. A. (2006). Welfare as we should know it: Social empathy and welfare reform. In K. M. Kilty, & E. A. Segal (eds.) *The promise of welfare reform: Rhetoric or reality?* Binghamton, NY: Haworth Press.

Segal, E. A. & Kilty, K. M. (2003). Political promises for welfare reform. *Journal of Poverty 7*(1/2): 51–68.

Segal, E. A., Kilty, K. M., & Kim, R. (2002). Social and economic inequality and Asian Americans in the United States. *Journal of Poverty 6*(4):5–22.

Shipler, D. K. (2004). *The working poor: Invisible in America*. New York: Alfred A. Knopf.

Social Security Administration. (2008). *Annual Statistical Supplement, 2007*. Washington, DC: Author.

Social Security Administration. (2005). *Annual Statistical Supplement, 2004*. Washington, DC: Author.

Social Security Administration. (2004). *Annual Statistical Supplement, 2003*. Washington, DC: Author.

Tenny, D., & Zahradnik, B. (2001). *The poverty despite work handbook*, 3rd ed. Washington, D.C.: Center on Budget and Policy Priorities.

U.S. Census Bureau. (2007). *Statistical abstract of the United States: 2008*. 127th ed. Washington, DC: U.S. Government Printing Office.

U.S. Census Bureau. (2001). *Statistical abstract of the United States: 2001*, 121st ed. Washington, DC: U.S. Department of Commerce.

U.S. Conference of Mayors. (2008). *Hunger and homelessness survey: A status report on hunger and homelessness in America's cities - a 25-city survey*. Washington, DC: Author.

U.S. Department of Housing and Urban Development. (2000). *Rental housing assistance: The worsening crisis*. Washington, DC: Author.

U.S. General Accounting Office. (1992). *Homelessness: Single-room-occupancy program achieves goal, but HUD can increase impact*. GAO/RCED-92-215. Washington, DC: Author.

Wilson, G. (1985). The juvenilization of poverty. *Public Administration Review 45*:880–884.

ECONOMICS: EMPLOYMENT, BUDGETS, AND TAXES

CHAPTER 9

Monika Graff/Getty Images

Current social welfare policies and programs have been shaped by both social factors and economic conditions. Social forces are central to the development of social welfare policy, but changes in the economic system have also played a crucial role in influencing public policy responses in the United States. The history outlined in Chapter 2 demonstrates numerous instances when economic change precipitated policy change. The best example was the impact of the Great Depression on the social welfare system: The Social Security Act was passed in response to the most significant economic downturn in history. Chapter 7 discussed how this legislation permanently altered the role of government in aiding individual economic well-being.

Although economic trends play a critical role in the development of social welfare policies, the role is often overlooked by those who provide direct human services. Social work and economics are often viewed as unrelated disciplines. Social workers are often not familiar with the subject of economics. The realm of economics seems to be technical and rigid to the social service provider, who is trained in human behavior.

Economics can be described as "the science of the production and distribution of wealth" (*Oxford American Dictionary*, 1999). Economics is viewed as a science, whereas social work is more often viewed as an art:

> A rigorous intellectual approach associated with scientific thinking is resisted ... It [rigorous intellectual assessment] is perceived on the one hand as a threat to the uniqueness of the individual. On the other hand, since it seems cold and impersonal, it is perceived as a threat to the skill of the social worker, to the sensitivity and the artistic element that are regarded as so important in social work. (Bartlett, 1970, p. 38)

The main difference between social work and economics appears to be the difference between an art and a technical science, but there are significant ideological differences between the two disciplines as well.

IDEOLOGICAL DIFFERENCES BETWEEN SOCIAL WORK AND ECONOMICS

There are three fundamental ideological differences between social work and economics. The first is the emphasis placed on competition for resources. The foundation of economics is the competitive marketplace, in which those who have the most to offer can outbid all others. Social welfare services are designed to minimize the extremes of competitive distribution. The second difference is the emphasis on cost/benefit analysis. Economics is concerned with finding the least expensive way to produce the greatest results. Social welfare workers are concerned with the best ways of helping people cope or adapt and with methods of producing environmental change. The cost of these "products" is not the ultimate concern, and the most effective policies are often not the least expensive alternatives. The third difference is the use of mathematical calculations and concrete criteria to explain social and human behaviors in economics as opposed to the use of case studies and practical experience to guide analyses of behavior in social work. These differences can lead to conflict between the ideologies of economics and social work.

COMPETITIVE MARKETPLACE

Social workers tend to believe that economists are predominantly interested in finding the most efficient system of transfer for the marketplace (Page, 1977). Efficient transfer of resources minimizes social welfare outlays and stresses a competitive economic model. Those who possess sufficient means are able to acquire what they need and, conversely, those with minimal resources are left with very little. The by-products of such competition are the economically deprived groups who lack the means to actively participate in the marketplace.

An unrestricted competitive marketplace may function economically from a theoretical standpoint, but in reality there are social repercussions. If all variables related to employment were relatively equal, such as educational opportunity and access to jobs, and if impediments such as racism, sexism, and other forms of discrimination were eliminated, then open competition would create a stable economy. Unfortunately, this is not the case.

> Structural unemployment, beyond the reach of macroeconomic demand policies, afflicts disproportionately certain vulnerable demographic groups, teenagers, young adults, minorities. Labor markets are very imperfectly competitive. The interests of unemployed outsiders are insufficiently represented. . . . (Tobin, 1986, p. 30)

COST/BENEFIT EMPHASIS

An outgrowth of the competitive nature of the marketplace is the emphasis on comparing the cost of a product with the benefits it generates. Marketplace success is achieved when a product makes more money than the cost of the process required to produce it. In social welfare services, the outcome is often intangible or immeasurable. Although the dollars spent for a given program can be tallied, the quantifiable dollar benefit of a nutrition program for infants, mental health services for suicidal clients, or literacy tutoring for unemployed adults is impossible to calculate.

Furthermore, emphasizing costs versus benefits ignores social responsibility and conscience. Social work ideology stresses empowerment, self-determination, and advocacy regardless of the potential for profitable return. Cost/benefit concerns often do not take human needs into account. Weighing costs against benefits is an aggregate function that does not recognize the uniqueness of each person.

For example, Charles Murray (1984) in his book *Losing Ground*, an indictment of government involvement in social welfare, used the analysis of cost versus benefit to support his argument against social welfare spending. Murray's point was that if the amount spent on antipoverty measures over the previous 30 years had been effective, poverty would no longer exist. Because poverty continues to exist, he concluded that there is no reason to continue spending money on social welfare services. Although there are numerous fallacies in Murray's logic (as well as erroneous calculations), the issue here is that Murray looked at poverty as simply a matter of cost versus benefit. There is no acknowledgment of inequality of opportunity, discrimination, or the human experience of poverty anywhere in Murray's book. Murray also ignores the possibility that if antipoverty measures had not been available, poverty in this country would be worse.

MATHEMATICAL CALCULATIONS

Many aspects of economics are based on mathematical concepts and computations. Mathematics is often an intimidating subject and alien to human service providers. Furthermore, mathematical calculations cannot measure or quantify the uniqueness of each individual. Human variability is a key element for social work professionals and clients. In order to capture the uniqueness of individuals, social workers examine clients on a case-by-case basis. Details of a person's individual history and current social and emotional conditions are used to choose appropriate interventions. This emphasis on the qualitative aspects of people's lives seems to conflict with the quantitative mathematical assessment techniques used by economists.

Regardless of the difficulties in quantifying social concerns, elected officials and policy analysts tend to regard mathematical calculations as a stronger basis for making policy decisions. Consequently, social workers often base their arguments on first-hand, unquantifiable experience when they are dealing with policy makers who base their arguments on broad-based statistical data. Success in policy advocacy requires an understanding of this difference, and hence an understanding of the economy.

KEY ECONOMIC CONCEPTS

In spite of the ideological differences between economics and social work, economics is an extremely important aspect of the public policy debate:

> The health of the economy, and therefore economic policy, is vital to the ability of the nation to undertake other policy goals. An economy that is growing at a healthy, moderate rate with low inflation can develop new programs and help those who need assistance. A stagnant economy does not allow for new programs or the expansion of old ones. (Rushefsky, 2002, pp. 53–54)

Because social welfare policy is interwoven with the economic structure of our society, social workers should have a working knowledge and understanding of economic phenomena. "Unless the relationship between economics and social work is strengthened, the ability of social work to influence social policy will tend to decrease" (Page, 1977, p. 49). The course of social welfare policy during the 1980s, 1990s, and 2000s seems to confirm this view. Before we can influence social welfare policy, we must understand economic policy. The rest of this chapter is devoted to coverage of the key economic issues relevant to social welfare policy and the relationship of economics to social well-being.

ROLE OF THE MARKETPLACE

One of the key concepts of the economic marketplace is the balance between **supply and demand**. The products and services offered constitute the **supply**, and the desire and ability to buy constitute the **demand**. When there is a high demand, the price of goods goes up. If the price goes up too much, consumers cannot afford to buy a product and demand for it decreases. The supply stacks up; prices are cut to encourage buying; and demand increases again. The reality of supply and demand is not as smooth as the theory. Interest in an item or service changes according to people's attitudes or because of unexpected negative publicity. Nonetheless, it is a fact that the U.S. economy experiences periods of expansion and high demand alternating with periods of contraction and low demand.

For example, suppose automobile manufacturers develop a new vehicle, such as a minivan. People like the vehicle and want to buy it, but few are available. Because the demand is greater than the supply, there is a shortage of minivans. People are still interested in buying them, so the price goes up and creates inflation. Because the price is driven up by demand, and not by an increase in manufacturing expenses, profit increases. Other automobile companies see the interest in minivans and the profits others are making, and decide to also make minivans. Now the supply increases rapidly. The market expands as the supply grows. Eventually, however, the number of people interested in buying minivans does not increase as fast as the supply increases. In order to encourage customers to buy their minivans, manufacturers reduce prices and offer special incentives. This causes deflation, or the lowering of prices. The amount of profit falls. If manufacturers lose too much money because of overproduction, some companies lay off workers or shut down production. This can result in a recession. After a period of low production, the supply decreases. Some people will still have the interest and means to buy, so the demand begins to grow once more. With growth in demand, the cycle begins again.

This simplified example illustrates the cyclical nature of the marketplace. However, the simple give and take between supply and demand may be impacted by other variables. The example of the minivan production demonstrates further complications with competing economic events. Consider the speedy rise in oil prices during the summer of 2008. The increase in the cost of gasoline pushed consumers to reconsider the purchase of low-mileage vehicles like the minivan. The sales of vehicles with low gas mileage declined. Thus, the economics of gasoline has an impact on consumption, and hence an impact on supply and demand. Sometimes other economic events play a strong role in affecting the balance between supply and demand. The existence of prolonged economic downturns and unexpected events suggests that the cyclical, self-correcting nature of the economy is not always adequate. The potential for negative outcomes was addressed by economist John Maynard Keynes during the 1920s. Keynes advanced the idea that lapses in the supply and demand cycle could be influenced by government policies. "The crux of Keynes's message was that government spending might be an essential economic policy for a depressed capitalism trying to recover its vitality" (Heilbroner & Thurow, 1982, p. 31). The acceptance of Keynes's ideas following the Great Depression led to the direct involvement of government in the supply-and-demand economy.

One major way for government to take a Keynesian approach is to provide money for those without employment so they can continue to purchase necessities. Therefore, from an economic viewpoint, the Supplemental Nutrition Assistance Program (formerly the Food Stamp program), which allows people in poverty to continue to purchase food at local grocery stores, is not just an antipoverty program but a stimulus to production. This issue arose during arguments about cutting back Food Stamps under the 1995 policy plans of the Republican Contract with America. Farmers and agricultural businesspeople argued against cutting back the Food Stamp program by pointing out that the billions of federal government dollars spent on Food Stamps indirectly helped agriculture by guaranteeing that people could buy food no matter how poor they were.

The economic stimulus checks of 2008 are another example of a Keynesian way to approach the economy. The Economic Stimulus Act of 2008 was an effort by the federal government to address a slowdown in economic growth by putting money back in the hands of workers and businesses. The program was designed to provide rebates of up to $600 for individuals and $1,200 for couples. On a small scale per household that may not seem like a significant infusion of cash. But the program was designed to cover 128 million households and transfer $152 billion, about one percent of the Gross Domestic Product of the United States (White House, 2008). While the program did contribute to Americans spending more through the summer, it appears to have only marginally diminished the economic downturn. What was especially unusual about this policy was that it was so strongly backed by a Republican President Bush, whose policies and party's positions typically oppose Keynesian economic interventions.

Some people argue that "desperate times call for desperate measures" and so opposition to government intervention wanes with economic downturns. The economic downturn of 2007 and 2008 precipitated the largest government intervention in the economy. Never in U.S. history have so many debt markets—mortgages, bonds, securities, student loans, corporate lending, home equity loans, credit cards—been disrupted. The response has been Keynesian. The federal government took over or guaranteed the economic standing of mortgage lenders, investment banks, student loans that had originated from private banks, and offered low interest loans backed by the public treasury to keep financial institutions afloat. The long-term cost of these interventions could total trillions of dollars (Cho & Irwin, 2008). The Troubled Assets Relief Program signed into law under President Bush authorized $700 billion and the American Recovery and Reinvestment Act of 2009 signed into law under President Obama authorized $787 billion. These two bills alone pushed government investment in the economy to over one and a half trillion dollars.

The debate as to the optimal extent of government involvement in the economy is at the center of much of today's social welfare policy action. Those who advocate federal involvement reflect the value of social responsibility, that is, the market system is not perfect and some people do not benefit from the economic system, and, therefore, the government must intervene to alleviate the harmful effects of economic policies. Those who feel the government should not intervene in the economy reflect the belief that the market should be left alone because government intervention can inhibit the incentive for individual work and economic growth. Most political disagreements about the extent and form of social welfare services reflect the struggle between these two positions.

EMPLOYMENT AND UNEMPLOYMENT

One of the most strongly held economic beliefs, which is connected to our social belief in individual responsibility, is that if a person works hard, she or he will be rewarded. This ideology stems from the earliest history of this country, when Americans embraced concepts such as "pull yourself up by your own bootstraps" and eagerly read Horatio Alger stories about a young man who rose from rags to riches. Implicit in this ideology is the belief that there are jobs available for everyone who wants to work and that all a person needs to do is find a job and stay with it. Although this belief permeates our social consciousness, it is not entirely realistic. The job market frequently fluctuates. The existence of a job does not necessarily mean that it is available to anyone who is looking. Obviously, education and ability play a part in employability. Location and unwillingness of employers to consider a wide range of applicants can block access to employment. Therefore, even when jobs are available, they may not be available to all who are looking for work. The result is that there are varying numbers of people who are unemployed and looking for work.

The Bureau of Labor Statistics keeps track of the official rate of unemployment and announces it on the first Friday of each month. The official definition of **unemployment** is the following:

> Unemployed persons comprise all civilians who had no employment during the reference week [the week in which the data were gathered that month], who made specific efforts to find a job within the previous 4 weeks (such as applying directly to an employer or to a public employment service or checking with friends), and who were available for work during that week, except for temporary illness. Persons on layoff from a job and expecting recall are also classified as unemployed. (U.S. Census Bureau, 2007, p. 370)

People who have given up on looking for a job; those who would like a job but do not apply for one because they cannot find child care or transportation to a job site; and those who are underemployed (i.e., working in jobs that do not use their skills or give them as many hours as they need) are not officially counted among the unemployed. Therefore, the unemployment rate does not reflect all people who are out of work. The true rate of unemployment may be significantly higher than the official rate.

In spite of the limitations in counting the number of people who are unemployed, the data provide a valuable indication of employment trends over the years. Box 9.1 lists selective average unemployment rates from 1960 to 2007. The rate of unemployment in this country fluctuates and typically reflects the strength of the economy. Since 1960, the highest annual rate was 9.7 percent in 1982 and the lowest was 3.5 percent in 1969. By 2009, the unemployment rate had risen to 8.1%, the highest it had been since 1983, with the largest monthly loss of jobs in January in almost 40 years (Economic Policy Institute, 2009).

BOX 9.1 | **MORE ABOUT UNEMPLOYMENT RATES**

Annual unemployment rates (in percent)

1960	5.5	2000	4.0
1965	4.5	2001	4.7
1970	4.9	2002	5.8
1975	8.5	2003	6.0
1980	7.1	2004	5.5
1985	7.2	2005	5.1
1990	5.6	2006	4.6
1995	5.6	2007	4.6

Source: *Economic Report of the President*, 2008.

Types of Unemployment   Not all unemployment is the same. There are a number of types of unemployment (Schiller, 2004). **Structural unemployment** reflects the structure of our economic system. Some people, in spite of wanting to work, find themselves unable to gain access to the training or education needed for the jobs available. For example, there may be numerous jobs open for data processing, but if a person has not attended a school that has up-to-date computers and software, or cannot afford post–high-school training, a data processing job is out of reach. The unavailability of suitable employment is also true for the **dislocated worker**, the person who was trained for and employed in an occupation no longer needed. Many manufacturing jobs have been phased out of existence with the development of computerized assembly systems.

Seasonal unemployment reflects changes in employment at different times of the year. Retailers sell most of their goods during the winter holiday season, so they hire more workers at that time. Construction jobs tend to be available in the spring and summer when the weather permits large building projects to be undertaken. Farm workers, particularly migrant workers, find employment during the harvest but not during the rest of the year. The time of year and season have an impact on the needs of employers.

Unemployment that is limited to a specific region or a specific type of work is referred to as **geographic** or **industry unemployment**. When steel mills closed during the 1980s, for example, many workers lost their jobs. Typically, this work was concentrated in specific geographic areas, such as the Northeast. Although other regions of the country were growing, communities that relied on specific industries were hurt economically.

To what extent is unemployment an ever-present reality in our nation? The policy goal of full employment has been vigorously debated since the Great Depression. Debates about it raise a number of important points. **Full employment** means there are very few workers available for jobs paying typical wages, and those looking for jobs can find them. The economic upheaval of the Great Depression demonstrated that the goal of full employment was difficult to achieve and that economic cycles could be severe. The Great Depression convinced people that government intervention might be a suitable means of maintaining economic stability. Supporters of government intervention wanted legislation that promoted full employment. Such legislation would have made the federal government an employer of those in need of jobs, typically through public works programs and civil service agencies. Major business and agricultural groups fought full employment legislation on the grounds that it would interfere with the free market. Instead of supporting full employment, policymakers supported the **Employment Act of 1946** (Weir, 1987). The Employment Act's goal was maximum employment through government actions such as spending and taxing to stabilize the economy (Axinn & Stern, 2008). Although the legislation did not commit the government to achieving full employment, it did place some responsibility for the economy and employment on the federal government.

Effects of Unemployment   To social workers, it would seem that unemployment is not a desirable or healthy condition. In fact, analysis of research on the impact of unemployment suggests that having a job is crucial to self-esteem and self-definition (Aldous & Tuttle, 1988). In spite of the psychological benefits of working, public policies for full employment have never been enacted. In fact, there is an economic incentive for continually maintaining a pool of unemployed workers (Schiller, 2004).

Some analysts argue that there is a trade-off between unemployment and inflation. When the rate of employment increases, more people are working and therefore have more to spend. When consumers have more money to spend, manufacturers often seek to make a greater profit by raising prices on goods and services. As prices rise, inflation can follow. If prices rise too quickly, inflation occurs faster than growth in wages. Workers begin to spend less, and supply outpaces demand. The result is a slow-down in productivity. Fewer workers are needed, and unemployment rises as inflation goes down. This trend is exacerbated by the benefit of unemployment to employers. If there are numerous people looking for work, employers can offer lower wages and quickly fill open positions. If the unemployment rate is low, then there are fewer people willing to accept less desirable employment.

The social welfare policy conflict rests on the short-term advantages of unemployment. Businesses tend to prefer having a pool of workers who are not in a position to make strong demands for high wages or working conditions that may seem costly to the employer. In reality, however, this short-term gain seems to be more than offset by the long-term liabilities. Low wages make for low consumption and, therefore, the economy as a whole suffers. Also, poor working conditions lead to worker dissatisfaction. Those who are unhappy in their work tend to be less productive and less loyal and are more likely to leave. Worker turnover can become costly over time.

IMPACT OF RACE AND GENDER ON EMPLOYMENT AND ECONOMIC WELL-BEING

Data reveal strong demographic trends that reflect the disparity in employment in this country. The statistics in Box 9.2 reveal the difference in unemployment by gender and race. Racial differences are most pronounced. African-American workers experience rates of unemployment that are twice as high as those for white workers. Unemployment rates for Latino workers have consistently been higher than for white workers.

BOX 9.2	MORE ABOUT UNEMPLOYMENT RATES BY RACE AND GENDER

Average Unemployment Rates (in percent)

Year	Males	Females	Whites	Blacks	Hispanics
1980	6.9	7.4	6.3	14.3	10.1
1985	7.0	7.4	6.2	15.1	10.5
1990	5.7	5.5	4.8	11.4	8.2
1995	5.6	5.6	4.9	10.4	9.3
2000	3.9	4.1	3.5	7.6	5.7
2005	5.1	5.1	4.4	10.0	6.0
2008*	6.8	5.6	6.3	11.5	8.9

Source: U.S. Census Bureau, 2007
*4th Quarter statistics (Bureau of Labor Statistics, 2009)

BOX 9.3 | CONSIDER THIS . . .

Economic Realities for Women

In the United States, a man earns an average of $155 more per week than a woman.

Women with a high school education earn 29 percent less than men with a high school education.

Female college graduates earn 27 percent less than male college graduates.

Fifty-four percent of female workers earn less than $25,000, compared with 36 percent of male workers.

Only 3.1 percent of senior executives at Fortune 500 companies are women.

Source: McAndrew, 2002

Until recent years, the rate of unemployment for women tended to be higher than for men. Even though the unemployment rate for women has leveled off compared with the rate for men, the economic well-being of women is significantly lower than that of men (see Box 9.3).

EMPLOYMENT AND JOB CREATION

As is typical of so many social welfare policies, the national approach to employment is residual in nature. Instead of actively promoting full employment, policy makers respond to unemployment when it becomes a significant problem. The country's economic history demonstrates that when left to its own, the employment market does not provide jobs or sufficient wages for all those who are looking, particularly for women and people of color.

If the employment arena does not provide enough jobs, one solution is to have the federal government intervene and help people become employed. The employment programs of the New Deal, such as the Works Progress Administration and the Civilian Conservation Corps (discussed in Chapter 2), represented the largest government effort at creating jobs. These programs employed millions of workers. The major government employment efforts for economically disadvantaged persons over the past 30 years centered on the Comprehensive Employment and Training Act of 1973 (CETA, P.L. 93-203), the Job Training Partnership Act of 1982 (JTPA, P.L. 97-300), and the 1998 Workforce Investment Act (WIA, P.L. 105-220). Efforts under the American Recovery and Reinvestment Act of 2009 are designed to reinforce existing systems by funding additional government projects to employ more people. These programs represent very different approaches to government-sponsored employment.

The goal of the **Comprehensive Employment and Training Act of 1973 (CETA)** was to create public service jobs. The CETA program was a federal, state, and local effort, which enrolled as many as 750,000 participants during the peak year of 1978 (Levitan & Gallo, 1992). Unfortunately, however, CETA developed a negative reputation because of poor administration and political pressures. Public service employment jobs were doled out as a form of political patronage by local politicians; cities used CETA workers in basic services so that they did not have to use city funds; some work sites were poorly supervised; and some positions never materialized into real jobs (Levin & Ferman, 1985). Research on CETA demonstrated that the program did not achieve the desired results (LaLonde, 1995).

In response to the negative publicity of the CETA program, the Reagan administration vowed to change the approach to employment services from job creation in the public sector to job placement in the private sector. In 1982, the **Job Training Partnership Act (JTPA)** was passed to replace CETA. JTPA placed the responsibility for program administration with state governments and the private sector. The goal was to link those looking for jobs with existing employment. Each community was to develop a council with representatives from private employers who would direct the employment services. Compared to CETA, JTPA received less funding, did not create new jobs, and provided less social service support for participants (Levitan & Shapiro, 1987).

The effectiveness of JTPA was minimal. Although JTPA included over 600 local programs providing services, most services were contracted out to private groups such as community colleges and trade schools. As one would expect, these organizations had difficulty creating jobs for those with employment deficits (Blumenthal, 1987). Investigation of JTPA programs revealed improper spending without adequate federal and state government oversight (U.S. General Accounting Office, 1991). Researchers concluded that although there may have been some short-term benefits from JTPA training, there was no significant improvement in earnings or employment 5 years after JTPA services were instituted (U.S. General Accounting Office, 1996).

As part of JTPA and other programs, the federal government was involved in employment training in many other areas. By the mid-1990s, 154 programs were administered through 14 different federal departments and agencies. These programs included numerous separate services for disadvantaged youth, disadvantaged adults, older individuals, summer employment, and dislocated workers (U.S. General Accounting Office, 1994a). Unfortunately, the effectiveness of these programs was questionable. Information on the outcomes or effectiveness of the programs was not adequately collected by agencies, and there was no evidence that participants who did find jobs were helped by the programs or would not have achieved the same results on their own (U.S. General Accounting Office, 1994b).

Unemployment rates have fluctuated with the economy. Unfortunately, efforts to increase employment through social welfare services have not been extremely effective. The average rate of unemployment for adult workers increased in each decade from the 1960s through the 1980s. Although the economic growth of the 1990s resulted in higher overall employment, in recent years the rate has begun to increase again. If employment and training efforts are not highly effective, then there is greater need for supportive services for those who are unemployed.

In an effort to consolidate the numerous employment programs and provide better outcomes, Congress enacted the **Workforce Investment Act (WIA)** (P.L. 105-220) in 1998, which replaced JTPA. The WIA requires states to offer employment services through a centralized system, with one-stop centers (Woodbury, 2000). The purpose of the centers is to offer all employment services at a single location. WIA services now include 17 programs funded through four federal agencies, all to be offered at one-stop centers (see Box 9.4) (U.S. General Accounting Office, 2002). Implementation of the WIA did not begin until 2000, so the success of the program has yet to be fully assessed. The WIA program does seem to offer improvements over the JTPA because the WIA provides a broader range of services

BOX 9.4	MORE ABOUT MANDATORY PROGRAMS UNDER THE WORKFORCE INVESTMENT ACT

Department of Education
  Adult Education and Literacy
  Vocational Rehabilitation Program
  Vocational Education (Perkins Act)

Department of Health and Human Services
  Community Services Block Grant

Department of Housing and Urban
  Development (HUD)
  HUD-administered employment and training

Department of Labor
  WIA Adult
  WIA Youth

WIA Dislocated Worker
Employment Service (Wagner-Peyser)
Trade adjustment assistance programs
Veterans' employment and training programs
Unemployment Insurance
Job Corps
Welfare-to-Work grant-funded programs
Senior Community Service Employment Program
Employment and training for migrant and
seasonal farm workers
Employment and training for Native Americans

Source: U.S. General Accounting Office, 2002

and does not use income to determine eligibility. The one-stop centers are open to anybody. With centralized services and broader use, employment success may be enhanced. Specialized programs are targeted to those in greatest need, such as dislocated workers and youth. However, the program is only designed to enhance people's employability. It does not address the quality of existing jobs or development of new employment opportunities.

During his campaign, President Barack Obama promised to bring back the kind of infrastructure building and job creation that was part of the New Deal. His intent was to take a 21st-century approach by using federal monies to invest in new technologies with an emphasis on developing alternative energy sources. So far, the efforts under the American Recovery and Reinvestment Act are to fund additional projects rather than create a new program or government agency. For example, additional resources will go to states to fund transportation construction projects and school improvements. These are not new programs, but will create additional jobs through expanding projects and existing systems. His economic stimulus plan has the potential to create a new era in government intervention in the employment arena.

TAXES

Paying taxes ranks high among peoples' dislikes, but taxes play a critical role in providing social welfare services and programs. **Taxes** are compulsory payments made to the government. The payments ensure that we have a government that will maintain law and order, protect property rights, and uphold civil rights. Without the power and strength of government, there would be no control over the social system and no protections for citizens. Therefore, taxes are the price citizens pay to feel safe and secure.

There are numerous forms of taxation. For example, taxes are paid on purchases (sales tax), property (real estate tax), stock sales (capital gains tax), and wages (income tax). The income tax dates back to 1913 when the Sixteenth Amendment to the Constitution was passed, giving Congress the authority to impose an income tax (Rushefsky, 2002). With the income tax, Congress was able to expand government services greatly.

Progressive taxes take an increasing percentage as income rises, whereas **regressive taxes** are proportionately higher on low incomes. The example of OASDI payroll taxes (see Chapter 7) demonstrates regressivity: people with lower incomes pay a greater proportion of their income to Social Security taxes. The individual income tax structure is an example of a progressive system. Box 9.5 outlines the tax rates for 2008. As a person's income increases, he or she pays a higher rate on the higher portions of income. It is important to note a misconception that people often have about tax rates. You might hear someone saying they do not want to earn more money because their tax rate will go up. As the rates in Box 9.5 demonstrate, one only pays a higher rate on that *portion* of the income that goes up.

The issue of who should shoulder the burden of taxes is controversial. Today, most people feel they pay too much in taxes and so tax cuts have become popular politically. Because the income tax is removed directly from our paychecks, it creates an individual sense of paying for government. At times, if government performs according to our wants, that personal connection is positive. When government spending does not reflect our wishes, we resent paying taxes and the connection is negative. And at times, there are people who favor government spending and those who do not. The two opposing sides create a conflict that contributes to controversy over taxes.

BOX 9.5 | **MORE ABOUT 2007 TAX RATES**

If your filing status is single:

If your adjusted gross income is over:	But not over:	Then your tax is:	Of the amount over:
$ 0	$ 8,025	10%	$ 0
$ 8,025	$ 32,550	$ 802.50 + 15%	$ 8,025
$ 32,550	$ 78,850	$ 4,481.25 + 25%	$ 32,550
$ 70,350	$164,550	$ 16,056.25 + 28%	$ 78,850
$164,550	$357,700	$ 40,052.25 + 33%	$164,550
$357,700	—	$103,791.75 + 35%	$357,700

If your filing status is married filing jointly:

If your adjusted gross income is over:	But not over:	Then your tax is:	Of the amount over:
$ 0	$ 16,050	10%	$ 0
$ 16,050	$ 65,100	$ 1,605+ 15%	$ 16,050
$ 65,100	$131,450	$ 8,962.50 + 25%	$ 65,100
$131,450	$200,300	$ 22,550 + 28%	$131,450
$200,300	$357,700	$ 44,828 + 33%	$200,300
$357,700	—	$ 96,770 + 35%	$357,700

Source: Joint Committee on Taxation, 2008

The tax burden in recent decades has declined. From 1979 to 2004, most income groups experienced a decline in the percent of their income paid in federal taxes. The income tax burden for medium-income families is down to an historical low of less than six percent of income paid for federal income taxes (Center on Budget and Policy Priorities, 2007). Tax rules are public policies set by legislators. As such, they are very political and subject to the beliefs and values of the majority. It is important to remember that paying taxes may be a requirement of government, but who pays what and how much can be changed. In fact, there are numerous exceptions to what parts of our income we must pay taxes for, as outlined in Box 9.6. Each year the federal government excludes or exempts parts of our gross income from taxes. These special exclusions include exemptions or deductions for contributions to our pension funds, mortgage interest paid on our homes, and contributions to charities. All these exclusions can be changed through policy and are subject to the legislative actions of the federal government. In 2008, almost $700 billion tax dollars were not collected by the federal government through these legal exclusions (Joint Committee on Taxation, 2008). Thus, when debating the extent of taxes we pay, whether it is too high or too low, we must also consider the taxes that we do not pay due to public policies of exemption, deduction, or exclusion.

BOX 9.6 | **CONSIDER THIS . . .**

Exclusions to Income Tax in 2008 (in billions)

The following list includes provisions of federal tax law that allow special exclusions, exemptions, or deductions from a person's gross income tax, which provides a special credit leading to a revenue loss or "tax expenditure" for the federal government:

Tax law provisions	Revenue lost in billions
Pension contributions	$141
Reduced tax rates on dividends and long-term capital gains	$128
Exclusion for employer contributions for health care insurance premiums	$117
Mortgage interest deduction	$80
Exclusion of capital gains at death	$54
Earned income tax credit	$47
Tax credit for children under 17	$45
Deduction for charitable contributions	$35
Deduction of state, local, and property taxes	$30
Total	$677 billion

Source: Joint Committee on Taxation, 2008

MAJOR ECONOMIC SOCIAL WELFARE PROGRAMS TIED TO ECONOMIC CONDITIONS

Economic policies are not always viewed as part of our social welfare system, and some social welfare programs are regarded as outside the domain of economics. The following programs, which are directly based on individual and social economic conditions, are integral parts of our social welfare system.

UNEMPLOYMENT INSURANCE

The previous chapter introduced the **Unemployment Insurance** program. Enacted as part of the 1935 Social Security Act, unemployment insurance was created as a joint program administered by both the federal and state governments. States decide the duration of, amount of, and eligibility requirements for benefits and directly administer the program. The federal government provides grants for administration of the program and is responsible for maintaining the Unemployment Insurance Trust Fund.

The Unemployment Insurance Trust Fund consists of state-collected payroll tax dollars from employers. Employers pay unemployment insurance tax according to the number of workers they employ. For each dollar paid, they receive up to a 90 percent credit against their federal tax (Social Security Administration, 2008). Because of this tax inducement, all states willingly comply with the program. Although every state participates in the Unemployment Insurance program, the specifics of the program vary widely from state to state.

Generally, eligibility is based on the extent of recent employment, willingness and ability to accept new employment, and involuntary termination from prior employment. Benefits are provided as a right and do not require a means test. Unemployment coverage provides a percentage of previous earnings for up to a maximum of 26 weeks in most states. In 2006, the average weekly benefit was $277 for an average of 15.2 weeks (Social Security Administration, 2008).

The Unemployment Insurance program is one of the few social welfare programs that tends to be universal in structure. As long as a person has been dismissed from a covered job, he or she is entitled to unemployment benefits, regardless of personal wealth, income, or age. Unfortunately, however, many people need to leave jobs for reasons that are not covered, such as caring for a family member who is ill or caring for children if no other care is available. Also, many people have part-time jobs and therefore do not qualify for unemployment benefits. For many unemployed workers, benefits run out before they have found new employment. This is particularly true during times of greatest need. For example, in 1991, during the peak of economic recession, 3.5 million recipients of unemployment insurance exhausted their benefits before finding new employment (Shapiro & Nichols, 1992). Between 1975 and 1996, coverage from unemployment insurance declined, from 76 percent of the unemployed to 36 percent (Miringoff & Miringoff, 1999). By 2003, almost two years after the previous recession had ended, there were still one million workers who had exhausted all of their unemployment benefits but had not found work (Center on Budget and Policy Priorities, 2003). With the recession of 2007 and 2008, many workers faced the same shortfall in benefits. By the end of 2008, more than one in five unemployed workers had been jobless for over half a year (Economic Policy Institute, 2008). Thus, more than two million unemployed workers had already reached or were near the end of benefit coverage. Although the Unemployment Insurance program provides a necessary safety net for people who lose jobs, it is not comprehensive and does not provide for all who are unemployed.

MINIMUM WAGE

Another public policy that is related to employment and provides wage security for workers is the minimum wage. The concept of a **minimum wage** is that the government intervenes to guarantee a base hourly wage. The instability of the market and the imbalance in power between employers and employees serve as the rationales for government intervention in wages. The minimum wage was discussed in the previous chapter because of its potential role in preventing poverty for low-income workers.

The aftermath of the Great Depression spurred lawmakers to investigate labor practices. Industry support of strike breaking, labor spies, and violent attacks on workers prompted the passage of the **Fair Labor Standards Act of 1938** (Axinn & Stern, 2008). In addition to standardizing work hours and controlling child labor, the legislation set a minimum wage below which employers could not legally pay workers. The hourly rate in 1938 was set at 25 cents an hour; it had risen to $4.25 an hour in 1991 (Social Security Administration, 1994). In 1996, President Clinton and Congress agreed to new legislation, the **Small Business Protection Act** (P.L. 104-188), which raised the minimum wage to $4.75 per hour as of October 1, 1996, and to $5.15 per hour as of September 1, 1997. In 2006, the minimum wage was once again raised through legislative action to amend the Fair Labor Standards Act. The rate was scheduled to increase incrementally from 2007 to 2009, rising to $5.85 in 2007, $6.55 in 2008 and $7.25 in 2009.

Critics argue that the minimum wage is inadequate and has not kept pace with the cost of living. As shown in Box 9.7, the value of the minimum wage shrunk over the years. The 2006 rate of $5.15 per hour was the lowest in constant dollars since the 1950s. With the increases for 2008 and 2009, the minimum wage provides a higher wage level, which should positively impact low wage earners.

The differences between working full-time at minimum wage and the poverty line are outlined in Box 9.8. Even with the increases, the disparity between minimum wage income and living in poverty in 2008 was more than five thousand dollars for a family of three. Based on these calculations, the minimum wage would have to be raised beyond the new levels to lift a family of three above the poverty line. Without public assistance or benefits through the Earned Income Tax Credit, full-time work at minimum wage still leaves a family below the poverty line. This difference highlights one of the many policy contradictions in our social welfare system. Although people are categorized as living in poverty with incomes below officially recognized levels, legislation that sets a minimum accepted level for wages does not set that level to pay wages that lift workers or their families out of poverty.

CONSIDER THIS ...

The Value of the Minimum Wage in 2008 Dollars

Value of the Minimum Wage

Year	Nominal dollars	2008 dollars
1947	$0.40	$3.42
1961	$1.05	$6.69
1975	$2.10	$7.44
1980	$3.10	$7.67
1985	$3.35	$6.36
1990	$3.80	$5.86
1995	$4.25	$5.93
2000	$5.15	$5.40
2005	$5.15	$5.65
2008	$6.55	$6.55

Source: Economic Policy Institute, 2008

BOX 9.8   **CONSIDER THIS ...**

Minimum Wage Earnings in Comparison to Poverty Line, 2008

$6.55 × 40 hours per week × 52 weeks per year = $13,624 per year

After Social Security taxes = $12,582 annual full-time income

Poverty line for family of three in 2008 = $17,600

The difference between full-time earnings at minimum wage and the poverty threshold for family of three = –$5,018

Even at the 2009 rate of $7.25 for minimum wage, after Social Security the full-time income would be $13,926, which does not even reach the 2008 poverty level for a family of two.

Source: Author calculations

Opponents of the minimum wage argue that government interference in setting pay levels destroys free enterprise and causes economic imbalances. They feel that if employers are forced to pay higher wages, there will be fewer jobs available. Research findings suggest this is not true. In a study done in New Jersey, labor economists found that when the minimum wage was increased, even during a state economic recession, the number of jobs actually increased (Epstein, 1995). The researchers theorized that higher wages attract people to jobs and keep them working; this results in more long-term employment, sparing employers the costs of frequent turnover.

Although the concept of a minimum wage is usually relegated to economic discussions, it has important implications for social work. Most low-paid workers lack economic security during recessions or changes in the employment market. Many are not covered by unemployment insurance and are consequently the most likely candidates for public assistance. If the minimum wages of available employment were adequate to support a family, it is likely that fewer people would be dependent on public assistance.

EARNED INCOME TAX CREDIT

Recent public policy efforts to make employment worthwhile centered on the **Earned Income Tax Credit (EITC)** program, which was discussed in Chapter 8. Enacted in 1975, the legislation allows for a decrease in taxes paid for low-income workers. The program is administered through the filing of a tax return and therefore does not involve additional federal agencies or administrators. The provisions of the EITC are complicated and vary according to income level and size of household. Generally, the lower the income, the higher the tax credit. In cases where the income is extremely low, families may qualify to receive a direct grant. As demonstrated in Chapter 8, the program can have a positive impact on the economic situation for low-income families who participate in the labor force and file an income tax return.

The program has received support from both political parties. It is supported because it rewards people for working, and it is efficient because it is handled through the existing Internal Revenue Service (Hutchinson, Lav, & Greenstein, 1992). Critics charge, however, that although the EITC helps low-income individuals, it also keeps wages low. Why should employers raise wages when the government subsidizes poor workers to accept the low wages? In effect, the EITC uses tax dollars to supplement poorly paid workers instead of placing the responsibility on the employers themselves (McDermott, 1994). This brings us back to the question of who should be responsible for determining wages: the government or the marketplace? Should wage levels be left entirely to the ebb and flow of economic conditions, or should the federal government intervene? If the government intervenes, what should that action be? Should employers be regulated, or should workers be supplemented? Those questions continually surface in the ongoing debates regarding economic policy and social well-being.

IMPACT OF THE FEDERAL BUDGET ON SOCIAL WELFARE POLICY

How do the workings of the federal budget affect social workers and their practice? The federal budget may seem far removed from the day-to-day activities of social service providers. As demonstrated throughout this book, the impact of government policies flows through all levels of our social welfare system and ultimately affects our direct practice. The federal budget is the main source of revenue for national social welfare programs and services. Federal money is used to fund services for children, families, health care, unemployment, retirement, education, national security, and other areas of social welfare. Budget cuts necessitate reductions in social welfare programs and services.

WHAT IS THE FEDERAL BUDGET?

Each year the federal government creates a plan for what and how much should be spent on the business of government. The process begins on or before the first Monday in February, when the president is required by law to submit to Congress a budget proposal for the following fiscal year. Box 9.9 outlines the timeline for the budget process. Part of the plan includes estimates for how much money will be taken in for taxes and how much the economy will grow. Because the plan is developed almost a year before it is implemented, the president's budget is the starting place for discussions and negotiations with Congress and government agencies. Congressional hearings precede voting on the appropriation measures. By September 30, on the eve of the new fiscal year, Congress and the president must enact the new budget.

WHAT ARE FEDERAL BUDGET SURPLUSES AND DEFICITS?

When the government ends the year with more revenue than was spent, it has a **surplus**. When the government overspends, it incurs a budget **deficit**. In order to continue financing its operations, the government must borrow to make up for the shortfall. The largest amount of borrowed money is financed through the selling of government treasuries to the public. This borrowed amount is referred to as the **public debt**. The public debt is the cumulative total of all federal deficits minus any surplus. By 2007, that amount had exceeded five trillion dollars (Congressional Budget Office, 2008).

From 1962 through 1997, the federal government had a deficit in every year except 1969. From 1998 through 2001, for the first time in decades, the federal government realized a budget surplus in consecutive years. Since 2002, the federal government has gone back to accruing a deficit annually. Box 9.10 lists the deficits and total debt for the past 30 years.

The budget surplus was short lived. The impact of the recession on lowering wages consequently lowered tax revenues. President Bush began his term in 2001

BOX 9.9 | **MORE ABOUT THE FEDERAL BUDGET PROCESS**

First Monday in February the president submits budget proposal to Congress

February through September	Congress works on budget resolution, setting the framework for expenditures and taxes, with the goal of passing the budget by April 15
	Congressional hearings are held on budget and appropriation bills
	Congress passes 13 annual appropriation bills, no later than September 30
October 1	Budget begins with new fiscal year

Source: Executive Office of the President, 2001; Meyer, 2002

BOX 9.10	MORE ABOUT ANNUAL DEFICITS AND OVERALL DEBT (IN BILLIONS OF DOLLARS)

	Deficit	Public Debt		Deficit	Public Debt
1975	53	395	1993	255	3,248
1976	74	477	1994	203	3,433
1977	54	549	1995	164	3,604
1978	59	607	1996	108	3,734
1979	40	640	1997	22	3,772
1980	74	709	1998	+69	3,721
1981	79	785	1999	+126	3,632
1982	128	919	2000	+236	3,410
1983	208	1,131	2001	+127	3,320
1984	185	1,300	2002	158	3,540
1985	212	1,499	2003	375	3,914
1986	221	1,736	2004	412	4,326
1987	150	1,888	2005	319	4,645
1988	155	2,050	2006	248	4,893
1989	153	2,189	2007	161	5,054
1990	221	2,410	2008*	407	5,461
1991	270	2,688			
1992	290	2,999			

Source: Congressional Budget Office, 2008; U.S. Census Bureau, 2007
*Projected

with tax cuts, further reducing incoming federal revenue, and increased defense spending to pay for homeland security and the war in Iraq. The annual deficit grew dramatically and pushed the public debt to the more than five trillion dollars. The costs for the wars in Iraq, Afghanistan, and other global war on terror operations totaled $805 billion from 2002 to 2008 (Congressional Research Service, 2008). Analysts predict that the costs of the wars and what will need to be spent to care for veterans and refurbish the military will exceed $1.5 trillion, and if the long-term costs to our economy that will be incurred over the years are added, the total is likely to exceed $3 trillion (Bilmes & Stiglitz, 2008). The federal government's interventions to stabilize the financial markets also pose unknown future costs. While the final numbers will not be known for years to come, we already have seen how these economic demands have pushed the deficit higher and added to the public debt. By the close of 2008, the federal government had pledged more than one trillion dollars to aid the U.S. economy and financial system. These efforts included $124 billion for an economic stimulus program; $300 billion in support of mortgage insurance; $200 billion for the takeover of Fannie Mae and Freddie Mac mortgage associations (there is more on this later in the chapter); and $700 billion for a Wall Street bailout (Montgomery & Eggen, 2008). The

American Recovery and Reinvestment Act authorized an additional $787 billion. These expenses and more to come will add significantly to the public debt.

CONSEQUENCES OF THE DEFICIT

The consequences of operating the federal government with such a high deficit are unclear. Some policy makers view this as dangerous to long-term economic health, whereas others consider it a fact of life for a large government. When the federal budget is decreased, resources for government programs are also decreased. As long as people will still invest in the government by purchasing securities, there is a cycle of transferring money from the public to the government and back again. Because there has never before been a time in history when the dollar amount of the total federal debt was so large, there is no precedent for interpreting the long-term impact of such a large deficit. It remains to be seen whether the cycle has become stable or whether economic distress will be the outcome of such an imbalance.

Contentious political debate surrounds deficit reduction. Although both the president and Congress agree that the budget must be balanced and the debt reduced, there is little consensus on how to accomplish this goal. Even when there was a surplus, Congress and the president did not produce budget plans that would save money for the future (Pianin, 2000). President Bush sent Congress budgets that simultaneously decreased taxes and increased expenditures, particularly defense expenditures. Between 2000 and 2004, tax revenues fell 76 percent, in part because of the recession and in part because of tax cuts proposed by President Bush and enacted by Congress (Center on Budget and Policy Priorities, 2004). With the decrease in revenues and increase in defense spending, the deficit soared. The impossible combination of tax cuts and increased spending has left the long-term problem of the deficit and public debt unresolved. Movement from deficit to surplus back to deficit demonstrates the unpredictability of economic conditions and, hence, the difficulty in controlling economic policy. Federal spending also provokes debate concerning the optimal size of government. Box 9.11 summarizes this conflict.

BUDGET PRIORITIES

The federal budget is in itself a social welfare policy. Each year, as Congress and the president debate the budget and work toward enactment of annual budget legislation, policy choices and options are discussed. How we spend our budget reflects national priorities and consequently shifts over time. Box 9.12 lists the main categories of spending in fiscal year 2007. Over half the budget went to cover Social Security, Medicare, and national defense. Interest on the debt required 9 percent of the national budget. Where do federal revenues come from? Most federal money comes from the personal income tax and social insurance retirement and health care taxes. For fiscal year 2006, 39 percent of the federal income came from personal income taxes; 32 percent from Social Security, Medicare, and other retirement taxes; 13 percent from corporate income taxes; and seven percent from excise, estate, and other miscellaneous taxes. Nine percent was borrowed to cover the deficit (Internal Revenue Service, 2008).

BOX 9.11 | CONTROVERSIAL PERSPECTIVES

The battle cry of conservatives used to be "Shrink the federal government!" Current changes in ideologies, however, are creating conflict:

When conservative Republicans took control of Congress in 1994, their platform for change included shrinking the size of the federal government by decreasing federal spending. The goal was to devolve administration back to state governments. This sentiment is captured in the words of then Senate Majority Leader Robert Dole, "If I have one goal for the 104th Congress it is this: that we will dust off the 10th Amendment and restore it to its rightful place in the Constitution. We will continue in our drive to return power to our states and our people" (quoted in VandeHei, 2005, p. 11). And for the next five years, that was the goal of the majority of members of Congress. Interestingly enough, the election of George W. Bush, an avowed conservative, changed the direction. In the words of another Republican member of Congress, Mike Pence of Indiana, "The Republican majority, left to its own devices from 1995 to 2000, was a party committed to limited government and restoring the balances of federalism with the states. Clearly, President Bush has had a different vision, and that vision has resulted in education and welfare policies that have increased the size and scope of government" (quoted in VandeHei, 2005, p. 11).

After taking office in 2001, President Bush increased federal government spending. In the final year of the previous presidency under Bill Clinton, the federal government spent $1.8 trillion and had an annual surplus of $236 billion. By 2008, the federal government spent almost three trillion dollars and had an annual deficit of more than 400 billion dollars. Regardless of the reasons for the increase in spending, this trend raises the question of what happened to the movement to decrease the size of the federal government and return control to state governments. And it also raises the question of how much is too much for annual deficits and government spending. Those who favor limiting government spending must be asking themselves, "Who is minding the store?" when such astronomical growth occurs under a conservative Republican president.

As a policy document, the federal budget prioritizes what congressional leaders and the president consider important. For example, spending for homeland security became a priority following the 9/11 terrorist attacks. The following two years, Congress had authorized $37 billion for homeland security (Center on Budget and Policy Priorities, 2004), which was more than the total spent on TANF and Food Stamps combined.

Even though having a large deficit may not have devastating effects on the economy, it does have a limiting effect on social welfare spending. Much of the budget is mandatory, and some of it is considered too important to cut. Social Security, Medicare, and interest on the debt are mandatory. National defense, particularly after 9/11 and the invasion of Iraq, is considered by many in political power to be untouchable. These costly items mean that the budget must be balanced by cutting back on other budget items; increasing tax revenue, a most disliked option

BOX 9.12	MORE ABOUT THE UNITED STATES BUDGET FY 2007

	TOTAL BUDGET	2,731 B	
	Receipts	2,568 B	
	(Deficit)	(163) B	

EXPENSES—partial list		Percent of total budget
National defense	549 B	20%
Social Security (OASDI)	581 B	21%
Medicare	436 B	16%
Interest on the debt	238 B	9%
Medicaid	1911 B	7%
TANF & Family Support payments	21 B	.8%
Food Stamps	35 B	1.3%
SSI	36 B	1.3%
Veterans	36 B	1.3%
Education, training, employment	75 B	2.8%
International affairs	37 B	1.4%
Science, space, technology	26 B	1%
Transportation	62 B	2.3%
Earned Income & Child Tax Credits	54 B	2%
SCHIP	6 B	.2%

Source: Congressional Budget Office, 2008

for politicians; or increasing the debt through larger annual deficits. Therefore, with greater demands on Social Security and national defense, the infusion of money into the financial and housing markets, dislike of taxes, and concern over the growing public debt, it is likely that social welfare programs will be cut. In this way, budget priorities and economic conditions directly affect the security of social welfare programs.

CORPORATE AMERICA

So far we have reviewed economic concerns in the public domain. No less important are the economic conditions and circumstances of the private sector. The largest piece of the private economy rests with the corporate sector. The connection between governmental economic policies and the corporate sector is significant. Numerous private businesses rely heavily on government subsidies and economic support. What is this support? Examples include business tax breaks that lower corporate tax bills. For example, in 2000, $22 billion was allowed for accelerated depreciation (allowing companies to subtract the costs of their equipment faster than the machinery wears out) and $14 billion was allowed for an Internal Revenue Service (IRS) tax exclusion on certain profits earned in other countries (Abramovitz, 2001). In 2008, more than $5 billion was set aside for subsidies to farmers with $178 billion already paid out from 1998–2006 (Environmental Working Group, 2008).

Other forms of government support to corporate America include emergency loans at reduced interest rates such as those given to the investment bank of Bear Stearns in 2008. In this case, the Federal Reserve Bank extended a loan at a reduced interest rate. The central bank lent another bank, JP Morgan, $29 billion to buy the troubled Bear Stearns and its liabilities. The risk to the Federal Reserve and to taxpayers is what happens with the weak investments in the future, because the federal government is now the insurer of those investments. On the other hand, if the federal government did not intervene, a very large and significant bank would go under, and that would have a major negative impact on the economy. This involvement of the federal government in the private market was one of several undertaken as part of the $700 billion authorized by Congress to support financial institutions with the goal of stabilizing the economy.

Although politically we often hear the pledge to "laissez faire" economics, that is the desire for a lack of interference from government into the private business sector, the federal government is often called upon to intervene to maintain equilibrium in the marketplace, as described previously. This is particularly true when major negative events occur, such as the support given to airlines after 9/11. These government efforts, while directed toward private corporations, have the effect of keeping the general economy stable, which in turn helps the entire nation. From a social welfare policy perspective, this principle of support is behind all government interventions, whether for corporate America or low-income individuals.

The federal government regularly subsidizes, either through tax breaks, direct grants, or loans with discounted interest rates, private agriculture and industry. The rationale for this support is that "What is good for business is good for the country," that is, that a strong private sector means jobs and that means individual economic well-being is enhanced. Although this is true, it also means that fewer resources are available for those whose lives are not improved by employment in the private sector. As stated in the opening of this chapter, the profit motive of corporations is not conducive to the social welfare of people on the margins of the economic system: the unemployed; underemployed; unemployed people who are disabled, elderly, or too young to work; and people who are economically limited due to discrimination and oppression. The challenge to policy makers is to find the balance between supporting the private sector and still having the resources to provide for the social well-being of all members of society.

CHANGES IN THE WORKFORCE

The concern for social welfare policy in relation to employment and economics rests with current and future service needs of work and people without work. The shortcomings of the system and some of the major current policies designed to address those social needs have been discussed here, but these policies reflect the state of the workforce in the past. Examination of demographic shifts suggests that new public policies will be needed in the future.

Over the past 55 years, the composition of the labor force has changed greatly. In 1950, 33 percent of women were actively engaged in the labor force and 86 percent of men (U.S. General Accounting Office, 1992). By 2006, almost 60 percent of women participated in the labor force and 74 percent of men (U.S. Census Bureau, 2007). With more women in the workforce, there are more two-parent families in which both parents are employed and more single-parent families headed by working mothers. In 1960, 32 percent of men who worked were married to women who were also in the labor force. By 1990, the percentage had increased to almost 70 percent (U.S. General Accounting Office, 1992). In 2005, 68 percent of married women with children and 73 percent of single women with children were in the labor force (U.S. Census Bureau, 2007).

Other changes have affected the workforce. Despite economic expansion following the downturn of 2001, the real income (that is, accounting for inflation) of the median family fell each year through 2004 (Mishel, Bernstein, & Allegretto, 2007). The median annual income for men was $31,275 in 2005, but for women it was $18,576 (U.S. Bureau of the Census, 2007). These changes reflect the recent decline in income as well as the earning gap between men and women. The result of an overall decrease in wages means that families are struggling to maintain their standard of living. Demographic and income changes will increase the need for social welfare policies that address the social and economic needs of all people.

Further complicating the changes in the demographics of the workforce are changes in the way industry creates jobs. Recent concern has risen over the tendency for companies to export jobs. Although manufacturers have done so in great numbers in the past two decades, high-tech firms are now following this practice. Recent research estimates that 3.3 million U.S. service-sector jobs will be outsourced to other countries over the next 15 years, taking along $136 billion in wages (Schneider, 2004). The financial gain for companies is evident. Computer programming jobs that pay $60,000 to $80,000 in the United States can be filled for less than $9,000 in countries such as China and India. This form of employment **outsourcing** has become possible with the technological advances of computers and worldwide access to telephones and satellite communications. The impact on the U.S. workforce is already being felt.

Another shift in the economy in recent years has been the growing distance between top earners and those at the bottom and in the middle. In Chapter 8, Box 8.5 lists the differences in income by households, with the highest group's share growing steadily over the past several decades. Income is only the immediate annual measure of a family's economic well-being. The accumulation of wealth through investments, savings, and home ownership provides long-term financial security. The disparity in wealth is even greater than the disparity in income. The top 20 percent of households controlled 85 percent of the wealth in the United States, with 15 percent shared by the other 80 percent of households (Mishel, Bernstein, & Allegretto, 2007). Although half of all families have direct or indirect stock holdings, that asset is skewed towards the top—less than 12 percent of the bottom fifth of families have any stock ownership with an average value of $7,500 compared to 93 percent of the top tenth of families with an average of $205,000 (U.S. Census

Bureau, 2007). Although there has always been disparity between the top earners and the bottom earners, what is particularly worrisome is the growing gap between the top and the bottom. The idea that increases in economic well-being trickle down and that support of high earners helps the entire nation is questionable given the data.

THE ECONOMIC IMPACT OF HOUSING AND MORTGAGES

Perhaps the economic story of recent years can be found in the housing market. Although the impact is still unfolding, the boom and bust of housing prices has had a significant impact on the economy as a whole. The quest for home ownership and economic gain found a lethal combination in the mortgage market during the 2000s. Subprime loans are riskier loans because they are intended for people who are unable to qualify for conventional loans at prevailing mortgage rates. These loans, to cover the risk of lending to someone who is financially less secure, charge higher interest rates. However, with minimal regulation and encouragement from policy makers to open the housing market to more Americans, these loans developed in more complicated fashions, with introductory loan interest rates that changed over time and minimal to no down payments. These practices were aided by, and in turn encouraged, rising home values. In effect, there was a cycle of high demand that pushed the value of the supply of housing up. In 1993, 100,000 home purchase or refinance loans were categorized as subprime, by 1999 that rose to one million, and by 2006, 20 percent of all home loans were subprime (Center for Policy Alternatives, 2007). With oversupply, housing values began to drop, and homes that were barely affordable to subprime borrowers became worth less, and even more difficult for people to afford. When people cannot afford to make mortgage payments, they walk away from the home and loan, leaving the banks with a house worth less and no payments coming in for the mortgage. The economic impact affected the entire economy. The biggest social concern with subprime borrowing is that it disproportionately covered people of color, elderly persons, and rural households. For example, in 2006, 54 percent of all loans made to African-American families were subprime compared to 18 percent for white families. And borrowers 65 years of age or older were three times more likely than borrowers younger than 35 years to hold a subprime mortgage (Center for Policy Alternatives, 2007).

Again the question of federal government intervention into the economy and private sector arose. With the housing market declining, and the impact of subprime mortgage lending practices gaining hold, the federal government decided to intervene. Historically, the federal government has been involved in the housing market, particularly through the creation of the Federal National Mortgage Association, now known as Fannie Mae, in 1938. As a government agency, Fannie Mae was authorized to purchase government-insured mortgages to replenish the available money for loans to help people buy homes. This program was another piece of the New Deal efforts to revitalize the economy following the Great Depression. In 1968, the structure of Fannie Mae changed, and it became a private company, but with a public mandate to increase home ownership under federal guidelines. A detailed discussion of Fannie Mae and the other government mortgage provider, Freddie Mac, is beyond the scope of this book, but it is important to know that these agencies are private but with a government charter. As described by the agency:

> During the course of our nearly 70-year history, Fannie Mae has worked to serve America's housing finance industry. Today, Fannie Mae continues to have a congressional charter that directs us to channel our efforts into increasing the availability and affordability of homeownership for low-, moderate-, and middle-income Americans. Fannie Mae's securities are not guaranteed by the U.S. government and Fannie Mae's business is self-sustaining and funded exclusively with private capital. Fannie Mae is a stockholder-owned corporation. Our common stock is listed on the New York Stock Exchange (NYSE) and traded under the symbol "FNM." (Fannie Mae, 2007, p. 2)

Although a private corporation, the impact of Fannie Mae is significant on the U.S. economy, and it is a government-sponsored enterprise. Although Fannie Mae was not involved in the subprime lending because its regulations did not allow such risky loans, it was caught up in the decline of the housing market, which meant that the value of the mortgages held by the corporation declined precipitously. Because of that impact, the federal government chose to intervene in 2008 by standing behind the loans and making sure that there would be financial support to keep the corporation solvent. Again, this is an example of Keynesian interventions.

CONFLICTING VALUES AND BELIEFS

Inherent in some of the technical aspects of economics are conflicts with social work values, as outlined at the beginning of this chapter. Those conflicts lead to competing values and beliefs. The most distinct conflict is the debate about individual versus social responsibility. Much of economics rests on individualism, whereas social work promotes social support. Our economic system reflects this dilemma: Individuals pay taxes to fund collective government services; the U.S. budget is a collective entity, but individuals often feel disappointed in the spending priorities; the marketplace requires large-scale citizen involvement in buying, but price competition is fiercely individual. The conflict between individual and social responsibility is pervasive in our economic system and reflects the struggle between self-sufficiency and social support.

Economics also brings several other conflicting beliefs into the fray. The issue of entitlement versus handouts surfaces in the economics of social policies. Employment training is a good example of this conflict. Are people entitled to an education and job preparation, or should they simply be placed in existing open employment? Whose responsibility is it to adequately prepare people for employment, the individual's or the state's? The format of economic redistribution, either through taxes or job creation, touches the belief in helping those we know versus helping strangers. The magnitude of the tax structure and the anonymity of job creation stress helping people we do not know. Because these dilemmas can be difficult at times, we struggle with willingness to pay taxes and support public economic programs.

The technical aspects of economics raise the conflict between rationality and emotionality. Economics, with its foundation of mathematical computations and quantifications, stresses rationality. On the other hand, human need touches our emotions. To what extent do we allow rationality to dictate social welfare policy, and to what extent do we allow emotions to influence policy?

FINAL THOUGHTS ON THE IMPACT OF THE ECONOMY

When examining the provision of social welfare services and the market economy, two questions must be asked. Can the market economy adequately provide for the social welfare needs of all its citizens? Second, should the marketplace and rules of the market economy dictate the provision and delivery of social welfare services? For example, is it best to leave medical care, nutritional needs, and housing needs to the cycles of supply and demand, or should there be government intervention? Are wage levels and unemployment protection the responsibility of industry and employers, or should the government intervene to compensate for the ups and downs of the economic system? These questions must be asked by anyone analyzing economic ideologies and social welfare policy. Social workers must be familiar with economic terms and concepts to be effective advocates for the social welfare needs of all members of society.

Key Terms

economics

supply and demand

unemployment

structural
   unemployment

seasonal
   unemployment

geographic
   unemployment

industry
   unemployment

full employment

taxes

progressive taxes

regressive taxes

unemployment Insur-
   ance program

minimum wage

Earned Income Tax
   Credit program

surplus

deficit

public debt

outsourcing

Questions for Discussion

1. How does economics differ from social work? What is the impact of those differences?
2. Discuss the relationship between supply and demand. Is the current state of the economy one of excess supply or demand? How does this affect the typical worker?

3. What is the effect of unemployment on individuals? Families? Communities? What social welfare policies should we institute to address unemployment?
4. Discuss the pros and cons of taxation.
5. When should the federal government intervene in the economy?

Excercises

1. Examine one of your pay stubs from a previous or current job. How much did you pay in taxes? What percentage of your wages did you pay in taxes? How much did you pay into FICA? Medicare? Does the total equal the required 7.65 percent?

2. Find out what unemployment benefits are available in your community and state. How many weeks are you eligible to receive benefits? What are the conditions or requirements for receiving benefits? What is the process for applying, and how long does it take to become eligible?

3. What kinds of jobs pay minimum wage in your community? Are there employers who offer more than minimum wage for entry-level, unskilled jobs? Where are those jobs? If so, why do you think they are offering more than minimum wage?

4. Conduct research on the current state of the federal budget. Go to the home page of the Office of Management and Budget and the Congressional Budget Office. Is the budget a deficit or a surplus budget? Compare the numbers from both agencies. What is the difference between the two? Why?

5. Visit the home page of Fannie Mae. Read through the description of the corporation. Does the structure of Fannie Mae seem helpful to our housing market? To what extent do you think the housing market should be private or public?

References

Abramovitz, M. (2001). Everyone is still on welfare: The role of redistribution in social policy. *Social Work* 46(4):297–308.

Aldous, J., & Tuttle, R. C. (1988). Unemployment and the family. In C. S. Chilman, F. M. Cox, & E. W. Nunnally (eds.), *Employment and economic problems*, pp. 17–41. Newbury Park, CA: Sage.

Axinn, J., & Stern, M. (2008). *Social welfare: A history of the American response to need*, 7th ed. Boston: Allyn and Bacon.

Bartlett, H. (1970). *The common base of social work practice*. Washington, DC: National Association of Social Workers.

Bilmes, L. J. & Stiglitz, J. E. (2008). Day of reckoning: The Iraq war will cost us $3 trillion—and it's the root of our economic problems too. *Washington Post National Weekly Edition* 25(22): 27.

Blumenthal, K. (1987, February 9). Job training effort, critics say, fails many who need help most. *Wall Street Journal*, p. 1.

Bureau of Labor Statistics. (2009). *Employment situation summary-February*. Washington, DC: US Department of Labor.

Bureau of Labor Statistics. (2002). *Value of the federal minimum wage 1938–2000*. Washington, DC: U.S. Department of Labor.

Center for Policy Alternatives. (2007). *Progressive agenda for the states 2008: Leadership for America*. Washington, DC: Author.

Center on Budget and Policy Priorities. (2007). *Federal tax burdens in historical perspective*. Washington, DC: Author.

Center on Budget and Policy Priorities. (2004). *Administration's FY 2005 budget an unbalanced and ineffective approach to fiscal discipline*. Washington, DC: Author.

Center on Budget and Policy Priorities. (2003). *New Unemployment Insurance extension neglects one million jobless workers*. Washington, DC: Author.

Cho, D. & Irwin, N. (2008, August 18–24). An unexpected rescue. *Washington Post National Weekly Edition* 25(44):22–23.

Congressional Budget Office. (2008). *The budget and economic outlook: Fiscal years 2008–2018*. Washington, DC: Government Printing Office.

Economic Policy Institute. (2008). *The real value of the minimum wage, 1947–2008*. Washington, DC: Author.

Economic Policy Institute. (2009, March 6). *Jobs picture: Unemployment at highest rate in over 25 years*. Washington, DC: Author.

Economic Report of the President. (2008). Washington, DC: U.S. Government Printing Office.

Epstein, G. (1995, January 23). A boost in the minimum wage doesn't always produce the expected result. *Barron's LXXV* (4): 42.

Environmental Working Group. (2008). *Total USDA subsidies in the United States*. http://farm.ewg.org/farm/progdetail.php?fips=00000&progcode=total&page=conc.

Executive Office of the President. (2001). *A citizen's guide to the federal budget*. Washington, DC: Author.

Fannie Mae. (2007). *An introduction to Fannie Mae.* Washington, DC: Author.

Heilbroner, R., & Thurow, L. (1982). *Economics explained.* New York: Simon & Schuster.

Hutchinson, F. C., Lav, I. J., & Greenstein, R. (1992). *A hand up: How state earned income credits help working families escape poverty.* Washington, DC: Center on Budget and Policy Priorities.

Internal Revenue Service. (2008). *1040 forms and instructions.* Washington, DC: Department of the Treasury.

Joint Committee on Taxation. (2008). *Overview of the federal tax system in effect for 2008.* JCX-32-08. Washington, DC: Senate Committee on Finance, U.S. Congress.

LaLonde, R. J. (1995). The promise of public sector-sponsored training programs. *Journal of Economic Perspectives* 9(spring):149–168.

Levin, M. A., & Ferman, B. (1985). *The political hand: Policy implementation and youth employment programs.* New York: Pergamon.

Levitan, S. A., & Gallo, F. (1992). *Spending to save: Expanding employment opportunities.* Washington, DC: Center for Social Policy Studies, George Washington University.

Levitan, S. A., & Shapiro, I. (1987). *Working but poor.* Baltimore: Johns Hopkins University Press.

McAndrew, S. (2002, August 2). Office cad a reminder women still face hurdles. *Arizona Republic,* p. D2.

McDermott, J. (1994, November 14). And the poor get poorer. *The Nation* 259(16):576–580.

Meyer, A. E. (2002). *Evolution of the United States budgeting.* Westport, CT: Praeger.

Miringoff, M., & Miringoff, M.-L. (1999). *The social health of the nation: How America is really doing.* New York: Oxford University Press.

Mishel, L., Bernstein, J., & Allegretto, S. (2007). *The state of working America 2006/2007.* Washington, DC: Economic Policy Institute.

Montgomery, L. & Eggen, D. (2008, October 27–November 2). Digging a deeper hole: Spending plans could push the deficit toward $1 trillion. *Washington Post National Weekly Edition,* 26, 2, p. 33.

Murray, C. (1984). *Losing ground: American social policy 1950–1980.* New York: Basic Books.

Office of Management and Budget. (2004). *FY 2005 budget.* Washington, DC: Government Printing Office.

Oxford American Dictionary. (1999). New York: Oxford University Press.

Page, A. N. (1977). Economics and social work: A neglected relationship. *Social Work* 22(1):48–53.

Pianin, E. (2000, October 30). Binges are part of the regular fare: Ignoring mandates, Congress's spending exceeds its plans by billions every year. *Washington Post National Weekly Edition* 18(1):30.

Rushefsky, M. E. (2002). *Public policy in the United States,* 3rd ed. Armonk, NY: M. E. Sharpe.

Schiller, B. R. (2004). *The economics of poverty and discrimination,* 9th ed. Upper Saddle River, NJ: Pearson Prentice Hall.

Schneider, G. (2004, February 9–15). Another kind of homeland security. *Washington Post National Weekly Edition* 21(6):18.

Shapiro, I. & Nichols, M. (1992). *Far from fixed: An analysis of the unemployment insurance system.* Washington, DC: Center on Budget and Policy Priorities.

Social Security Administration. (2008). *Annual statistical supplement, 2007.* Washington, DC: U.S. Department of Health and Human Services.

Social Security Administration. (2004). *Annual statistical supplement, 2003.* Washington, DC: U.S. Department of Health and Human Services.

Tobin, J. (1986). The economic experience. In D. R. Obey & P. Sarbanes (eds.), *The changing American economy: Papers from the fortieth anniversary symposium of the Joint Economic Committee* (Senate Hearing 99–637). New York: Basil Blackwell.

U.S. Census Bureau. (2007). *Statistical abstract of the United States: 2003,* 127th ed. Washington, DC: U.S. Department of Commerce.

U.S. Census Bureau. (1992). *Workers with low earnings: 1964 to 1990.* Current Population reports, P-60, No. 178. Washington, DC: U.S. Department of Commerce.

U.S. General Accounting Office. (2002). *Workforce Investment Act: Improvements needed in performance measures to provide a more accurate picture of WIA's effectiveness.* GAO-02-275. Washington, DC: U.S. Government Printing Office.

U.S. General Accounting Office. (1996). *Job Training Partnership Act: Long-term earnings and employment outcome.* GAO/HEHS-96-40. Washington, DC: U.S. Government Printing Office.

U.S. General Accounting Office. (1994a). *Multiple employment training programs: Conflicting requirements underscore need for change.* GAO/T-HEHS-94-120. Washington, DC: U.S. Government Printing Office.

U.S. General Accounting Office. (1994b). *Multiple employment training programs: Most federal agencies do not know if their programs are working effectively.* GAO/HEHS-94-88. Washington, DC: U.S. Government Printing Office.

U.S. General Accounting Office. (1992). *The changing workforce: Demographic issues facing the federal government.* GAO/GGD-92-38. Washington, DC: U.S. Government Printing Office.

U.S. General Accounting Office. (1991). *Job Training Partnership Act: Inadequate oversight leaves program vulnerable to waste, abuse, and mismanagement.* GAO/HRD-91-97. Washington, DC: U.S. Government Printing Office.

VandeHei, J. (2005). So much for limited government. *Washington Post National Weekly Edition* 22(17):11.

Weir, M. (1987). Full employment as a political issue in the United States. *Social Research* 54(2): 377–402.

White House. (2008). *Fact sheet: Bipartisan growth package will help protect our nation's economic health.* Washington, DC: Office of the President of the United States.

Woodbury, S. A. (2000). New directions in reemployment policy. *Employment Research* 7(3): 1–4.

Childhood is one phase of life that we all have shared. Our experiences in childhood vary greatly, however. Many of us remember childhood as a happy time, but others remember it as a time of stress and family breakdown. During difficult periods, family members may turn to outsiders for help and guidance.

Traditionally, the family has been responsible for the care of its children. Over the past 60 years, however, there has been a shift in focus. The family is still seen as the main caregiver for children, but various forms of public intervention in family functioning have become more accepted. When a family is deemed incapable of caring for a child or dangerous to a child's well-being, for example, the government intervenes. Education for all children has become a public responsibility. Public intervention in relation to children and families has been mandated and guided by social welfare policies. The rules and guidelines are generally referred to as **child welfare policy**. The constellation of public services designed to protect and promote the well-being of children is the **child welfare system**. In a narrow sense, the child welfare system is concerned with public intervention when a family cannot or does not properly care for a child. This book will take a broader view of child welfare, however. It will look at the development, focus, and extent of child and family social welfare policies for protection as well as more extensive policies and programs, such as health and education, which affect the well-being of children. The social and political values and beliefs that have shaped these policies will also be discussed.

OVERVIEW OF CURRENT CONDITIONS

There are about 74 million children in this country, or 25 percent of the total population. These numbers are estimated to grow by 25 million in the next 40 years (U.S. Census Bureau, 2007). Box 10.1 presents demographic characteristics of children in America. More than 39 million households include children under 18 years of age. Box 10.2 provides a breakdown of family composition by race and head of

BOX 10.1

MORE ABOUT DEMOGRAPHICS OF CHILDREN AND YOUTH (UNDER 18 YEARS OF AGE) IN 2006 (IN MILLIONS)

	Total Number of Children and Youth	Percent of Reference Group
Total	73.7	25%
White	42.5	21%
Black	11.4	30%
Hispanic*	15.0	34%
Asian	3.0	24%
American Indian	0.8	28%

*Persons of Hispanic origin may be of any race.
Source: U.S. Census Bureau, 2007.

BOX 10.2	MORE ABOUT HOUSEHOLD COMPOSITION IN 2006

Households with Children under 18 Years of Age (in thousands)

	Total	Two-Parent	Female-Headed	Male-Headed
All	39.4	26.5 (67%)	10.4 (26%)	2.5 (6%)
White	24.6	18.1 (74%)	4.9 (20%)	1.5 (6%)
Black	5.6	2.1 (38%)	3.1 (55%)	0.4 (7%)
Hispanic*	6.9	4.5 (65%)	2.0 (30%)	0.4 (6%)

*Hispanic persons may be of any race.
Source: U.S. Census Bureau, 2007.

household. Overall, in 2006, 32 percent of households with children and adolescents were headed by a single parent. In African-American families, the proportion was almost twice as high, at 62 percent, and in Hispanic families, it was 36 percent. These demographics demonstrate some of the unique concerns about families today. More children will spend part or all of their childhood living with only one parent, particularly African-American children. As discussed elsewhere, more and more parents are working, both in two-parent and single-parent households.

Other demographic changes seem to greatly affect children. The proportion of children in the total population is decreasing. In 1990, children under the age of 18 years constituted 36 percent of the total population. At the same time, people 65 years old and over made up 9 percent of the population. Today, more than 12 percent of the population is 65 years old and over, and by 2050, this group is expected to increase to 21 percent (U.S. Census Bureau, 2007). Child welfare advocates fear that the shift in population age groups may cause competition for funding between child welfare programs and elderly welfare programs. As discussed in Chapter 8, the economic well-being of children is already precarious. Children are proportionately the poorest population group in the United States. These facts show that the needs of children are increasing but at the same time are becoming less of a priority. The services and support of child welfare programs will become increasingly important to the well-being of families.

It would seem that a group this large and diverse would be one of the most important social welfare concerns. It is a trite but true observation that children are the future of our nation. Although many people speak emphatically about the well-being of children and families in this country, social welfare policy does not respond emphatically. The United States lacks a coherent and comprehensive social welfare system for the care and protection of children. The existing child welfare system is a collection of programs and policies that have evolved incrementally, with little planning or coordination. Social problems such as poverty and unequal access to resources and opportunities have contributed to poor coordination of services. Racism further exacerbates the problems. Services for children of color have historically been inadequate (Gustavsson & Segal, 1994). Families of color often receive inferior services or are held to different standards because of their race and

| BOX 10.3 | CONSIDER THIS . . . FACTS ABOUT CHILDREN IN THE UNITED STATES |

Every day in America

- Two children under the age of five die in homicides.
- Five young people commit suicide.
- Eight young people die from firearms injuries.
- More than 1,800 babies are born to parents without health insurance.

- More than 2,400 babies are born into poverty.
- Almost 2,300 high school students drop out of school.
- Almost 8,000 children are reported abused or neglected.
- Four children are killed by abuse or neglect.

Source: Children's Defense Fund, 2007.

the stereotypes associated with race. Although child welfare services are an integral part of social welfare policy, there are problems that still need to be addressed if families and children are to be served adequately. Box 10.3 highlights the condition of children in the United States today.

THE CHILD WELFARE SYSTEM

The numerous federal programs and countless state and local programs that are "Designed to promote the well-being of children by ensuring safety, achieving permanency, and strengthening families to successfully care for their children" (National Clearinghouse on Child Abuse and Neglect, 2004, p. 1) make up the child welfare system. This system is primarily responsible for preventing the unnecessary separation of children from their families. In cases where separation is necessary, child welfare agencies assist families in solving problems so that children can be returned to their families as soon as possible. If it is impossible for children to be returned, they are placed in adoptive homes. Services that are typically part of the child welfare system include child protective services (CPS), foster care, adoption, and family preservation.

CPS, foster care, and adoption are part of a larger system of child and family policies. The broader panoply of child welfare services includes mental and public health care for children and families, public education, juvenile justice and family court services, and income maintenance programs. Therefore, the social welfare policy debate on children and families is extremely broad. Furthermore, child welfare services in one state are often very different from those in other states or unavailable in other states. Levels of assistance and gaps in service also vary across the country. This variability and complexity make our child welfare system difficult to understand.

Almost all public social services for children and families focus on problems that have already occurred, not on preventing problems. Most programs have evolved out of publicly recognized need or breakdown. This residual approach has resulted in a patchwork of services, sometimes overlapping or leaving needs unmet. For the majority of programs, the rules and regulations are federally mandated and state administered. Examination of the main programs reveals the variability and residual nature of child welfare policy.

HISTORICAL DEVELOPMENT OF CHILD AND FAMILY POLICY

As outlined in Chapter 2, the historical foundation of social welfare policy for children in this country rests on the belief that needs and problems should be dealt with privately and that the family should be the key social resource. Only in the most significant times of need should the public intervene. Before the early 1900s, the federal government had no role in child welfare. The first major congressional policy was initiated in 1916, for the protection of children from labor abuses (see Box 10.4). The earliest efforts at public intervention took place at the state, not the federal, level.

BOX 10.4 | **MORE ABOUT GOVERNMENT LEGISLATION AND CHILDREN**

The history of public involvement in the care of children and the regulation of families dates back to the 1800s. The following chart outlines the evolution of public legislation and major private child welfare organizations.

Timeline for Child Welfare Legislation and Organizations

Year	State	Federal	Private
1824	House of Refuge, New York, first state-funded institution for juvenile delinquents		
1836	Child labor law enacted in Massachusetts		
1853			Children's Aid Society founded
1867	County homes for children authorized in Ohio		
1868	Foster homes for orphans funded in Massachusetts		
1875			Society for the Prevention of Cruelty to Children established
1899	First juvenile court established in Chicago		
1900	32 states have compulsory education		
1904			National Child Labor Committee formed
1909		White House Conference on Children and Youth	
1911	First Mother's Aid law enacted in Illinois		

continued

BOX 10.4	**MORE ABOUT GOVERNMENT LEGISLATION AND CHILDREN** *continued*

		Source of Action	
Year	**State**	**Federal**	**Private**
1912		Establishment of U.S. Children's Bureau in Department of Labor	
1916		Congress passes Child Labor Bill	
1920			Child Welfare League of America organized
1921		Maternity and Infancy Act (Sheppard-Towner Act) passed	
1929		Repeal of Sheppard-Towner Act	
1935		Aid to Dependent Children	
		Maternal and Child Health Services	
1961		Juvenile Delinquency and Youth Offenses Control Act	
1964		Food Stamp Act Head Start	
1965		Medicaid Elementary and Secondary Education Act	
1966		Child Nutrition Act	
		Supplemental Food Program for Women, Infants, and Children (WIC)	
1967		Child Health Act	
1973			Children's Defense Fund established
1974		Title XX, Social Services Block Grant	
		Child Abuse Prevention and Treatment Act	
		Juvenile Justice and Delinquency Prevention Act	

continued

BOX 10.4 | MORE ABOUT GOVERNMENT LEGISLATION AND CHILDREN *continued*

		Source of Action	
Year	State	Federal	Private
1975		Education for all Handicapped Children Act	
1978		Indian Child Welfare Act	
1980		Adoption Assistance and Child Welfare Act	
1983		Creation of House Select Committee on Children, Youth, and Families	
1984		Child Support Enforcement Amendments	
1988		Family Support Act	
1990		Individuals with Disabilities Education ACT (IDEA)	
1993		Family and Medical Leave Act	
		Child welfare amendments, family preservation	
1994		Multiethnic Placement Act	
1996		Temporary Assistance for Needy Families Block Grant (TANF)	
1997		Adoption and Safe Families Act	
		State Children's Health Insurance Program	
2001		No Child Left Behind Act	
2003		Keeping Children and Families Safe Act	
2006		Child and Family Services Improvement Act	

Source: Administration for Children and Families, 2008c; Axinn & Stern, 2008; Children's Defense Fund, 2002 & 2004; House Committee on Ways and Means, 1994; Katz, 1986; Kimmich, 1985; Segal, Gerdes, & Steiner, 2010; Stein, 1991; Trattner, 1999.

Policies and programs as diverse as juvenile justice, public education, foster care, child labor regulation, and cash assistance all began with state legislation. Often the push for these efforts came from private groups. Six key periods of federal government involvement in child and family welfare can be identified. The first wave occurred during the early 1900s, when the nation was experiencing tremendous social and economic change with the growth in industrialization, urbanization, and immigration as well as geographic expansion.

THE PROGRESSIVE ERA

As indicated in Box 10.4, by 1920 most of the major private organizations for the protection and advocacy of children had been founded. As early as 1853, the **Children's Aid Society (CAS)** was founded in New York to care for children who were orphaned, whose families were too poor to care for them, or who had left their families. The goal of CAS was to remove children from urban slums and place them with rural families (Hasci, 1995). This goal paralleled the general social reforms of the period, which focused on care provided by institutions outside the family. As the progressive era took hold around the turn of the century, child welfare advocates were successful in securing a number of key policy initiatives. Recognition that youths were different from adults spurred the development of the juvenile court system. For the first time, children charged with crimes were tried with sensitivity to their young age. Compulsory education, first mandated by law in Massachusetts in 1852, was commonplace by the early 1900s (Katz, 1986). Also during this period, child abuse gained limited recognition as a social concern.

Awareness of the need to care for children on a national level grew during the progressive era. The exploitive and unhealthy treatment of children as economic entities—laborers—was targeted by reformers. The growing middle class and the social reform movement spurred the desire for change. Children were no longer thought of only as economic entities but also as family members with sentimental value (Zelizer, 1985).

Social reformers advocated the end of child labor through the National Child Labor Committee. The first formal federal effort toward recognizing child welfare occurred in 1909, with the White House Conference on Children and Youth. The first federal agency for child welfare was established in 1912 as the Children's Bureau in the Department of Labor. Congress regulated child labor in 1916 with the passage of the Child Labor Bill. Although the bill was deemed unconstitutional by the Supreme Court, it set the stage for state regulations, which covered all jurisdictions by the 1930s. The opposition to child labor demonstrates the conflict inherent in public intervention in private family matters and the resistance of the private marketplace. Although protection of children was viewed as a worthy goal, removal of children from the labor market had a negative impact on poor families (Stadum, 1995). Many families relied on the economic contributions of their children. Furthermore, private industry was strongly opposed to any government regulation that was perceived as interfering with the free market.

THE GREAT DEPRESSION AND THE NEW DEAL

The next period of permanent federal involvement came with the Great Depression. The Maternity and Infancy Act (commonly referred to as the Sheppard-Towner

BOX 10.5	MORE ABOUT CURRENT CHILD WELFARE COMPONENTS OF THE SOCIAL SECURITY ACT

Temporary Assistance for Needy Families	Title IVA	Maternal and Child Health	Title V
		Medicaid	Title XIX
Child Welfare Services	Title IVB	Social Services Block Grant	Title XX
Child Support Enforcement	Title IVC	State Children's Health Insurance Program	Title XXI
Foster Care and Adoption Assistance	Title IVE		

Act), which was passed in 1921, provided for health care and assistance for pregnant women, mothers, and their children. Funding and support for the act were meager, however, and it was repealed eight years later. The legislation was repealed because it was viewed as interfering with the rights of states (Jansson, 2009). Despite its brief existence, the act set the stage for permanent federal intervention on behalf of mothers and children. The Great Depression cemented the role of the federal government in child and family welfare policy. As discussed in Chapter 8, the **Aid to Dependent Children** cash assistance program was enacted in 1935 as part of the **Social Security Act.** The Social Security Act also included the **Maternal and Child Health Act.** These pieces of legislation and subsequent amendments to the Social Security Act formed the core of today's child welfare assistance and preventive social service programs (see Box 10.5).

THE WAR ON POVERTY

The period of the 1960s and the War on Poverty was the third period of key federal involvement in child welfare. The progressive nature of the War on Poverty was evident in child welfare efforts. During the 1960s, the **Food Stamp** program, child nutrition services, and the **Supplemental Food Program for Women, Infants, and Children (WIC)** were enacted. Health needs were met by **Medicaid** and the Child Health Act. Social opportunities were expanded through the **Head Start** programs and the **Elementary and Secondary Education Act.** These programs represented a significant expansion of care for low-income children.

THE 1970S AND CHILD PROTECTION

The fourth period of federal expansion of child welfare legislation came during the 1970s. Recognition of the problem of **child abuse and neglect** grew during the 1960s following medical "discovery" of the phenomenon. The legislative response came with the **Child Abuse Prevention and Treatment Act of 1974 (CAPTA).** This legislation provides for federal assistance to states to enable the development of prevention and treatment programs for abuse and neglect. The act also established the **National Center on Child Abuse,** which serves as a clearinghouse for current data and information on child abuse and neglect.

Also in 1974, social services were added to the Social Security Act under a new program, **Title XX**. In 1981 its format was changed to grants to states as the **Social Services Block Grants (SSBG)**. SSBG provides funds for a variety of social services. A significant portion is spent on children's services, including child care, abuse and neglect prevention programs, and programs for the prevention or reduction of unnecessary institutional care. SSBG is a capped entitlement program that provides grants to states in proportion to their populations. States have a great deal of discretion in the use of the funds. In 2000, 7.5 million children, or 54 percent of recipients, benefited from the services of SSBG. Federal appropriations have decreased over the years, from $2.8 billion in 1995 to $1.8 billion in 2000 (Administration for Children and Families, 2002b).

In 1978, the federal government passed the **Indian Child Welfare Act (ICWA)**. This bill was enacted in response to concerns that American Indian children were being taken out of their homes and placed with non-Indian families. At the time, up to 35 percent of American Indian children were removed from their families and placed in non-Indian foster or adoptive homes (Wilkins, 2004). The goal of the legislation was to keep American Indian children in their homes, if possible, and in cases where removal was necessary, to place them in alternative homes that maintained a link to their tribal culture (Mannes, 1995).

The passage of ICWA was positive recognition of the right of Native American parents and tribes to decide what is best for their children. Unfortunately, implementation has not been highly successful. A disproportionately large number of children are removed from American Indian families compared with other ethnic groups, and Native American foster and adoptive homes are still in short supply (Halverson, Puig, & Byers, 2002).

Removal of children from their homes and placement of them in substitute care became a major concern during the 1970s. In response, Congress passed the **Adoption Assistance and Child Welfare Act of 1980** (P.L. 96-272). This legislation is the foundation of all protective services today. The goals of the legislation are, first, to prevent the unnecessary removal of children from their homes and, second, to place a child that must be removed in the most permanent situation possible. Reunification with the family is a high priority. When that fails, adoption is the optimal goal (Gustavsson & Segal, 1994).

THE 1980s AND 1990s: WELFARE REFORM AND PRESERVING FAMILIES

The fifth wave of child welfare policies was a more restrictive era, with a closer focus on individual responsibility. Numerous legislative efforts during the 1980s and 1990s were concerned with the economic efficiency of public assistance. Efforts to amend the AFDC program during the early 1980s were punitive and designed to cut people off from public assistance. The **Child Support Enforcement Amendments of 1984** and the **Family Support Act of 1988** amended the AFDC program, so that ways could be found to get child support payments from noncustodial parents and to help custodial parents to work and become economically self-sufficient.

Although welfare reform was still a concern, other issues of child welfare arose. In keeping with the civil rights atmosphere of the 1970s and the intent of policies such as the Indian Child Welfare Act, states had created policies to limit transracial adoptions and emphasized that children of color should be placed with adoptive parents of their own race or ethnic group (Hollingsworth, 1998). The more restrictive atmosphere of the 1990s changed that approach with passage of the **Multiethnic Placement Act of 1994.** This legislation prohibited federally funded agencies from denying anyone the opportunity to become an adoptive or foster parent solely on the basis of their race, color, or national origin. Racial sensitivity was urged, but adoption and foster care were to be conducted transracially. Members of nondominant groups found this reversal problematic and viewed it as a return to earlier times, when children's racial and ethnic identities were not recognized or preserved.

The **Personal Responsibility and Work Opportunity Reconciliation Act of 1996 (PRWORA)** was the culmination of years of debate about how to enforce economic self-sufficiency among poor families. The creation of the **Temporary Assistance for Needy Families (TANF)** program affected the lives of millions of poor children (see Chapter 8). TANF represented a major shift in federal policy toward children in need. Parental responsibility and individual self-sufficiency became the primary focus, and the federal government no longer guaranteed support. This shift was a major departure from the child support services of the previous 60 years.

One piece of legislation during this time had a more preventive tone. Advocates had tried for almost ten years to develop legislation guaranteeing job protection for employees who needed to take time off to care for children or sick dependents. Business interests were strongly opposed to the legislation, and George H. W. Bush twice vetoed it during his presidency. The election of Bill Clinton opened the door, however. The **Family and Medical Leave Act** was passed in January of 1993. The law represents one of the few times the federal government has taken a preventive approach to child and family welfare. The legislation allows workers to take up to 12 weeks of unpaid leave to care for a newborn or newly adopted child or to care for a sick dependent without losing their jobs.

Another policy effort was the addition of new preventive services for child welfare. Funding for **family preservation** and family support services—programs that emphasized permanency or keeping families together—were included in federal budgetary legislation (P.L. 103-66) in 1993 (House Committee on Ways and Means, 1994). The legislation created the Family Preservation and Support Services program under Title IVB of the Social Security Act. The goal of family preservation is to "serve families where child abuse or neglect has occurred or where children have been identified as representing a danger to themselves or others. These families risk having their children temporarily or permanently placed outside the home" (U.S. General Accounting Office, 1997, p. 4). Services were tailored to each family's need to keep the family intact and deal with the underlying issues that endangered the child.

This period marked government intervention with an emphasis on the private responsibility of families instead of the provisions of the public child welfare system. For example, during the 1990s, courts became more reluctant to remove children from their homes and returned children to their biological families. Two highly publicized cases of adoption, one in Michigan and one in Illinois, demonstrate the trend of courts to return children to their biological parents. In both cases, adoptive families were mandated through court decisions to relinquish their children. In the Illinois case, the biological father claimed he had not known about the existence of the child, known to the public as "Baby Richard." In spite of the fact that the baby had been legally adopted and had lived with his adoptive family from birth to age 4 years, in April 1995 the courts negated the adoption and returned him to the biological parents he had never known. Emphasis on keeping a child with his or her family reflects the value that the family of origin is the primary place for a child.

THE NEW MILLENNIUM

The emphasis on "permanency" and keeping families intact has come under scrutiny. In the previous example, was the removal of "Baby Richard" from his adoptive family in his best interest? Is keeping a child with his or her biological family always preferable? The family preservation program, in theory, was a way of keeping families together and thereby improving everyone's well-being. Adapting this small-scale experimental program for use in large urban child welfare agencies has been difficult. Child welfare agencies are serving more families with deep, intractable problems exacerbated by poverty and racial discrimination at the same time that agency staffing levels and the hiring of highly trained professionals have declined (Hutchinson, 2002). The impact of the family preservation program has not been as great as was hoped. A new policy direction that addresses the structure of the child welfare system and systemic social problems is needed for the care of children and families.

During the early 2000s, child welfare advocates hoped that a greater emphasis would be placed on prevention with the No Child Left Behind movement. With the advent of the new millennium, the Children's Defense Fund, a nonprofit children's rights organization, adopted the trademarked slogan "Leave No Child Behind" (Children's Defense Fund, 2002). Advocates pushed for preventive services to improve the well-being of children, including health insurance coverage for all children, Head Start for every eligible child, rebuilding of public schools and reduction in classroom sizes, Food Stamps for all eligible families, and safe and affordable housing for the millions of families living in dangerous neighborhoods and substandard homes. In response to this initiative, President George W. Bush campaigned to adopt the general goal of leaving no child behind, and the result was the **No Child Left Behind Act of 2001** (P.L. 107-110) (NCLB).

NCLB was much smaller in scope than what the Children's Defense Fund and other advocates had proposed. NCLB focuses only on education. The purpose of NCLB is to mandate higher teaching outcomes for public schools. Though it is still too early to assess the impact of NCLB, problems with implementation have already surfaced. States, which have a mandate to adopt NCLB, have received no funding to implement the act. States must pay for this **unfunded mandate** from their own coffers. They are required to increase teacher salaries, recruit and train new teachers, and increase teacher certification, all during a period of decreasing state revenues (Congressional Quarterly, 2004). Presidential budgets have proposed even less economic support than when the NCLB bill was passed (Children's Defense Fund, 2002). In fiscal year 2005, almost all school districts received less dollars under NCLB than had been promised (Children's Defense Fund, 2004) This is an example of the divergence between funding promises and actual delivery of services.

In recent years, legislation has been passed to strengthen the child welfare system. The Keeping Children and Families Safe Act of 2003, in addition to reauthorizing CAPTA, emphasized improving linkages between CPS and other agencies such as public health, mental health, and developmental disabilities. This recognized the complexity of caring for children and the numerous interrelationships between government agencies. In 2006, the Child and Family Services Improvement Act was enacted. This law reauthorized programs to improve permanency outcomes for children with greater emphasis on state flexibility. The laws of recent years reaffirm the child welfare approaches of permanency planning and family preservation, although the difficulty in achieving these goals is better understood. Preserving families must still be weighed against the best interest of the child, and this continues to be the challenge when there is government intervention in the privacy of families.

MAJOR FEDERAL PROGRAMS PROVIDING AID AND SERVICES TO CHILDREN AND FAMILIES

The constellation of social welfare policies outlined serves as the legislative foundation for the majority of programs and services for children and families. As in other areas of social welfare policy, child welfare programs are mandated by the federal government and implemented on the state level. The consequence of this duality is that child welfare programs vary from state to state. In addition, statutory laws, regulations, and court decisions shape child welfare policy. The state variations are too voluminous to cover here. The main federal provisions are discussed here.

The key areas of child welfare services are income assistance, food and nutrition, health, protective services, education, employment, corrections, and social services. Child welfare services can be organized into three types: supportive, which help families cope with problems; supplementary, which provide needed resources; and substitutive, which take the place of the family (Kadushin & Martin, 1988). Supportive services include family preservation, child care, and parenting skills. Supplementary services include cash assistance, health care, and nutrition services. Substitutive services primarily involve foster care and adoption programs. These three domains broadly define child welfare services. In the following sections, the major child welfare programs and policies are outlined.

INCOME ASSISTANCE

Temporary Assistance for Needy Families (TANF)   The TANF program is most often thought of as a poverty program, yet it has also been a significant child welfare program (see Chapter 8). In 2005, 5 million people received benefits through TANF; 75 percent of the recipients were children (Office of Human Services Policy, 2007). Although the number of recipients has declined, the concentration of children has increased. Over the years, TANF has become less of a family program and more of a children's support program as the proportion of children as recipients has grown. In 2000, 40 percent of the children receiving TANF were under the age of 6 years, and only 8 percent were older than 15 years (Administration for Children and Families, 2002a). The average TANF family was made up of a mother and two children.

Therefore, TANF has been primarily a program for young children living with their mother and a crucial source of economic support for needy children and their families. Although the program has been extremely important for the financial well-being of families, benefits are set at a level that keeps a family below the poverty threshold. In 2005, the average family payment through TANF was $370 per month, or about $4,440 a year (Office of Human Services Policy, 2007).

As discussed previously, the original ADC program was not designed to be a permanent part of the social welfare system. When it was enacted in 1935 as part of the Social Security Act, it was seen as a temporary program that would last only until all workers were covered by the Social Security system. It was built on the demographic assumptions of the 1930s: Children live with two parents, and their fathers have good jobs that are covered by Social Security. Families and economic conditions have changed over the past 75 years. The number of single-parent families has grown. More women head households and have never been married, so they are ineligible to be survivors of workers who participated in Social Security. As already discussed, there are many shortcomings in the TANF program and the employment market does not provide the economic support needed by all families. The weakened economy of recent years has meant fewer jobs, more families in need, and decreases in welfare-to-work services and benefits in most states (Children's Defense Fund, 2007). In spite of these limitations and low levels of cash assistance, the TANF program provides a much-needed safety net for poor children and their families.

Child Support Enforcement   Another program designed to provide economic support for families is the **Child Support Enforcement** program. Created as part of the AFDC program, it was established in 1975 as Title IVD of the Social Security Act to enforce the payment of court-mandated child support by noncustodial parents (U.S. General Accounting Office, 1996). The program was expanded in 1984, 1988, and again in 1996. Today, eligibility for TANF rests on the enforcement of child support through state and local Child Support Enforcement agencies. The program assists custodial parents in receiving payments from noncustodial parents. The program is designed to assist non-TANF individuals as well. Money collected on behalf of TANF families is used to offset the costs of the program, and money collected on behalf of non-TANF families goes to the non-TANF family. In 2006, 16 million TANF and non-TANF cases were handled (U.S. Census Bureau, 2007). The majority of support payments collected, 91 percent, are for non-TANF cases. Through Child Support Enforcement efforts, the government provides public services for custodial parents to collect past-due child support payments.

FOOD AND NUTRITION

Most food and nutrition programs for children are designed for children from low-income families. The largest food program for poor children is the Food Stamp program, now known as the Supplemental Nutrition Assistance Program. As discussed in Chapter 8, it is based on financial need and provides coupons, or credit, toward buying groceries. In 2005, more than 26 million people received Food Stamps, and 48 percent were children (Office of Human Services Policy, 2007). Another program targeted specifically to children is the **WIC program**, known officially as the

Supplemental Food Program for Women, Infants, and Children. This program provides nutrition and health assistance for pregnant women and their children up to the age of 5 years. WIC served 8.1 million people in 2006 (U.S. Census Bureau, 2007). Other efforts such as the School Breakfast and Lunch programs also serve poor children by providing meals through schools. More than 30 million children participated in the National School Lunch program in 2006, and almost 10 million children participated in the School Breakfast Program. Because proper child development depends on good nutrition and early health care, these programs play a critical role in child well-being for the poorest families. Although cash assistance has declined in recent years, poverty has not and food assistance programs have become even more important. These programs have seen increased participation in every year since 2000.

HEALTH CARE

More details on the health of children is presented in Chapter 11. However, it is important to highlight the major health care social welfare policies for children here. Improved physical health contributes to a child's abilities to learn, socialize, and develop into a productive adult. Discussion of overall well-being must include attention to children's health.

Medicaid   Chapter 11 covers the Medicaid program in detail. Medicaid serves financially needy persons. For poor children, Medicaid is the key public medical insurance program. In 2005, more than 26 million dependent children received Medicaid services, constituting 46 percent of the total Medicaid population. This group of children were responsible for only 15 percent of the program expenses, however (Social Security Administration, 2008). Most of the money paid out for Medicaid assists aged, blind, and disabled people. Nevertheless, Medicaid is the most important health service for poor children. As employment-based health insurance has declined for children, Medicaid coverage has become more important.

State Children's Health Insurance Program (SCHIP)   Medicaid has provided health care coverage for poor children since the 1960s. Even so, a large group of children was still unprotected: millions of families in which some members were employed and earned too much to make them eligible for Medicaid but did not earn enough to pay for health insurance. Either their job benefits did not include health insurance coverage or it was too expensive. The surge in numbers of these people led to a public debate on national health insurance. President Clinton attempted to make national health insurance a cornerstone of his administration but was met with strong resistance. Although significantly lesser in scope, the Clinton proposal for health insurance for children was an important contribution to child welfare. Congress concurred, and in 1997 the **State Children's Health Insurance Program (SCHIP)** was created.

SCHIP is a federal-state program whereby states have flexibility within broad federal guidelines. The flexibility includes operating SCHIP as an extension of Medicaid or as a stand-alone program. If states choose to link SCHIP to Medicaid, they must offer all Medicaid services to all who are eligible. If they choose to use SCHIP as a stand-alone program, services can be limited and enrollment capped.

In 2002, 16 states had created Medicaid expansion programs, 16 had stand-alone SCHIP programs, and 19 had created a combination of the two approaches (U.S. General Accounting Office, 2002). By 2006, almost 7 million children received health care through SCHIP with combined state and federal spending topping $7 billion, up from $2 billion just six years earlier. Enrollment in the program doubled between 2000 and 2006 (U.S. Census Bureau, 2007). One of President Obama's first legislative initiatives after he took office was to reauthorize and extend the program through 2013 with coverage increased to include an additional 4 million children.

Maternal Health Care   Infant mortality is a major health concern. It is used as a measure of the well-being of a nation's children. In the 1930s, the infant mortality rate in the United States was one of the highest among industrialized nations. In addition, significant numbers of children were born with severe physical disabilities. These phenomena prompted Congress to develop legislation to provide health care for all mothers and children (National Commission to Prevent Infant Mortality, 1988). The Maternal and Child Health Act was included in the original 1935 Social Security Act. Amended to become a block grant program, the Maternal and Child Health Services Block Grant (Title V, Social Security Act) provides health services for low-income mothers and children. The program is designed to reduce the incidence of infant mortality, treat and prevent communicable diseases, and provide prenatal and postpartum care. Services today include immunizations, genetic disease testing, and treatment for children with physical disabilities. Unlike so many other social services proposals, the legislation mandates a number of preventive programs. The need for such programs is real, but, regrettably, funding for them has been limited. In 2001, federal spending totaled $2.7 billion, which held steady for several years and then dropped in 2005 (U.S. Census Bureau, 2007). The greatest need is among African-American families. The mortality rate for African-American infants is twice as high as for white infants due to lower incomes and less availability of prenatal care for African-American mothers (Federal Interagency Forum on Child and Family Statistics, 2005).

CHILD PROTECTIVE SERVICES

Abuse and Neglect/Maltreatment   Although historically there has been public hesitancy to interfere with the rights of parents to raise their children as they see fit, government intervention is a central part of child welfare services. Until the 1870s, families raised their children with complete autonomy. The first officially documented case of child abuse occurred in 1874 (Tower, 1989; Watkins, 1990). Legend has it that the case of "Little Mary Ellen" was publicized through the efforts of the New York Society for the Prevention of Cruelty to Animals (SPCA). Neighbors found Mary Ellen physically and emotionally abused by her foster parents. Concerned about her welfare, they approached the only organization protecting the rights of animals. The SPCA had never handled a case concerning a child. In response to this gap in service and to the growing recognition that children were vulnerable and deserved protection, the Society for the Prevention of Cruelty to Children was founded. Although this version of the story is found in many accounts of child welfare history, it has most likely been embellished. The Mary Ellen case inspired public action because of other factors, including journalistic attention from a strong women's rights movement and the growing strength of the judiciary system (Costin, 1991). These factors led to organized efforts to protect children. For the next several decades, most efforts to protect children centered on private organizations.

The impetus behind today's policies stems from the 1960s, when documentation of the vulnerability of children was publicized. In 1962, a medical doctor, C. Henry Kempe, documented the impact of abuse and neglect, developing the term *battered child syndrome* (Kempe, et al., 1962). Battered child syndrome was based on growing medical evidence of physical abuse of children. Professional and public attention to this report and related research began to raise awareness that many children were abused and neglected within their families.

The **1974 Child Abuse Prevention and Treatment Act (CAPTA)** (P.L. 93-247) elevated the protection of children from abuse and neglect to the federal level. The act provided grants to states on the condition that they must have a mandatory reporting law requiring professionals to report suspected cases. Immunity for those who reported suspected incidents of child abuse and neglect was also a requirement (Costin, Bell, & Downs, 1991). Today, all states have such provisions. Mandated reporters include health care providers, teachers, social workers, police officers, and foster care providers. The development of mandatory reporting gave rise to the collection of statistics documenting the incidence of child abuse and neglect. Each state sets its own definitions, but they must reflect minimum standards outlined by federal law.

It is difficult to accurately assess the number of abusive or neglectful acts committed. Statistics represent cases that are actually reported to authorities. Although many cases go unreported, the numbers are revealing. Over the years, the incidence of reported cases of child maltreatment has increased. According to data submitted by states to the National Child Abuse and Neglect Data System, a federally mandated collection service, 3.3 million reports alleging abuse and neglect of 6 million children were filed with state children's services agencies in 2006. About 60 percent (3.6 million children) were accepted for investigation. During 2006, 905,000 children were determined to be victims of child abuse or neglect, and 1,530 children died from an injury caused by abuse or neglect (Administration for Children and Families, 2008b). Children under one year of age are most at risk, with the highest rate of victimization. More than half of child victims are girls. The most common maltreatment was neglect (60 percent) while seven percent involved sexual abuse. Although a strong belief in family privacy still exists, without public intervention millions of children are at risk of serious injury, neglect, and even death. Box 10.6 outlines the struggle between family privacy and state intervention.

Foster Care and Adoption   Although preventive efforts have sporadically been funded and supported, the main public response to abuse and neglect is to document the abuse and remove the child from the dangerous environment. Removal can be temporary through **foster care** or permanent through **adoption**. Foster care and adoption are the major social program interventions. The number of children in foster care fluctuated over the years, but data were only estimates. In 1986, Congress mandated the Department of Health and Human Services to establish a system for collecting national

BOX 10.6 | CONTROVERSIAL PERSPECTIVES . . .

When discussing the care of children, nothing raises more controversy than whether the state should or should not intervene in families, and, if so, how.

State child protective services (CPS) agencies are the government agents responsible for protecting children from abuse and neglect. Check the mission of any state CPS office and you will find admirable and worthwhile goals. For example, the Department of Child Services in Indiana "protects children from further abuse and neglect and prevents, remedies, or assists in solving problems that may result in abuse, neglect, exploitation, or delinquency of children." This goal is repeated in 49 other states across the United States. Yet there are harsh critics of CPS. One visit to the web site fightcps.com will tell you a different story. This is the mission of this site: "To provide information and support for families facing false accusations of child abuse or neglect, and for researchers working to

protect and encourage natural family rights." This group rejects state intervention into the family. And there is yet a third position adding to the controversy, that of people who feel that we need an improved public system. Consider the goal of an organization called Justice for Children, which was developed "in response to the inadequacies and failure of child protective system to protect abused and neglected children." Arguing for better protection of children, this group calls for overhaul of the CPS systems.

The conflict is multifaceted: There are laws that mandate the state to protect children; there are families in our nation who do not think the state should intervene at all; and there are advocacy groups who feel that state intervention should be done very differently. Who is right? This is an example of how difficult it is to get public agreement on a policy approach to a very important social issue, the protection of children from abuse and neglect.

data on foster care. It took seven years for HHS to issue regulations, however. The system finally became operational in mid-1995 (U.S. General Accounting Office, 1994). Since that time, states have been required to submit data semiannually to the Administration for Children and Families, an agency within the Department of Health and Human Services. In 2006, there were 510,000 children in foster care (Administration for Children and Families, 2008a).

During the 1960s and 1970s, child welfare advocates noted with concern that more and more children were spending more time in foster care. Some children remained in foster care on a permanent basis, often drifting from one placement to another. Little effort was made to keep children in their own homes. Disproportionate numbers of children of color were placed in foster care, and poverty was often a precursor to foster care placement. Furthermore, awareness was growing about the negative consequences of children growing up separated from their families (Pecora, Whittaker, & Maluccio, 1992). These trends prompted child welfare advocates to push for changes. The result was the **Adoption Assistance and Child Welfare Act of 1980** (P.L. 96-272).

Advocates regarded the legislation as a new era in foster care and adoption. The law implemented a number of services and guidelines designed to correct imbalances in the system. Foremost was the goal of **permanency planning**. Permanency planning stressed the concept that foster care was a temporary service and that children should either be returned to their family or placed for permanent adoption in the shortest time possible (Lindsey, 1994). Components of the

Adoption Assistance and Child Welfare Act required a case review of each child at least once every six months; a mandatory hearing after 18 months to promote the achievement of a permanent placement; expanding the role of the courts by requiring a judicial finding that all reasonable efforts had been made to keep the child in the family; expanding Title IVB of the Social Security Act to provide greater child welfare services; and creation of Title IVE of the Social Security Act to develop the state-federal partnership in funding services related to foster care and adoption.

The initial impact of the 1980 legislation on foster care was evident in the numbers of children in placements. From 1980 to 1985, the number of children in foster care dropped by about ten percent, from over 300,000 to 269,000. After that initial drop, the numbers increased. By 1992, more than 440,000 children were placed in foster care; 43 percent had been in continuous care for more than two years (House Committee on Ways and Means, 1994). These numbers and the growing lengths of stay raised concern about the effectiveness and quality of foster care. The structure of the child welfare system did not promote family preservation:

> The current federal system for financing child welfare programs offers little incentive for states to provide services designed to achieve the 1980 legislative goals of keeping families together and averting the need for foster care (U.S. General Accounting Office, 1993).

Child welfare advocates engaged in efforts to pass new legislation that would revise the 1980 legislation and emphasize ways to keep families together.

Emphasis on prevention and treatment in child welfare services expanded. In response to the growth in foster care placements, services promoting **family preservation** evolved. The federal government supported those efforts by including family preservation and support provisions as part of the Omnibus Reconciliation Act of 1993 (P.L. 103-66). Five-year plans were developed by states in 1994 and implemented that year. As discussed earlier, family preservation efforts were insufficient to address the volume of demand and complexity of cases.

By the late 1990s, the emphasis on family preservation and reunification had abated. A new focus was achieving permanent solutions through adoption. Several high-profile cases of children who were returned to their families only to be abused again, some so severely that they died, prompted this approach. In 1997, Congress passed the **Adoption and Safe Families Act (ASFA)** (P.L. 105-89). ASFA amended Title IVE of the Social Security Act (Foster Care and Adoption Assistance) to emphasize the health and safety of the child when making efforts to preserve and reunify families. Although this is laudable, child welfare experts raise concerns that ASFA, in an attempt to correct the perceived mistakes of family reunification efforts, may go too far in the opposite direction and encourage a return to the practice of removing children from homes when it is not necessary (Stein, 2000).

Although ASFA was passed to emphasize permanent placements for children, the evidence over the past 25 years suggests that the impact of the legislation was short term. Assessment of this child welfare legislation is harsh:

> The new policy [AFSA] reflects old themes. Parents remain ultimately responsible for the care of their children—child maltreatment remains a personal, not a social, problem. Interventions are remedial and residual; previous levels of financial support have been reduced; and CPS workers maintain their dual role of helping/policing families... these policies have generated practices that have not been particularly effective in either

protecting children or preserving families. It becomes obvious that a re-evaluation of policy is necessary. (Smith & Fong, 2004, p. 125)

In 2003, the Keeping Children and Families Safe Act was passed to reauthorize CAPTA and emphasize adoption of older foster care children, greater training for mandated reporters, and enhanced linkages between CPS and other service systems to promote comprehensive treatment for victims of maltreatment. For the 510,000 children in foster care in 2006, the average age was ten years old, and the children stayed in foster care for an average of 28 months. Most children were in foster care for less than two years, with only 13 percent in the system for five or more years. For most children, foster care is temporary, two thirds return to their families or live with relatives. In 2006 though, 25 percent of the children in foster care were waiting to be adopted and these children had been in foster care for an average of three and a half years (Administration for Children and Families, 2008a).

The system of removing children from their homes is entirely residual in nature and has been resistant to preventive efforts. The need for improving the social environment and providing support for families also should be addressed when developing policies to protect children. How can families be better equipped to care for children? For legislation to be effective over a longer time, policies must be developed that support families socially and economically and help families develop the skills and resources to care for children in the home.

EDUCATION

Compulsory education laws have given all children access to schooling. Education has proved to be an effective way of increasing earning potential and providing a means of achieving economic self-sufficiency. In general, the more years of education a person has, the higher his or her earnings will be. Data from 2005 showed

 **BOX 10.7** | **MORE ABOUT EDUCATION AND EARNINGS**

Educational Level	Median Earnings in 2005
9th to 12th grade but no diploma	$19,915
High school graduate	$29,448
Some college but no degree	$31,421
Associate degree	$37,990
Bachelor's degree	$54,689
Master's degree	$67,898
Doctorate	$92,863
Professional degree	$119,009

Source: U.S. Census Bureau, 2007.

significant variation in earnings (see Box 10.7). In every category, the household income increased as the level of education increased. The relationship between educational level and economic well-being is clear.

Although public education is available, the quality of education varies widely. In a classic review of public education, Jonathan Kozol (1991), a journalist who investigates social issues, visited a number of public schools across the country. He compared schools in wealthy communities with schools in poor communities and discovered incredible disparities. He found almost total racial segregation, huge differences in per pupil spending, and classroom resources ranging from nonexistent to state of the art. In Chicago, the suburban schools spent 78 percent more per pupil than did the city schools; in New York City, the difference was more than 100 percent; and in New Jersey, the difference was almost 120 percent. Kozol's assessment of the state of children's education was that "in public schooling, social policy has been turned back almost one hundred years" (p. 4) and "I often wondered why we would agree to let our children go to school in places where no politician, school board president, or business CEO would dream of working" (p. 5). Research during the 1990s on the state of school facilities concluded that the majority of students attend schools with inadequate building or environmental conditions. Schools with the most problems were located in central cities; more than 50 percent of their students were from nondominant groups and 70 percent or more were poor (U.S. General Accounting Office, 1996). Recent assessment reconfirms the disparity between schools with nonwhite and poor students and schools with predominantly white and economically advantaged students. Teachers' education, experience, credentials, knowledge, and skills are higher in schools with students who are white and economically advantaged.

> Poor schools also offer less music and visual arts instruction than their nonpoor counterparts, and they have more buildings in need of repair. Minority schools have fewer support staff, such as counselors, than whiter schools, and they are more likely to be extremely overcrowded. African American and Latino students are also more likely than white students to avoid certain places at school and to fear being attacked (Phillips & Chin, 2004, p. 510).

The disparity in schools reflects the dependence on local authority and local funding by property taxes. Because public schools rely heavily on funding from property taxes and, hence, the economic level of their surrounding communities, those in wealthy areas receive more money than those in poorer communities. For example, in New York, the wealthiest school system spends almost $14,000 per pupil, whereas the poorest system spends $7,500 (Shipler, 2004). The role of the federal government has been to provide funding only in cases where there are special needs, so local property taxes dictate the funds available for school systems. Poor neighborhoods have low tax bases and, hence, less money for schools. Unfortunately, federal funding for children's education has declined since 2004, dropping about 9 percent (First Focus, 2008). This has left schools in poor neighborhoods even farther behind.

Children with Disabilities   The major policies intended to provide education to all children include the **Elementary and Secondary Education Act of 1965**, the **Education for all Handicapped Children Act of 1975**, and the **Individuals with Disabilities Education Act (IDEA) of 1990**. The 1965 legislation provided federal funds to support education for severely handicapped children; the 1975 legislation expanded coverage of the program; and the 1990 legislation reauthorized the program with an emphasis on making every effort to educate a disabled child in the child's neighborhood rather than a special school outside the child's neighborhood. In 1997 the law was amended to include services for a wider array of health impairments (Altshuler & Koppels, 2003). States administer the program and determine eligibility. Educating children with disabilities requires special services and training. The IDEA program ensures that schools will make the effort to provide those educational opportunities. Although the IDEA program has not been applied uniformly and there are differences in expenditures and services, it has been successful in providing education for children who would otherwise have received little or no schooling.

Head Start   The **Head Start Program** is both an educational and an antipoverty program. Established in 1964 as part of the Economic Opportunity Act, it serves low-income preschool children. The program provides funds to states for education, socialization, and on-site nutrition at Head Start preschools. The goal is to help economically disadvantaged children be better prepared for school and therefore be on the same starting line as more advantaged children. In 1995 the program was expanded to reach low-income infants and toddlers. This expansion, Early Head Start, has been effective in improving language and problem-solving skills and in promoting better parenting (Mathews, 2002). In spite of research documenting the success of Head Start, its funding has never been high enough to reach all eligible children; 40 percent of eligible children are not served (Children's Defense Fund, 2004). In 2006, 909,000 children were enrolled in Head Start (U.S. Census Bureau, 2007).

No Child Left Behind Program   Earlier in this chapter, the **No Child Left Behind Act of 2001** was introduced. As an education program, it sets annual targets in student achievement that schools must meet. The goal of the Act is to ensure that all children are at grade-level proficiency in reading and math by 2014. Unlike previous education programs, it tends to take a hard approach to performance, mandating outcomes that are uniform across the nation. When schools do not meet those standards, even if there is improvement, they are penalized. Both the strict outcome measures and implementation problems are regarded by some school educators as limiting the effectiveness of the program. Research on NCLB found that "The law's tangled rules have mystified—and demoralized—many," and "Schools should be rewarded for elevating achievement levels by some degree, rather than penalized for not meeting an absolute, unrealistic standard" (Fuller, 2004, p. 23). Early results from NCLB are difficult to assess. NCLB has brought more publicity to what schools are doing, but the impact is almost impossible to assess—what changes in schools are directly related to NCLB is difficult to determine because most states started testing as a result of the law, so there are no before and after comparisons. Critics argue that teachers will teach to the test, raising scores but not necessarily educating better (Mantel, 2005). Overall, assessment of NCLB by a bipartisan commission found the principles to be worthy, but that not enough has been accomplished. "The problems that NCLB was intended to address remain" (Commission on NCLB, 2007, p. 2). NCLB does represent a bipartisan effort to create legislation to improve schooling for children. Before the program deteriorates because of poor implementation and unrealistic expectations, legislators need to seriously examine it and make necessary changes so that children will receive a better education.

EMERGING SOCIAL CONCERNS

In spite of our reluctance to interfere in the privacy of families, child well-being has become a national concern. This is evident through the numerous programs and policies that have been described in this chapter. Thus, we should be aware of issues that are looming in the future and that have already garnered interest in federal involvement by child welfare advocates. Health and well-being of children are critical social policy concerns. Health issues are further discussed in the next chapter. However, two health concerns affect children greatly, and are important to mention while discussing child welfare.

The number of overweight children in this country has become a public health concern. In 1976–1980, only six percent of children ages 6–17 were overweight. By 2000, this percentage had risen to 15 percent. Most recently, in 2005–2006, 17 percent of children ages 6–17 were overweight (Federal Interagency Forum on Child and Family Statistics, 2008). Because weight affects health, there is growing public concern that today's children will be less healthy than previous generations and will require costly health care. In addition, healthy children become productive adults, and compromising children's early life health can mean that their ability to work and contribute to society may be diminished. This represents a major public challenge—what and how much children eat seems to be a personal and family choice, yet the consequences can have significant costs to the larger society.

Another child welfare concern is the mental health of children. Recent research on the impact of stress on children, particularly over prolonged periods of time, found severely negative effects on health. In children, toxic stress can impair brain development, as well as suppress immunity to infections, and do permanent damage that affects learning and memory (Centers for Disease Control and Prevention, 2008). The link between stress in childhood and adult health is significant. Studies have found that adverse childhood experiences are common among people in the United States, and the consequence is distressing. Based on responses of over 17,000 adults, researchers from the Adverse Child Experience study found that almost two thirds reported at least one adverse childhood experience, and 25.5 percent reported three or more adverse experiences (Centers for Disease Control and Prevention, 2006). The ACE study documented that as the number of adverse experiences increases, the risk for negative health outcomes increases. These negative outcomes include alcoholism and alcohol abuse, depression, illicit drug use, heart disease, sexually transmitted diseases, smoking, and suicide attempts. Researchers have documented the interrelationship of stress and trauma with mental well-being, and the long-term negative impact on people's health over time. Thus, the intervention of government has significant health and well-being implications for children throughout their lives.

CONFLICTING VALUES AND BELIEFS

When talking about children and families, the values that are prevalent include privacy of the family and caring for children because they are our future. Our social welfare policy often reflects the first value but is inconsistent on the second. Public intervention is often seen as a necessary evil, a process that should not be used until there is a problem severe enough to warrant it. This perspective maintains the privacy of the family; however, it also promotes an after-the-fact response to problems, a response that sometimes comes too late to save children from harm. On the other hand, one must remember that few people would welcome constant surveillance of their families by public officials. If public policy for children and families could shift to an institutional and preventive focus, there would be less of a need for interventions that disrupt the privacy of families. Such an approach relies on a belief in social responsibility over individual responsibility. As has been discussed so many times before, this is a nation of individualists, and as such, it is reluctant to embrace social responsibility, even for the well-being of children and our own families.

Children and families would also benefit if social welfare efforts were not predominantly in response to crisis—abuse, poverty, failing health—but instead took a preventive approach. Programs such as Head Start and WIC and family preservation are combinations of this approach. Designed for low-income families or ones with identified problems, these programs try to prevent future problems. This blend may be the compromise that will resolve the conflict between the wish to respond to a crisis and the hesitancy to offer programs without a problem already in place. Most child welfare policies are developed out of feelings of sympathy; feeling bad for the plight of disadvantaged children. But if we could move to a place of empathy, identifying with children because we have all been children, we might create different ways of caring for children and their families. If an empathic stance is taken, we would ask what all children need to ensure well-being, and create policies that fulfill that need.

FINAL THOUGHTS ON CHILDREN AND FAMILIES

The policies described in this chapter represent the key areas of child welfare policy. Almost all of them share a number of characteristics. The vast majority of child and family social welfare policies have only been concerned with pressing social problems. Foster care and adoption are responses to family breakdown; abuse and neglect services identify children after maltreatment has occurred; and cash assistance programs are available to families only after all resources have been exhausted. The challenge confronting policy makers is to create social welfare policies that address the current needs of children and families and, at the same time, redress the structural inequalities and obstacles that place children at risk. Preventive approaches to caring for children and their families are both socially responsible and cost-effective. For example, immunization can prevent childhood diseases and save thousands of dollars in health care costs; early childhood education and compensatory learning can prevent a student from dropping out of high school, becoming unemployable, and requiring welfare assistance; and job creation and training can help adults find jobs so they can provide for their children and not need unemployment compensation or other family assistance. Preventing social problems not only alleviates immediate suffering but may help to solve the problems entirely.

Key Terms

child welfare policy

child welfare system

child abuse and neglect

Child Abuse Prevention and Treatment Act of 1974 (CAPTA)

Social Services Block Grant (SSBG)

Adoption Assistance and Child Welfare Act of 1980

Indian Child Welfare Act (ICWA)

Multiethnic Placement Act of 1994

Family and Medical Leave

Family Preservation

No Child Left Behind Act

unfunded mandate

Temporary Assistance for Needy Families (TANF)

Child Support Enforcement

State Children's Health Insurance Program (SCHIP)

foster care

adoption

permanency planning

Adoption and Safe Families Act

Elementary and Secondary Education Act of 1965

Education for all Handicapped Children Act of 1975

Individuals with Disabilities Education Act (IDEA) of 1990

Head Start

Questions for Discussion

1. Do you think children are a priority in this country?
2. How have the role and position of children in our society changed over time?
3. Most child welfare services are residual. Can you identify institutional and preventive services that would benefit children? How would you design an institutional approach to child welfare services?
4. What should be the role and responsibility of families in caring for children? What should be the role and responsibility of government in caring for children?
5. Why is education important when discussing child welfare?

Exercises

1. Each state has laws including a mandate on who must report suspected cases of child abuse and neglect. What are the laws in your state? To whom does the mandate apply? Does it apply to you, as a social work student? Does it apply to professionals?
2. You are interested in providing foster care. What requirements are there for becoming a foster parent in your community? Can anyone become a foster parent? What about single adults? Gay adults? Why or why not?
3. Call your local office for child protective services (CPS). Ask if you can meet with a CPS worker to learn more about his or her job. What does the worker do? How does the worker feel about serving as a state intermediary in families' lives? How large is the caseload? Does the worker feel that he or she can serve each family adequately? Why or why not?
4. Visit a local elementary school. What types of facilities are available? What type of student is served? Is the school different or

similar from the school you attended? Are social work services provided at the school?

5. Exercise and recreation are important for healthy child development. What programs and opportunities are there for children in your community? How do exercise and recreation opportunities vary for children? Why?

References

Administration for Children and Families. (2008a). *Adoption and foster care analysis and reporting system report.* Washington, DC: U.S. Department of Health and Human Services.

Administration for Children and Families. (2008b). *Child maltreatment.* Washington, DC: U.S. Department of Health and Human Services.

Administration for Children and Families. (2008c). *Major federal legislation concerned with child protection, child welfare, and adoption.* Washington, DC: U.S. Department of Health and Human Services.

Administration for Children and Families. (2002a). *Characteristics and financial circumstances of TANF recipients, October 1999 to September 2000.* Washington, DC: U.S. Department of Health and Human Services.

Administration for Children and Families. (2002b). *Social Services Block Grant program annual report.* Washington, DC: U.S. Department of Health and Human Services.

Altshuler, S. J., & Koppels, S. (2003). Advocating in schools for children with disabilities: What's new with IDEA? *Social Work* 48(3):320–329.

Axinn, J., & Stern, M. J. (2008). *Social welfare: A history of the American response to need,* 7th ed. Boston: Allyn & Bacon.

Centers for Disease Control and Prevention. (2008). *The effects of childhood stress on health across the lifespan.* Atlanta: Author.

Centers for Disease Control and Prevention. (2006). *Adverse childhood experience study.* Atlanta: Author.

Children's Defense Fund. (2004). *The state of America's children 2004.* Washington, DC: Author.

Children's Defense Fund. (2002). *The state of children in America's union: A 2002 action guide to leave no child behind.* Washington, DC: Author.

Children's Defense Fund. (2007). *Annual report, 2006.* Washington, DC: Author.

Commission on No Child Left Behind. (2007). *Beyond NCLB: Fulfilling the promise to our nation's children.* Washington, DC: Author.

Congressional Quarterly. (2004, April 9). Unfunded mandates: Education. *CQ Weekly.* http://library.cqpress.com/cqweekly/document.php.

Costin, L. B. (1991). Unraveling the Mary Ellen legend: Origins of the "cruelty" movement. *Social Service Review* 65(2):203–223.

Costin, L. B., Bell, C. J., & Downs, S. W. (1991). *Child welfare: Policies and practice,* 4th ed. New York: Longman.

Federal Interagency Forum on Child and Family Statistics. (2008). *America's children in brief: Key national indicators of well-being 2008.* Washington, DC: U.S. Government Printing Office.

Federal Interagency Forum on Child and Family Statistics. (2005). *America's children: Key national indicators of well-being 2005.* Washington, DC: U.S. Government Printing Office.

First Focus. (2008). *Children's budget 2008.* Washington, DC: Author.

Fuller, B. (2004, February 9–15). No politics left behind: Bush's education plan has flaws, but both parties can work to retool it for the long run. *Washington Post National Weekly Edition* 21(6):23.

Gustavsson, N. S., & Segal, E. A. (1994). *Critical issues in child welfare.* Thousand Oaks, CA: Sage.

Halverson, K., Puig, M. E., & Byers, S. R. (2002). Culture loss: American Indian family disruption, urbanization, and the Indian Child Welfare Act. *Child Welfare* LXXXI(2):319–336.

Hasci, T. (1995). From indenture to foster care: A brief history of child placing. *Child Welfare* LXXIV(1):162–180.

Hollingsworth, L. D. (1998). Promoting same-race adoption for children of color. *Social Work* 43(2):104–116.

House Committee on Ways and Means. (1994). *Overview of entitlement programs: 1994 green book.* WMCP: 103-27. Washington, DC: U.S. Government Printing Office.

Hutchinson, J. R. (2002). *Failed child welfare policy: Family preservation and the orphaning of child welfare*. New York: University Press of America.

Jansson, B. S. (2009). *The reluctant welfare state: A history of American social welfare policies*, 6th ed. Pacific Grove, CA: Brooks/Cole.

Kadushin, A., & Martin, J. A. (1988). *Child welfare services*, 4th ed. New York: Macmillan.

Katz, M. B. (1986). *In the shadow of the poorhouse: A social history of welfare in America*. New York: Basic Books.

Kempe, C. H., Silverman, F., Steele, B., Droegmueller, W., & Silver, H. (1962). The battered-child syndrome. *Journal of the American Medical Association* 181:17–24.

Kimmich, M. H. (1985). *America's children: Who cares?* Washington, DC: Urban Institute Press.

Kozol, J. (1991). *Savage inequalities: Children in America's schools*. New York: Crown.

Lindsey, D. (1994). *The welfare of children*. New York: Oxford University Press.

Mannes, M. (1995). Factors and events leading to the passage of the Indian Child Welfare Act. *Child Welfare LXXIV*(1):264–282.

Mantel, B. (2005). No Child Left Behind. *CQ Researcher* 15(20):471–486.

Mathews, J. (2002). The earlier the better: Head Start shows gains in very young children and their families. *Washington Post National Weekly Edition* 19(3):34.

National Clearinghouse on Child Abuse and Neglect. (2004). *How does the child welfare system work?* Washington, DC: Administration for Children and Families.

National Commission to Prevent Infant Mortality. (1988). *A historic day for children*. Washington, DC: Authors.

Office of Human Services Policy. (2007). *Indicators of welfare dependence: Annual report to Congress 2007*. Washington, DC: U.S. Department of Health and Human Services.

Pecora, P. J., Whittaker, J. K., & Maluccio, A. N. (1992). *The child welfare challenge*. New York: Aldine de Gruyter.

Phillips, M., & Chin, T. (2004). School inequality: What do we know? In K. N. Neckerman (ed.), *Social inequality*, pp. 467–519. New York: Russell Sage Foundation.

Segal, E. A., Gerdes, K. E., & Steiner, S. (2004). *Social work: An introduction to the profession*. Belmont, CA: Thomson Brooks/Cole.

Shipler, D. K. (2004). *The working poor: Invisible in America*. New York: Alfred A. Knopf.

Smith, M. G., & Fong, R. (2004). *The children of neglect: When no one cares*. New York: Brunner-Routledge.

Social Security Administration. (2008). *Annual statistical supplement 2007*. Washington, DC: U.S. Department of Health and Human Services.

Stadum, B. (1995). The dilemma in saving children from child labor: Reform and casework at odds with families' needs. *Child Welfare LXXIV*(1):33–55.

Stein, T. J. (2000). The Adoption and Safe Families Act: Creating a false dichotomy between parents' rights and children's rights. *Families in Society 81*(6): 586–591.

Stein, T. J. (1991). *Child welfare and the law*. New York: Longman.

Tower, C. C. (1989). *Understanding child abuse and neglect*. Boston: Allyn & Bacon.

Trattner, W. (1999). *From poor law to welfare state*, 6th ed. New York: Free Press.

U.S. Census Bureau. (2007). *Statistical Abstract of the United States*, 127th ed. Washington, DC: U.S. Government Printing Office.

U.S. General Accounting Office. (2002). *Children's health insurance*. GAO-02-512. Washington, DC: U.S. Government Printing Office.

U.S. General Accounting Office. (1997). *Child welfare: States progress in implementing Family Preservation and Support Services*. GAO/HEHS-97-34. Washington, DC: U.S. Government Printing Office.

U.S. General Accounting Office. (1996). *School facilities: America's schools report differing conditions*. GAO/HEHS-96-103. Washington, DC: U.S. Government Printing Office.

U.S. General Accounting Office. (1994). *Child welfare: HHS begins to assume leadership to implement national and state systems*. GAO/AIMD-94-37. Washington, DC: U.S. Government Printing Office.

U.S. General Accounting Office. (1993). *Foster care: Services to prevent out-of-home placements are limited by funding barriers*. GAO/HRD-93-76. Washington, DC: U.S. Government Printing Office.

Watkins, S. A. (1990). The Mary Ellen myth: Correcting child welfare history. *Social Work 35*(6):500–505.

Wilkins, A. (2004). *The Indian Child Welfare Act and the states*. Washington, DC: National Conference of State Legislatures.

Zelizer, V. A. (1985). *Pricing the priceless child*. New York: Basic Books.

HEALTH CARE POLICY

One of the most important areas of people's lives is their physical and mental well-being. Poor health impairs every aspect of daily living. It affects one's social and economic participation in society, including one's involvement in work, education, and family life. Therefore, the health of the population is a national concern. This chapter explores the policies and programs through which the United States has attempted to care for its citizens' physical and mental welfare. As in other areas of social welfare, the term *health care system* is often used to describe national efforts toward the physical and mental care of people. It is important to note that health care in America is not delivered in a defined system, although people in the health care field often use that term. The nation lacks a universal health care program; instead, it has a patchwork of services of unequal availability and that is overly expensive for individuals. This chapter outlines the collection of policies and programs that make up the national response to health care and identifies major areas of concern.

OVERVIEW OF HEALTH CARE POLICY IN THE UNITED STATES

Like so many of today's social issues, health and well-being have historically been personal and family concerns. It was not until the mid-1800s that public involvement in health care began. The few hospitals that existed in that era were charities for the poor, often attached to almshouses (Katz, 1986). Medical care at the time was harsh and not very effective. Home remedies were often as effective as medical treatments, or more so.

With industrialization, immigration, and urbanization, cities of the 1800s became overcrowded, and people lived in unhealthy environments. Filthy conditions favored the rapid spread of disease in cities. Leaders recognized that organized efforts to promote public sanitation were necessary. What really changed the state of health in this country, however, was the introduction of scientific techniques in medicine. When science showed how diseases were spread, significant medical advances were accomplished. Science helped to "establish the cultural authority of medicine" (Starr, 1982, p. 59). From 1890 to 1910, public health efforts expanded with the enactment of hygiene laws, creation of inoculation programs, and segregation of those who were carriers of disease (Trattner, 1999). Public awareness grew, and the professions of health care and medicine gained respect.

Although public health was an important part of the social reform agenda at the turn of the 20th century, most policies were directed at local intervention. Cities developed public sanitation services in response to pressure from groups such as settlement workers, who knew firsthand about the problems associated with urban living. These services included the establishment of public trash collection and sewage systems and emphasized public sanitation more than health care.

Federal legislation addressing health care was first developed in 1921, with passage of the Sheppard-Towner Act. The act provided resources for improving maternal and infant health care. Public health education was provided by public health workers. Private physicians and the American Medical Association (AMA) opposed the act because they felt that health care belonged to medical specialists (Starr, 1982). The act was in effect for only eight years, after which time the care of mothers and young children was taken over by states and localities (Axinn & Stern, 2008).

Even during the Great Depression, when social welfare policies were expanded and institutional efforts gained support, health care remained focused on individual curative care. Health care concerns were addressed primarily within the domain of private practice, with an emphasis on curing illness rather than preventing poor health (Starr, 1982). This emphasis reflects the trend in social welfare policy toward a residual response and an individual focus. Advocates of a national health insurance system that would take an institutional approach to health care pushed hard for national legislation during the New Deal, but they were not successful. Although the Maternal and Child Health Services program was part of the 1935 Social Security Act, it was one of the smallest components of the act and received limited funds.

It took an additional 30 years to achieve federal health care legislation. For some population groups, national health insurance was provided in 1965, with passage of amendments to the Social Security Act. **Medicare** (Title XVIII) health insurance for the elderly and **Medicaid** (Title XIX) health coverage for the poor were added to the Social Security Act. These programs followed the structure of income support policies already implemented through the act. Medicare, which is part of the social insurance program, is available to people who have been employed for their working life and have paid in during that time. Medicaid is for people who are too poor to afford health care coverage on their own.

Medicare and Medicaid met with stiff opposition from organized medical groups, such as the AMA, and organized insurance groups. After World War II, most coverage for health care was included in group insurance policies at places of employment. Government involvement was perceived as interference. In reality, however, millions of people were not covered because of the limitations of the private insurance system. A person who did not have a job with health care benefits, or was too old to work, or could not afford an individual health insurance policy had no health care. The enactment of legislation providing national health insurance for the elderly and medical assistance for low-income people was the last major social welfare policy area to be covered by the Social Security Act.

Medicare and Medicaid provide medical coverage for millions of people. In 2006, 43.3 million people were enrolled in Medicare and 58 million people were recipients of Medicaid services—almost a third of the U.S. population (Social Security Administration, 2008). Despite public and private insurance, many others are not covered by any form of health insurance; 47 million people did not have health insurance during 2006 (De-Navas Walt, Proctor, & Smith, 2007), including almost nine million children. These uninsured people represent a major social welfare policy concern.

In 1985, Congress addressed the issue of working persons who needed to maintain health insurance coverage after they lost or quit a job through passage of the **Consolidated Omnibus Reconciliation Act (COBRA)** (P.L. 99-272). The COBRA program allows a person to keep his or her group coverage for up to 18 months after leaving employment. The person must pay the entire cost, including the portion previously paid by the employer, but is guaranteed the same coverage for the 18-month period. The COBRA program provides some protection for workers who are already insured, but it does nothing for the person who is uninsured.

During the 1992 presidential election and President Clinton's first two years in office, proposals for **national health insurance** were hotly debated. Political infighting and interest group pressures blocked passage of any legislative initiatives for health care reform. Republican control of Congress in 1995 and 1996 shifted the focus from consideration of national health care coverage to incremental adjustments and cost containment of existing programs. Congress and the President came to agreement on an adjustment to current health care insurance policies with the **Health Insurance Portability and Accountability Act of 1996 (HIPAA)** (P.L. 104-191). Workers who lose or leave a job can now qualify to purchase individual coverage from their previous insurer. If the person was covered for at least 18 months while working, is not eligible for coverage under any other group plan, and has exhausted COBRA coverage, she or he is entitled to purchase an individual policy through the insurer. In addition, the legislation limits to 12 months the period during which insurers can refuse or limit coverage of a new enrollee for a previously treated or diagnosed condition for which the enrollee has sought treatment in the last six months, and insurers cannot refuse coverage or renewal because of an employee's health status (Langdon, 1996). HIPAA, like COBRA, is primarily directed toward persons who are already insured. The issue of national health insurance coverage for the millions of people without any health care benefits remains unresolved.

In an effort to address part of the uninsured problem, Congress passed the **State Children's Health Insurance Program (SCHIP)** in 1997. As described in Chapter 10, SCHIP is a federal-state program that provides health coverage for low-income children. Although SCHIP provides additional coverage for uninsured low-income children, the number of people who lack health insurance has increased in recent years. Box 11.1 presents the numbers of people lack health insurance in the United States.

| BOX 11.1 | CONSIDER THIS . . . |

Each year, more people lack health insurance coverage, with improvement for children disappearing.

	Total without Health Insurance	Children under 18 Years
2007	45.7 million	8.1 million
2006	47.0 million	8.7 million
2005	44.8 million	8.1 million
2004	45.8 million	7.7 million
2003	45.0 million	8.1 million
2002	43.6 million	8.2 million
2001	41.2 million	8.2 million
2000	39.8 million	8.4 million

Source: DeNavas-Walt, Proctor, & Smith, 2008.

Although programs such as SCHIP serve children in need, the issue of national health insurance remains critical and must be addressed.

In 2003, Congress expanded the Medicare program to include prescription drug coverage. This legislation was an attempt to assist seniors in purchasing medications. It is discussed in more detail later, however it is important to note that it represents the other key health care concern—the rising cost of medical care. Health insurance coverage and medical costs are the preeminent health care policy concerns today.

OVERVIEW OF MENTAL HEALTH CARE POLICY IN THE UNITED STATES

The history of mental health care parallels the history of public health care in general. Until the mid-1800s, mentally ill persons were cared for at home or in almshouses. Professional mental health treatment was nonexistent. People with mental illnesses were tolerated at best, and punished and treated poorly at worst. The health care advocate Dorothea Dix, who lived from 1802 to 1887, is credited with bringing national attention to the needs and concerns of people with mental illness (Stroup, 1986). Dix believed that the government had an ethical, legal, and medical obligation to care for mentally ill people. Her advocacy led to the establishment of more than 30 state hospitals by the mid-1800s (Fellin, 1996). Although Dix and other advocates were not successful in gaining national support, they were able to gain state support. By the late 1800s, however, funds for maintaining institutions were minimal and state hospitals were perceived as places for economically destitute people with mental illness (Jansson, 2009).

Although inadequate state funding led to overcrowding and custodial care at some institutions, continued development of state institutions was supported by the growing belief that people with mental problems could be treated, cured, and released rather than locked away (Starr, 1986). This belief, coupled with the creation of state institutions, led to the development of professional mental health specialists. Following World War I, the mental hygiene movement emerged. Emphasis was placed on psychology and local community care. Therefore, although state hospitals continued to be the major providers of care, the scope of services expanded to include community care (Fellin, 1996). The psychological wounds of veterans returning from World Wars I and II were a factor in the further development of mental health care (Trattner, 1999).

In 1946, the federal government became involved in the delivery of mental health services through the National Mental Health Act, which provided limited funds to states to develop community mental health centers and created the National Institute of Mental Health (Axinn & Stern, 2008). Although some efforts were made to provide community-based care, most mental health services continued to be provided by state institutions. When medications became available that could help people function outside of institutions, Congress passed the **Community Mental Health Centers Act of 1963**. This legislation provided federal funds for communities to build mental health centers and, thereby, provide outpatient services (Jansson, 2009).

The development of mental health centers was never fully funded. In the 1970s, as the public became aware of the realities of life in an institution and the possibility that it might be less costly to treat people outside of institutions, the **deinstitutionalization** of thousands of people with mental illness occurred. In theory, deinstitutionalization promised freedom and community integration for people newly released from state hospitals; however, the reality was different. Inadequate resources and a lack of community mental health centers caused many people to be left with little or no care. From 1955 to 1980, the number of people in state institutions dropped from 559,000 to 138,000, a 75 percent decrease. By the new century, there were fewer than 60,000 resident patients in public mental hospitals (Mechanic, 2001). The system of community mental health centers that was to have been established in conjunction with deinstitutionalization never fully materialized. More than half of the anticipated need was unmet (U.S. General Accounting Office, 2000). The result of this shift was inadequate care for countless persons. For many, the outcome has been reinstitutionalization—not in mental health facilities but in substandard nursing homes—or a precarious existence in tenements, in homeless shelters, or on the streets (Trattner, 1999).

There are concerns about some people who may have been discharged but should not have been. Such people, who do not function well in society, may have become homeless, victimized, or violent themselves. Although deinstitutionalization has not been a perfect solution for severe mental illness, experts recognize that it has had some benefits:

> The traditional custodial mental hospital ruined many lives. But many communities, even now, have yet to develop the networks of community services essential to an effective system of deinstitutionalized care. Nevertheless, the evidence is overwhelming that most clients are immeasurably better off in the deinstitutionalized care system than they ever could be in mental hospitals. It remains less clear, however, whether reduced hospitalization has been too extensive and is now introducing unacceptable risks to persons with complex mental health needs (Mechanic, 2001, p. 178)

In spite of insufficient funding and limited availability, community mental health centers are vital because they provide mental health services that many people could not obtain otherwise. For people who do not have private insurance or cannot pay for services themselves, these centers are their only source of care. The creation of community mental health centers provided greater access to mental health services for many people.

MAJOR HEALTH PROGRAMS

Although the United States lacks a national health program, there are numerous social welfare programs that provide needed services. Since the 1930s, the federal government has developed public health care programs for its most vulnerable citizens: elderly people, low-income families, and children. Unfortunately, these programs vary greatly in eligibility, coverage, and services offered.

MEDICARE

Medicare is health insurance for individuals who are eligible to receive Social Security benefits (Social Security Administration, 2008). Basic coverage is provided for inpatient hospital services and care after release from the hospital. The Medicare program for basic coverage consists of two separate plans: Hospital Insurance, or Part A, and Supplementary Medical Insurance, or Part B. Hospital Insurance is a social insurance program that covers inpatient hospital services, skilled nursing facility services for people who have been released from the hospital, home health services, and hospice care.

Supplementary Medical Insurance is a voluntary program subsidized by the government. It covers health needs that Hospital Insurance does not, such as physician services, outpatient services, physical and outpatient therapy, and diagnostic tests. Participants pay a monthly premium ($96.40 in 2008, with additional costs for higher incomes), have an annual deductible amount, and are responsible for co-payments for services. Generally, Medicare pays 80 percent of the cost of services under Part B, and the participant is responsible for the remaining 20 percent.

Taxation for Part A Hospital Insurance is assessed in the same way as for the Old-Age, Survivors, and Disability Insurance (OASDI) program. The tax is paid based on workers' earnings in covered employment and the matching monies paid in by employers. Part B is optional, and those who elect to use it must pay a monthly premium.

The overall administrative responsibility for Medicare rests with the Department of Health and Human Services (HHS). The Centers for Medicare and Medicaid Services (CMS), an agency within HHS, handles the direct management. Currently, CMS makes contracts with Blue Cross/Blue Shield and other insurers to handle the processing of claims. Medicare recipients can choose to receive their care through managed care providers if they wish.

Although Medicare is comprehensive, it does not cover all costs. For example, it does not cover long-term care. It pays for stays of up to 100 days in skilled nursing facilities but not for longer stays. Many older people elect to purchase additional health coverage through Medigap insurance. **Medigap** is private insurance that pays for health services not covered by Medicare. Although it is private, in 1990 the federal government passed legislation to regulate it, and included regulations that prohibit companies from denying coverage, discriminating against insurees, or overpricing premiums.

The major shortfall in Medicare coverage was lack of payments for prescription medications. In 2003, Congress enacted legislation that expanded the scope of Medicare. The **Medicare Prescription Drug, Improvement, and Modernization Act of 2003 (MMA)** (P.L. 108-173) amended Title XVIII of the Social Security Act. This amendment codified options for private-sector health plans in Part C, and added prescription drug coverage through a new Part D. This legislation has been the largest expansion of benefits since the Medicare program began. It is now possible to receive prescription drug coverage from Medicare, and funds are also available for coverage of rural health care services and the creation of health savings accounts.

The major change comes with prescription drug coverage. The program officially began in 2006, when private companies began to offer prescription drug insurance coverage. Subscribers must pay a monthly premium and make co-payments for services. They are also responsible for a low annual deductible amount. The formula for benefits is extremely complicated and changes each year to keep up with inflation. In 2008, the plan reimbursed 75 percent of drug costs (after a $275 deductible amount had been met), up to $2,510 a year. Once expenses exceeded $2,510, coverage was not available until drug costs reached $4,050. The plan then paid for 95 percent of drug costs over $4,050 (Social Security Administration, 2008).

After years of debate and rejection of proposals, the compromises needed to pass the MMA resulted in a complex piece of legislation. Early analysis of the legislation found that appeasement of all sides in the debate made the program extremely complicated. It does not cover all medication costs and will be expensive to administer (Dallek, 2003). Estimates place the cost of the program to be $635 billion over the first 10 years (Congressional Budget Office, 2008). The options for private-sector health plans, known as Medicare Advantage, has not gone well either. Instead of saving money, it has cost the federal government more. The private plans, using attractive reimbursement rates to entice private insurance companies to participate, has cost the federal government $10 billion more annually than would the government run Medicare program (Whelan, 2008). With the high cost of prescription drugs and the increasing numbers of elderly people in the United States, the Medicare program will become more central to federal efforts to provide health care coverage.

MEDICAID

Under Medicaid, the federal government matches state funds for covering the cost of medical care and services for low-income individuals (Social Security Administration, 2008). Medical coverage includes physician care, inpatient hospitalization, outpatient services, diagnostic tests, home health services, nursing home care (including long-term care), and early and periodic screening and diagnostic treatment for those under 21 years of age. States may elect to offer additional services such as dental care and payment for medications and eyeglasses; they may receive federal matching grants for these services. The program covers all TANF recipients, most SSI recipients, and some children in foster care.

States can also choose to extend Medicaid coverage to people who are "medically needy." If medical costs would deplete the financial resources of a person or family to the point that they would become impoverished, they are eligible for Medicaid coverage in many states. Typically, people "spend down," or pay for medical care until their finances reach a prescribed level. When this point is reached, Medicaid covers the rest of the costs.

Medicaid payments are usually made directly to the provider of services rather than the recipient. This format reflects the nature of public assistance, where the low-income recipient is given in-kind benefits.

Medicaid is administered by the CMS under the HHS, but each state designs and administers its own program in keeping with federal standards. States establish standards; set the type, amount, and duration of services; and establish the rate of payment for services. Therefore, unlike Medicare, the Medicaid program varies from state to state.

Medicaid is often thought of as a program for poor young families. TANF families are typically covered by Medicaid. Less than eight percent of Medicaid recipients are 65 years of age or older, about 14 percent are people with disabilities, and 48 percent are children. Most costs paid by Medicaid cover services for elderly and disabled people. Twenty-three percent of Medicaid costs are for elderly people and 43 percent for people with disabilities, compared to 17 percent of Medicaid costs going for children (U.S. Census Bureau, 2007). For example, in 2004 per child Medicaid payments averaged $1,615 compared to $13,295 for elderly persons (Social Security Administration, 2008). Therefore, Medicaid is an important safety net for poor elderly people and people with disabilities whose medical costs are high. The existence of both Medicaid and private insurance has resulted in a two-tiered medical care system, with one level for those who can afford to pay and the other for those who cannot.

SCHIP

The **State Children's Health Insurance Program (SCHIP)** was enacted in 1997 as Title XXI of the Social Security Act. SCHIP funds are targeted at uninsured children in families whose income is too high to qualify for Medicaid but is below 200 percent of the federal poverty level. A child who already has health insurance, even if the coverage is inadequate or limited, is prohibited from coverage by SCHIP. SCHIP is not meant to replace existing private or public health insurance. It was created to fill gaps in coverage. States can offer coverage to adults in families with children who qualify for SCHIP coverage if it is cost-effective to do so and there is no other insurance available. SCHIP participants follow the eligibility regulations and benefit amounts of the Medicaid program and receive services as an extension of Medicaid. States receive federal matching dollars for SCHIP. Efforts to raise the eligibility level to cover more children failed in 2008 when it was vetoed by President Bush. In 2009, a month after President Obama took office, the program was reauthorized and expanded. Once these changes are implemented, the program name will be shortened to CHIP.

IMMUNIZATION

One of the most effective preventive health measures for children has been routine immunization. It has proved effective in guarding children against preventable diseases such as measles, mumps, pertussis, rubella, and polio. Keeping children healthy results in lower costs for health care over the years of childhood. It is estimated that for every dollar spent on vaccinations for measles, mumps, and rubella, $16 is saved because these infections do not have to be treated (Children's Defense Fund, 2004). Although immunizations are cost-effective, the U.S. immunization program is not as comprehensive as it should be.

Because of school regulations, almost all children are immunized against most preventable childhood diseases by the age of 5 years. Some infants and toddlers, however, are not fully immunized. Many health insurance programs do not cover the cost of preventive measures such as immunizations. People lacking health care coverage cannot afford to pay for childhood immunizations. Free vaccines are available through Medicaid or public health clinics, but lack of awareness of this service, inadequate resources such as insufficient staffing at clinics, and clinic locations that are inaccessible for some people contribute to underimmunization of children who are at risk for disease. Overall, the majority of children in this country are immunized against major childhood illnesses, although the rates are lower for newer vaccines (U.S. Census Bureau, 2007). Eighty percent of children aged 19 to 35 months old were immunized in 2007. However, rates vary by state, with lows of 65 percent immunized in Nevada and 74 percent in Louisiana and Mississippi, compared to 88 percent in Connecticut and Massachusetts (Kaiser Foundation, 2008). Prevention of childhood illnesses through immunization was a major breakthrough in modern medicine. Today, immunization programs must be maintained to ward off easily preventable illnesses.

DISABILITY INSURANCE

Programs to support people with disabilities include protection of rights and cash assistance. The **Americans with Disabilities Act (ADA)**, discussed in Chapter 5, is the foundation ensuring equality under the law for people with disabilities. Cash assistance is provided by two main programs: one for workers' compensation and another for low-income people.

Part of the OASDI program includes coverage for people who must stop working because of a disability. Added to the Social Security Act in 1956, the program provides monthly cash benefits for eligible workers. It is part of the social insurance provisions of the Social Security Act. The program pays monthly benefits to a disabled worker under 65 years of age equal to the amount that the worker would receive during retirement. To qualify, the person with a disability must have paid in for at least 20 quarters (5 years) during the previous 40 quarters (10 years) (Social Security Administration, 2008). There are some provisions for working while still receiving benefits.

The **Disability Insurance (DI)** component of OASDI also includes medical care through the Medicare program, but Medicare coverage does not begin until after the person has received benefits for 24 months. There were 8.6 million recipients of DI in 2006, with disabled workers receiving an average of $978 per month (Social Security Administration, 2008).

SUPPLEMENTAL SECURITY INCOME

As discussed in Chapter 5, Congress developed the **Supplemental Security Income (SSI)** program, Title XVI of the Social Security Act, in 1972. SSI replaced the previous categorical federal/state programs of Old-Age Assistance and Aid to the Blind, which were original provisions of the 1935 act, and Aid to the Disabled, which had been added in 1956. These three programs had a multiplicity of eligibility requirements and benefit payment systems. The SSI program consolidated them and created a unified federal operation.

The SSI program is a means-tested program that provides cash payments to people who are 65 years or older, blind, or disabled and whose income places them below the poverty line. The payments are reduced by any other income received, including wages or other program benefits. The Social Security Administration administers SSI, and the program is funded by the federal government. There were 7.2 million recipients of SSI in 2006, receiving an average of $455 per month (Social Security Administration, 2008).

It is important to understand that SSI is different than OASDI. Among some social service providers, the term SSDI, which stands for Social Security Disability Insurance, is sometimes used for the disability component. There is often confusion between these two programs, but they are radically different. Although both programs serve people with disabilities and people over 65 years of age, the funding and eligibility criteria differ greatly. SSI is an antipoverty program that provides cash assistance to seniors and people with disabilities if they fall below the poverty line. It is residual in its approach. OASDI is social insurance, and people who have previously worked and paid into the program receive monthly benefits when they reach retirement age or become disabled. Therefore, OASDI takes an institutional approach. SSI is funded through general tax revenues, and OASDI is funded through FICA payroll taxes.

Although SSI is not directly a health care program, it is significant to the financial well-being of many medically needy individuals. Disability at any age and illness in old age can cause severe financial stress. For persons who are not covered through the disability funds of OASDI, particularly young workers who have not worked long enough to be eligible for adequate social disability insurance, this program offers the only source of economic support.

COMMUNITY MENTAL HEALTH CENTERS

Care of people with mental illness is provided through both inpatient and outpatient treatment. Federal support of mental health care is provided predominantly through funding of the **Community Mental Health Centers Act of 1963** (P.L. 88-164). The original intent of the legislation was to support the construction of **community mental health centers** throughout the country to replace state institutions and provide inpatient and outpatient care, emergency and day care services, and follow-up care for people released from mental health facilities (U.S. General Accounting Office, 2000). The goal of the act was to help people who had been hospitalized for mental illness return to their communities. The program designers hoped that community mental health centers would replace institutions; prevention would be emphasized; and continuity of care would develop, with the centers offering the least restrictive mental health care environment (Fellin, 1996).

Many people face times when their mental health is stressed. The death of a loved one, a divorce, the loss of a job, or physical illness can affect a person's mental health. In the past, public services targeted people with **severe** or **serious mental illness (SMI)**. SMI is usually defined as an illness that has a diagnosable mental, emotional, or behavioral disorder that meets the criteria outlined by the American Psychiatric Association and that interferes or limits one or more major life activities. Serious mental disorders affect about 11 percent of the adult population, which includes 25 million people. Less than half receive treatment (Substance Abuse and Mental Health Services Administration, 2007). Among children, 12 percent have serious emotional disturbances, yet only one-third receive mental health services (Hochman, 2006).

Forty-five years after passage of the Community Mental Health Act, mental health services are still inadequate. Most people with mental illness remain untreated. Although inadequate funding has left a shortage of needed services, the community mental health policy has made mental health services accessible to the public and established a framework for community-based treatment.

CURRENT NEEDS AND POLICY ISSUES

America's changing health care needs present new challenges with each generation. We have seen resolution of the public health problems of sanitation and hygiene during the 1800s, followed by awareness and sensitivity to mental illness and medical technological breakthroughs during the 1900s. Yet there are still serious social concerns related to health care in this country. Our social welfare system is confronted by millions of people without health care coverage, as well as escalating costs, new diseases, and increases in existing health problems. These emerging issues must be addressed through social welfare policies and programs. Box 11.2 presents data on some of the health care problems we face today.

LACK OF HEALTH INSURANCE COVERAGE

One of the most pressing health issues of the first decade of the 21st century is the lack of health insurance coverage for millions of Americans. In 2007, 46 million people lacked any form of coverage (DeNavas-Walt, Proctor, and Smith, 2008). Young adults and part-time workers were most likely to lack health insurance coverage. This problem has been growing in recent years. The number of people who do not have health insurance increased by almost 20 percent from 2000 to 2007. It is interesting to note while the number of uninsured people declined slightly from 2006 to 2007, the number of people covered by government health insurance increased. And at the same

---

BOX 11.2 | **CONSIDER THIS . . .**

In spite of all the medical advancements made over the past several decades, health care in America is in critical condition. According to research on the state of health care across the United States

- Public health departments are understaffed, with an estimated need of 10,000 to 30,000 more employees just to meet current needs (Congressional Quarterly, 2004);
- About one fifth of adults in America suffer from mental illness, yet only half seek treatment, in large part because resources and facilities are inadequate (Substance Abuse and

Mental Health Services Administration, 2007);

- With the aging of our population, the need for long-term care is growing. "Long-term care threatens to bankrupt Medicaid and the states that pay for it" (Congressional Quarterly, 2004, p. 46);
- The cost of prescription drugs has risen dramatically, almost eight percent a year since 1994 (Center for Policy Alternatives, 2007); and
- Lack of a national health insurance program has left 46 million people without insurance (DeNavas-Walt, Proctor, & Smith, 2008).

time, private direct purchase insurance declined, and employment-based health insurance barely increased. This suggests that more people are turning to and qualifying for government health insurance. One area of growth in government health insurance has been the coverage of children. However, in spite of the creation of SCHIP, not all children in low-income families are insured. It is estimated that 4 million children are in low-income families who are not poor enough to qualify for Medicaid, but are still not covered by SCHIP. The 2009 reauthorization is designed to address this shortfall. The numbers may understate the extent of the problem. Many workers move in and out of employment. The numbers of people who may have been uninsured for some amount of time during the year are difficult to count, likely making the total number of uninsured people even higher.

A person who does not have health insurance is less likely to receive needed medical care. Without coverage, people do not receive preventive services and tend to wait longer to seek medical treatment. When they do, they most likely seek emergency care at a hospital. This type of care is more costly than preventive care or immediate medical attention for a health problem.

HIGH COST OF MEDICAL CARE

The cost of health care is another pressing concern. In 2005, national health care expenditures in the United States totaled $2 trillion, an increase of about seven percent over the previous year (Centers for Disease Control and Prevention, 2007a). This represented 16 percent of the gross domestic product, a greater share than in any other industrialized nation (U.S. Bureau of the Census, 2007). Out-of-pocket expenses for health care are higher in the United States than in any other country, averaging $3,180 per person, an 81 percent increase over the past ten years (U.S. Census Bureau, 2007). The increase in national expenditures was due in part to the development of new technology as well as to expanded coverage for elderly and low-income people through Medicare, Medicaid, and SCHIP.

The high cost of health care is not only affecting individuals and government programs but businesses as well. For example, a car manufactured in the United States costs the manufacturer $1,300 in health care costs for employees. General Motors spent $4.5 billion in 2003 on health care for its 1.2 million American workers and retirees (Downey, 2004). In Canada, which has government-funded universal health care, a car manufacturer incurs no extra costs for health care for its employees.

The containment of costs for health care is further complicated by the mixture of public and private health coverage. Health coverage is based primarily on a market system: Those who are covered or can afford care receive treatment, whereas people without coverage must use public medical facilities. When public resources are diminished, uninsured people have a harder time finding health care. For-profit medical facilities can choose who they want to serve, leaving those who are uninsured to be served by government-supported institutions. This practice has further fueled the cost of medical care because costs are inflated for those who can pay. Health care providers prefer to treat privately insured people because they can receive higher fees than if they treat publicly funded individuals. In 2005, 40 million adults did not receive medical health services because they could not afford them (Centers for Disease Control and Prevention, 2007a).

MANAGED CARE

The movement toward managed care is affecting the entire health care field. **Managed care** is the system in which a person's medical care is controlled by the insurer. The goal of managed care is to minimize unnecessary and questionable health care services and maximize procedures known to be effective. Managed care is usually provided through group plans and administered by for-profit organizations, typically **Health Maintenance Organizations** (HMOs) and **Preferred Provider Organizations** (PPOs). The number of managed care plans is on the rise. In 1990, 33 million Americans were enrolled in HMO plans, and by 2006, that number had increased to 74 million (U.S. Census Bureau, 2007).

Each insured person in a managed care program receives regulated care as determined by administrators of the plan. This practice has raised concerns. For example, in the early 1990s, HMOs decided that women who had given birth should be released from the hospital 12 hours after the delivery, instead of after the usual stay of 2 days. The reason was that this saved the HMO $2,000 (Sherrill, 1995). Many questioned whether this early release was good health care. In response to this specific practice, Congress enacted federal legislation in 1996 that mandated insurance coverage for a minimum hospital stay of 2 days for a normal delivery and at least 96 hours for a Cesarean section (Pear, 1996). This is precisely the concern with managed care: Is the final decision concerning medical care based on cost or on adequacy of the treatment? It is unlikely that Congress can regulate each medical decision as it did for hospital stays following childbirth.

Even state governments are turning to managed care for their public health care programs. In an effort to cut costs, state governments are reorganizing their Medicaid programs to follow the managed care model. Arizona was the first state to do so, in 1982. The state redesigned its Medicaid program and created the Arizona Health Care Cost Containment System (AHCCCS). The AHCCCS program, which is state-operated and state-regulated, delivers services through health plans selected on a county-by-county basis. The state calculates the funding for each plan according to the number of patients and adjusts the yearly fees to reflect a county's population. Therefore, if a plan serves more people with higher-cost procedures, calculations of the next year's funding reflect those greater expenses. Whether managed care can be beneficial to states over time remains to be seen.

Concern over whether health care decisions are being made by medical personnel or by insurance administrators continues to be a hotly debated issue. These issues contribute to the debate surrounding national health insurance. The policy push for national health insurance dates back to the early 1900s. Groups have advocated for a system of health care that is provided by the federal government and equally covers all Americans, regardless of their income, employment status, or age. Opposition to such a system has been strong, with groups such as AMA and the insurance industry fighting such legislation. The most recent major attempt to change the health care system was by the Clinton administration in 1993. Like previous proposals, it was defeated. National health insurance was an issue in the 2004 and 2008 presidential elections. President Obama has pledged to bring national health insurance to the forefront of legislative action under his administration.

Managed care programs seem to be a permanent part of our health care system. Whether national health insurance will be created as an alternative or replacement remains to be seen. But there is no doubt that it raises the question of how health care should be funded (see Box 11.3).

EMERGING HEALTH CONCERNS

There are numerous health concerns requiring the attention of policy makers and the public. For social work practitioners, the increased incidence of acquired immunodeficiency syndrome (AIDS) and human immunodeficiency virus (HIV) infection, Alzheimer's disease, diabetes, obesity, and problems with alcohol and drug use are a challenge. The following discussion highlights the social welfare policy implications of these health concerns.

HIV INFECTION AND AIDS

Until the 1980s, no one had heard of AIDS or HIV infection. Today, AIDS and HIV are common terms. These diseases have deeply touched the social welfare of our country. AIDS and HIV are first and foremost health concerns, but they are also related to economics and social values. The social welfare policy response to HIV/AIDS was slow, reluctant, and, at times, hostile. Addressing the problem on a social welfare policy level was not easily accepted by the U.S. government. Randy

---

| BOX 11.3 | CONFLICTING PERSPECTIVES . . . |

Who should pay for health care, the private sector or the public sector?

Currently, most people get health care coverage through their places of employment or as family dependents of workers. Those who are too poor can qualify for Medicaid, and those who are over 65 years of age can qualify for Medicare. However, employer coverage has diminished over the years. From 1990 to 2007, private insurance coverage dropped from 73.2 percent to 67.5 percent, causing more people to remain uninsured or to turn to public programs (DeNavas-Walt, Proctor, & Smith, 2008). Should we rely on employers to be the source of health insurance? Should the federal government step in

and develop a program that covers all citizens, regardless of age or income?

The strongest argument for federal intervention is that health care is a right and should not be a perk of employment. Lower-paying jobs may involve substantial hours of labor, but employers do not provide health insurance. Why? Because it is expensive and, as private entities, they do not have to include health insurance for every worker. The result is that private businesses make profit a higher priority than health care coverage. Therefore, advocates argue that the government should intervene, as it has to ensure other rights. Universal health care will protect life and liberty, as guaranteed by the Constitution.

Shilts (1987) documented the disdain and reluctance of federal government officials toward taking public action to prevent the spread of HIV/AIDS. He wrote:

> The bitter truth was that AIDS did not just happen to America—it was allowed to happen by an array of institutions, all of which failed to perform their appropriate tasks to safeguard the public health. This failure of the system leaves a legacy of unnecessary suffering that will haunt the Western world for decades to come. ...In those early years, the federal government viewed AIDS as a budget problem, local public health officials saw it as a political problem, gay leaders considered AIDS a public relations problem, and the news media regarded it as a homosexual problem that would not interest anyone else. Consequently, few confronted AIDS for what it was, a profoundly threatening medical crisis. (pp. xxii–xxiii)

Incidence of HIV Infection and AIDS   AIDS is often referred to as a pandemic as opposed to an epidemic. In medical terms, a **pandemic** is an epidemic that is occurring across a large geographic region. A pandemic is an accurate description of AIDS because of its worldwide impact and spread. The World Health Organization (2007) estimates that 33.2 million people are living with HIV/AIDS worldwide, of whom 2.1 million are children. In 1981, the Centers for Disease Control and Prevention documented 189 cases of AIDS in the United States. By 2006, that number had risen to more than a million cases (Centers for Disease Control and Prevention, 2007b). New cases have numbered about 36,000 for the past several years, and the rate seems to have leveled off from a peak of over 70,000 new cases in 1995. Overall patterns based on research suggest that the rate of spread of HIV remains stable, although the rates are still higher among gay men, intravenous drug users, and black populations (Centers for Disease Control and Prevention, 2007b).

Several significant trends have developed over the years. The number of AIDS cases among children has decreased by 64 percent, the number of deaths of persons with AIDS has declined 17 percent, and the number of people living with HIV/AIDS has increased steadily from 2003 through 2006 (Centers for Disease Control and Prevention, 2007b). Research has found that once a person enters medical care with HIV, projected life expectancy is 24.2 years, compared to less than 7 years in 1993 (Shackman et al., 2006). Advanced medical care has greatly extended life expectancy. However, this care comes at a cost. The lifetime costs will run from $385,000 to $620,000.

Social Policy Efforts   The only federal policy implemented as a direct response to the AIDS pandemic has been the **Ryan White Comprehensive AIDS Resources Emergency (CARE) Act of 1990** (U.S. General Accounting Office, 1995). This legislation was passed after years of pressure from advocacy groups for a government response. The law authorizes federal funds to support health care services for people who have AIDS or are HIV-positive. Services include home and community-based care and provisions for early intervention, prevention, research, and education.

Critics argue that the federal response was slow in coming until people other than gay men and intravenous drug users contracted the disease. The bill was named after a young boy with hemophilia who contracted AIDS through a blood transfusion. His case highlighted the divisiveness surrounding social welfare policy and AIDS. Because marginalized groups were initially predominant among those infected, public opinion and federal policies viewed people with AIDS as responsible for their illness. Children such as Ryan White are viewed differently. Because his was a case of transmission through a medical procedure and not as a result of individual behavior, cases like his were viewed as "innocent victims." No other life-threatening disease is viewed with such a clear distinction. This social value delayed public response to a growing health problem. The conflict between social policy and social values hampered the legislative response to health care interventions and the HIV/AIDS pandemic.

The spread of HIV in the United States has disproportionately affected populations who are poor and oppressed. Groups who lack civil rights protection and are continually discriminated against make up a disproportionate number of the people who live with HIV/AIDS. People who are stigmatized by skin color, drug use, poverty, and sexual orientation lack strong political and economic advocates in this country. Although the rates have stabilized, HIV and AIDS continue to spread through our population. With improved medical care and medication, the cost in dollars and lost human lives grows greater each year. HIV/AIDS is a social problem that must continue to be addressed by policy makers, however difficult that may be.

ALCOHOL AND ILLEGAL DRUGS

The use of illegal drugs and alcohol is not a new social concern. Federal involvement has increased, however, in response to shifts in public attitudes and signs that use of these substances is increasing. The early 1900s was the first period of federal involvement in control of illegal drugs. Laws were enacted in 1914 to regulate the sale and use of narcotics. In 1937, legislation was passed that controlled the use and distribution of marijuana (Hogan & Doyle, 1989). Alcohol was made an illegal substance in 1919, when laws prohibited the manufacture and sale of liquor. Prohibition laws were extremely difficult to enforce, and they were repealed 14 years later (Axinn & Stern, 2008). Since the 1930s, American attitudes toward alcohol have become more and more tolerant and alcohol continues to be a legal substance. However, ambivalence toward the use of alcohol still exists today. The policy issue is whether to treat alcohol as a drug to be legislatively controlled in the same manner as narcotics and marijuana, or to allow individuals to decide.

In spite of its addictive qualities, alcohol is legal and its use is a major part of our society: More than 85 percent of adults report having used alcohol (U.S. Census Bureau, 2007); more than half (50.9 percent) of Americans age 12 years and older drink alcohol; and more than one-fifth (23 percent) have participated in binge or heavy drinking (Substance Abuse and Mental Health Services Administration, 2007). Currently, alcohol is a legal substance and, therefore, its use is prohibited only for people younger than 21 years of age. Nevertheless, underage drinkers gain access to alcohol and are at great risk of addiction.

The sale, possession, and use of other drugs such as heroin, cocaine, and marijuana are illegal. Differentiation between legal and illegal drugs was codified in the Controlled Substances Act of 1970. This legislation controls and regulates drugs and identifies levels of enforcement (Gray, 1995). Further efforts to use public policy to control behavior related to drug use took place in 1973. Congress created the U.S. Drug Enforcement Administration (DEA) as part of the Department of Justice. The DEA was empowered to enforce federal drug laws (Dye, 2008).

Federal control of illegal substances peaked with passage of the Anti–Drug Abuse Act of 1988 (PL 100-690). Much of the legislation involved control strategies rather than treatment. Although there are laws against drug use, over 20 million people aged 12 or older were current illicit drug users in 2006. This represents eight percent of the population. The highest rate of current use was 22 percent among 18 to 20 year olds (Substance Abuse and Mental Health Services Administration, 2007). Almost 60 percent of people between the ages of 18 and 25 years reported having tried an illicit drug at some point, with marijuana the most common. For all people over 12 years of age, 46 percent reported having ever used an illicit drug (U.S. Census Bureau, 2007). Thus, although illegal, drug use is a reality in American society. The social welfare policy struggle in **substance abuse** involves two ideologies. Should the use and abuse of drugs be controlled through punishment and law enforcement, or should it be a health care concern treated through medical and mental health interventions? There are almost 14,000 treatment centers for drug and alcohol abuse. These service agencies had more than 1.1 million clients in 2006 (U.S. Census Bureau, 2007). The debate between enforcement and treatment has yet to be resolved. Until it is, social welfare policies related to drug use and abuse will reflect these two conflicting philosophies.

An additional issue is the medical use of marijuana. Some medical professionals have called for the legalization of marijuana for use as a medical treatment, particularly to relieve nausea during chemotherapy. Some states have legalized its medical use. The debate over what makes one substance legal and another illegal is not new. Because the legality of substances and alcohol has politically changed over time, public policy is key in the argument for and against the medical use of marijuana. At this point, this argument is being fought on the state level with local ordinances and ballot propositions.

ALZHEIMER'S DISEASE

Alzheimer's disease (AD) is emerging as a growing health concern. As people live longer, the likelihood of developing mental dementia increases. Alzheimer's disease is a form of brain dementia that seriously impairs a person's ability to carry out the activities of daily living. It is most prevalent among older people. Scientists estimate that between 2.4 and 4.5 million people have Alzheimer's disease, and most of them are over 60 years of age (Alzheimer's Disease Education and Referral Center, 2008). Although about five percent of people age 65 to 74 years old have AD, nearly half of people age 85 years and older have the disease. Researchers have found that after 65, the number of people with AD doubles with every five year age-interval, which means as our population lives longer, the incidence of AD will exponentially increase (Alzheimer's Disease Education and Referral Center, 2008). The disease is progressive. Over time, a person experiences greater impairment of memory and can manage fewer and fewer tasks of daily living. As with other illnesses, individuals with AD are cared for primarily by family members and friends. As people live longer and more develop AD, more public attention and resources will need to be devoted to AD treatment. The cost of care is estimated to be more than $100 billion each year, with Medicare covering about two thirds. At the current rate of increase in the disease, the cost to Medicare by 2015 could rise to almost $200 billion (Alzheimer's Disease Education and Referral Center, 2008). Although there is not a specific public policy directed toward AD, government spending on research and clinical trials are underway through the National Institute on Aging.

DIABETES

Diabetes is not a new illness, and treatments have improved over the years. Nonetheless, the incidence of diabetes is on the rise. The prevalence of diabetes in the adult population was 7.8 percent or 23.6 million people in 2007 (Centers for Disease Control and Prevention, 2008). Diabetics have high levels of blood glucose and low levels of insulin. The challenge with diabetes is that it complicates all other medical conditions, can be taxing on a person's general health, and can result in premature death. Complications from diabetes are costly. The disease costs the nation about $174 billion a year ($116 billion in direct medical costs and $58 billion in lost productivity) (Centers for Disease Control and Prevention, 2008).

The increasing incidence of diabetes may in part result from the increasing rate of obesity in the American population. Two thirds of adults are overweight, with one third obese. The rate for adolescents, 19 percent, was more than three times higher than it was 20 years ago (Centers for Disease Control and Prevention, 2007a). Many contributing factors can be minimized through prevention, such as losing weight and keeping physically active. However, legislating personal behaviors is difficult; Americans do not embrace prevention. The cost of diabetes is becoming a social welfare concern. Health care costs for persons with diabetes were 11 percent of the national health care expenditures in 2002. The annual health care cost for a person with diabetes is more than five times as much as the cost for a person without diabetes (Centers for Disease Control and Prevention, 2004).

HEALTH NEEDS OF VETERANS

The war in Iraq and Afghanistan poses significant challenges to the veterans' health system as well as the physical and mental health resources of our general health care system. It is estimated that as many as 20 percent of soldiers returning from Iraq have Post-Traumatic Stress Disorder (Zoroya, 2008). Veteran's Affairs disability pay has jumped 150 percent in recent years (Priest & Hull, 2007). Medical advances have saved lives on the combat field, but that means more survivors with disabilities and greater need for medical care. Analysis of veterans' health needs upon their return, after the first three and a half years of the war, found that the Veterans Health Administration (VHA) was already overwhelmed by the number of veterans and the degree of care they needed. Survival rate has been far higher than any other war in U.S. history, with more than 50,000 soldiers wounded by September of 2006. The VHA was already incapable of handling all the pending claims and volume in 2006, and the cost over the course of the returning veterans' lives is estimated to be between $350 and $700 billion (Bilmes, 2007). These amounts will grow with continuation of the war. The length of the war and multiple tours of duty will tax our health care system and increase the national costs of physical and mental health care for years to come.

CONFLICTING VALUES AND BELIEFS

As with so many social welfare concerns, the question of individual versus social responsibility predominates. Our health care system is a combination of public programs and private services. The fact that national health insurance proposals have been defeated for decades demonstrates the tenacity with which citizens hold onto the value of private provision of health care. As more people need care, however, and families are stretched to their financial and emotional limits, national health insurance may be created. In the meantime, policies such as the **Medicare Modernization Act of 2003** will probably combine public and private efforts and create complicated systems of health care.

The tendency of people in the United States to respond to crises rather than take a preventive approach is most evident in the health care arena. In spite of a tremendous amount of research demonstrating the benefits of preventive health care, obesity rates are on the rise, as are other preventable health risks. Individuals are as likely to wait until a crisis occurs before they take care of themselves as the population as a whole is to respond to health care issues. Because of this tendency, the health care system will probably face costly crises that will be difficult to address without preventive efforts.

FINAL THOUGHTS ON HEALTH CARE POLICY

Health care and medical services are significant issues at the forefront of social welfare policy debate. The need for national health insurance has been debated for decades and will continue to be the central issue in social welfare policy proposals. Health concerns such as HIV/AIDS, substance abuse, Alzheimer's disease, and diabetes are major challenges for policy makers and providers of social welfare services. With rising costs, more people facing medical problems, and the aging of the population, social welfare policy will need to adapt to meet the challenge of health care in America in the coming years.

Key Terms

Medicare

Medicaid

Consolidated Omnibus
   Reconciliation Act
   (COBRA)

national health
   insurance

Health Insurance
   Portability and
   Accountability Act of
   1996 (HIPAA)

State Children's Health
   Insurance Program
   (SCHIP)

community mental
   health centers

deinstitutionalization

Medigap

Medicare Prescription
   Drug, Improvement,
   and Modernization
   Act (MMA)

Americans with
   Disabilities Act
   (ADA)

Disability Insurance (DI)

Supplemental Security
   Income (SSI)

severe or serious mental
   illness (SMI)

Managed care

Health Maintenance
   Organizations (HMOs)

Preferred Provider
   Organizations (PPOs)

pandemic

Ryan White
   Comprehensive AIDS
   Resources Emergency
   (CARE) Act of 1990

substance abuse

Alzheimer's disease (AD)

Medicare Moderniza-
   tion Act of 2003

Questions for Discussion

1. Is health care a right, or should it be linked to employment?
2. What are the differences between the Medicaid and Medicare programs?
3. Do you think managed care is a good way to provide health care coverage?
4. Discuss the differences between drug treatment and drug enforcement. Which is preferable for dealing with substance abuse? Why?
5. Should the government get involved with personal health decisions such as the choice to smoke cigarettes, drink alcohol, overeat, or use illicit drugs? Why?

Excercises

1. Find out whether there is a community mental health center in your community. If not, why? Where do people go for mental health services? If there is one, visit it. What services do they offer? How accessible and affordable are the services?
2. As you may have done in the exercise from Chapter 6, apply for an entry-level job. Ask about health care benefits. Are they available? Is the coverage affordable? Can dependents also be covered?
3. In class, identify several managed care companies in your community. Divide into groups, with one group for each company. Each group should call its company and ask for information on their services. Is it a private or public agency? Nonprofit or for-profit? What services are covered? What services are not? What is the cost? Who decides what treatments are provided, a primary care physician or a case manager? Do doctors get bonuses for keeping costs down? Compare the information about your company with the information obtained by other groups. How are the services different or similar? Which company would you prefer? Why?
4. Interview a medical provider. Has he or she treated people with diabetes? If so, what are his or her impressions of the disease and what does he or she think should be the role of government in dealing with diabetes?
5. Find out the laws in your state regarding the medical use of marijuana. Are there neighboring states with different laws? What do you think might be the implications of these differing laws?

References

Alzheimer's Disease Education and Referral Center. (2008). *Alzheimer's disease: Unraveling the mystery*. NIH Publication No. 08-3782. Washington, DC: U.S. Department of Health and Human Services.

Axinn, J., & Stern, M. J. (2008). *Social welfare: A history of the American response to need*, 7th ed. Boston: Allyn and Bacon.

Bilmes, L. (2007). Soldiers returning from Iraq and Afghanistan: The long-term costs of providing Veterans Medical Care and Disability Benefits. *Faculty Research Working Paper RWP07-001*. Cambridge, MA: Harvard University John F. Kennedy School of Government.

Centers for Disease Control and Prevention. (2004). *Diabetes: Disabling, deadly, and on the rise*. Atlanta, GA: Author.

Centers for Disease Control and Prevention. (2007a). *Health, United States, 2007*. Atlanta, GA: Author.

Centers for Disease Control and Prevention. (2007b). *HIV/AIDS Surveillance report*. Atlanta, GA: Author.

Centers for Disease Control and Prevention. (2008). *National diabetes fact sheet, 2007*. Atlanta, GA: Author.

Center for Policy Alternatives. (2007). *Progressive agenda for the states 2008. Leadership for America*. Washington, DC: Author.

Children's Defense Fund. (2004). *The state of America's children 2004*. Washington, DC: Author.

Congressional Budget Office. (2008). *The budget and economic outlook: Fiscal years 2008 to 2018*. Washington, DC: Congress of the United States.

Congressional Quarterly. (2004). A case of neglect: Why health care is getting worse, even though medicine is getting better. *Governing*, February.

Dallek, G. (2003). A prescription for confusion. *Washington Post National Weekly Edition* 21(8):22.

DeNavas-Walt, C., Proctor, B. D., Smith, J. (2008). Income, poverty, and health insurance coverage in the United States: 2007. *Current Population Reports*, P60-235. Washington, DC: U.S. Census Bureau.

Downey, K. (2004). A hefty dose to swallow. *Washington Post National Weekly Edition* 21(21):18.

Dye, T. R. (2008). *Understanding public policy*, 12th ed. Upper Saddle River, NJ: Pearson Prentice Hall.

Fellin, P. (1996). *Mental health and mental illness: Policies, programs, and services*. Itasca, IL: F. E. Peacock.

Gray, M. C. (1995). Drug abuse. In *Encyclopedia of social work*, 19th ed., pp. 795–803. Washington D. C.: NASW.

Hochman, M. E. (2006). Children of depressed parents are more vulnerable. *Health Science*, June 5:C3

Hogan, H., & Doyle, C. (1989). The drug problem and the federal response: A growing problem. *CRS Review* 10(10):11–13.

Jansson, B. S. (2009). *The reluctant welfare state*, 6th. ed. Belmont, CA: Thomson Brooks/Cole.

Kaiser Foundation. (2008). *Percent of children who are immunized, 2007*. http://www.statehealthfacts.org.

Katz, M. B. (1986). *In the shadow of the poorhouse: A social history of welfare in America*. New York: Basic Books.

Langdon, S. (1996). Health insurance. *CQ Weekly Report* 54(31):2197–2200.

Mechanic, D. (2001). Mental health policy at the millennium: Challenges and opportunities. In R. W. Manderscheid & M. J. Henderson (eds.). *Mental health, United States, 2000*. Washington, DC: U.S. Department of Health and Human Services.

Pear, R. (1996, September 20). In Congress, leaders agree on insurance plans. *New York Times*, p. A11.

Priest, D. & Hull, A. (2007, June 25–July 8). The war inside: Veterans encounter a mental-health system that makes healing difficult. *Washington Post National Weekly Edition* 24(36 & 37):6–8.

Shackman, B. R., Gebo, K. A., Walensky, R. P., Losina, E., Muccio, T., Sax, P. E., Weinstein, M. C., Seage, G. R., Moore, R. D., & Freedberg, K. A. (2006). The lifetime cost of current Human Immunodeficiency Virus care in the United States. *Medical Care* 44(11):990–997.

Sherrill, R. (1995). The madness of the market. *The Nation* 260(2):45–72.

Shilts, R. (1987). *And the band played on*. New York: Penguin Books.

Social Security Administration. (2008). *Social security bulletin: Annual statistical supplement, 2007*. Washington, DC: U.S. Department of Health and Human Services.

Starr, P. (1982). *The social transformation of American medicine*. New York: Basic Books.

Stroup, H. (1986). *Social welfare pioneers*. Chicago: Nelson-Hall.

Substance Abuse and Mental Health Services Administration. (2007). *Results from the 2006 National Survey on Drug Use and Health: National finding*. Washington, DC: U.S. Department of Health and Human Services.

Trattner, W. I. (1999). *From poor law to welfare state*, 6th ed. New York: Free Press.

U.S. Census Bureau. (2007). *Statistical abstract of the United States 2008*, 127th ed. Washington, DC: U.S. Department of Commerce.

U.S. General Accounting Office. (2000). *Mental health: Community-based care increases for people with serious mental health issues*. GAO-01-224. Washington, DC: U.S. Government Printing Office.

U.S. General Accounting Office. (1995). *Ryan White CARE Act*. GAO/HEHS-95-49. Washington, DC: U.S. Government Printing Office.

Whelan, D. (2008). Unfilled prescription. *Forbes* 181(8): 40–46.

World Health Organization. (2007). *AIDS epidemic update*. Geneva, Switzerland: UNAIDS.

Zoroya, G. (2008, March 7). A fifth of soldiers at PTSD risk: Rate rises with tours. *USA Today*, p. 11A.

Aging and Social Welfare Policy

Aging, like childhood, is part of the human condition. With good health and care, most people in our society are likely to live into their 70s, and many will live 10 or 20 years longer. Life expectancy has risen over the years, from less than 50 years of age at the turn of the 20th century to almost 78 years for a person born in 2004 (U.S. Census Bureau, 2007). From 1900 to 2006, the number of elderly people in this country increased twelve-fold, from 3.1 million to 37.3 million (Administration on Aging, 2008c). In 2006, 37.3 million people were 65 years of age or older, representing 12.4 percent of the total population. From 1980 to 2002, the number of people older than 85 years grew by almost 2.4 million (Administration on Aging, 2003). A person who reaches the age of 65 years today can expect to live an additional 18 years (Administration on Aging, 2008c). One result of the growing elderly population and longer life span has been a need to consider social welfare policies that provide care and support for people as they age.

Historically, families have cared for their elderly members. The percentage of older people in the general population was relatively small, so there were more people to share in their care and support. The value of family care is still very strong and most caregivers are unpaid family or friends. There are 44 million people who are informal caregivers (Administration on Aging, 2008a). However, because of the increasing proportion of elderly people in the population, not all families are able to provide all the care that their aging relatives need. As a result, families increasingly look to the government to help care for and support the older generation. This chapter will examine the social welfare policies and programs that have been developed to assist aging Americans.

HISTORY OF SOCIAL WELFARE POLICIES RELATED TO AGING

During the 19th century, most people worked throughout their lives. In fact, the concept of retirement is relatively new (Richardson, 1993). The idea of leaving the workforce at a specific age began to receive public support after the 1930s and was formalized with policies and programs that evolved over the years, starting during the Great Depression and lasting into the 1960s.

The Great Depression hit older people particularly hard. Most lost their life savings and homes, and families were dispersed. These events gave rise to a political movement of elderly citizens. During the 1930s, thousands of older people organized to push for the creation of federal old-age pensions (Torres-Gil, 1992). This was the first time that older adults had formed a voting bloc to support legislation. The economic devastation of the Great Depression combined with organized political pressure from older people resulted in passage of the **Social Security Act of 1935**. As discussed in Chapter 7, the major social welfare policy of this act was the **Old Age, Survivors, and Disability Insurance (OASDI)** program, commonly referred to as Social Security. This program is the foundation of today's Social Security coverage and the largest social welfare program in the nation. During the 1930s, there was significant resistance to such a broad social welfare effort by the federal government; however, the social insurance system established by the Social Security Act is now strongly supported.

Thirty years passed after passage of the Social Security Act before the other major public program for the elderly, **Medicare**, was passed. As discussed in

Chapter 2, advocates had tried repeatedly to get legislation passed that would provide federal support for health care insurance for older people. Not until 1965 was the Social Security Act amended to include Title XVIII, Health Insurance for the Aged and Disabled, the official designation of the Medicare program. When Medicare is included, the entire program is sometimes referred to as the **Old Age, Survivors, Disability, and Health Insurance (OASDHI)** program. In this book, to maintain clarity, Medicare and OASDI are discussed separately.

Also in 1965, the **Older Americans Act (OAA)** was passed. Although it was not as significant and comprehensive as OASDI and Medicare, this legislation furthered the policy gains made by older adults. The details of the OAA and its programs are discussed later in this chapter. The civil rights movement of the 1960s influenced the creation of another critical social welfare policy for older people, the **Age Discrimination in Employment Act of 1967**. This act, which is administered by the Equal Employment Opportunity Commission, protects people who are 40 years of age or older from employment discrimination based on age.

Public assistance for poor elderly people was addressed in Title I of the original Social Security Act as the **Old Age Assistance** program. In 1972, it was consolidated with assistance programs for the blind and disabled in the amendment that became Title XVI of the Social Security Act, the **Supplemental Security Income for the Aged, Blind, and Disabled (SSI)** program. This amendment changed old age assistance from a state-level program with federal guidelines to a federal program overseen by the Social Security Administration. Eligibility requirements and federal payment standards are nationally uniform as a result. Although most SSI services are for people with disabilities, 28 percent of recipients are aged people (Social Security Administration, 2008).

Since the 1970s, legislation relevant to aging in America has centered on retirement and economic security. These policy efforts emphasized savings programs through the private sector. Most policies were based on federal tax incentives for individual retirement savings accounts, pension plans, and employer-sponsored retirement programs. Therefore, Social Security and the aging policies of the 1960s were social welfare policies based in government provision of services. Aging policies of the past 30 years have focused on government support of services provided through the private sector. OASDI, Medicare, SSI, OAA, and ADEA provide a full spectrum of national social welfare services for elderly people, and pensions and private health insurance provide individual security.

SERVICES FOR PROMOTING AND PROTECTING ELDERLY PEOPLE

Key social welfare interventions for elderly populations center on services to enhance daily living and to protect people from abuse and discrimination. These interventions have been created through major legislative efforts over the past 45 years. Services to promote well-being and provide protection are guided primarily by two social welfare policies, the OAA and ADEA.

OLDER AMERICANS ACT OF 1965

The growth of social welfare programs during the 1960s expanded services for the elderly. In 1961, the first White House Conference on Aging was held (Axinn &

Stern, 2008). It highlighted the growing needs of older people and was partly responsible for passage of the **Older Americans Act (OAA) of 1965** (P.L. 89-73). The OAA established the Administration on Aging and ensured the well-being of older persons with programs that included in-home services, transportation, legal assistance, and outreach. The programs are facilitated and monitored by distinct planning and service areas coordinated by the **Area Agencies on Aging (AAA)** (Administration on Aging, 2003). Core services funded by the OAA include support, nutrition, preventive health, elder rights, and caregiver supports.

The legislation also authorized a number of social services to be overseen by the AAAs. Each local agency has a great deal of discretion in planning and implementing the services. The general services supported by OAA funds include transportation, outreach, case management, senior centers, recreation and nutrition programs, visiting homemakers, home health aids, and health-related programs such as immunizations, financial counseling, and representation in guardianship proceedings. The overall goal of the act was to create a governmental agent that would coordinate various existing services and create new ways to better serve older people. Some of the specific programs coordinated today through the OAA include routine health screenings, Meals-on-Wheels, senior centers, adult day care centers for older people with impairments, in-home care, exercise and fitness programs, and employment services. The OAA is also a vehicle that advocates for and serves elderly American Indians, Alaskan Natives, and Native Hawaiians. Their services are comparable to those of all AAAs but emphasize the cultural identities of these groups.

Several amendments have expanded the scope of OAA. In 1992, Congress created and funded Title VII, which addressed the prevention of abuse, neglect, and exploitation of older people. The next section of this chapter has more information about these services.

In 2000, the OAA was amended again. The National Family Caregiver Support Program (NFCSP) was created. The program provides information, assistance, and support to caregivers; counseling and training to help caregivers make decisions and solve problems related to their roles as caregivers; and respite care to temporarily relieve caregivers from their responsibilities. This legislation also included provisions for a specialized Native American Caregiver Support Program. The OAA was reauthorized in 2006, and added more services to emphasize long-term care options for people to maintain their independence.

In general, the services offered through OAA are available to all persons 60 years of age and over, regardless of means. In practice, however, limited resources and low funding levels over the years have caused services to be directed to those most in need (Torres-Gil, 1992). The struggle between universality and targeted services developed because of incremental cutbacks in federal and state funds over the past 20 years. As is true in so many areas of service, the expanding population of older people will challenge the resources of OAA programs. Most likely, demands for social welfare policy changes will be heard over the next several years.

PROTECTIVE SERVICES FOR ELDERLY PEOPLE

Title VII of the OAA, the Vulnerable Elder Rights Protection law, was created by Congress in 1992, "to protect and enhance the basic rights and benefits of vulnerable older people: individuals who may need advocacy on their behalf because their physical or mental disabilities, social isolation, limited educational attainment, or limited financial resources prevent them from being able to protect or advocate for themselves" (Administration on Aging, 2003, p. 4). This legislation includes the Long-Term Care Ombudsperson program, Programs for the Prevention of Abuse and Exploitation, and State Legal Assistance. All are coordinated by geographic region, as set up by the AAAs. Although Congress enacted these three services, the legal rights section has never been funded (National Center on Elder Abuse, 2003). These programs are primarily concerned with prevention and legal advocacy.

Provision of **Adult Protective Services (APS)** emerged at the state level during the 1970s. The first programs were funded by the social services monies of Title XX of the Social Security Act. Under this federal mandate, states created APS units. All states have some form of Adult Protective Services that receive some funds through the OAA. However, there are no federal statutes directly related to the delivery of APS, so each state has developed its own system. Although the systems vary, most states have placed the APS unit under their state human services agency, separate from the state geographic unit on aging and the AAA (National Center on Elder Abuse, 2001). APS unit workers are typically the first responders to reports of abuse, neglect, and exploitation of adults. Based on the data collected by state APS programs and voluntarily submitted, there were 565,747 reports of elder/adult abuse in 2004, up 20 percent since 2000. More than 80 percent of these cases were investigated, and almost half were substantiated. The majority of victims were women (66 percent), three fourths were white (77 percent), and more than two in five were 80 years of age or older (43 percent) (National Center on Elder Abuse, 2006). For more details, see Box 12.1. The true dimensions of the problem are difficult to assess because there is no system of national mandatory reporting. Undocumented cases could be in the millions. The majority of perpetrators of elder abuse are intimately known to the victims—they are family members or partners. The privacy of the family adds to the difficulty in assessing the extent of the problem.

BOX 12.1 | **MORE ABOUT ELDER MALTREATMENT**

In 2003, of 191,908 substantiated reports of abuse, neglect, and exploitation:

The most frequent reasons were:		The relationship to the victim of the identified perpetrator was:	
Self-neglect	37%		
Caregiver neglect or abandonment	20%	Adult child	33%
Financial exploitation	15%	Other family member	22%
Emotional/psychological/verbal abuse	15%	Unknown	16%
		Spouse/intimate partner	11%
Physical abuse	11%	Other	18%
Sexual abuse	1%		
Other	1%	Source: National Center on Elder Abuse, 2006	

If indeed there is a greater prevalence of elder maltreatment than reported, this problem is likely to increase as the elderly population increases. Although federal legislators have begun to recognize the problem, federal standards are still minimal. Over time, federal regulations to ensure data collection and create uniform systems for protection may become part of the social welfare policy system.

AGE DISCRIMINATION IN EMPLOYMENT ACT (ADEA)

Under the ADEA, it is illegal to discriminate against a person because of his or her age in employment practices. This includes privileges of employment; procedures for hiring, firing, and promotion; and compensation, benefits, work assignments, and training. Although employers are not prohibited from asking an applicant's age or date of birth, that information cannot be used in any discriminatory way. In 1990, the ADEA was amended to include the Older Workers Benefit Protection Act. This policy prohibits employers from denying benefits to older employees. Certain benefits such as health insurance can be more costly for older workers. This legislation protects older workers from being excluded from having benefits because of the greater cost. At the same time, it allows employers to offer reduced benefits based on age, as long as the cost of providing benefits for older workers is the same as the cost of providing benefits for younger workers (U.S. Equal Employment Opportunity Commission, 2004).

New interpretations and rulings by the EEOC in 2004 allow employers to reduce or eliminate health benefits for retirees when they become eligible for Medicare (AARP, 2004b). Previously, employers who provided health coverage as part of company retirement benefits could not take that coverage away when a person became eligible for Medicare. That was considered a form of discrimination. As a result, some employers began to take the health coverage benefit away from all retirees, even those too young for Medicare, to save money. In an effort to protect younger retirees and keep employers from discriminating against them, the EEOC ruled that employers could terminate health care coverage when a retiree became eligible for Medicare. This compromise was a way of encouraging employers to continue health coverage for those who would otherwise have to pay for private insurance. This debate highlights the struggle between private and public provision of health insurance, and the importance of legislation that protects workers' rights. With an aging population and more people choosing or needing to work later in life, the protections of the ADEA are important.

FINANCIAL SECURITY

As the population ages and more people live longer, financial security becomes even more integral to social well-being. The Great Depression demonstrated how vulnerable older workers were in times of economic downturn. As a result, the Social Security Act was created to provide financial support for people when they age. Although Social Security is a critical component of financial security for older Americans, it does not provide all the financial security needed. Retirement guidelines and resources suggest that financial security for aging citizens should be a "three-legged stool" made up of Social Security payments, pensions, and private savings. Of the three, only Social Security is guaranteed through the federal government.

The other two depend on corporations' and individual's behaviors. For a small number of elderly people, the three financial resources are not enough. This group depends on public assistance, which is a fourth source of economic support for people who are aging. Two thirds of the almost 37 million older Americans receive at least 50 percent of their income from Social Security, for one third of the seniors in this country Social Security constitutes more than 90 percent of their total annual income, and for one out of five seniors it is the only source of income (Social Security Administration, 2008). The three legs of the stool and public assistance are critical for the well-being of the elderly population.

INCOME ASSISTANCE: SUPPLEMENTAL SECURITY INCOME (SSI)

Poverty among elderly people has become less common, in large part because of Social Security. In 1959, 35 percent of older people lived in poverty (Federal Interagency Forum on Aging-Related Statistics, 2004). In 2007, 3.6 million people age 65 years and older (9.7 percent) were officially living below the poverty line (DeNavas-Walt, Proctor, & Smith, 2008). In spite of Social Security, some elderly people still need public assistance. Under SSI, low-income persons who are eligible receive a monthly cash assistance benefit. In 2006, 2 million aged people received SSI benefits, with an average payment of $457 per month (Social Security Administration, 2008). Although the monthly benefit was small, it was the primary income for most of the recipients. Other supports for low-income elderly people are provided through in-kind services such as food assistance and subsidized housing. Although these services provide only minimal support, they are vital to the lives of very poor people over age 65 years.

RETIREMENT SECURITY

Most people who reach retirement age rely on the three major sources of income: Social Security, pensions, and private savings. More and more people, however, are choosing an additional source of income: continued employment. Although employment is not typically considered a resource for retirement after people have *retired from* work, income from jobs is becoming a larger part of the economic livelihood of people over age 65 years. Over the next 25 years, the number of people 65 years of age and older is expected to double and become 20 percent of the population (Federal Interagency Forum on Aging Related Statistics, 2008). Although people know they will grow older, many do not plan for retirement. Almost 60 percent of workers have not calculated how much money they need to save for retirement; that percentage drops minimally for people 55 years and older (Employee Benefit Research Institute, 2004). Research suggests that of households in 1998, in which a person was between the age of 47 and 64 years, about 20 percent will fall into poverty when they retire and 43 percent will not be able to replace even half of their current income when they retire (Economic Policy Institute, 2003). For women and people of color, the prospect for financial well-being in retirement is less secure. Single women are most likely to be low-income in retirement, with 60 percent likely to have income less than twice the poverty line. Fifty-seven percent of African American and Hispanic households are likely to have income less than twice the poverty line, compared to only 23 percent of white households (Weller & Wolff,

2005). The impact of gender and race in the economic marketplace carries over into retirement—the lifetime lower earnings of women and people of color are reflected in their lower retirement income.

Most people do not think seriously about retirement until the time comes. In a comprehensive survey of recent retirees, 70 percent reported serious consideration of retirement occurred less than two years before they retired. One out of five retirees seriously considered it less than 6 months before retiring (Employee Benefit Research Institute, 2008). Retirement security will continue to be a major social welfare concern.

Social Security   For the majority of older people in this country, Social Security payments make up their primary income. Ninety-one percent of elderly persons receive some Social Security benefits. Box 12.2 shows the distribution of sources of income for the aged. On average for the typical retiree, 40 percent of annual income comes from Social Security, continued employment provides 24 percent, pensions provide 18 percent, and asset income provides 15 percent. However, for two thirds of recipients, Social Security provides more than half of their total income,

| **BOX 12.2** | **MORE ABOUT SOURCES OF INCOME FOR THE AGED** |

Where the elderly get their income:

Social Security	91%
Asset income	58%
Retirement benefits other than Social Security	40%
Earnings	22%
Public assistance	5%
Veterans' benefits	4%

Source: Social Security Administration, 2003

Average sources of income for all elderly:

Social Security	39%
Earnings/employment	24%
Pensions	18%
Asset income	16%
Other	3%
Total	100%

Source: U.S. Census Bureau, 2005

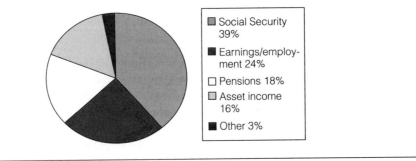

- Social Security 39%
- Earnings/employment 24%
- Pensions 18%
- Asset income 16%
- Other 3%

and for one third, 90 percent or more of their income. Assets and pensions are significant for a much smaller proportion of the elderly.

Clearly, Social Security benefits are the major form of retirement income for millions of elderly people. As stated in Chapter 7, Social Security is not meant to be a person's total retirement income; rather, it is a safety net. The average Social Security retirement benefit in 2006 for retired workers was $1,044 per month (Social Security Administration, 2008), or $12,258 a year. Although this amount of Social Security was higher than the poverty threshold, clearly it is not a great sum of income. The median household income for seniors in 2006 was $27,798 (DeNavas-Walt, Proctor & Smith, 2008). Although most senior households supplement their Social Security benefits, the overall additional income is low. More than 60 percent of households headed by someone 65 years or older had total incomes below $50,000 (Administration on Aging, 2008c). Social Security plays a vital role in ensuring people's financial security as they age. Nevertheless, Social Security is not enough to fully fund a person's retirement. Even the maximum monthly benefit possible for someone retiring at 65 of $2,027 in 2006 would have provided only $24,324 a year—and that would mean a person paid in maximum amounts for every working year prior to retirement (Social Security Administration, 2008). For a person to achieve financial security in retirement, the two other legs of the stool, pensions and savings, are vital.

Pensions   A pension, which is a form of retirement savings, may be one of two primary types: **defined contribution (DC)** and **defined benefit (DB)**. DB plans are often called "traditional pension plans" and provide employees with a guaranteed level of retirement income based on years of service. The guaranteed income can also be influenced by age at retirement and level of income over the working years. Although private companies may provide DB plans, they are insured by the federal government through the Pension Benefits Guaranty Corporation. Thus, they are an example of a private economic program that is ultimately supported by the federal government. In 2005, among private-sector employment of all workers with retirement benefits, only 10 percent of active workers participated in a defined benefit plan, another 27 percent were invested in both a DB and DC plan, and the rest, 63 percent had only a defined contribution plan (Employee Benefit Research Institute, 2007).

The most popular DC plan is the *401(k) plan*. Employees must contribute a portion of their income to an individual account. In some plans, employers also make contributions or match the employee's contribution. DC plans do not provide a guaranteed level of retirement income, because they are not insured and rely on private investment programs such as stock market–based mutual funds to create income growth. Although traditional pensions are insured by the federal government, and companies and individuals get tax subsidies for defined contributions, only 48 percent of workers participated in a workplace retirement plan in 2004, a drop from just four years earlier (Economic Policy Institute, 2006).

The configuration of pensions in the United States has shifted over the past 20 years (Crenshaw, 2004). The number of traditional pensions dropped from 130,000 to 32,000. In place of them, companies have opted for 401k-type plans. In 1980, eight percent of workers had k-plans, but by 1998, that number had increased to

27 percent. As mentioned, by 2004 63 percent of private-sector workers participated only in a DC plan (Employee Benefit Research Institute, 2007). Although both DC and DB plans can provide financial security, the DC, or k-type, plans are riskier. If DC plan investments do well in the private market, the employee retires in good financial stead. If the investments do poorly, the employee may retire with less than he or she had before entering the plan. The bottom-line difference between DB and DC plans is that "where the company once had to be sure it had enough money to pay pensions way out into the future, now the employee/retiree bears all the investment risk" (Crenshaw, 2004, p. 20). The shift from DB to DC pensions has been a shift from shared risk and responsibility to individual risk and responsibility.

The solvency of defined benefit programs, as previously stated, is guaranteed by the federal government through the Pension Benefits Guaranty Corporation. In 2006, the federal government, in response to private corporations' bankruptcies and inadequate funding of their pension plans, passed the Pension Protection Act. This legislation made significant improvements to U.S. retirement laws. Among those changes were stronger requirements for companies to adequately fund their pension plans, as well as creating incentives for employees in contribute more to their defined contribution plans (Day, 2006).

Private Savings Individuals have total control over their private savings for retirement. Less than 70 percent of workers report that they or their spouses have saved for retirement. Those who do save tend to put away a small amount of money (Employee Benefit Research Institute, 2004). Federal Reserve data on consumer finances show that two thirds of those families whose chief earner is likely to retire within the next decade had less than $88,000 in retirement savings in 2004 (Cranford, 2007). In recent years, the personal saving rate has been minimal, only .4 percent of disposable income in 2006 (*Economic Report of the President*, 2008). This should concern social policy planners, but it depends on other economic factors. Although personal savings rates have declined, when other forms of asset accumulation increase, particularly contributions to retirement accounts, housing values, and capital gains through stock purchases people's savings are augmented by these assets. People may not be saving in the traditional sense, but they are accumulating assets. The point at which this becomes problematic is when the economy plummets, as in 2008. When housing prices and retirement accounts drop significantly, seniors who rely on their home values as a major asset and payments from retirement accounts to provide income face severe economic hardship. Without adequate savings, they find themselves in precarious economic situations. Planning for retirement with personal savings becomes a way to weather financial downturns in the financial and housing markets.

Employment after Retirement By definition, retirement implies that paid employment has ended. Many people, however, feel that they are still young at the age of 65 and choose to continue working. Others find it economically necessary to continue working. In 2006, 34 percent of men ages 65 to 69 and 24 percent of women in that age group were active participants in the labor force. Even after the age of 70, 14 percent of men and 7 percent of women participated in the labor force (Federal Interagency Forum on Aging Related Statistics, 2008). It is difficult to know how many people are working because of need. About 80 percent of adults between the ages of 38 and 57 years plan to work in some capacity when they retire. Of those planning to work, more than a third anticipate that they will need to work (AARP, 2004a). Although numerous variables affect financial security in retirement, it is likely that some people who reach retirement age will have to continue to work.

VARIABILITY IN FINANCIAL SECURITY BY RACE AND GENDER

A pattern of inequality exists among races and between men and women in the United States. The rate of poverty for older women is higher than for men, one out of eight women over 65 live in poverty compared with one out of twelve men (U.S. Bureau of the Census, 2005). This difference is further troubling because women have longer life expectancies than men. Thus, financial insecurity not only hits women more deeply, it means more years of living in poverty. In 2006, as outlined in Box 12.3, the racial differences in poverty continue into old age.

One of the reasons women are less secure in retirement than men is due to the disparity in participate and receipt of pensions. In 2000, 43 percent of men age 65 years received defined benefit (pension) income, compared with only 29 percent of women. Furthermore, the dollar amount differed significantly, with men receiving an average of $14,232 and women receiving $8,734 (Economic Policy Institute, 2003). Over time, the gap is closing, although white men still have the highest pension coverage, as shown in Box 12.4. Lower pensions for women combined with lower average Social Security benefits over more years of life mean that the economic status of older women is more precarious than that of older men. Pension coverage is particularly low among Hispanic seniors.

Many factors contribute to the disparity. Divorce, family care responsibilities, childbearing, and longer life expectancies place women at greater financial risk in retirement. Women earn less than men over the course of their lives, both in terms of wages earned and length of time in the labor market. Differences in earnings by race lay the groundwork for disparities in retirement. These differences all contribute to lower Social Security benefits, less savings, and lower pension benefits.

The most vulnerable group seems to be women age 55 to 64 years, who are approaching retirement. Fifty-four percent of these women work full or part time.

BOX 12.3 | **CONSIDER THIS . . .**

Poverty rates for people 65 years and older in 2007:

White	7.4%
Black	23.2%
Hispanic	17.1%
Asian	11.3%

Source: DeNavas-Walt, Proctor, & Smith, 2008

BOX 12.4	CONSIDER THIS . . .

Pension Coverage According to Race in 2000

	Men	Women
African American	43.6%	42.6%
Hispanic	27.5%	30%
White	57.6%	51.8%

Source: Economic Policy Institute, 2003

Workers Participating in Workplace Retirement Plans in 2004

All	48.3%
Males	49.4%
Females	47.2%
White	52.8%
African American	45.9%
Hispanic	28.7%

Source: Copeland, 2007

Many of them do so because of "desperation;" they have no savings or insurance as they near retirement age. This desperation leads to the need to work, not the desire to work (Finkel, 2003). Net worth, the value of real estate, stocks, bonds and other assets, minus debt, also reflects lifelong patterns. In retirement, the net worth of older white households was six times greater than in black households, and this disparity was significantly greater than in 1985 when the difference was four times greater (Federal Interagency Forum on Aging Related Statistics, 2008). Although financial security is a concern for the majority of people approaching retirement, it is particularly worrisome for women and people of color.

HEALTH CARE FOR AN AGING POPULATION

Chapter 11 covers health care and, specifically, the Medicare program. In this chapter, we look at the issues of health particularly relevant to people as they age. The major consideration that has emerged for older people is the cost of health care. Although Medicare guarantees coverage for retirees who are eligible through OASDI, Medicare costs have gone up and not all health care needs are covered. Seniors are spending more money of their own to insure their health care coverage.

HEALTH EXPENSES

Health care costs have increased significantly for older Americans over the past 15 years. Since 1992, the average annual cost for health care for Medicare enrollees rose 51 percent, after accounting for inflation (Federal Interagency Forum on Aging Related Statistics, 2008). In 2003, out-of-pocket medical costs for people age 65 years and older averaged $2,487, or about 14 percent of the average senior's income (Kaiser Family Foundation, 2007). The cost of health care increases with age. For example, health care costs in total, both out-of-pocket and insurance expenditures, were $9,702 in 2004 for people 65 to 74 years old and jumped to $21,907 for people age 85 years and older (Federal Interagency Forum on Aging-Related Statistics,

2008). Prescription drug costs have been particularly high for the elderly. Many seniors have some form of insurance for prescription drugs. Medicare did not cover the cost of prescription drugs until the **2003 Medicare Modernization Act** was passed, as discussed in Chapter 11 (and that coverage did not start until 2006). The impact of that coverage should begin to be felt by seniors as more of them are covered by the program. However, because most seniors are covered by Medicare, the rising cost of health care will be felt most acutely by the federal government.

MEDICARE

As described previously, Medicare operates in much the same way as the OASDI program. Part of the Social Security tax all employees and employers pay goes toward funding Medicare. When a person becomes eligible to receive Social Security benefits, he or she is also eligible for Medicare coverage. The health care components of the Medicare program are discussed more fully in Chapter 11.

As a program for the elderly, Medicare is extremely important. It provides coverage for many routine medical procedures as well as very specialized procedures. Because of rising medical costs and the development of new procedures over the past 40 years, the cost has become a major policy problem. The average annual expenditure for health care for a person over 75 years old is almost three times more than for a person 25 to 34 years old (author calculations based on data in U.S. Census Bureau, 2007).

What amount should be spent on health care? Who should pay for it? These are pressing social welfare policy questions. As the population ages and medical technology advances, the expense of health care will increase. Currently, Medicare pays for a large portion, but not all of, the health care costs for elderly people who are covered by the Social Security system. Almost all seniors are covered by Medicare, and thus have a strong dependence on the program. The cost of Medicare has grown faster than other social welfare programs. One estimate to close the gap between what will be paid in to Medicare by workers and what will be needed to pay out for beneficiaries will require raising the payroll tax to 8 to 12 percent (McArdle, 2008). This presents a major economic concern for policy makers faced with increasing budget deficits and workers' aversion to paying more taxes.

LONG-TERM CARE

One of the most costly health care concerns is long-term care. **Long-term care** covers a wide array of services for elderly, chronically ill, and disabled persons. The services are necessary for day-to-day living and personal care. Although Medicare covers some long-term care costs, it does not cover all of them. For example, Medicare covers skilled nursing home care for a period of up to 100 days. After that period has ended, an elderly person must either use private insurance or personal finances to pay for continued nursing home care. Because of this shortfall in Medicare coverage, people often deplete their financial assets and become eligible for Medicaid, which does provide unlimited nursing home care. People cannot intentionally give away assets to qualify for Medicaid, but they can legally "spend down" their assets to qualify.

About 1.3 million older Americans lived in nursing homes in 2004, of whom three fourths were women and about half were 85 years or older (Federal Interagency Forum on Aging Related Statistics, 2008). Countless other older people are in assisted living facilities. The difference tends to be that nursing homes provide continuous skilled nursing care, whereas assisted living facilities provide care for people who cannot live independently, but do not need intensive medical care. There are numerous types of assisted living facilities, and licensing criteria vary by state. Different terms are used to refer to assisted living facilities, including residential care, congregate care, and senior care. Assisted living facilities can be stand-alone facilities or part of a retirement community, senior housing complex, or nursing home. Costs vary considerably, ranging from $10,000 to more than $50,000 a year. The average monthly rate across the United States is $1,800 or $21,600 a year (Administration on Aging, 2008a). The majority of these costs are paid privately. Medicare does not cover assisted living; Medicaid covers it when it is a medical necessity for eligible low-income people. With the growth in assisted living facilities and home health care options in recent years, residents in nursing homes tend to be older and frailer.

Caring for people as they age is becoming extremely costly for individuals and the government. Public and private spending for long-term care totaled $183 billion in 2003, or 13 percent of all health care expenditures (U.S. General Accounting Office, 2005). Medicaid spending on Long-term care tripled between 1991 and 2005, costing the federal government $95 billion in 2005 (Clemmit, 2006). The issue of long-term care has yet to be adequately addressed. As people age, the issue takes on greater significance. Six percent of noninstitutionalized people age 65 to 74 years needed assistance with performing daily activities because of health problems, as did 18 percent of people 85 years of age and older, and 25 percent of people age 65 to 74 years had limited activity due to a chronic condition, which increased to 44 percent for people over 75 years of age (U.S. Census Bureau, 2007). Reliance on Medicare and Medicaid is costly for taxpayers, but private insurance, personal savings, and family member support cannot meet the need. Alternative solutions to long-term care are needed as our population ages. Other services such as home health care and day treatment programs for senior citizens attempt to fill the need for such care. The goal of these services is to keep senior citizens at home and out of institutions for as long as possible. Often, these services must be paid for privately.

MEDICAID

Medicaid is administered under numerous social welfare categories. It is primarily a health care program with emphasis as an antipoverty program because it is targeted to people with low incomes. Medicaid has broad federal guidelines under which each state establishes its own eligibility standards, services offered, and rates of payment for services. As such, Medicaid varies from state to state. Typically when we think of government health care for seniors, we think of Medicare. However, Medicaid is also an elder care program, providing health care to low-income seniors. Although Medicaid provides care for low-income people of all ages, it is used heavily by the elderly, as discussed in the previous chapter. Although, less than eight percent of Medicaid recipients were 65 years and over, they accounted for 23 percent of money spent in the program (Social Security Administration, 2008).

Types of Caregiving and Caregivers

One of the growing social welfare needs related to aging is caregiving. Who will provide care for the growing numbers of elderly people? How will that care be provided? Who will pay for care and how will they pay for it? These are emerging questions that need to be addressed by our social welfare system.

Most caregivers are family members or other unpaid informal caregivers. As many as 44 million Americans provide unpaid care and financial support for a person with a chronic illness or disability. The economic value of these family and informal caregivers has been estimated at $306 billion per year (Administration on Aging, 2008b). The typical caregiver is a woman, 46 years old, who provides more than 20 hours of care a week to her mother (AARP Public Policy Institute, 2005). Sixty-four percent of elderly people with a disability received all their care from a family member or other informal unpaid caregiver (U.S. General Accounting Office, 2002). Because the typical caregiver is a middle-aged woman who is responsible for both the care of her aging parents and the care of her children, the term "sandwich generation" has been used to describe them. Many caregivers are caught between two generations and responsible for both. In addition, the typical caregiver is employed. Almost half of unpaid caregivers are employed full time (AARP Public Policy Institute, 2005).

Not all care can be given by family members. Millions of older people live in skilled nursing and assisted living facilities and are cared for by paid caregivers. Unfortunately, the nation is facing a critical shortage of front-line caregivers in long-term facilities. Positions now go unfilled. Over the next 25 years, the number of patients over 85 years will double but the traditional care giving worker population is projected to increase minimally (Wright, 2005).

The **Family and Medical Leave Act**, which addresses the care of children, was discussed in Chapter 10. This legislation is also important for caregivers of elders. It offers 12 weeks of unpaid leave, which can be used to care for an ill family member. Although the legislation preserves a person's job while they are gone, the leave is unpaid, making it difficult for many workers to take advantage of the policy.

Family and informal unpaid caregivers obviously make significant contributions within the private domain to the care of older people. This informal system will become more heavily strained as individuals live longer. Caregivers who reach retirement age may still have parents to care for who are in their 80s and 90s. It is likely that this phenomenon will push policy makers to develop additional public resources for the care of the elderly.

POLITICAL POWER

Although older adults constitute a minority of eligible voters, their political power is strong. As more people live longer, the emphasis on programs and services for seniors gains strength. The **baby boom generation**, Americans born between 1946 and 1964, has 78 million people, all of whom are approaching retirement over the next 25 years. One of the notable characteristics of the baby boom generation is that they have commanded national attention as every wave of their development has occurred. As the largest population wave born in the United States and as the generation born into the prosperity of the post–World War II years, the baby boomers have had a major influence on social, economic, and political trends. The size and social dominance of this age cohort will likely greatly influence the way people age.

Voting

Rates of voting and voter registration are highest among those who are 65 years of age and older (U.S. Census Bureau, 2007). From 1972 to 2000, voter turnout decreased in every age group except the 65-years-and-older group. The rate in this group grew from 63.5 percent to 67.6 percent, the highest proportion of voters of all age groups (Freeman, 2004). In 2006, 75 percent of people 65 years of age and older were registered to vote, double the rate for 18 to 20 year olds (U.S. Census Bureau, 2007). Preliminary tabulations suggest that the rate of youth registering and voting increased for the 2008 election, but older voters still outpaced the young in numbers and rate. The voting strength of older citizens keeps policy makers politically tied to support of senior citizen programs and sensitive to the wishes of this substantial voting group. The political power of elders is an advantage for advocates of social welfare aging issues, but it is a concern for advocates of other social welfare issues.

Intergenerational Relations: Conflict or Cooperation?

The political power and influence of senior citizens has brought attention to what is sometimes described as the public policy divide between the young and the old (Pearlstein, 1993) (see Box 12.5). Child welfare advocates argue that several forces have combined to encourage spending on the elderly over spending on children. There is a sense of self-interest involved:

> While we cannot recapture our own childhoods, all of us anticipate being old someday. At some level we all perceive programs and benefits for the elderly as *mechanisms through which we transfer resources to ourselves in the future*. (Hewlett, 1991, pp. 187–188)

BOX 12.5 | **CONTROVERSIAL PERSPECTIVES . . .**

Care for the old, or care for the young?

The public cost for health care for a child averages $1,475, compared with $12,764 for an elderly person (Congressional Quarterly, 2004).

People who retire in 20–30 years will most likely receive less of their preretirement income (about 15 percent less) from Social Security than retired people of 2006. If the system does not change, the decline will be even greater for those retiring in 40 years (Butrica, Iams, & Smith, 2003/2004).

Between 1967 and 2006, the number of people over 65 years of age living in poverty decreased from 29.5 percent to 9.4 percent. The number of children under 18 years of age living in poverty increased (16.6 percent in 1967 to 17.4 percent in 2006) (Federal Interagency Forum on Aging-Related Statistics, 2008).

Social services and social welfare policies have aided those who are older in our society. Some people ask if it is worth it. Should we be spending resources on young people who have their full lives ahead of them? Or do we have an obligation to care for those who have already made contributions to our society throughout their lives?

Another way to view the evolution of senior services is to recognize that government support for people as they age has freed the younger generation from responsibility (Torres-Gil, 1992). The benefits and services provided over the past 40 years have helped to reduce the proportion of poor elderly, to extend life expectancy, and to enhance the political power of older Americans. These social welfare policies have not only given the elderly more autonomy but have allowed their children to be more mobile and relieved some of their worry about day-to-day responsibilities and cost of care for their parents.

The public policy divide between the young and the old will likely focus on resources. The two major entitlement programs for older Americans, Social Security and Medicare, today account for almost eight percent of the nation's gross domestic product (GDP). By 2050, that percent is estimated to increase dramatically, to 22.2 percent of GDP (Greenblatt, 2007).

Without addressing this economic situation, we run the risk of polarizing social welfare services. There is a tremendous danger in viewing social welfare policy in divisive terms. To pit the old against the young is counterproductive. Spending disproportionately on the aging population ignores the needs of the young, and they are the future workers and caregivers who will support the economy and the aging population. The challenge is to develop social welfare policies and programs that do the same for children, families, and younger adults that they do for seniors, provide for their well-being, while keeping the economy balanced.

More social welfare programs should be patterned after Social Security. The idea of investing in a social insurance system that helps ensure the health and well-being of a future generation of taxpayers could be incorporated into programs that serve children. At the same time, the cost for these programs needs to be spread evenly across the population and generations. By creating similar program structures for seniors and children, the intergenerational divide could disappear.

CONFLICTING VALUES AND BELIEFS

The primary belief that dominates our care of the elderly in this nation is the belief in self-reliance over social responsibility. Although Social Security, Medicare, and Medicaid are public programs, the contribution of these programs is to provide a safety net to keep elderly people from falling into destitution. A comfortable retirement without financial stress rests heavily upon personal savings and pension contributions. Long-term care must be provided by the family or by the elderly person's private funds.

A second belief that influences social welfare policy for the aged is the crisis over prevention. Although most social welfare policies are residual, the impetus in aging policy has overwhelmingly been crisis care. Planning for old age is not something individuals do well, nor does society. If one waits too long to plan for retirement, one can neither save enough nor build a foundation for healthy living. Aging, more than many areas of social well-being, requires advance planning. Prevention strategies should be at the top of social welfare policy agendas for aging in the United States.

FINAL THOUGHTS ON AGING AND SOCIAL WELFARE POLICY

As the population of elderly persons continues to grow, the political power of senior citizens will also increase. Policy makers will need to be more attentive to the wishes of the aged. Advocacy groups such as the American Association of Retired Persons (AARP), with over 30 million members, represent very powerful special interests. The high level of voting and political involvement among seniors will promote their views and needs among policy makers. As such, they will dominate discussions of issues related to aging, as well as other social welfare issues. Therefore, social welfare policies relevant to aging in America will remain a critical part of our social welfare system.

Key Terms

Old Age, Survivors, and Disability Health Insurance (OASDHI)

Medicare

Older Americans Act of 1965

Age Discrimination in Employment Act (ADEA)

Supplemental Security Income (SSI)

Area Agencies on Aging (AAA)

Adult Protective Services (APS)

Pensions

defined contribution

defined benefit

long-term care

Questions for Discussion

1. Why is Social Security the most important social welfare program for elderly people?
2. What protections does the law provide for elderly people?
3. Do you think you will be financially prepared for retirement? What might you do to better prepare?

4. Health care is vital to people as they age. What changes should be made to improve health care policy in the United States?
5. What do you think of when you hear the term "baby boomer"? In what ways do you think the baby boomer generation will affect the nation over the next 20 years?

Excercises

1. Contact a relative, neighbor, or friend who is 65 years of age or older. Ask if he or she would be willing to sit and discuss with you the senior services and benefits he or she receives. Are they adequate? What would he or she like to see increased or changed?
2. Visit a senior center in your community. What services are available? What activities are available for people who come to the center? How is the senior center funded? Who administers the programs? Are social workers involved? If so, how?
3. Visit an assisted living facility in your community. What does the residence look like?

What services are available? Is the facility what you expected? Explain.
4. Interview someone who was born between 1946 and 1964. What do they think of Social Security? Medicare? Have their opinions of these programs changed over the years? Did they think differently about the programs when they were in their twenties? Thirties? Forties?
5. Visit the AARP home page on the web. What services does the organization offer? Who is the targeted membership? See if you can find the organization's financial information.

References

AARP. (2004a). *Baby Boomers envision retirement II: Key findings*. Washington, DC: Author.

AARP. (2004b). *Perceptions of the EEOC ruling among the 50+ population: Results of a national survey*. Washington, DC: Author.

AARP Public Policy Institute. (2005). *Caregiving in the United States*. FS Number 11. Washington, DC: AARP.

Administration on Aging. (2008a). *Assisted living*. Washington, DC: U.S. Department of Health and Human Services.

Administration on Aging. (2008b). *National Family Caregiver Support Program*. Washington, DC: U.S. Department of Health and Human Services.

Administration on Aging. (2008c). *A statistical profile of older Americans aged 65+*. Washington, DC: U.S. Department of Health and Human Services.

Administration on Aging. (2003). *Older American's Act: A layman's guide*. Washington, DC: U.S. Department of Health and Human Services.

Axinn, J., & Stern, J. (2008). *Social welfare: A history of the American response to need*, 7th ed. Boston: Allyn and Bacon.

Butrica, B. A., Iams, H. M., & Smith, K. E. (2003/2004). The changing impact of Social Security on retirement income in the United States. *Social Security Bulletin* 65(3):1–13.

Clemmit, M. (2006). Caring for the elderly. *CQ Researcher* 16(36)841–864.

Congressional Budget Office. (2003). *Baby boomers' retirement prospects: An overview*. Washington, DC: Congress of the United States.

Congressional Quarterly. (2004, February). Why health care is getting worse. In *Governing: The magazine of states and localities*. Washington, DC: CQ Press.

Copeland, C. (2007). *How are retirees doing financially in retirement?* Issue Brief No. 302. Washington, DC: Employee Benefit Research Institute.

Cranford, J. (2005). Averting the saving crunch. *CQ Weekly* (April 9, 2007):1028–1034.

Crenshaw, A. B. (2004, June 14–20). The benefits bust. *Washington Post National Weekly Edition* 21(34):20–21.

Day, K. (2006). What the Pension Protection Act means. *Washington Post Weekly Edition* 23(45):19.

DeNavas-Walt, C., Proctor, B. D., & Smith, J. C. (2008). Income, poverty, and health insurance coverage in the United States: 2007. *Current Population Reports*, P60-235. Washington, DC: U.S. Census Bureau.

Economic Policy Institute. (2006). *Retirement security*. Washington, DC: Author.

Economic Policy Institute. (2003). *Retirement security*. Washington, DC: Author.

Economic report of the President. (2008). Washington, DC: Office of the President of the United States.

Employee Benefit Research Institute. (2008). *Recent retirees survey: Report of findings*. Washington, DC: Author.

Employee Benefit Research Institute. (2007). *Retirement trends in the United States over the past quarter-century*. Washington, DC: Author.

Employee Benefit Research Institute. (2004). *2004 Retirement Conference Survey Fact Sheet: Saving and retiring in America*. Washington, DC: Author.

Federal Interagency Forum on Aging-Related Statistics. (2008). *Older Americans 2008: Key indicators of well-being*. Washington, DC: U.S. Government Printing Office.

Federal Interagency Forum on Aging-Related Statistics. (2004). *Older Americans 2004: Key indicators of well-being*. Washington, DC: U.S. Government Printing Office.

Finkel, D. (2003). Over 50 and a slave to health insurance. *Washington Post National Weekly Edition* 20(51):19–20.

Freeman, R. B. (2004). What, me vote? In K. M. Neckerman (ed.). *Social inequality*. New York: Russell Sage Foundation.

Greenblatt, A. (2007). Aging baby boomers: The issues. *CQ Researcher* 17(37)867–873.

Hewlett, S. A. (1991). *When the bough breaks: The cost of neglecting our children*. New York: Harper Collins.

Kaiser Family Foundation. (2007). *The burden of out-of-pocket health spending among older versus younger adults*. Menlo Park, CA: Author.

McArdle, M. (2008). No country for young men. *The Atlantic Monthly* 301(1)80–87.

National Center on Elder Abuse. (2006). *Abuse of adults 60+ 2004 survey of adult protective services*. Washington, DC: Author.

National Center on Elder Abuse. (2003). *Laws and legislation: Older Americans Act*. Washington, DC: Author.

National Center on Elder Abuse. (2001). *A response to the abuse of vulnerable adults: The 2000 survey of state Adult Protective Services*. Washington, DC: Author.

Pearlstein, S. (1993). Battling for a slice of the pie: The young challenge their elders. *Washington Post National Weekly Edition* 10(17):22.

Richardson, V. E. (1993). *Retirement counseling*. New York: Springer.

Social Security Administration. (2008). *Annual Statistical Supplement*, 2007. Washington, DC: Author.

Social Security Administration. (2003). *Income of the aged chartbook, 2001*. Washington, DC: Author.

Torres-Gil, F. M. (1992). *The new aging: Politics and change in America*. New York: Auburn House.

U.S. Census Bureau. (2008). *Statistical abstract of the United States 2007*, 127th ed. Washington, DC: U.S. Department of Commerce.

U.S. Census Bureau. (2005). *65+ in the United States: 2005*. Washington, DC: U.S. Department of Commerce.

U.S. Equal Employment Opportunity Commission. (2004). *Age discrimination*. http://www.eeoc.gov/types/age.html.

U.S. General Accounting Office. (2005). *Long-term care financing*. GAO-05-564T. Washington, DC: U.S. Government Printing Office.

U.S. General Accounting Office. (2002). *Long-term care*. GAO-02-1121. Washington, DC: U.S. Government Printing office.

Weller, C. & Wolff, E. N. (2005). *Retirement income: The crucial role of Social Security*. Washington, DC: Economic Policy Institute.

Wright, B. (2005). *Direct care workers in long-term care research report*. Washington, DC: AARP Public Policy Institute.

United States Social Welfare Policies and International Comparisons

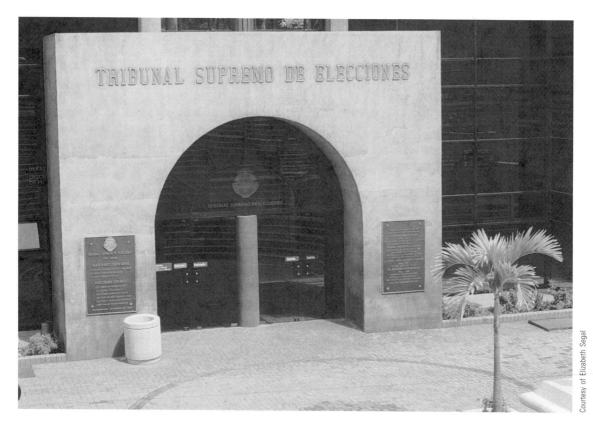

The United States of today has a distinct identity, and its citizens have distinct values and beliefs. From the earliest days of the nation, people from many cultures with varying belief systems have made up the population. Although they have gradually created an American identity, their integration has not always been smooth or sensitive to people's needs and well-being. The integration of foreign people who still come to the United States and the interaction of the United States with other nations continue to be areas of concern. The 21st century is an era of enhanced technology and communication systems that can link distant parts of the world economically and socially. Hokenstad and Midgley (2004) sum it up well:

> The U.S. is a geographically insulated, demographically diverse, and politically power-ful nation. For these and other reasons, its policies reflect a curious blend of interna-tionalism and isolationism. The terror of 9/11 was a wake-up call: No nation can ignore international interdependence in the 21st century. This nation's interaction with both other nations and the international community has a direct impact on the welfare of America's people as well as people everywhere. (p. 2)

Although it is important to understand the workings of the American social welfare system and the dynamics of immigrant integration into American life, it is also helpful to look at the policies of other countries. We need to investigate our role in the international community and economic markets. First, we will review our history as a nation of immigrants from numerous countries, with backgrounds that vary in every way imaginable, including ethnicity, race, religion, class, lan-guage, education, and ability.

FORCED RELOCATION AND ENSLAVEMENT

Some of the earliest settlers of America were subjects of forced relocation and im-portation as slaves. The earliest settlers who came to America by their own choice were primarily Northern Europeans, who believed that the land was theirs to in-habit. There were also many indigenous people living in this country—probably millions of them (Mann, 2002) (see Chapter 2). Through the late 1700s, almost 600,000 Europeans came to America, and 300,000 Africans were brought here as slaves (Daniels, 1990). In spite of their numbers, indigenous people and slaves were not allowed to participate in economic life or political decision making. Euro-pean settlers, although immigrants themselves, controlled all of the political, social, and economic governance and established themselves as the first Americans. They settled primarily along the eastern seaboard. Immigrants who arrived later faced this initial nucleus of settlers and had to integrate their customs and norms into the cultural fabric that had already been established.

Western expansion caused more international conflict. The region that is now the states of Texas, New Mexico, Arizona, and California was explored and claimed by the Spanish government as colonial territory during the 1500s and 1600s. Spain also claimed control of Mexico and much of Latin America. Indigenous people in these regions were ignored. The westward expansion of the United States worried the Spanish colonial rulers, but their biggest worry of the time was unrest among their co-lonists. In 1821, Mexico gained its independence from Spain. At that time, Mexico's struggle with the United States over border policies also began.

For the next 25 years, economic exchange between the northern territory of Mexico and the United States was relatively unregulated, in large part because the area was far from the heart of the U.S. and Mexican governments. U.S. expansion continued and relations flared when the Texas Revolution of 1846 pitted American settlers against Mexican soldiers. This conflict set the stage for the Mexican-American War. In 1848, the Treaty of Guadalupe Hidalgo officially ended the war. In exchange for an end to hostilities, the Mexican government accepted payment and peace and surrendered the present-day states of Texas, New Mexico, Arizona, and California and parts of Colorado, Nevada, and Utah (Massey, Durand, & Malone, 2003). Mexican citizens living in these regions were entitled to all the protections and privileges of American citizens, but, in fact, only a small number of people of Mexican descent were given those privileges (Foley, 2004). Therefore, relations across the 2,000 miles of the border between the United States and Mexico evolved out of conflict, war, and broken promises. In addition, the economies of the two countries have always varied greatly, with Mexico lagging behind the United States. The economic lure of the United States has brought people from all over the world to its shores, including people from Mexico and Latin America.

IMMIGRANTS AND REFUGEES

The United States is a nation of immigrants and refugees, except for its indigenous peoples, who today make up less than one percent of the population. **Immigrants** are people who choose to relocate and emigrate to a new country. **Refugees** are people who leave their countries of origin to escape political turmoil or persecution.

The first settlers who made their own choice to live in America came as immigrants. Although all new arrivals added to the culture, the biggest influx came during the 1900s. The immigration numbers of the past century are listed in Box 13.1. From the day when the first colonial settlers arrived until 1965, most voluntary immigration was from Europe. Leaving one's home and adjusting to a new land is difficult for all immigrants. However, the immigrant experience was not the same for all groups. Those who came from Northern and Western European countries, such as England and France, were welcomed to the United States, whereas other immigrants, such as those from Ireland and Italy, were not. In part, this was due to economics and religion. People already established in this country were afraid that poor Irish and Italian immigrants would work for lower wages and take their jobs, and bring Catholicism to the predominantly Protestant established population. Today, differences between people of English, Irish, and Italian descent are hardly noticed, but animosity between established residents and new arrivals is still very much a reality.

Immigrants from Asia, Southern and Eastern Europe, the Pacific Islands, and Africa often experienced racism and class bias. Starting in the early 1900s, laws were established to restrict immigration and establish quotas. Immigration quotas were based on the percentage of each ethnic group already living in the United States, so that ethnic composition would not be altered by the influx of immigrants. The **Immigration and Nationality Act of 1965 (INA)** (P.L. 89-236) replaced the quota system with broader regulations and led to increased immigration from Latin America, Asia, and Eastern and Southern Europe. The INA and its amendments account for

| BOX 13.1 | MORE ABOUT IMMIGRATION FROM **1901** TO **2007** |

Years	Number of People Obtaining Legal Permanent Resident Status to the United States in Millions
1901 to 1910	8.8
1911 to 1920	5.7
1921 to 1930	4.1
1931 to 1940	0.5
1941 to 1950	1.0
1951 to 1960	2.5
1961 to 1970	3.3
1971 to 1980	4.4
1981 to 1990	7.3
1991 to 2000	9.1
2001 to 2007	7.2

Source: U.S. Department of Homeland Security, 2007; 2008

most of the immigration laws today. **Legal permanent residents (LPR)**, commonly referred to as "green card" recipients (based on the early permit card that was green), are defined as people who have been granted permanent residence in the United States. People who are legal permanent residents may live and work anywhere in the United States, own property, join some branches of the Armed Forces, and apply to become U.S. citizens. The concept of *preference* is used to designate categories for LPR status. Preference is given under immigration law to foreign nationals who have a close family relationship with a U.S. citizen, who possess needed job skills, who are from countries with low levels of prior immigration, or who are refugees or seeking asylum (terms that are explained in the next section). The Immigration Act of 1990 set an annual limit of 416,000 to 675,000 immigrants for preference priority (U.S. Department of Homeland Security, 2008).

One of the concerns following 9/11 was immigration. Numerous proposals were introduced into Congress to address what many perceived as lax investigations into the backgrounds of people coming to this country. The Department of Homeland Security created measures to improve background checks and scrutinize visa applications more closely. The initial fallout from international terrorism was particular scrutiny of people from Middle Eastern countries and Muslim backgrounds. The "**Patriot Act**," passed in 2001, allows the long-term detention of noncitizens viewed to be terrorist threats. The office of the attorney general decides who should be detained; it has tremendous leeway in implementing the policy and determining what a terrorist threat may be (Lee, 2004).

In recent years, concern over immigration has focused on people who are in the United States illegally. In 2006 it was estimated that there were 11.5 to 12 million un-authorized people living in the United States, of whom more than half (56 percent) were thought to be from Mexico and 22 percent from the rest of Latin America (Passel, 2006). The most prevalent occurrence of undocumented people has been found in the states that border Mexico, as this has been the transit route for migrants from Mexico and the rest of Latin America. However, people who lack legal documentation can be found living throughout the United States.

Although immigration is not new for this country, in recent years attention has focused on the "danger" that is posed by the surge in immigrants who either overstay their visas or permits to visit or sneak over the border. Since 2005, the Department of Homeland Security (DHS) has increased efforts to detain undocumented immigrants and remove them from the United States. (National Immigration Law Center, 2007). These efforts have been accompanied by increasing state and local enforcement of immigration law. Although the initial impetus was in response to the illegal entry of the terrorists from the 9/11 attacks on the World Trade Center, it has become focused primarily on undocumented Latino immigrants. Enforcement of immigration laws was minimal prior to 2000. From 1996 to 2000, less than 12,000 people had been deported and barred from re-entry; in 2006 alone, more than 13,000 people were barred from re-entering the United States for ten years (Gonzalez, 2008). The difference is not in the actual laws on the books, which have not been changed, but on the enforcement of those laws.

Tighter restrictions on immigration have not deterred people from wanting to come to the United States, although civil liberty advocates worry that tighter restrictions will erode rights and protections for international visitors and immigrants. Immigration detainees are held under civil law, not criminal law. As such, they are legally entitled to better living conditions than convicted prisoners or pre-trial detainees (American Civil Liberties Union, 2007). Civil law covers issues such as property rights, child custody, divorce, contracts and agreements, and are not considered crimes. Therefore, under law, undocumented people are to be tried for a breach of contract, not for committing a crime. However, the reality of detaining thousands of undocumented people in recent years has led to accusation of abuses of their rights.

The DHS detainee population exceeds 261,000 annually (Nugent, 2007). The detention is civil and not punitive, yet the vast majority is held in actual prisons housed with criminal convicts. Other than entering or staying in the country illegally, the detainees have not committed any other crime. However, if proof can be found that a person has been using an unauthorized social security number, then the issue becomes a form of identity theft, which can be a criminal offense. The numbers of undocumented people in prisons and requiring legal authorities' attention has grown dramatically, particularly in the border states of California, Arizona, and Texas. The cost for the increase in incarceration is growing, and the extra efforts at border control are costly.

One of the rationales for this increase is to combat crime. This is a controversial issue. Do immigrants, particularly undocumented immigrants, cause more crime? Although there may be a public perception as such, studies indicate that may not be true. Research indicates that the opposite may be the case—crime decreases with growth in immigrant populations (Press, 2006). Immigrant communities are often tight-knit and there is an informal system of social control.

Most immigrants come to this country for economic opportunity. To find employment, immigrants who do not speak English and are uneducated will take low-paying jobs. This contributes to the perception that immigrants keep wages low. In most cases, however, such jobs are the only ones available, and because of necessity, immigrants take those jobs without demanding higher wages. This pattern dates back to the immigrants of the 1800s. Over time, as ethnic groups became acclimated and new generations were born in this country, the economic status of earlier immigrant groups improved. This trend lends credence to the belief of new immigrants that the United States is the land of economic opportunity. In fact, research suggests that today immigrants assimilate faster into American culture than previous generations (Aizenman, 2008). Where people may be held back is in terms of the advances that legal status confers. For example, public education is a right for all children, including unauthorized children. However, children who came to this country at a young age and may have excelled in school will not have the higher education or employment opportunities that similarly educated and accomplished children with citizenship have. Federal law prohibits the hiring of workers who are in the country illegally, therefore unauthorized students are ineligible for federal financial aid in the form of work-study. Federal legislation also discourages states from granting educational benefits such as qualifying for in-state tuition rates (Congressional Research Service, 2008). In some states, such as Arizona, state laws have been passed to explicitly bar undocumented students from qualifying for in-state tuition, regardless of how long they have actually lived in the state.

This dilemma has given rise to bills that have been introduced to several Congresses to allow unauthorized students to be eligible for LPR status. These bills have been referred to as the DREAM Act (Development, Relief and Education for Alien Minors Act). There have been numerous variations of the DREAM Act, but the key provisions of the proposed bills include ways for young people who have been living in this country for at least five years, came here at an age younger than 16, have graduated high school, and have been admitted to college to have their immigration status adjusted to legal permanent resident status. Although debated and voted down as of the 110th Congress, immigration advocates are hopeful that some form of the DREAM Act will be passed with a new Congress and President.

The issue of immigration will not disappear. By 2007, the immigrant population in the United States had reached 38 million, 12 percent of the total population, and it is estimated one third are in the country illegally (Camarota, 2007). In 20 percent of the homes in this country, another language besides English is spoken (U.S. Census Bureau, 2007). The issue of immigration is complicated and involves larger economic and international concerns.

Refugee and asylum-seeking status differ from the immigration discussion. In the United States, refugee status is a legal classification. By law, **refugees** are people fleeing persecution in countries officially recognized by the U.S. government as oppressive of certain groups of people. For example, people leaving Cuba are considered refugees. Thousands of Southeast Asian people who fled Vietnam after the end of the Vietnam War were also considered refugees. Passage of the **Refugee Act of 1980** (P.L. 96-212) gave legal status to refugees and provided additional social services for the resettlement of refugees. On the other hand, people coming from Mexico are not considered refugees and, hence, are not entitled to special services and assistance in resettlement.

GLOBALIZATION

As the discussion on immigration makes clear, the United States is intimately connected socially and economically with many other countries of the world. The United States is a global economy. Its citizens buy products from dozens of other countries and sell products in nations all over the world. If you travel to any major country in the world, you are likely to see American restaurants and products in the heart of its largest cities. Many of us work for companies that operate internationally, some of which are owned by people outside of the United States. This phenomenon points to the globalization of our economy and social order. **Globalization** refers to the interconnection of the world's economies.

One of the most publicized economic policies linking the United States to other nation's economies is the **North American Free Trade Agreement (NAFTA) of 1993.** This controversial piece of legislation cut tariffs or taxes between Mexico, the United States, and Canada. The purpose of this agreement was to stimulate economic activity across borders, relieving companies of tax burdens by producing and selling goods within all the countries of North America. Critics worried that cheaper labor costs would encourage companies to close their factories and eliminate jobs in the United States and move to other countries, particularly Mexico. Supporters argued that opening trade would bring more business to each country and thereby improve the economy in all three nations.

Tracing economic consequences directly to NAFTA has been difficult, as the economies of Canada, Mexico, and the United States are so intertwined. It is likely that there have been benefits, such as cheaper and more plentiful products for consumers, and deficits, such as companies leaving the Unites States to set up production in Mexico, where labor is less costly. What may be the outcome is that globalization has done both—raise our national income, and at the same time reduce the incomes of many workers (Bivens, 2007). In simple terms, global economics means that producers of goods can consider all countries as possible production sites. Because labor is the most expensive part of manufacturing, globalization allows American companies to shop around for international sites where labor will be significantly cheaper than in the United States. Moving production elsewhere displaces jobs here, but allows developing countries and workers to earn more income through hosting the production. This creates growing demand abroad for American products. Those products that are more likely to only be made in America are based in more professionalized arenas, such as technology. So as developing countries grow, they will purchase American technology or invest in American financial markets. The overall net effect is to create greater national income from globalization. However, the increase in resources tends to be concentrated in areas with less employment from manufacturing, which was displaced. The end result is more overall national wealth but a loss of lower wage jobs.

The globalization of our economy means that policy makers cannot ignore international events or make policies in the United States in a vacuum. Understanding the impact of globalization requires analyses on many levels. With the help of technology, borders and geographic distance become less limiting. For example, there is one cell phone for every two people in the world. From 1982 to 2008, the world went from zero to 3.3 billion active cell phones and is likely to add another

2 billion in the next five years (Garreau, 2008). The cell phone has connected re-mote areas that still lack indoor plumbing or running water to the industrial and technological world. In underdeveloped areas where landlines have been absent, the ownership of cell phones has grown, and with it people have gained a mobile portal to the worldwide web. Globalization of our economy and the international link between the United States and countries all over the world is here to stay.

BORDER POLICIES BETWEEN MEXICO AND THE UNITED STATES

As discussed previously, the issue of immigration from Latin America through the shared border with Mexico has been an international concern. A history of war and broken promises between the border states and Mexico has set the stage for a relationship of conflict. NAFTA was viewed as a way to close the economic gap and improve relations across the border. As had been promised with NAFTA, the integration of economies and trade across the U.S.–Mexican border has been rapid. Yet the United States has been reluctant to integrate in one area, the labor market.

> Even as the United States has committed itself to integrating most markets in
> North America, however, it has paradoxically sought to prevent integration of one
> particular market: that for labor. Indeed, since 1986 the United States has embarked on
> a determined effort to restrict Mexican immigration and tighten border enforcement.
> U.S. policy toward Mexico is inherently self-contradictory, simultaneously promoting
> integration while insisting on separation. (Massey, Durand, & Malone, 2003, p. 83)

As discussed in relation to overall immigration, the growing numbers of **undocu-mented workers**, people who are employed but are living illegally in the United States, is a major social welfare issue. Box 13.2 describes the terms used to describe people who are not authorized to legally live in the United States. There are two conflicting sides to the issue of undocumented immigrants. The first concern is that people come illegally without resources or employment and, once here, use services and need pub-lic support. On the other hand, many undocumented people take jobs that American citizens are not filling, and employers depend on them. Examples of such jobs include migrant farm work, meat-packing and textile factory jobs, and landscape and domes-tic work. Recognition of the struggle between preventing illegal entry and needing workers to fill low-level jobs has been recognized in policy-making circles as high as

| BOX 13.2 | CONSIDER THIS . . . |

An **undocumented immigrant** is a person without proper documents proving that he or she has legally entered the United States. A term often used to refer to an undocumented person is *illegal alien*. This term is often considered offensive, as an alien is an abnormal, hostile being who comes from another world. Some advocates prefer the term *unauthorized*, suggesting that it is just a matter of time before legal recognition can be secured. When one is working with immi-grant groups, one should be culturally sensitive to the most preferable term and be aware that it can be perceived as offensive to refer to people as illegal aliens rather than undocumented or unauthorized immigrants.

the President. In 2004, President George W. Bush proposed reform of U.S. immigration laws to create a temporary worker program "to match willing foreign workers with willing U.S. employers when no Americans can be found to fill the jobs" (National Conference of State Legislatures, 2004, p. 1).

Congress has introduced similar proposals. These policy makers have acknowledged that people coming from other countries to make a living are important to the success of our economy, as was true for so many of our ancestors who came to this country during the 1800s and 1900s. However, by the close of President Bush's tenure as president, Congress had not passed any immigrant reform legislation. Enforcing the current law became one way to focus on the issue. In May of 2008, the federal government, under the guidance of the Bush administration, conducted the largest crackdown on illegal hiring. Three hundred and eighty nine immigrants were arrested at a meatpacking plant in Postville, Iowa, in May of 2008. Authorities alleged that three fourths of the almost 1,000 employees had used false or suspect Social Security numbers (Hsu, 2008). However, the economics of illegal immigration are strong. As one local merchant summed up the situation, "People who can afford to eat meat only once or twice a week in Guatemala, while earning $4 a day, can earn $60 a day in Iowa, enough to eat beef or chicken three times a day" (Hsu, 2008, p. 33), the economics of immigration will keep people crossing the borders and staying beyond the limits of their visas.

Therefore, in addition to the crackdown on finding people who are illegally here, there has been a growing effort at worksite enforcement. This approach focuses less on the individual immigrant and more on the employers. Even though for 20 years it has been against the law for an employer to knowingly hire or continue to employ a person who is illegally living in the United States, until recently little has been done to enforce the law. Now, the federal government and many state governments have increased scrutiny on employers.

In June of 2008, President Bush, failing to get Congress to agree to any new immigration legislation, passed an Executive Order that further enforced the workplace compliance requirements of the Immigration and Nationality Act. An Executive Order can only be used to enhance existing laws, not create new ones. Therefore, this Executive Order was created to further the economy and efficiency of government procurement contracts by ensuring compliance with the existing prohibitions against hiring undocumented workers. Contractors with the federal government were to electronically verify employment eligibility of all workers performing work within the United States on the federal contract as well as those who are hired during the contract term starting in January of 2009 (Office of the President, 2008). The system to be used is called E-Verify, and it is jointly operated by the U.S. Citizenship and Immigration Services and the Social Security Administration. Enforcement of this new provision places the responsibility on the employer for ensuring that undocumented workers are not hired. The risk of not doing so is loss of the federal contract and penalties for noncompliance with the Immigration and Nationality Act. Implementation of the Executive Order was delayed for 6 months with the change in presidents from Bush to Obama. The new administration explained that the time lag would allow for examination of the policy and assessment of the effectiveness of the E-Verify system.

It is too soon to tell what the impact of this new policy will be if fully implemented. If businesses that have previously relied on undocumented workers cannot find replacements for them, it is likely that business leaders will push harder for some kind of temporary worker program. Immigration advocates will continue to push for ways that undocumented people can work and attend school legally and earn the opportunity to follow a path toward citizenship should they choose to. And those who oppose increases in immigration will oppose temporary worker programs and policies such as the DREAM Act. The conflict is likely to be at the forefront of federal politics in the years to come.

HOW DOES THE UNITED STATES COMPARE WITH OTHER NATIONS?

Countries have different ways of implementing social welfare, making comparisons between them difficult. One way to view international differences is to compare the proportion of the gross domestic product (GDP) spent on social welfare. Box 13.3 provides an historical view. In almost all the nations listed, the percentage of the GDP committed to social welfare spending increased from 1970 to 1990.

Box 13.4 shows how the United States compares with 25 other industrialized nations. The United States is the wealthiest nation, topping the list in gross domestic product and health technology, but it ranks 14th in efforts to raise children out of poverty, 18th in the rate of children living in poverty, and 23rd in infant mortality (Children's Defense Fund, 2004). These statistics suggest that compared with other industrialized nations, we are a nation of resources but not a nation of social services aimed at preventing poverty and poor health.

BOX 13.3 | **MORE ABOUT SPENDING ON SOCIAL WELFARE**

Percentage of gross domestic product spent on social welfare

Country	1990	1970
Hong Kong	8	5.3
New Zealand	8.3	4.9
Russia	13.4	23.2
Japan	13.7	5.8
Australia	18	11
United States	18.5	14.3
Canada	24.7	18.8
Italy	27	21.3
Germany	29	26
South Africa	31	n/a
Sweden	36	20

Source: Alcock, 2001, p. 20

BOX 13.4 | CONSIDER THIS . . .

Among 25 industrialized nations, the United States ranks:

First in Gross Domestic Product

First in military technology

First in the number of millionaires and billionaires

First in health technology

First in defense spending

Eighteenth in the proportion of children living in poverty

Fourteenth in efforts to lift children out of poverty

Thirteenth in the gap between rich and poor children

Twenty-third in infant mortality

Last in protecting children against gun violence

Source: Children's Defense Fund, 2004

SOCIAL WELFARE POLICIES SUPPORTING WORK

The right to work is well protected in the United States, particularly for different racial and ethnic groups, genders, ages, and disabilities. As discussed previously, the **Age Discrimination in Employment Act of 1967** prevents age discrimination, the equal employment sections of the **Civil Rights Act** prevent race and gender discrimination, and the **Americans with Disabilities Act of 1990** protects the rights of people with disabilities in employment. These are important public policies that make work safe and accessible for most Americans. Where the United States lags behind other nations is in its support of working conditions, particularly for those who need to care for children and other family members. The only U.S. legislation that provides support is the **Family and Medical Leave Act of 1993**. As discussed in Chapter 10, this legislation provides up to 12 weeks of unpaid leave for the birth or adoption of a child, or care of an ill family member, and a job (the previous position or an equivalent one) upon return. In contrast, 163 other countries provide guaranteed paid leave for women in connection with childbirth; 45 countries ensure that fathers have a right to paid paternity leave; 37 countries guarantee paid leave for major family events; and 96 countries mandate paid leave by employers, which the U.S. does not require (Heymann et al., 2004).

SOCIAL WELFARE AND HEALTH

Part of a nation's social well-being is the health of its people. Typically, nations with more resources have better health care and, consequently, people live healthier and longer lives. As discussed in Chapter 11, the United States has an extensive system of health care services but, at the same time, is faced with numerous health problems. Other nations are faced with the same dilemma.

Health Care Spending   One way to evaluate health in various nations is to compare how much a nation spends on health care with the outcome measures of healthy living. Box 13.5 provides this comparison for a number of large countries.

BOX 13.5	**MORE ABOUT HEALTH EXPENDITURES AND HEALTH CONDITIONS**

	2004 Expenditures % of GDP	1990 Expenditures % of GDP	Life Expectancy		Infant Mortality Rate
			Fem	Male	
United Kingdom	8.3	6.0	n/a	n/a	5.1
Japan	8.0	5.9	85.6	78.6	2.8
New Zealand	8.4	6.9	n/a	n/a	n/a
Italy	8.4	8.0	n/a	n/a	5.8
Sweden	9.1	8.2	82.7	78.4	n/a
Australia	9.2	7.8	83.0	78.1	4.6
France	10.5	8.6	83.8	76.7	3.4
Germany	10.9	8.5	81.4	75.7	4.1
United States	15.3	13.0	80.4	75.2	6.4

Source: U.S. Census Bureau, 2007

The United States spends the largest portion on health care but ranks below most other industrialized nations in life expectancy and infant mortality, two commonly cited indicators of good health. Why is this so? There are many theories. The high amount spent may have to do with the very expensive technology used; lower life expectancy with higher rates of violent death; and higher infant mortality with the imbalanced distribution of health care, which leaves poor families with inferior care. Although it is difficult to pinpoint reasons for this disparity, it is clear that in spite of spending an enormous amount of money on health care, the United States has poorer health outcomes than other comparable nations.

As discussed in Chapter 11, the United States has chosen a system of health care based in the private sector through employment. It is interesting to consider how differently other nations approach the social need for health care. Canada is geographically, and in many ways demographically, similar to the United States. Yet the health care system differs greatly. Canada has a national system of health care. People may go to public or private practitioners of medicine; all the billing for services is submitted directly to the provincial or territorial health insurance plan, which is government operated and financed. The cost for these services was about $4,500 per person, and health expenditures accounted for 9.8 percent of the gross domestic product. The comparable expenses in the United States were $7,500 per person, accounting for 15.3 percent of the gross domestic product. Do greater expenditures result in better health? Possibly as a result of national health care, Canada has better health outcomes. Two leading indicators of health demonstrate that Canada does better than the United States. Life expectancy in Canada is 80.2 years compared with 77.8 years in the United States, and the infant mortality rate in Canada is 5.3 per 1,000 live births compared with 6.8 per 1,000 live births in the United States (Landers, 2007). The question is, why does the United States resist having a national health insurance program? As stated in Chapter 11, the private health care sector is well established and most of it is profit based. Therefore, it has not favored a national health insurance system.

The fear of a national health insurance system, sometimes referred to as "socialized medicine," is that consumers will lack choices, government will control everything, and worse health care will result. Although the example of Canada suggests this fear is unwarranted, we do not have to look at other countries to the success of public health insurance. Consider the Medicare program—once fiercely opposed, it has become a successful national health care program. Since legislated cost controls in the 1980s, Medicare expenditures have grown at a slower rate than spending on private insurance, with higher consumer satisfaction than privately insured patients report (Hacker, 2008). Even corporations are beginning to support some form of national health insurance. The realization that the best way to cover everyone, while still controlling costs, rests with the federal government is gaining ground. With a new president and Congress, it is likely that the issue of national health insurance will be addressed.

HIV/AIDS Illnesses and diseases know no borders. The spread of HIV/AIDS worldwide has demonstrated how the interconnectedness of nations can create global health problems. Almost 40 million people carry the virus, with the highest rates in sub-Saharan Africa and increased spread in Asia and Eastern Europe. Over four million people were infected in 2006, the majority in sub-Saharan Africa (U.S. Census Bureau, 2007). Although preventive efforts have been instituted through international organizations, the spread has not abated. The HIV/AIDS pandemic is the leading cause of adult death in many countries. This high rate leaves children orphaned, and they are often infected with the virus themselves. Nations face a shrinking working population, escalating health costs, impoverished families, and growing numbers of children that must be raised by the state. In countries already stressed economically, the toll of HIV/AIDS is mounting, threatening the stability and health of entire nations. One in every four new infections is occurring in Asia, and sub-Saharan Africa already has 25 million people who are infected (U.S. Census Bureau, 2007). As discussed in Chapter 11, survival rates have improved significantly in the United States. However, poor regions rarely have antiviral drugs that can keep people alive. The future is bleak for people in these regions and, consequently, for their governments.

SOCIAL SECURITY PROGRAMS

Social security programs in most countries include old-age, disability, and death coverage, sickness and maternity care, work injury coverage, unemployment compensation, and family allowances. The United States has institutionalized national services in three of these categories, old-age, disability, and death coverage; work injury coverage; and unemployment compensation. There are no national sickness and maternity benefits and there is no standardized family or child allowance program. All five forms of social security are available in many countries today, although the degree of institutionalization and coverage vary.

Most industrialized countries provide a family allowance, or economic support for families with children, regardless of their economic situation. The United States has never had a universal family allowance but does have policies that support children. The dependent credit for income taxes provides a deduction for each dependent child. Although this tax policy recognizes the economic needs of families raising children, it is not universal, as a family allowance would be. Only people who earn enough to pay taxes and file returns are eligible for the deduction. The other income support programs for children are means tested and not universal.

Social Security is the only U.S. program that is provided universally and is not based on economic need. Compared with other developed nations, we have the lowest number of universal social services and rely more heavily on the private family and marketplace for programs such as maternity care and health coverage. The United States is characterized by the expectation that public welfare should be available only for the poor and needy. The entrepreneurial nature of this country has opposed the development of a strong, centralized social welfare state (Alcock, 2001).

POVERTY

Worldwide poverty, even with different standards of living, is staggering. The number of people living on less than one dollar per day was 980 million in 2004, down from 1.25 billion in 1990. The proportion of people living in extreme poverty worldwide fell from nearly one third in 1990 to less than one fifth in 2004 (United Nations, 2007). Although this overall decrease is encouraging, it is not evenly distributed. In sub-Saharan Africa, 41 percent of the population lived in extreme poverty in 2004. Using a slightly higher measure reveals how extensive poverty is—2.5 billion people live on less than $2 a day, more than 40 percent of the world's population (World Bank, 2008). The impacts of such extreme and widespread poverty are many. Poverty has been linked to social unrest and political upheaval, poor health and spread of communicable diseases such as HIV/AIDS, and national growth and progress.

Poverty exists in the United States, in spite of the nation's wealth and development (see Chapter 8). Worldwide poverty reflects deeper and more debilitating economic conditions, as it is found in countries far poorer than the United States. Half the population in the developing world lack basic sanitation (United Nations, 2007). Hunger and malnourishment are extensive. In industrialized nations, people spend about 10 to 20 percent of their income on food, but in developing countries, the cost to consumers is 60 to 80 percent (Faiola, 2008). For the very poor of the world, food is their most significant expense, and survival becomes a daily struggle of acquiring food. The global interconnectedness of our food supply means that we in the United States cannot ignore the production of food, nor the health and well-being of people in other nations.

Some people argue that standards are different in different countries, and that a dollar in the United States has a different value than a dollar in a developing country. Although this is true, the needs for nourishment, safe drinking water, and sanitation are the same everywhere. Worldwide poverty keeps these basic needs from being fulfilled and has led to high levels of infant mortality, increased spread of illnesses, low worker productivity, and poor national economic development. These deficits affect the world because war and conflict arise out of poverty and struggles for survival. Also, as part of a global economy, we in the United States benefit from higher international productivity and safety. Policies addressing world-wide poverty include increasing aid from wealthier nations as well as supporting programs for self-sustenance for developing nations.

CLIMATE AND NATURAL DISASTERS

Weather and climate conditions also know no boundaries. Intense debate surrounds the issue of changing global weather conditions. There is general agreement that the primary methods used for economic development are carbon-intensive. A recent report examining human development concluded that the use of carbon-based fuels to spur economic prosperity is ecologically unsustainable (United Nations Development Programme, 2007). Five areas of concern due to climate change are cited:

1. Adverse climate conditions affect rainfall and temperature and will decrease agriculture production and food security;
2. Changed glacial melt, drought, and flooding will increase water insecurity;
3. Global temperature increases lead to rising sea levels, which would displace millions of people;
4. Transformation of ecosystems and biodiversity will lead to species extinction;
5. More extreme summer and winter conditions will strain public health resources and lead to spread of major diseases.

Each of these areas may initially be confined to geographic regions, but the consequences will spread worldwide. Concern regarding climate change and the potential for increasing incidents of natural disasters such as drought and flooding are increasingly important to global well-being.

Since 1970, more than 7,000 major disasters have been recorded worldwide, with $2 trillion in damages and 2.5 million lives lost; the likelihood of a natural disaster is four times greater today than in 1970 and the impact is also much greater, displacing more people and costing seven times more. Although the exact role of climate change is difficult to assess, "the scientific community has no doubt that the link does exist" (United Nations, 2008, p. 13).

Policies on agriculture and energy have historically been specific country focused. Most planning in the United States has been done in the context of our nation, with recent trade policies reflecting our connection with our neighbors to the north and south. However, future policies on agriculture and energy, as well as ecology, will need to be developed in the global context. The reality of today is that our food and energy supplies, weather, and health are all without boundaries. The decisions of one country affect others. For example, the lack of oversight on food production in one country can result in tainted food being imported into another. The change in global climate can have adverse affects on suppliers of food, making worldwide poverty more extensive. Worldwide poverty can create instability and lead to civil wars and impact productivity. Examples of productivity impact include the closing down of oil fields in producing countries due to civil unrest. The unexpected rapid increase in global food costs in 2008 led to riots in more than a dozen countries with at least 30 more nations at risk, and potentially 100 million more people pushed into poverty. The federal government recognized the potential threat to U.S.

national security and in response released $200 million in emergency wheat stores for developing countries (Eggen, 2008). The United States historically has been involved in international policy-making, including donations of food aid and response to natural disasters. Today that role needs to be reexamined and further developed, particularly in the arenas of agriculture, climate, and energy, and in relation to national security.

INTERNATIONAL RELATIONS

The United States has been a large international power for decades and has received both positive and negative responses from other nations. Recent events have tarnished that image and led to stronger anti-American sentiments around the world. Immediately following the attack on September 11, 2001, international attitudes toward the United States were sympathetic and concerned about the well-being of American citizens. However, the invasion of Iraq changed those views (see Box 13.6). Negative feelings toward the United States escalated following the Iraq war. A nine-country survey found that a year after the war in Iraq:

> Discontent with America and its policies has intensified rather than diminished. Opinion of the United States in France and Germany is at least as negative now as at the war's conclusion, and British views are decidedly more critical. Perceptions of American unilateralism remain widespread in European and Muslim nations, and the war in

---

BOX 13.6 | **CONFLICTING PERSPECTIVES**

Should we have gone to war in Iraq?

The attack of September 11, 2001, evoked strong emotions and forced all Americans to think about international concerns. The war in Iraq followed in the wake of the anger, fear, and frustration with terrorism. Small but vocal groups opposed the war, although a majority of Americans supported the war and President Bush's actions in entering the war. The international perception has been different. Anti-American sentiment reflects the international perception that the United States is trying to control oil supplies in the Middle East and dominate the world (Pew Research Center, 2004). The conflict centers on whether the U.S. government engaged in the war to protect the safety of its citizens or for the reasons the international community is proclaiming. Unfortunately, recent evidence suggests that the latter may be the case. "The U.S. occupation of Iraq is a debacle not because the government did no planning but because a vast amount of expert planning was willfully ignored by the people in charge" (Fallows, 2004, p. 53). Weapons of mass destruction, which were touted as the reason for instigating the war, were never found, and predictions of a quick entry and exit strategy were not fulfilled. The war in Iraq has created an international controversy that may haunt the United States for years to come: "When the decisions of the past eighteen months [since the war] are assessed and judged, the Administration will be found wanting for its carelessness. Because of warnings it chose to ignore, it squandered American prestige, fortune, and lives" (p. 74). From 2002 through 2007, Congress appropriated $602 billion for military operations in Iraq and Afghanistan. Depending on the level of engagement over the next ten years, the cost would include an additional $570 billion to $1.1 trillion (Congressional Budget Office, 2007).

Iraq has undermined America's credibility abroad. Doubts about the motives behind the U.S.-led war on terrorism abound, and a growing percentage of Europeans want foreign policy and security arrangements independent from the United States. (Pew Research Center, 2004, p. 1).

International views of the United States have not changed positively in recent years, and in fact have declined in many countries. From 2002 to 2008, the portion of people with a favorable opinion of the United States dropped appreciably: from 75 to 53 percent in Great Britain, 62 to 42 percent in France, 60 to 31 percent in Germany, 61 to 46 percent in Russia, 61 to 37 percent in Indonesia, 30 to 12 percent in Turkey, 64 to 47 percent in Mexico, and 72 to 50 percent in Japan (Pew Global Attitudes Project, 2008).

The image of the United States internationally has faded considerably since 2001. Although the United States is a large and powerful nation, it is also a member of the international community. As discussed previously, we depend on the global economy to help balance our economy. Operating without international cooperation can lead to isolation, which in turn can damage our standing and, potentially, our economic well-being.

CONFLICTING VALUES AND BELIEFS

The most pressing issue involving beliefs is whether to aid people we know or whether to aid strangers. Asking the American people to support populations in countries far away that most have never visited and are not likely to visit is a difficult proposition. We are inclined to feel territorial about our efforts, because they reflect the American values of individualism and independence. Once again, the effort to broaden social welfare policy depends on the willingness of people to shift their values from individualistic to collective efforts. That is a difficult change, and it is more so when those in need of assistance do not speak our language, have different religions, and live very far away.

Distance and "foreignness" can provoke feelings of sympathy, but feelings of empathy are more difficult to engender. Empathy, or understanding what a person is going through and realizing that under different circumstances, you could be going through the same thing, is difficult for Americans who have not been exposed to other nations and cultures. Therefore, international social welfare assistance typically is based on sympathy, which is feeling bad for someone else's plight but not personally connected to it. Sympathy is related to the reluctance to help strangers, as discussed earlier. Taken together, these conflicting beliefs create a great deal of tension around social aid and support of other nations.

FINAL THOUGHTS

The life of a typical American today is filled with international connections. Automobiles, clothing, food items, electronic devices, and, in fact, most everyday products are produced partly or totally in other countries (see Box 13.7). Through the wizardry of electronics, a phone call for information about a refrigerator, car, or computer you bought may be answered by someone overseas, and you do not

BOX 13.7	CONSIDER THIS . . .

Familiar products in the United States are international:

Brand	Owned by a company in
Taster's Choice coffee	Switzerland
Holiday Inn	United Kingdom
Mellon Bank	Scotland
Random House	Germany
Columbia Pictures	Japan
Chicago Sun Times	United Kingdom
Jeep	Germany
7-Up	United Kingdom
Baby Ruth candy	Switzerland
Universal Studios	France

Source: Reid, 2002

even know it. We are a global economy, and American influence is felt in most major cities of the world. Our role as the wealthiest and most powerful nation in the world is significant. We can dictate public policies on trade and commerce and even social welfare. The decisions U.S. citizens make, or do not make, can have an impact on future generations and their relationships across the world.

Key Terms

immigrants

refugees

Immigration and
Nationality Act
of 1965 (INA)

Legal permanent
residents (LPR)

Patriot Act

globalization

North American Free
Trade Agreement
(NAFTA)

undocumented workers

Questions for Discussion

1. What is the difference between a person who is an immigrant, a person who is a refugee, and an undocumented person?
2. What services and programs do you think we should provide for immigrants? Refugees? Undocumented people?
3. How does the history of slavery and relocation in this country impact the

acceptance and integration of racial and ethnic groups?
4. Are there policies or programs in other countries that you think would be beneficial to adopt here? Explain.
5. What do you think about climate change? Is it an issue important to the United States? Why?

Excercises

1. Locate a neighborhood that has a large population of international residents. Visit the shops and restaurants of the neighborhood. What is the area like? Is it similar or different than the neighborhood in which you live? How so?

2. Identify a social service agency that serves immigrants and refugees. What services do they offer? What languages are spoken? What cultures are represented?

3. Spend a week reviewing a major daily newspaper, looking for articles on international social welfare policy issues. What did you find? How are these issues the same or different than those in the United States?

4. Trace your family history. When did your family first arrive to the United States? From what country did your ancestors originate? How did they come to this country? Why?

5. View the movie *An Inconvenient Truth*. What do you think? Does it seem well-researched and true, or sensationalized and politically motivated? Do some research on other views of the movie and see how those assessments compare with your own.

References

Aizenman, N. C. (2008, May 19–25). Newcomers to the U.S. assimilate rapidly. *Washington Post National Weekly Edition 25*(31):33–34.

Alcock, P. (2001). The comparative context. In P. Alcock & G. Craig (eds.). *International social policy*, pp.1–25. Great Britain: Palgrave Press.

American Civil Liberties Union. (2007, January 24). *ACLU sues immigration officials and for-profit corrections corporation over dangerous and inhumane housing of detainees*. New York: Author.

Bivens, L. J. (2007). *Globalization and American wages: Today and tomorrow*. Washington, DC: Economic Policy Institute.

Camarota, S. A. (2007). *Immigrants in the United States, 2007: A profile of America's foreign-born population*. Washington, DC: Center for Immigration Studies.

Children's Defense Fund. (2004). *The state of America's children 2004*. Washington, DC: Author.

Congressional Budget Office. (2007). Estimated costs of U.S. operations in Iraq and Afghanistan and of other activities related to the war on terrorism. CBO Testimony before the Committee on the Budget U.S. House of Representatives. Washington, DC: Author.

Congressional Research Service. (2008). *Immigration legislation and issues in the 110th Congress*. RL34204. Washington, DC: U.S. Congress.

Daniels, R. (1990). *Coming to America: A history of immigration and ethnicity in American life*. Princeton, NJ: Harper Perennial.

Eggen, D. (2008, May 5–11). Caught off guard, the U.S. scrambles to respond. *Washington Post National Weekly Edition 25*(29):11.

Faiola, A. (2008, May 5–11). The economics of hunger: A brutal convergence of events has hit an unprepared global market. *Washington Post National Weekly Edition 25*(29):6–8.

Fallows, J. (2004). Blinding into Baghdad. *The Atlantic 293*(1):52–74.

Foley, N. (2004). Straddling the color line: The legal construction of Hispanic identity in Texas. In N. Foner & G. M. Fredrickson (eds.). *Not just black and white: Historical and contemporary perspectives on immigration, race and ethnicity in the United States*, pp.341–357. New York: Russell Sage Foundation.

Garreau, J. (2008, March 3–9). The whole world's talking: Cellphones have fueled the fastest revolution in human history. *Washington Post National Weekly Edition 25*(20):11.

Gonzalez, D. (2008, February 17). U.S. immigration law drives husband, wife apart. *Arizona Republic*, p. A1, A18.

Hacker, J. S. (2008, March 21–April 6). Take it. You'll feel better: Public health insurance isn't a poison pill. *Washington Post National Weekly Edition 25*(24):26.

Heymann, J., Earle, A., Simmons, S., Breslow, S. M., & Kuehnhoff, A. (2004). *The work, family, and equity index: Where does the United States stand globally?* Boston: Project on Global Working Families, Harvard School of Public Health.

Hokenstad, M. C., & Midgley, J. (2004). *Lessons from abroad: Adapting international social welfare innovations.* Washington, DC: NASW Press.

Hsu, S. S. (2008, May 26–June 1). Raid on a small town: In Iowa illegal workers are arrested. *Washington Post National Weekly Edition* 25(32):33.

Landers, J. (2007, November 16). Canadian health system may be cure for U.S. *Arizona Republic*, p. A28.

Lee, E. (2004). American gatekeeping: Race and immigration law in the twentieth century. In N. Foner & G. M. Fredrickson (eds.). *Not just black and white: Historical and contemporary perspectives on immigration, race and ethnicity in the United States*, pp.119–144. New York: Russell Sage Foundation.

Mann, C. C. (2002). 1491. *The Atlantic Monthly* 289(3):41–53.

Massey, D. S., Durand, J., & Malone, N. J. (2003). *Beyond smoke and mirrors: Mexican immigration in an era of economic integration.* New York: Russell Sage Foundation.

National Conference of State Legislatures. (2004). *Immigration reform.* Washington, DC: Author.

National Immigration Law Center. (2007). *Overview of key immigration issues facing the immigrants' rights movement.* Washington, DC: Low-Income Immigrant Rights Conference.

Nugent, C. (2007, November 8). Testimony before the House Subcommittee on Immigration, Citizenship, Refugees, Border Security, and International Law on *H.R. 750, the "Save America Comprehensive Immigration Act of 2007."* Washington, DC.

Office of the President. (2008). *Executive Order: Amending Executive Order 12989, as Amended.* Press release, June 9, 2008. Washington, DC: Author.

Passel, J. S. (2006). *The size and characteristics of the unauthorized migrant population in the US.* Washington, DC: Pew Hispanic Center.

Pew Global Attitudes Project. (2008). *24-nation Pew global attitudes survey.* Washington, DC: Pew Research Center for the People and the Press.

Pew Research Center for the People and the Press. (2004). *Mistrust of America in Europe ever higher, Muslim anger persists: A nine-country survey.* Washington, DC: Author.

Press, E. (2006, December 3). Do immigrants make us safer? *New York Times*, http://www.nytimes.com/2006/12/03/magazine/03wwln_idealab.html.

Reid, T. R. (2002). Buying American? Many brands that look homegrown are actually European-owned. *Washington Post National Weekly Edition* 19(31):20.

United Nations. (2008). *World economic and social survey 2008: Overcoming economic insecurity.* New York: United Nations Department of Economic and Social Affairs.

United Nations Development Programme. (2007). *Human development report 2007/2008—Fighting climate Change.* New York: United Nations.

United Nations. (2007). *The millennium development goals report.* New York: United Nations Department of Economic and Social Affairs.

U.S. Census Bureau. (2007). *Statistical Abstract of the United States*, 127th ed. Washington, DC: U.S. Government Printing Office.

U.S. Department of Homeland Security. (2008). *U.S. legal permanent residents: 2007, Annual Flow Report (March, 2008).* Washington, DC: DHS Office of Immigration Statistics.

U.S. Department of Homeland Security. (2007). *2006 yearbook of immigration statistics.* Washington, DC: DHS Office of Immigration Statistics.

World Bank. (2008). *Poverty analysis.* http://go.worldbank.org/JAIVP73S80.

THE IMPACT OF SOCIAL WELFARE POLICY AND POLICY PRACTICE IMPLICATIONS

CHAPTER 14

Courtesy of Elizabeth Segal

This chapter is a review of the power that social welfare policy has to affect lives and how you can use that power. By now, you have learned a great deal about the social welfare system in America. You should have an understanding of how values and beliefs shape the policy-making process. Insight into those values and beliefs can help us to change policies, so that social welfare policies can shape a more just society and provide for the well-being of all people.

Typically, students who are required to take courses that cover social welfare policy do not start out understanding how the course is relevant to their lives. This is particularly true in social work where public policy analysis and assessment of social welfare programs do not seem to be critical when working with individuals. This chapter attempts to pull together all that has been covered in order to answer the question of why one needs to understand social welfare policy.

Every year in my class on social welfare policy, I ask my social work students, "How many of you would take this class if it were not required?" Out of 20 or 25 students, 1 or 2 typically say they would, and once in a while, 3 or 4 students express interest in the subject. The rest admit that they are taking the course only because it is required. I understand this feeling. As a social work student, I too wanted to get to the "real stuff"—how to work with people and affect their lives. Public policy did not feel like social work. Now, my goal in each social welfare policy course I teach is to show my students that social welfare policy does affect people's lives, and, therefore, all social workers should understand how the social welfare system works. This has also been my goal in writing this book. This chapter attempts to pull together all that has been covered in order to answer the question of why we need to understand social welfare policy.

HOW IMPORTANT IS SOCIAL WELFARE POLICY TO SOCIAL WORKERS?

The social work profession is built on the principles of social justice, nondiscrimination, improving people's lives, and advocating for social change. These principles are part of our day-to-day practice. How do we ensure that our clients are not discriminated against in their jobs, schools, and neighborhoods? If we are meeting with a client on a regular basis, we can certainly discuss actions that are discriminatory and help formulate personal ways to deal with that discrimination. But if a school system regularly discourages children of color from attending, or if a factory never hires women, or if, as was true in the past, an African-American person cannot enter a restaurant because of the color of his or her skin, our individual interventions will not eradicate these discriminatory practices. The reduction of discriminatory practices in this country is in large part due to changes in social welfare policy. The increased opportunities for women, people of color, and people with disabilities are all a result of public policy changes. Therefore, when social workers strive to meet the mission of their profession, they are able to do so because of the power of social welfare policy to effect social change.

As we know, the U.S. Constitution was the first social welfare policy document that addressed public involvement in improving people's lives. It established the system of government and outlined the first protections of individual rights. Today, the Constitution serves as the foundation of all legal discussions and decisions related to social well-being. The Constitution and its amendments protect civil rights in many ways. We are free to practice any religion we choose, speak out for or against any cause, peaceably assemble, vote, own land, and be tried by a jury. We may consider these basic rights, but they are not all available in many nations of the world and they were not easily achieved. Countless civil clashes, even war, led to the establishment of these rights.

THE POWER OF SOCIAL WELFARE POLICY

Box 14.1 illustrates the power of social welfare policy to have positive and negative impacts on basic rights. The U.S. government has enacted policies that have both promoted and prohibited racism, sexism, ethnocentrism, homophobia, and classism. Also, some policies have been more effective in bringing about change in some areas than others.

 BOX 14.1 | **CONSIDER THIS . . .**

The Power of Social Welfare Policy

Racism

Policies promoting:

Slavery of Africans

Jim Crow laws

Policies opposing:

Fourteenth Amendment

Civil Rights Act of 1964

Ethnocentrism

Policies promoting:

Policies on early land ownership

Native American treaties

Policies opposing:

Constitutional equality

Reparations

Sexism

Policies promoting:

Women not allowed to own land

Women denied the right to vote

Policies opposing:

Constitutional equality

Women's suffrage, Nineteenth Amendment

Homophobia

Policies promoting:

Antisodomy laws

Legality of violence based on sexual orientation

Policies opposing:

Equal rights ordinances

Hate crimes legislation

Classism

Policies promoting:

Nobility through inheritance

Political access based on ability to pay

Policies opposing:

Constitutional equality

Campaign finance reform

ADDRESSING RACIAL DISCRIMINATION

Without the power of the Constitution and the federal government, it is highly unlikely that all states and localities would have ended slavery or given people of color the right to vote. Starting with the abolition of slavery in the Fourteenth Amendment, and including legal battles and passage of the Civil Rights Act of 1964 and the Voting Rights Act of 1965, legislation became the tool for publicly outlawing discriminatory practices that took away people's civil liberties and their right to vote. For example, Jim Crow laws were legally sanctioned forms of racial oppression and discrimination. Enactment of civil rights laws overturned these laws. Executive orders and agency regulations promoted affirmative action, so that discrimination in hiring practices could be overcome. Although racial discrimination has not been completely eradicated in America, the constitutional amendments, court cases, and other social welfare policies have outlawed many blatantly discriminatory practices. In addition, social and economic opportunities have improved for marginalized and oppressed groups of people over the past 100 years.

ADDRESSING GENDER DISCRIMINATION

The passage of the Nineteenth Amendment in 1920, which guaranteed women the right to vote, and legislation such as Title IX and equal employment policies have opened many social and economic opportunities for women. Again, although these policies guaranteed rights to women, equality has not been achieved. Women's earnings are less than men's, even in equivalent jobs. Title IX has enforced efforts to equalize resources and opportunities through federally funded educational systems, but here too equality has not yet been achieved.

SECURING RETIREMENT

Social Security has an impact on the economic well-being of millions of Americans. Without Social Security, almost half of all elderly people would be in poverty. Social Security has been paying benefits for more than 70 years, and for 45 years it has included health care coverage. Social Security affects more Americans than any other social welfare policy in the United States. Most people are recipients, dependents, survivors, or contributors. These roles shift over the span of a person's life; involvement in the program starts when workers are young and continues throughout their lives. Social Security is an excellent example of how social welfare policy can be an institutional program, can prevent poverty, and can emphasize social responsibility. Furthermore, it is supported by people with different values and beliefs. It serves as a model for a social welfare policy that improves all of our lives and is strongly supported by constituents and policy makers.

ENSURING PUBLIC SAFETY

People count on the state to ensure their safety. They rely on publicly funded police and fire protection. Government agencies are expected to protect children and elders from abuse and neglect, and families from domestic violence. People who break laws are prosecuted through our public legal system, and government-sanctioned safe homes are found for those who must be relocated. A cabinet level agency, the Department of Homeland Security, has been created to help protect everyone. Public policies govern and provide funding for all the agencies responsible for protecting and ensuring the public's safety.

PROVIDING PUBLIC EDUCATION

Education is a social policy. The mandate for public education for all children until the age of 16 years and the extent of public funding for education from the preschool and kindergarten levels through the university level demonstrate the legislated aspects of education. More than many social welfare policies, education has the potential to provide people with tremendous social and economic advantages. Unlike so many social welfare policies in our country, education is institutional and universal, making it potentially one of the strongest policies for promoting social justice. Consider the economic implications of education discussed in Chapter 10. Box 14.2 outlines the differences in income by level of education. There is a strong correlation between the amount of education a person receives and the income he or she will likely earn. With such a clear relationship, it makes sense for the nation to develop policies that promote completion of education to the highest levels possible. However, as Box 14.3 demonstrates, only 28 percent of adults have a four-year college degree or more, and 15 percent do not even have a high school diploma. The differences in education, earnings, and race demonstrate another area in which public social welfare policies can make a difference. In 1960, 41 percent of the adult population was a high school graduate or higher, and that rose to 86 percent by 2006. Over those same years, the proportion of black adults with a high school diploma or higher rose from 20 percent to 81 percent. However, for Latino adults, although progress has been made, in 2006 the rate was only 59 percent, far lower than the national average. The disparity in terms of college education is also significant by race. From 1960 to 2006, the 28 percent of adults with a college degree or higher

 BOX 14.2 | **MORE ABOUT INCOME BY LEVEL OF EDUCATION**

Educational Level	Median Earnings in 2005
9th to 12th grade but no diploma	$19,915
High school graduate	$29,448
Some college but no degree	$31,421
Associate degree	$37,990
Bachelor's degree	$54,689
Master's degree	$67,898
Doctorate	$92,863
Professional degree	$119,009

Source: U.S. Census Bureau, 2007

| BOX 14.3 | **MORE ABOUT EDUCATIONAL ATTAINMENT** |

Percentage of population 25 years old and over whose highest level was:

Some high school	14.5%
High school graduate	31.7%
Some college, no degree	17.0%
Associate's degree	8.7%
Bachelor's degree	18.3%
Advanced degree	9.7%

Source: U.S. Census Bureau, 2007

was a four-fold increase nationally. For blacks, the rate grew six times greater, to almost 19 percent in 2006. For Latinos, although the rate grew, it was 12.4 percent in 2006, less than half that for the white population (U.S. Census Bureau, 2007). Thus, progress has been made since passage of civil rights legislation and judicial decisions opening access to education. However, there are still significant disparities and hence room for improvement in educational opportunities.

Because it is so clear that earnings and opportunities are linked to education, the question must be asked why public policies do not do more to facilitate education. Education creates a stronger workforce. Innovations and technological advancement can be nurtured through education. Educating children is a positive institutional and preventive long-term social welfare policy. The infrastructure for schools and universities exists, but widespread access to them is not promoted. Attending institutions of higher education is costly, even if they are public schools. The average cost for a public four-year institution is about $12,000 a year, and for a private institution the average is about $23,000 per year. The average total amount of federal financial assistance, including loans, is about $7,400 per student each year (U.S. Census Bureau, 2007). With the power of education to improve people's employment opportunities and, hence, their economic well-being, providing higher education opportunities for more adults should be a top social welfare priority.

HOW DOES SOCIAL WELFARE POLICY CHANGE?

Social welfare policies are created and enacted in several different ways. Throughout the book numerous federal laws that have contributed to social change have been discussed. In addition to legislation passed by Congress and signed into law by presidents, judicial decisions, executive orders, and agency regulations have resulted in social welfare policies. All of these forms of legislating social welfare policy occur at the highest levels of government and contribute to uniformity and universality in guaranteeing civil rights. The three levels of government, **Legislative, Executive,** and **Judicial,** account for the policies made at the national level. Although all states, tribes, and local jurisdictions are bound by federal laws, these levels also pass laws that impact people's lives.

It is important to note that although the processes discussed in this chapter outline a clear process, the actual passage, interpretation, implementation, and supervision of the laws of the land do not follow a clear and straightforward process in reality. The process is full of politics and subject to values and beliefs of participants at all levels—elected and appointed officials, staff, and constituents. Although the process is outlined here, trying to trace the process as it is happening is complicated, nontransparent, and confounding. Do not despair, this is the art of policy-making and the more one investigates it, the easier it will be to understand.

The phrase often used to describe the government is that it is a system of "checks and balances." What this means is that the three major government branches, Legislative, Executive, and Judicial, all have powers that balance and control one another. It is a democracy, which means that all citizens participate in the election of representatives, and therefore the electorate also serves as a balance in the law-making process. The Constitution is the primary basis for this system, which has been in effect continuously for more than 200 years. This fact alone sets the United States apart from almost all other nations—the same form of government in place since the founding of our nation over two centuries ago, even enduring a civil war. In that same time, countries throughout the world have had various forms of government.

CONGRESS AND HOW LAWS ARE MADE

The Legislative branch at the federal level consists of the U.S. Congress. The **Congress** is made up of two bodies, the **Senate** and the **House of Representatives**. Here too there is a system of checks and balances. Each body is constructed differently to complement and balance the other. The Senate consists of 100 voting members, with each state having two representatives. This form of representation means that each state, regardless of size, has equal representation. The House of Representatives has 435 voting members, each representing an even proportion of the population. As the U.S. population grows, the 435 elected positions remain constant, so the number of people represented increases over time. Currently, each district represents about 700,000 people, with even the smallest state allowed at least one representative should their population fall below the threshold. This form of representation is proportionate, reflecting the size of a state, as opposed to equal as in the Senate. For example, in 2009, California had two senators and 53 representatives, while Vermont had two senators and only one representative. The balance in this format is that because all laws must be approved by both the Senate and the House, all states have a say in the process, and can both weigh in equally and proportionately.

Additionally, lengths of terms differ in the Senate and House. Each Senator serves for a six-year term and terms are staggered. In every national election held in November of the even-numbered years, one-third of the Senators are up for reelection. House members serve two-year terms and their offices are voted on in every national election. This too is a form of checks and balances. Senate members, with longer duration, are thought to be less sensitive to public demands, and can legislate more deeply. Representatives are voted on more frequently and therefore are thought to be more sensitive to public wishes and are therefore more responsive to their constituents. Also, as there are more House members with fewer constituents to represent, they can be more representative of the people who directly elect them. Consider again the example of California. With a population of about 35 million people, the two senators have a lot of public opinions to consider. In contrast, a House member represents a much smaller geographic region of about 700,000 people. Although still a sizeable number, it is more manageable and likely to be more homogenous than the population of the entire state.

Box 14.4 outlines the official process for how laws are made in Congress. Although the official process must be followed, much goes on behind the scenes in terms of advocacy, persuasion, and decision-making. It is during this process that constituents, lobbyists, and other interested parties can make their opinions known to elected representatives. Participation in the formal process is primarily conducted by elected officials. Later in this chapter, ways to be involved in this process are discussed.

Each Congress convenes for two years, and each year is called a session. Congresses are consecutively numbered and start in January of the odd-numbered year, which follows the November election. In 2007, the 110th Congress opened its first session in January, finished the session in the late fall of 2007, took a recess, reconvened for its second session in January of 2008, and concluded the 110th Congress in the fall of 2008. In January of 2009, the 111th Congress opened with all the members elected in the November 2008 election. Each Congress starts the bill-making process over in terms of bills to be discussed. If something was introduced into the previous Congress, in order to be considered, it must be reintroduced into the new Congress. This is not an automatic process.

If a bill is successful, and is passed through both chambers and then signed by the president (or passed by two-thirds majority if the president vetoes it), then it becomes federal law. Each law is numbered as it is approved and listed by the Congress in which it was passed. For example, the Hope for Homeowners Act passed in 2008 in response to the mortgage lending meltdown is P.L. 110-289—the 289th bill passed in the 110th Congress and enacted into public law (P.L. stands for public law). All public laws are then consolidated and codified by subject into the master of permanent laws of the United States, known as the **United States Code**. All bills, public laws, and the U.S. Code can be accessed through a number of web portals, as described in the research section of Chapter 6.

EXECUTIVE ORDERS

Some ways of creating and enacting social welfare policies are easier to track than others. Major policy decisions, such as the modernization of Medicare in 2003, captured newspaper headlines and tremendous television coverage. Other ways are more subtle and require diligence on our part to follow. For example, as may be recalled from the example of affirmative action, a presidential executive order initiated it and agency regulations institutionalized it. The **executive order** is the major way presidents intervene in agency processes. The President cannot make law. However, through an executive order, the President can clarify or further a law that was passed by Congress or is established based on the Constitution. When a president puts forth an executive order, it should identify to which specific law the

BOX 14.4 | MORE ABOUT HOW PUBLIC LAWS ARE MADE

Nothing can be discussed or acted upon without introduction. Each chamber processes its respective bills under different rules, although similar in structure and intent. For a bill to be sent on to the President to become a public law, it must be agreed upon by both chambers and passed in exactly the same final format. Once introduced, there is no guarantee that the bill will go through the entire process. In the last Congress, about 11,000 bills were introduced, with only four percent enacted into law.

HOUSE OF REPRESENTATIVES	**SENATE**
Bill is introduced	**Bill is introduced**

Each bill is consecutively numbered as it is entered, starting with HR 1 in the House and S 1 in the Senate. When each new Congress opens every two years, the numbering starts over and all bills to be discussed are introduced anew.

Referred to committee	**Referred to committee**

Usually a bill is referred to a committee and subcommittee based on the substance of the bill. It is sent to committees with jurisdiction or knowledge of the issue. However, the decision for referral is made by the majority leader's office and can have political undertones. For a bill to go to the next level, it must be voted on and receive a majority vote in the full committee.

Referred to subcommittee	**Referred to subcommittee**

Discussion and public hearings may be held to examine and debate the issues.

Reported by full committee	**Reported by full committee**

For a bill to go to the next level, it must be voted on and receive a majority vote in the full committee.

Rules are set for floor action

This action typically only occurs in the House; in the Senate the bill voted on by committee goes directly to the floor. This is in part a way for the larger House to handle discussion with so many more members.

Floor action	**Floor action**

The bill is discussed and debated with the full membership.

House debate	**Senate debate**
Vote	**Vote**

It can be amended and is then passed or defeated. If it is passed, it must go to the other chamber and also be passed. If the other chamber has already passed it, and the versions differ, they go to a joint conference to work out the differences.

Conference Action

Members from both chambers form a committee to work out the differences. The revised version that is agreed upon in the conference committee is then sent to each chamber for final approval.

Sent to President

The President can sign the bill into law or veto it and return it to Congress. If Congress chooses to override the veto, it must do so by a two-thirds majority vote in both the House and Senate. The bill would then become law without the President's signature.

Source: House of Representatives, 2003

order refers. Executive orders can be used to establish requirements for agencies and departments. For example, in the previous chapter the executive order that mandated employers choosing to contract with the federal government to conduct immigration background checks was discussed. Executive orders can change with presidents. Since the federal government was first instituted, more than 14,000 executive orders have been issued. Congress has the power to overturn an executive order by passing legislation, but it would likely be vetoed by the president, and then would require a two-thirds majority to override the president's veto. Thus, the executive order is a way for the president to participate in shaping the implementation of public laws. However, a future president cannot issue a new executive order that could amend orders from previous presidents.

The Executive Branch, headed by the President, includes the Vice President, all the cabinet level departments, and federal agencies and commissions. The Cabinet currently consists of 15 departments, including the Departments of Agriculture, Defense, Education, Health and Human Services, and Labor. Updated information on all the cabinet members and departments can be found on the White House web site. Each department head is recommended by the President and approved by the Senate. Each person serves the President and in turn is responsible for upholding the policies of the President in facilitating each department and its agencies. However, the rules of each agency must reflect the public laws, so there tends to be a mix of interpretations of implementation when legislation is passed by Congress and implemented by the agencies headed up by presidential appointees.

JUDICIAL PROCESS

The Judicial branch is headed up by the United States Supreme Court, and includes U.S. Courts of Appeals and U.S. District Courts. There are nine justices of the Supreme Court and they are appointed for life. Because they are appointed, they are considered to be immune to public opinion and voting constituencies. Presidents appoint them with confirmation from the Senate. One justice is appointed to serve as Chief Justice and oversees the court process. Although the members of the court are regarded as apolitical, they too have their own values and beliefs and those positions influence their decisions and interpretations. Also, the appointment process is very political. When a vacancy arises, whoever is President at the time chooses the nominee. And depending on what political party is in the majority in the Senate, that party has the majority of votes for the confirmation. Thus, although the checks and balances were designed to place the courts outside the political process, the selection and appointment process can be very political.

All the decisions of the Supreme Court are to be based on Constitutional law, which involves interpretation of the Constitution and prior laws. The Supreme Court acts as another body to assess and contribute to law-making. Major public policies were decided in the courts, not in Congress or through Presidential orders. For example, the legalization of abortion across the nation was established through the Supreme Court decision of *Roe v. Wade* in 1973. The Supreme Court ruled that abortion was a right based on the Fourteenth Amendment, which was interpreted to protect personal liberty and personal privacy, rights under which the court found abortion to belong. Although congressional laws and presidential efforts and subsequent court rulings have made changes, they have been marginal and the original court decision still stands. That is not to say that Congress could not outlaw abortion, but since 1973 the only congressional legislation that has been passed and enacted into law has amended the law, not overturned it.

STATE AND LOCAL GOVERNANCE

Each state has its own form of state government. Typically, state governments reflect the same structure as the federal government. The legislative branch, often referred to as the State Legislature, consists of two bodies, a state senate and a state house of representatives. The State level executive branch is headed by the governor who oversees all the state agencies. And the judicial branch at the state level consists of a State Supreme Court, courts of appeal, and trial courts. Each state is subject to federal laws, but there are numerous areas of law decided at the state level. The Constitution built in a significant amount of state power as another form of balance. The federal government could never become too powerful if some decisions and power remained at the state level. For example, the National Guard is an outgrowth of state militias and is considered the reserve force for the federal United States Department of Defense. Technically, should the president need additional military support, as has been the case with the war in Iraq, the president requests that each governor "loan" the state's National Guard to the federal government. The actual structure of each state's government differs in terms of representation, terms in office, and operations.

Further down in the policy chain are local governments. The variety of local legislative bodies is great, and varies among municipalities. There are cities, towns, villages, boroughs, districts—all with different forms of governing. All share a public focus and as such individuals can find out information on their local government and attend policy-making meetings and events. With the power of the web, information and access has been greatly enhanced. Agendas for town councils are accessible and the meetings are open to the public.

TRIBAL GOVERNANCE

Each federally recognized tribe can form its own governing body. Each tribe is subject to all federal laws, but not necessarily all state laws. The laws and jurisdictions are complicated and vary from state to state. The form of governing varies by tribe as well. The Bureau of Indian Affairs is the federal department under which tribal governments operate. Positions, terms of office, representation, and election procedures are determined by each tribe. For example, a number of tribes have Tribal Councils with elected representatives and a chair elected to head the council. Some bodies elect a governor or president and council members are representatives or members.

THE INFLUENCE OF ADVOCACY GROUPS

Elected and appointed officials are not the only players in the policy-making arena. In 2003, when members of Congress and President George W. Bush were trying to get approval for their version of Medicare reform, they knew that interest groups would be a key factor. With 35 million members age 50 years and older and high national visibility and credibility, the **American Association of Retired Persons (AARP)** was the advocacy group whose endorsement could make or break the bill (Broder & Goldstein, 2003). AARP did endorse the proposal, and for many constituents, that endorsement suggested that the policy was favorable to seniors. Although the policy is flawed and very costly (see Chapter 11), the influence of a large advocacy group swayed public opinion. For the public, the endorsement of an established and respected advocacy group strengthened the policy makers' decisions and legitimized the proposal. This influence can be felt when other issues are being debated also.

One criticism of our political system is that financial means provide people with access to and, hence, influence of policy makers. In 2002, for the first time in more than 30 years, Congress passed legislation to curb spending on political campaigns with the Bipartisan Campaign Reform Act (BCRA) (P.L. 107-155) (Congressional Research Service, 2008). This legislation is also known as the McCain-Feingold bill, named for its two lead senate sponsors. BCRA banned large corporations and unions from making donations to national political parties, known as soft money. Soft money consists of those political donations used for general political efforts and education about issues. Hard money consists of those donations made to fund a specific candidate or issue. The legislation also put limits on political advertising preceding elections. Although this was considered a major breakthrough, it has since then been tied up in legal battles, court cases, stalled nominations to the Federal Election Commission, and further legislation trying to implement the policy.

The impetus for campaign finance reform was the large sums of money spent by the national parties to elect candidates. However, the actual legislation did not cap the amounts, rather it closed off two large sources, corporations and unions, from making donations directly to the national parties. The thinking was that the two parties had become too powerful in fundraising, and then in turn could choose which issues or candidates to support and have too much control over the election. During the 2000 and 2002 elections, almost $500 million flowed through the Democratic and Republican parties to influence the outcomes of individual campaigns. By 2004, following the BCRA, that amount had been eliminated. However, by 2006 total spending was on the rise. In 2000, $457 million in soft money was raised by state political parties, almost evenly divided between the Democrats and Republicans. In 2002, it had risen to $569 million, prompting the need for campaign finance legislation. In 2004 the amount dropped to $297 million, only to rise in 2006 to $455 million (Barber, 2007). Fundraising for the 2008 election eclipsed those numbers. Over one and a half billion dollars was raised by the candidates running for president in 2008. What happened? Campaign finance reform was successful in limiting corporations and unions from playing a key roll in donating to the national parties. However, other donors stepped up and donations were shifted from the national level to state levels. Donations from individuals and businesses increased. In the 2008 election, Barack Obama did what no other candidate had done before, he raised most of his money through individuals giving small donations and accepted virtually no contributions from Political Action Committees. Over 90 percent of his fundraising came from individual donors, of which half the dollars raised came through donations under $200 (OpenSecrets.org, 2008).

Arguments against campaign finance stress the rights of people to support the candidates of their choice without limits. Supporters still voice concern that the amount of money one is willing to contribute affects the level of influence. Campaign finance reform is an example of the potential of social welfare policy to regulate our political process, however the actual success of crafting legislation and implementing it remains to be seen.

LIMITATIONS OF SOCIAL WELFARE POLICY

Social welfare policy can implement laws and regulations to govern people's actions, but it may not change people's beliefs. It may be illegal to discriminate against a person because of his or her skin color, but people can still be prejudiced. It may be illegal to refuse to hire a qualified woman to work on a construction crew, but once she gets there she may not be welcomed by her co-workers.

Remember Charles Lindblom's thesis that policy is incremental and changes slowly and in small ways. The incremental nature of social welfare policy limits its impact as well. Due to differing beliefs and compromises made in getting policy passed, the changes may be small and, consequently, very slow in taking effect. Advocates for change may get discouraged and lose momentum after seeing incremental change occur, even though the bigger issue at stake has not been resolved. However, if we take a longer-term view of policies, we can see that even incremental changes can accumulate to become a significant change. Although actions can be regulated but a person's beliefs cannot, changes in actions can eventually lead to changed beliefs. Although homophobia is still very real in America, tolerance of LGBT people has increased in the decades since the Stonewall riot of 1968. Therefore, changes in attitudes can follow legislation but often take time.

POLICY PRACTICE

Once armed with a framework, and an understanding of the process, how does one actually go about changing social welfare policy? **Policy practice** can affect the policy-making process. Policy practice is using knowledge of how policies are made to take an active role in influencing the outcome of the process. The most powerful way to conduct policy practice is to participate in the political system. People often think that "participation" means they must run for political office. Some social workers have chosen to do so and have been successful in securing a political office. Box 14.5 lists social workers who have been elected to public office. However, getting elected is just one way to influence social welfare policy.

THE POWER OF VOTING

Public officials are all responsible to their constituents, especially if they want to stay in office and get reelected. Therefore, the voices of the people who elect them can be very important. One of the easiest ways to participate in the

BOX 14.5 | MORE ABOUT SOCIAL WORKERS ELECTED TO PUBLIC OFFICE

According to the National Association of Social Workers:

Social workers in elected offices:

	2003	2008
U.S. Congress	6	10
State legislatures	44	71
County/borough	17	29
City/municipal	62	51
School board	35	30
Other	10	1

Social workers in federal offices in 2008:

State/district	Name	Party
MD	Senator Barbara Mikulski	D
MI	Senator Debbie Stabenow	D
CA-53	Congresswoman Susan Davis	D

State/district	Name	Party
CA-09	Congresswoman Barbara Lee	D
TX-23	Congressman Ciro Rodriguez	D
NY-10	Congressman Ed Towns	D
IL-4	Congressman Luis Gutierrez	D
OH-11	Congresswoman Stephanie Tubbs Jones (deceased August of 2008)	D
PA-13	Congresswoman Allyson Schwartz	D
NH-1	Congresswoman Carol Shea-Porter	D

policy-making process is to vote. Voting is a civil right available to all citizens of the United States. Each person's vote has equal weight, and candidates who get the most votes typically win the election. In spite of this simple democratic process, millions of people who are eligible to vote do not do so. In the 2000 presidential election, 51.2 percent of eligible voters turned out to cast a vote, a rate that is lower than the rate in more than 20 western democracies (Polsby & Wildavsky, 2004). In the midterm election of 2002, only 42 percent voted, while in 2004 that proportion rose to 55 percent and dropped again in 2006 to 44 percent (U.S. Census Bureau, 2008). Initial tabulations of voter turnout for the 2008 election suggest that the rate was higher than in previous presidential elections. This pattern is well documented over the decades, during presidential election years more people register and turn out to vote than for the elections in-between presidential years.

Data reveal a number of interesting voting patterns. The higher a person's income, the higher a person's educational attainment, and the higher a person's age are all correlated with a greater likelihood to vote. Box 14.6 lists those data. Women tend to register and vote at slightly higher levels than do men. Candidates running for office are well aware of these statistics. Because the goal of campaigning is to

BOX 14.6	MORE ABOUT VOTING

Voting by Age	2004	2006	Voting by Income	2004	2006
18 to 24 years	47%	22%	Less than $20,000	48%	31%
25 to 34 years	56%	34%	$20,000 to $29,999	58%	44%
35 to 44 years	64%	46%	$30,000 to $39,999	62%	48%
45 to 54 years	69%	54%	$40,000 to $49,999	69%	53%
55 years and older	72%	63%	$50,000 to $74,999	72%	54%
65 to 74 years	73%	64%	$75,000 to $99,999	78%	57%
75 years and older	69%	61%	$100,000 and over	81%	64%

Source: U.S. Census Bureau, 2008

Voting by Education	2004	2006
Less than high school	40%	27%
High school graduate or GED	56%	41%
Some college or assoc degree	69%	49%
Bachelor's degree	78%	61%
Advanced degree	84%	70%

get elected, one improves those chances by focusing on those people who are most likely to vote. However, recent efforts to register people who have not been involved previously and encouraging them to turn out and vote seem to be playing a part in recent elections. In close elections, increasing the number of previously uninvolved potential voters can shift the outcome. One of the most famous presidents, John F. Kennedy, was elected president with a plurality of 119,450 votes out of almost 69 million votes cast, less than 0.2 percent of the total of votes. Registering a handful of new voters in each district and getting them to vote can change the outcome of any election.

When we consider social justice in America, voting is powerful. All votes are equal, and they are completely anonymous so people are protected from pressure and threats. At the same time, people of lower income, less education, and from different racial backgrounds vote in smaller proportions to their numbers, effectively lessening their voice and power. Full representation means that all who are eligible to vote actually vote. Efforts to increase voter registration have often met with resistance from groups who have benefited from the disproportionate involvement in the voting process. History of the Voting Rights Act demonstrates the struggle to gain the right to vote and then to actually be able to exercise that right once it is granted. Educating people about public policy issues, candidates, and political positions is a very important part of the policy practice arena. But if a person is not registered to vote, it is impossible to participate no matter how much knowledge and understanding one has. Voter registration and getting people out to vote on election days is a very powerful policy practice tool.

ADVOCACY—GETTING ONE'S VOICE HEARD

Voting is one way of actively engaging in the policy arena. Making one's opinion count can be accomplished in numerous other ways as well. Some people choose to be active in a campaign and canvass for a candidate or an issue. Throughout the policy-making process it is possible to contact elected officials and let them know of your position on an issue. The following sections outline some of the ways to get one's voice heard and become an active policy practitioner.

Lobbying   When the term **lobbying** is mentioned, people think of a professional activity, typically undertaken by wealthy corporate interests to influence politicians. Indeed, numerous professionals and well-financed groups fit this profile. The reach of public policy is extensive, and impacts numerous groups and special interests. Thousands of professionals work at the local, state, and federal levels as lobbyists. Organizations and groups with professional lobbyists on their staff include commercial enterprises, industrial groups, labor unions, ideological, religious, educational, health-related organizations, just to name a few. Even state and local governments employ the use of lobbyists to influence the policy-making process. The nation's capitol is full of Washington-based offices for all sorts of groups with trained personnel to monitor the legislative process and act to influence, inform, and educate elected officials about topics important to their constituents.

In general, lobbying is action used to persuade policy makers. Writing letters or emails to representatives can be influential. It is a form of lobbying, of trying to make a position known and convincing the elected representative to vote according to that position. Personal meetings are another way. Most elected officials welcome the opportunity to meet with constituents, and if they are busy, their staff will meet with constituents. These forms of contact can be ways for social workers to educate policy makers about people's needs and concerns. Social workers can try to paint pictures of people's lives to help teach those who are in decision-making positions.

Letter Writing   In this day and age of advanced technology, writing a letter may seem out-dated. Precisely because it takes longer and is used less today makes it a powerful tool for advocacy. If a person takes the time to sit down and craft a letter, the issue is likely to be important enough that the person will follow through and vote accordingly. Elected officials have to keep this in mind when receiving letters from constituents.

The letter should be typewritten (word processed) or very clearly written if by hand. Keep the letter to one page, make it brief, and clearly state the reason for writing and the position taken. It may seem obvious, but being polite is better than being angry. Also, be aware of the proper salutations and headings, it shows respect and engages the reader better. Being a voting constituent strengthens your position. Typically, writing to one's own member of Congress or statehouse representative is more influential. It might be worth adding why you are interested in this issue. A personal reason or experience with the issue can be very convincing and help to illuminate the points being made. Always thank the legislator for taking the time to read the letter (even though a staff person may be handling the letter, depending on the size of the office or the issue, some do go directly to the elected official). Include your address on the letter to improve the possibility of a return note. This also acts to demonstrate your connection to the elected official as a voting resident of his or her district. Also ask for the elected person's position on the issue and ask for a response. It will tell you something about the office of the elected official whether you get a response or not. Numerous votes are given or withheld on the simplest of actions—a call returned, a letter answered, information given. As a constituent, the elected official serves the public and you are part of that public.

Email   It may be similar to letter-writing, but it is easier and faster to send an email. This makes it a useful form of policy practice, but not necessarily as persuasive as a well-written letter. The content and structure should be the same as a written letter. Be careful about the email address you use to send a message. The law prohibits public employees from using their government job as a place from which to lobby for a candidate. The use of your title or organization can appear to be an endorsement, and that too is illegal. You should not use a public employer's logo or letterhead unless you are authorized by the organization to take a position. It is best to use your personal email address for any political emails that you might send.

Telephone Calls   The information given in a telephone call is very similar to what would be put in a letter or email. The information does not change, only the mode of delivery. Because a telephone call is easy to place, it may not seem as powerful a tool for advocacy. But hundreds of phone calls taking a position on an issue can be very compelling and persuasive. With the speed of communication through the Internet, a phone campaign can easily be organized. But elected officials know that it still takes time to make the call, and it is likely that a caller who is more committed to the particular issue will be more likely to vote. Thus, the telephone call is still a strong tool for advocacy.

Organized Letter Writing and Calling Campaigns   A note of caution about the power of these modes of lobbying. The power of a written letter, email, or phone call can be diluted if it is obviously orchestrated by an organization and may not really be an issue about which a person is passionate. To increase the numbers of participants in a lobbying campaign, try to find ways to individualize the messages. One way is to develop a list of points to be made, and call together people for a "writing party" where everyone joins together to talk about the issue, but writes his or her own letter. A strategy to strengthen this approach is to have different types of envelopes and stationery and stagger sending out the letters. This helps to promote the issue as a more widespread concern rather than an orchestrated effort by one organization or group. Petitions are often seen as a weak form of advocacy for the same reason. It is easy to sign something, and may not mean that a person has any real commitment to the issue.

In-Person Meetings   It is one's right to meet with elected officials, they are public servants and we elect them. However, their schedule is busy and they typically have staff who are overextended. If it is during the legislative session, their time will be at more of a premium. Be understanding of their schedule when asking for a personal meeting. Meeting with a staff person can be effective as well, especially if trying to educate on a position—the staff person may be the one doing all the background research for the elected official and will serve as a consultant as the elected official develops his or her position.

Be polite, be brief, stick to the issue, and do not complicate the meeting by discussing other issues. Ask for the legislator's position. Do not confront him or her, and try and find a point you agree on. Usually the general goal (helping people, making the community safer, improving opportunities) can be agreed upon. From there, calmly state your position, reminding the legislator of the common general goal. Because you will have specific points you want made but may not have the time to do so, bring a one- or two-page fact sheet. Make the fact sheet clear, concise, and factual. With today's software programs, it can look professional and compelling, and should strive to do so. Leave on a positive note so that you will be welcome in the future. Send a note afterward thanking the elected official for the time spent with you. Information can be added to your thank you note that may have been missed during your meeting or for clarification. Offer to be a future resource. If new information becomes available, send that along in the future. Keeping the line of communication open allows the opportunity to lobby for an issue over time. Most public policy is slow to evolve and can take multiple legislative sessions to be enacted, so having an ongoing relationship can be an asset for policy practice.

Town Halls or Community Meetings   Some of the most obvious aspects of setting up a meeting can often get lost in the political frenzy of lobbying for an issue important and meaningful to people. The better organized a public meeting is, the more influential it can be. Be sure to contact the elected official you are most interested in having attend and clear a date and time that fits best for the official. Confirm it in writing so that you have a definite commitment. Often things come up at the last minute, so have a back-up plan if the elected official must decline. Select a convenient location, and try to find something that adds to the purpose of the meeting. For example, if lobbying for more support for public education, meeting at a local school after hours might be appropriate. If there are grounds to tour afterwards, check whether that can be added to the official's schedule. The rules of running a good meeting are key—start on time, be efficient, keep things moving, speakers should be brief and concise, have variety in the format, and try to be creative and engaging. Include a one-page handout that highlights the points you want to get across. This can serve as a reminder later for the elected person and also ensures that the information you most want shared is made available and clearly outlined.

Prepare written invitations or flyers and be sure to include all the information needed to attend—date, time, location, map, and a phone number to call for more information. Be clear who is sponsoring the event and why. Make attendance as easy as possible and as inviting as possible.

A well-attended meeting can be more influential. Be sure that you can count on attendees, even if you have to fill the room with staff to be sure it looks full. It is always better to be packed into a smaller room than lost in a larger room. That is the one rule for effective meetings you may want to break—you want the impression that this issue is important and people are packing the room to make sure their voices are heard. Letter of invitations, follow-up phone calls, and "assignments" for participants can enhance the turnout. Also, be sure that photographs are taken, it is good public relations and can be sent to the elected official as a follow-up to keep the relationship going. If media coverage can be arranged, all the better. Even a local newsletter provides free publicity for your cause and for the elected official. It can persuade the official that his or her time spent with your group will be beneficial politically. Have refreshments, it sends a message of welcome and helps people to connect with one another. Use nametags, that way everyone can be "known" and feel a part of the meeting. A sign-in sheet can be beneficial for contacting people later for future advocacy efforts and networking. Definitely send a thank you note to the elected official and any staff who attended. If time permits, send a thank you note to all the participants.

CONFLICTING VALUES AND BELIEFS: WHERE DO WE GO FROM HERE?

In each chapter, the values and beliefs that relate to certain policies have been discussed. Recognizing those differences helps to explain the conflict in developing social welfare policies. Such recognition is important. But what should be done once those differences are understood? If one group strongly favors social responsibility and another group feels individual responsibility is most important, how those opposing viewpoints be accommodated in our social welfare policies?

One way is to openly acknowledge the values and beliefs that differ. Typically, policy discussions center on specifics or the outcomes desired but do not address the differences in beliefs. For example, when welfare reform was debated prior to passage of PRWORA in 1996, the outcome was the focus, that is, getting people off of welfare and helping them to become economically self-sufficient. There was not much disagreement on the goal. The disagreement was on how to *accomplish* the goal. Therefore, policy discussions centered on program requirements, and, at times, beliefs and facts were intertwined. Is it a belief or a fact that a person is better off "making it on his or her own" (or getting help)? Is it a belief or a fact that welfare makes people complacent (or lazy)? The values and beliefs of individual lawmakers were the foundation for all of the discussions. Some lawmakers believe that the only way a person can be economically self-sufficient is to do it on his or her own, get a job, work hard, and stick with it. Others strongly believe that society needs to help people prepare, either by training them or by changing the structure of workplaces. These are two very different approaches to welfare reform. The position emphasizing individual responsibility won out and became the foundation of the legislation. What might have happened if policy makers had first discussed their beliefs on individual responsibility versus social responsibility? What if the legislation had addressed those two viewpoints? Is it possible that a compromise piece of legislation could have been developed that might have included parts reflecting both beliefs?

DEVELOPING SOCIAL WELFARE POLICIES THAT PROMOTE SOCIAL JUSTICE

To tackle social problems in the United States and change the conditions that perpetuate disparity and exclusion, the conflict of values and beliefs must be addressed. For example, consider the problem of poverty. People who have never been poor, never experienced discrimination that has prevented them from educational and employment opportunities, and never been aware of what it feels like to grow up poor in America, will likely have trouble understanding values such as prevention and social support. If your frame of reference is that everything in life depends on individual effort and you have been rewarded for your own efforts, then you may not see any value in social responsibility. Lack of experience and insight into what it means to grow up poor in America may limit a person's ability to see the value of a social response to poverty. What if everyone experienced what it feels like to be poor? Shared experience or understanding can develop social empathy which in turn can lead to better social policies (Segal, 2006). **Social empathy** is the capacity of people to understand and experience other people's social conditions. Should all policy makers be forced to spend time in poverty-stricken circumstances? That may be a good idea but, of course, it is not possible. Instead, we should strive toward teaching social empathy.

A person may never have been hit by a car, but he or she knows not to walk in front of a moving vehicle and risk being hit. Why? He or she has been told since a young age that it is dangerous. People are taught to avoid dangerous situations. They can remember previously experiencing pain (e.g., falling off a bicycle) and know that the pain felt if hit by a car would be much worse. It is possible to learn from other people's experiences through stories and the media. Being well-versed in the consequences of being hit by a car, means that people avoid such an accident as much as possible. In fact, so many things that we "know" are taught to us by others rather than being personally experienced. With the example of poverty, if more time was taken to teach others about living in poverty, about economic and social disadvantage, it would be possible to create a deeper understanding of what it means to be poor. With that deeper understanding, it is more likely the social conditions that lead to poverty and are a consequence of it will be addressed.

The continued existence of poverty in the United States seems contradictory to the growth and expansion that has occurred in American society. Concentrations of wealth have created greater disparities between those at the top and those at the bottom. The likelihood of someone with wealth knowing or understanding the day-to-day life of someone poor is small today. Yet people learn best from experience and first-hand knowledge. How do we close the experience gap between those at the top and those at the bottom? We must begin to find ways to teach policy makers, voters, and people who have never experienced poverty and other social problems what it is like. Ways need to be found to develop social empathy, the ability to feel and understand what others are experiencing in our society.

Teaching empathy is difficult, yet it is considered an important part of social functioning. On a personal level, empathy is a key ingredient in change (Watson, 2002). Empathy is critical to becoming an emotionally intelligent person

BOX 14.7	CONSIDER THIS . . .

Values and beliefs that influence our feelings about the role of government

Unlikely to support government social programs	More likely to support government social programs
Undeserving: Seen as able to be responsible for self	*Deserving*: Worthy of help
Personal Failure: Conditions of need brought on by individual's failure	*System Failure*: Conditions of need brought on by economic, political, and social conditions
Self-sufficiency: People should take care of themselves; no outside support	*Social Support*: We are all responsible for each other; society should care for all
Helping those we know: Inclined to help when there is a personal relationship	*Helping strangers*: Willing to help people unknown to us
Crisis: Mobilize for a critical event	*Prevention*: Provide services before there is a problem

(Goleman, 1994). With empathy, people are more likely to understand social needs and develop ways to build a better social environment for others and themselves.

Values and beliefs need to be clarified so people's positions on social welfare are understood. For example, consider the role of government in social support. Box 14.7 outlines the values and beliefs that conflict when people are deciding whether to support government social programs. If a person holds beliefs in the first column, he or she is more likely to expect individuals to be responsible for the conditions of life. If a person holds beliefs in the second column, he or she would more likely believe in social support. Rather than argue for or against more government programs, these important values and beliefs need to be addressed and what they mean explored. Then policies can be created that address those conflicts and challenge people's beliefs. Although ideological discussions are difficult, they are the most likely venue for change—not debates about legislative rules and regulations.

FINAL THOUGHTS ON THE IMPACT OF SOCIAL WELFARE POLICY

Social welfare policy has great power to influence and change social well-being. Legislation has opened doors to opportunities for people who have been excluded because of their race, gender, age, or ability. It has altered the social fabric of our society. Such power is critical to creating a just society and ending discrimination and oppression. Public policies and public programs can make a difference and improve social well-being. Cutting the number of poor Americans in half, providing health coverage to tens of millions, keeping elderly people living safely and comfortably in their homes, helping airlines to recover from an industry freefall following terrorist attacks, shoring up the housing market and helping people to stay in their homes even after lenders were loose with lending practices, all these interventions demonstrate the power of government to act and improve the quality, security, and safety of our lives.

BOX 14.8 | CONTROVERSIAL PERSPECTIVES . . .

Do we do too much?

"I work hard and pay taxes, and nobody helps me out. Why should we have social programs?"

This is a common sentiment in our country, and it is often the reason people oppose social welfare policies and programs. After reading this book, what is your response to this question? How might you answer the person's complaint that hard-working people don't get help?

Do we do enough?

"I have tried to get a job, and I want to work, but I can't. I count on the services of government programs to help me get by. These resources are a vital part of my survival. Why aren't there more social programs?" There are hundreds of social welfare programs on the local, state, and federal levels. Private organizations also offer services. After reading this book, how do you answer the question of why there are not more social programs?

We also need to clarify values and understand the impact of competing values and beliefs. If those in positions of power and policy-making tend to share values that are individualistic in nature, then they are unlikely to support government social welfare programs. Rather than argue for funding or specific programs, the fundamental beliefs that people hold need to be addressed. Are these beliefs realistic, given the structure of society? Are there different program approaches that can be created to appeal to people's differing values and beliefs? Box 14.8 raises questions common to social welfare advocates. These are beliefs that must be addressed in the classroom, in legislative sessions, and in all discussions of social welfare.

Key Terms

Legislative branch

Executive branch

Judicial branch

Congress

Senate

House of
    Representatives

U.S. Code

executive order

campaign finance
    reform

social empathy

policy practice

lobbying

Questions for Discussion

1. Do you think social welfare policy has had an impact on your life? If so, describe the impact.
2. What difference do you think education will make in your life?
3. How might you influence policy makers? What can you do?

4. What are some of the limitations of social welfare policy?
5. How would you describe social empathy? Can you find examples of policies or programs that have been built on social empathy?

Excercises

1. Social welfare policies contribute to our social well-being. Identify three pieces of legislation that you think have directly affected your own well-being. Explain.

2. List three ways you could present your ideas to an elected official to try and influence him or her to vote in favor of a position you hold. What are the strengths of each strategy? What are the weaknesses?

3. Write a letter to an elected official taking a position on a social welfare issue.

4. Attend a public meeting. Who were the principal participants? How did they run the meeting? Was the public made to feel welcome? Were you able to follow the format and what was happening in the meeting?

5. Think of a social condition you know very little about, for example, poverty or drug addiction. How might you develop greater awareness and, hence, social empathy about the condition? Visit a poor neighborhood, and imagine yourself living there. What might it be like? Can you identify the conditions that are the result of individual decisions and the conditions that are the result of social system failures?

6. Go back to Chapter 1 and review the conflicting values and beliefs in Box 1.6 and Figure 1.3. Have your beliefs changed since you began reading this book? If so, how?

References

Barber, D. R. (2007). *Closing the gap: State party finances four years after BRCA*. Helena, MT: National Institute on Money in State Politics.

Broder, D. S., & Goldstein, A. (2003). How the GOP wooed AARP. *Washington Post National Weekly Edition 21(5)*:11.

Congressional Research Service. (2008). *Campaign finance: Legislative developments and policy issues in the 110th Congress*. CRS Report RL34324. Washington, DC: U.S. Congress.

Goleman, D. (1994). *Emotional intelligence*. New York: Bantam Books.

House of Representatives. (2003). *How our laws are made*. Document No. 108-93. Washington, DC: U.S. Government Printing Office.

OpenSecrets.Org. (2008). Candidate comparison: Source of funds 2008 cycle. http://www.opensecrets.org/pre08/sourceall.php?cycle=2008.

Polsby, N. W., & Wildavsky, A. (2004). *Presidential elections: Strategies and structures of American politics*, 11th ed. New York: Rowman & Littlefield.

Segal, E. A. (2006). Welfare as we should know it: Social empathy and welfare reform. In K. M. Kilty & E. A. Segal (eds.). *The promise of welfare reform: Results or rhetoric?* Binghamton, NY: Haworth.

U.S. Census Bureau. (2008). *Voting and registration in the election of November 2006*. Current Population Reports P20-557. Washington, DC: U.S. Department of Commerce.

U.S. Census Bureau. (2007). *Statistical abstract of the United States: 2008* 127th ed. Washington, DC: U.S. Government Printing Office.

Watson, J. C. (2002). Re-visioning empathy. In D. J. Cain & J. Seeman (eds.). *Humanistic psychotherapies: Handbook of research and practice*, pp. 445–471. Washington, DC: American Psychological Association.

GLOSSARY

Absolute poverty a fixed, predetermined income level that defines people as poor

Adoption permanent placement of a child

Adoption and Safe Families Act legislation emphasizing the health and safety of children when making efforts to preserve and unify children and families

Adult Protective Services programs for the protection of elderly people from maltreatment

Affirmative action efforts to correct historical imbalances in opportunities due to race and gender

Age Discrimination in Employment Act (ADEA) legislation that protects people who are 40 years of age or older from employment discrimination based on age

Alzheimer's disease a disease causing mental dementia

Americans with Disabilities Act of 1990 (ADA) federal legislation that mandates protection from discrimination for people with disabilities

Area Agencies on Aging agencies responsible for planning and coordinating services for older people

Belief an opinion or conviction

Bill of Rights first ten amendments to the Constitution, which identify central tenets of civil rights

Biological determinism ideology that heredity predetermines, or at least strongly influences, the social and economic position a person will achieve

Blaming the victim concept that explains why poverty and other social concerns are viewed as personal rather than collective social problems

Campaign finance reform legislation to curb spending on political campaigns

Cash assistance government payment of money from general taxes to those in need

Cause and function two aspects of social work: cause is the belief in a moral position to improve society, and function is the day-to-day efforts to provide services

Charity Organization Societies (COS) early private social welfare agencies developed to eliminate poverty through discovering its causes among individuals and then removing those causes on an individual basis

Child abuse and neglect the maltreatment of children

Child welfare policy the rules and regulations governing public intervention in relation to children and families

Child welfare system the constellation of public services designed to protect and promote the well-being of children

Civil rights the rights to which people are entitled because they are members of society

Civil Rights Act of 1964 codified protection of racial minorities; it required desegregation of public facilities and prohibited discrimination in employment hiring

Commercial private for-profit social service provider

Community mental health centers federally funded mental health centers

Congress Elected body consisting of the House of Representatives and the Senate at the federal legislative level

Consolidated Omnibus Reconciliation Act (COBRA) program that allows a person to continue group health insurance coverage for up to 18 months after leaving employment

Contracting out funding services through public money but delivering the services through private organizations

Critical theory examination of social life with the goal of evaluating our social order, the ways in which power and domination affect people's lives, and the ways in which that effect can be changed

Culture of poverty ideology asserting that those who are born poor are in turn socialized to remain poor

Deficit the situation in which the government ends the year with less revenue than the amount it has spent

Deinstitutionalization the movement of people out of mental health institutions and into the community

Disability Insurance (DI) coverage for people who must stop working because of a disability

Discrimination the action of treating people differently based on their identity; it is linked to prejudice

Dislocated worker person who was trained and employed in an occupation that is no longer needed

Distributive justice the social obligation of the state to provide agreed-upon social benefits for all of its citizens that are not merely fair but also contribute to the betterment of society

Earned Income Tax Credit program (EITC) federal program designed to lift families with full-time, year-round workers above the poverty level

Economic development form of social investment that is specifically designed to enhance community and individual economic growth

Economic Opportunity Act legislation that outlined policies and programs to fight poverty during the War on Poverty

Economics the science of production and distribution of wealth

Elite power idea that a handful of people control the policies that govern all of society

Elizabethan Poor Laws British laws that greatly influenced the earliest form of legislated social welfare policy in the Thirteen Colonies

Entitlement programs that are mandated by public law for all who are eligible, regardless of the total cost in any given year or fiscal period

Equal Rights Amendment (ERA) constitutional amendment written, but never passed, that would have extended civil rights protections for women and prohibited discrimination based on sex

Equality equivalent opportunities and access to resources

Executive Branch The federal government branch that houses the President and Vice President

Executive order action by which the president can intervene in agency

processes; it establishes requirements for agencies and departments

Family and Medical Leave Act federal legislation that mandates employers to guarantee unpaid leave for workers after the birth or adoption of a child, or during the illness of a dependent or family member

Family Preservation programs that emphasize permanency for children or keeping families together

Federal Insurance Contribution Act (FICA) federal legislation that mandates the payment of contributions to the Social Security Trust Fund from employment wages

Feminization of poverty the likelihood that women will be in a state of poverty more than men

Food Stamp program federal program for the alleviation of hunger in America

For-profit organizations agencies that charge fees for services; making a profit is the underlying economic structure of these organizations

Foster care placement for temporary removal of a child from his or her family

Full employment situation in which very few workers are available for jobs paying typical wages and those looking for jobs can find them

Geographic unemployment unemployment limited to a specific region

Globalization the increasing connectedness of the world's economy

Hate crime laws legislation for tracking the occurrence of illegal discriminatory acts and for creating stricter punishments for crimes motivated by discrimination

Head Start services for aiding poor preschool children and their families

Health Insurance Portability and Accountability Act (HIPAA) legislation that adjusted health care insurance policies to allow for coverage after a person leaves his or her employment

Homeless living without a permanent residence

House of Representatives federal government legislative body that houses the elected members from all states' congressional districts

Human rights civil rights with emphasis on political and humanitarian concerns

Ideologies ideas or bodies of thought that guide us

Immigrants people who choose to relocate and migrate to live in a new country

Implementation the putting into practice of a public policy

Incrementalism theory that public policy is developed through small changes to existing policies

Indian Child Welfare Act (ICWA) legislation regulating the placement of American Indian children outside of their homes

Indoor relief institutions focused on serving the needs of the poor

Industry unemployment unemployment limited to a specific industry or type of work

In-kind benefits services or commodities provided for eligible recipients

Institutional racism public laws and regulations used to differentiate and discriminate according to race

Institutional social welfare policy the existence of social welfare programs as part of the social structure and normal function of society

Judicial branch federal government branch that houses the Supreme Court and federal courts

Juvenilization of poverty the likelihood that children will be in poverty

Legislative branch The federal government branch that houses the Congress (House of Representatives and the Senate)

Lobbying actions to persuade policy makers to enact or support certain programs

Long-term care an array of services for elderly, chronically ill, and disabled persons that are necessary for day-to-day living and personal care

Magnitude theory that dramatic events create openings for public policy

Managed Care system in which a person's medical care is controlled by the insurer

Medicaid federal health care program, primarily for low-income people

Medicare federal health care program, primarily for elderly people

Medicare Prescription Drug, Improvement, and Modernization Act legislation that expanded Medicare coverage to pay for prescription drugs

Medigap private insurance that pays for health services not covered by Medicare

Minimum wage federally mandated lowest hourly wage that employers may legally pay their workers

National Health Insurance health insurance coverage provided by the federal government for all citizens

New Deal the policies of President Franklin D. Roosevelt following the Great Depression

No Child Left Behind Act federal legislation mandating higher teaching outcomes for public schools

Nondiscrimination absence of discrimination

Nonprofit organizations voluntary charity groups that fall under Internal Revenue Code section 501(c)(3)

North American Free Trade Agreement (NAFTA) legislation that cut tariffs and taxes between Mexico, the United States, and Canada

Old-Age, Survivors, and Disability Insurance (OASDI) the program commonly referred to as Social Security

Older Americans Act of 1965 policy for developing a nationwide network to coordinate services for elderly people

Oppression widespread systematic discrimination

Outsourcing trend in which jobs that were formerly held by U.S. workers are given to workers in other countries

Pandemic epidemic occurring across a large geographic region

Paradigms patterns or models that provide a conceptual framework

Pensions a form of retirement savings, typically tied to prior employment

Permanency planning concept that foster care is a temporary service and that children must either be returned to their families or placed for adoption as quickly as possible

Personal Responsibility and Work Opportunity Reconciliation Act (PRWORA) federal legislation that changed the structure of public assistance; guaranteed support for poor families was replaced with time-limited support

Policy practice using knowledge of the policy-making process in order to take an active role in influencing the outcome of the process

Postindustrial era period beginning in the 1980s that emphasized service delivery

Poverty guidelines simplified level of the poverty thresholds for administrative use

Poverty threshold the dollar amount set for the federal poverty measure

Prejudice belief or attitude of dislike for a group based on myths and misconceptions

Private social service agencies organizations separate from the government that provide social services

Progressive era era from 1875 to 1925 during which communities and the government took on more responsibility for social welfare

Progressive tax a tax that is proportionally higher for people with high incomes than for people with lower incomes

Provider the organization that creates or manages social services

Public social services social services provided by the federal, state, local, or tribal government

Public assistance government-funded effort to provide economic assistance to people who fall below a certain income level and are considered to be in poverty

Public housing federally funded housing assistance programs for low-income people

Public policy general term for the decisions, laws, and regulations put forth by governing bodies

Rational policy making form of public policy development that stresses knowledge of all values, possible policy alternatives, and consequences of those alternatives when making policy

Recipient the person or group who is in receipt of social services

Refugees people who leave their countries of origin to escape political turmoil or persecution

Regressive tax a tax that is proportionally greater for people with low incomes than for people with higher incomes

Relative poverty poverty based on societal standards for assessing the minimum needed for a reasonable living situation

Residual social welfare policy public intervention that is organized only when

the normal resources of family and marketplace break down

Seasonal unemployment changes in employment over different times of the year

Selectivity restriction of services to those who can demonstrate need through established eligibility criteria

Senate federal government legislative body that houses the two elected senators from each state

Settlement Movement approach to social services that emphasized workers living among the people in order to best serve the community

Severe or serious mental illness (SMI) having a diagnosable mental, emotional, or behavioral disorder that interferes with or limits one or more major life activities

Social construction shared reality that occurs when those who are dominant in a society define a group's characteristics and determine the group's value to society

Social control actions of those in positions of power that control and direct the behavior of the needy

Social empathy use of insight gained about people's life conditions to develop public policies that are sensitive to people's needs based on the realities of their living situations

Social insurance collectively funded program for workers and their dependents that provides economic resources at the conclusion of employment due to retirement, disability, or death

Social investment spending public money to create ways for people and communities to grow and develop; the outcome is increased social well-being

Social justice the level of fairness that exists in society, and the goal of achieving fairness

Social Security Act of 1935 single most significant piece of federal legislation for the development of income support for poor people and retired workers and their dependents

Social Security Trust Fund account in which the federal government holds the tax contributions for the OASDI program

Social Services Block Grant (SSBG) federal funds for a variety of social services, primarily children's services

Social welfare the well-being of society

Social welfare policy collective responses to social problems for the maintenance of social well-being

Social welfare policy analysis the investigation and inquiry into the causes and consequences of public policies

Social welfare programs the products or outcomes of social welfare policies

Social welfare system the organized efforts and structures used to provide for societal well-being

State Children's Health Insurance Program (SCHIP) health insurance program for children

Street-level bureaucrats service workers at the lowest levels of the social welfare system

Structural unemployment inability to find employment due to lack of necessary education or training required for the jobs available

Substance abuse the misuse of alcohol or illegal drugs, or both

Supplemental Food Program for Women, Infants, and Children (WIC) federal program designed to provide nutrition and health assistance for low-income pregnant and postpartum women, infants, and children

Supplemental Security Income (SSI) federal program that provides cash assistance for any person who is aged, blind, or disabled and whose income falls below the poverty line

Supply and demand the interplay between products and services offered and the extent of the desire and ability to buy those products and services

Surplus situation in which the government ends the year with more revenue than the amount it spent

Taxes compulsory payments made to the government

Temporary Assistance for Needy Families (TANF) the public assistance program created by 1996 legislation that replaced the federal guarantee of support for poor families with time limits and other restrictions

Theories systems of ideas to explain something

Undocumented workers people who are employed but are not legally living in the United States

Unemployment lack of paid employment

Unemployment Insurance program (UI) public program that provides benefits in the event of unplanned unemployment

Unfunded mandate federally mandated initiatives that require state governments to create programs but do not provide the additional funding needed for the programs

United States Code the master collection of permanent federal laws of the United States

Universality social services that provide benefits for all members of society, regardless of their income or means

Unworthy poor those who do not deserve to receive aid

Value the worth, desirability, or usefulness that we place on something

Violence Against Women Act (VAWA) legislation to protect women from violence, particularly domestic violence

Voluntary private nonprofit social service provider

Vouchers aid earmarked for a specific service or commodity

War on Poverty the government policies and programs of the 1960s that were designed to alleviate poverty

Window of opportunity the time period in which political or social events or changes in personnel open the way for a policy to be adopted

Working poor people who live in poverty even though they are employed

Worthy poor those who deserve to receive aid

INDEX

Note: Page numbers followed by t refer to Boxes or Tables